THE UNIVERSITY, STATE, AND MARKET

The University, State, and Market

The Political Economy of Globalization in the Americas

Edited by
ROBERT A. RHOADS
and
CARLOS ALBERTO TORRES

STANFORD UNIVERSITY PRESS

STANFORD, CALIFORNIA, 2006

Stanford University Press
Stanford, California

Printed in the United States of America on acid-free,
archival-quality paper

Library of Congress Cataloging-in-Publication Data

The university, state, and market : the political
economy of globalization in the Americas / edited
by Robert A. Rhoads and Carlos Alberto Torres.
    p. cm.
  Includes bibliographical references and index.
  ISBN 0-8047-5168-4 (cloth : alk. paper)—
ISBN 0-8047-5169-2 (pbk. : alk. paper)
    1. Education, Higher—Economic aspects—
North America.   2. Education and globalization—
North America.   3. Education, Higher—Economic
aspects—Latin America.   4. Education and global-
ization—Latin America.   I. Rhoads, Robert A.
II. Torres, Carlos Alberto.

LC67.68.N67U55 2006
338.4'3378—dc22   2005017982

Original Printing 2006

Last figure below indicates year of this printing:
15   14   13   12   11   10   09   08   07   06

Typeset by G & S Book Services in 10/14 Janson

To my best friend and wife, Jia Li. Thanks for your love and support and the hope of many years to come.

Robert A. Rhoads

Writers always search for sources of inspiration. Social scientists are no exception. There cannot be sources of inspiration without the consistent, always refined, unconditional love of one's family. In all these years, I continue to draw support, love, and affection from my children, Carlos, Pablo, and Laura, and of course from E. C. F., always there, always mine. Together, they offer me the best of life.

Carlos Alberto Torres

Special thanks to Kate Wahl for believing in this project and helping to bring it to fruition. We also wish to acknowledge and thank Shannon Calderone for her helpful edits and work on the book's index.

Contents

List of Figures and Tables

Contributors

ESTELA MARA BENSIMON is a professor of higher education at the Rossier School of Education in the University of Southern California and the director of the Center for Urban Education. Her research interests include academic leadership, organizational change, social action research, urban colleges and universities, and women and minority faculty in higher education. In spring 2002 she was a Fulbright fellow at Universidad Nacional Autónoma de México. She is a leading scholar in the field of higher education and the author of several books, including *Promotion and Tenure: Community and Socialization in Academe* (with William G. Tierney, SUNY Press) and *Redesigning Collegiate Leadership* (with Anna Neumann, Johns Hopkins University Press).

ATILIO ALBERTO BORON graduated with a Ph.D. in political science from Harvard University. Currently he holds the Chair of Political Philosophy at the Faculty of Social Sciences of the University of Buenos Aires and is the executive secretary of CLACSO, the Latin American Council of Social Sciences. He is highly recognized throughout Latin America, the United States, and Europe for his work in the area of political philosophy, higher education finance, and theories of democracy, capitalism, and imperialism. Among his notable recent works published in English are the following: *State, Capitalism, and Democracy in Latin America* (Lynne Rienner Publishers) and *Empire and Imperialism: A Critical Reading of Michael Hardt and Antonio Negri* (London: Zed Books)

ANDREA BREWSTER is a doctoral candidate in social sciences and comparative education at the University of California, Los Angeles. She is currently investigating faculty life in her dissertation, titled "Gender Equity in the University: A Study of Women's Higher Education Experiences in Mexico and the United States." Her research interests include international human rights; the interplay between gender and globalization, development, and education; and social and feminist theories and research methodologies.

NOAM CHOMSKY joined the staff of the Massachusetts Institute of Technology in 1955 and in 1961 was appointed full professor in the Department of Modern Languages and Linguistics (now the Department of Linguistics and Philosophy). From 1966 to 1976 he held the Ferrari P. Ward Professorship of Modern Languages and Linguistics. In 1976 he was appointed Institute Professor. Professor Chomsky has written and lectured widely on linguistics, philosophy, intellectual history, contemporary issues, international affairs, and US foreign policy. His works include *Aspects of the Theory of Syntax*; *Cartesian Linguistics*; *Sound Pattern of English* (with Morris Halle); *Language and Mind*; *American Power and the New Mandarins*; *At War with Asia*; *For Reasons of State*; *Peace in the Middle East?*; *Reflections on Language*; *The Political Economy of Human Rights, Vol. I and II* (with E. S. Herman); *Rules and Representations*; *Lectures on Government and Binding*; *Towards a New Cold War*; *Radical Priorities*; *Fateful Triangle*; *Knowledge of Language*; *Turning the Tide*; *Pirates and Emperors*; *On Power and Ideology*; *Language and Problems of Knowledge*; *The Culture of Terrorism*; *Manufacturing Consent* (with E. S. Herman); *Necessary Illusions*; *Deterring Democracy*; *Year 501*; *Rethinking Camelot: JFK, the Vietnam War, and US Political Culture*; *Letters from Lexington*; *World Orders, Old and New*; *The Minimalist Program*; *Powers and Prospects*; *The Common Good*; *Profit over People*; *The New Military Humanism*; *New Horizons in the Study of Language and Mind*; *Rogue States*; *A New Generation Draws the Line*; *9-11*; *Understanding Power*; *On Nature and Language*; *Pirates and Emperors, Old and New*; *Chomsky on Democracy and Education*; *Middle East Illusions*; and *Hegemony or Survival*.

ANA LOUREIRO JUREMA is an associate professor in the Graduate School of Education and the Department of Psychology and Educational Orientation at the Federal University of Pernambuco in Brazil. She also has served at the Government School and Public Policies of the Joaquim Nabuco Foundation. Her areas of interest include technology in education, higher education, comparative education, social psychology, and distance education. She is actively involved in developing educational policy for the public school system in northeastern Brazil and in professional development for distance education teachers throughout the country. Her work has been published in numerous books and journals and she has coauthored (with Ken Kempner) several published pieces on Brazil's resistance to externally imposed economic solutions.

KEN KEMPNER is the dean of Social Sciences and Education and a professor of international studies and education at Southern Oregon University. His research addresses the role of higher education in social and economic development, most recently in Brazil, Mexico, and Japan. Recognized as a leading comparativist of higher education, his work has been published in a variety of international journals and he has been invited to lecture on educational development and organizational theory in several countries, including Chile, China, Taiwan, and Thailand. He is senior editor of the *Association for the Study of Higher Education (ASHE) Reader on Comparative Education* (first edition) and co-editor of the *Social Role of Higher Education: Comparative Perspectives*.

MARCELA MOLLIS is a professor of history of education and comparative education and director of the Research Program on Comparative Higher Education at the Research Institute of Education (IICE) in the School of Philosophy and Literature at the University of Buenos Aires. In addition, Professor Mollis is the Latin American coordinator for the Latin American Center of Social Sciences (CLACSO) of the research group on society and university and is a highly regarded scholar of higher education. Her latest book is *La Universidad Argentina en Tránsito: Un Ensayo para Jóvenes y no tan Jóvenes* (Fondo de Cultura Económica, Buenos Aires).

RAYMOND A. MORROW is a professor of sociology and an adjunct professor of educational policy studies at the University of Alberta. He has gained world renown for his work in the area of social theory. He specializes in the areas of critical theory and culture and education. Among his current projects is research on Mexican intellectuals and democratic transition. His book *Critical Theory and Methodology* (Sage) was selected as a 1994 *Choice Magazine*

Academic Book of the Year. In collaboration with Carlos Alberto Torres, he also has published *Social Theory and Education: A Critique of Theories of Social and Cultural Reproduction* (SUNY Press) and *Reading Freire and Habermas: Critical Pedagogy and Transformative Social Change.*

IMANOL ORDORIKA is a professor at the Instituto de Investigaciones Económicas at the Universidad Nacional Autónoma de México (UNAM) and the Frank Talbott Jr. Visiting Professor at the Curry School of Education at the University of Virginia. He is also affiliated with the Seminario de Educación Superior at UNAM. His research interests include the politics of higher education, academic governance, and organizational change. Professor Ordorika is well known for his work on reform and political struggle at UNAM, covered in his book *Power and Politics in University Governance: Organization and Change at the Universidad Nacional Autónoma de México* (Routledge Farmer).

GARY RHOADES is professor and director of the Center for the Study of Higher Education (CSHE) at the University of Arizona. A well-known scholar in the study of the academic profession and academic restructuring, Professor Rhoades's recent books include *Managed Professionals: Unionized Faculty and Restructuring Academic Labor* (SUNY Press) and *Academic Capitalism and the New Economy: Markets, State, and Higher Education* (with Sheila Slaughter, Johns Hopkins University Press).

ROBERT A. RHOADS is a professor of higher education and organizational change in the Graduate School of Education and Information Studies and a faculty affiliate of the Latin American Center and the Center for Chinese Studies at the University of California, Los Angeles (UCLA). Professor Rhoads is a noted scholar of higher education with interests in the United States, Latin America, and China. His most recent books include *Freedom's Web: Student Activism in an Age of Cultural Diversity* (Johns Hopkins University Press), *Community Service and Higher Learning* (SUNY Press), and *Democracy, Multiculturalism, and the Community College* (with James Valadez, Garland Press).

BOAVENTURA DE SOUSA SANTOS is a leading international sociologist and professor at the School of Economics of Coimbra University in Portugal, where he also serves as the director of the Center for Social Studies. He is also a Distinguished Legal Scholar at the Law School of the University of Wisconsin, Madison. He has written and published widely on the issues of globalization, sociology of law and the state, and epistemology. His books in English include *Toward a New Common Sense: Law, Science, and Politics in the Paradigmatic Transition* (Routledge), *Toward a New Legal Common Sense: Law, Globalization, and Emancipation* (Butterworths), and three forthcoming edited volumes: *Another Democracy Is Possible: Beyond the Liberal Democratic Canon* and *Another Production Is Possible: Beyond the Capitalist Canon* (both by Verso) and *Law and Counterhegemonic Globalization: Toward a Cosmopolitan Legality* (Cambridge University Press).

DANIEL SCHUGURENSKY is an associate professor of adult education and counseling psychology at the Ontario Institutes for Studies in Education at the University of Toronto. His research interests include linkages between adult education and the political economy of higher education, Latin American education in comparative perspective, and lifelong citizenship education. Highly regarded for his critical analysis of education, his most recent work has appeared in *Higher Education, Comparative Education Review*, the *Journal of Educational Policy*, and the *International Journal of Lifelong Education*.

SHEILA SLAUGHTER is a professor and the Louise McBee Chair of Higher Education at the University of Georgia. A leading policy scholar in the field of higher education, her research focuses on the political economy of higher education and academic science and technology policy, as evidenced in three of her recent books: *The Higher Learning and High Technology: Dynamics of Higher Education Policy Formation* (SUNY Press), *Academic Capitalism: Politics, Policies, and the Entrepreneurial University* (with Larry Leslie, Johns Hopkins University Press), and *Academic Capitalism and the New Economy: Markets, State, and Higher Education* (with Gary Rhoades, Johns Hopkins University Press). Her most recent project is funded by the National Science Foundation: "Virtual Values: Universities in the Information Age" (with Jennifer Croissant and Gary Rhoades).

CARLOS ALBERTO TORRES is director of the Latin American Center and a professor of education in the Graduate School of Education and Information Studies at the University of California, Los Angeles (UCLA). Professor Torres is a highly regarded scholar of Latin America and has published more than 20 books on education in the United States and Latin America. Among his recent books are the following: *Globalization and Education: Critical Perspectives* (edited with Nicholas Burbules, Routledge), *Democracy, Education, and Multiculturalism: Dilemmas of Citizenship in a Global World* (Rowman & Littlefield), *Social Theory and Education: A Critique of Theories of Social and Cultural Reproduction* (with Raymond Morrow, SUNY Press), *Reading Freire and Habermas: Critical Pedagogy and Transformative Social Change* (with Raymond Morrow, Teachers College Press), and *Comparative Education: The Dialectic of the Global and the Local* (with Robert Arnove, Rowman & Littlefield).

Critical Theory, Globalization, and Higher Education: Political Economy and the Cul-de-Sac of the Postmodernist Cultural Turn

Raymond A. Morrow

The importance of this volume can be readily presented in a prefatory, summary way as signaling a reintegration of critical social theory and political economy in the study of higher education in the Americas. Although political economic approaches have come upon hard time since the heyday of the early 1980s, they remain—especially in the new forms that have emerged—more important than ever in the context of globalization. The new challenges relate especially to taking into account a new understanding of the state in the context of neoliberal globalization and the downsizing of the welfare state as well as the paradoxical effects of the cultural turn in the human sciences and its uses and abuses in political culture.

It is necessary to have some historical perspective here in recognizing that higher education has had a distinctive fate in this context. Although post-secondary education initially remained relatively autonomous relative to lower levels, it has subsequently lost control of its pact with the devil in opening itself to commercialization in the name of its public responsibility, although most administrators in the United States in particular would be unwilling to accept this conclusion (Stein 2004). On the one hand, in accepting the principle of overt public accountability (even if hedged with caveats about protecting autonomy), public college and university institutions since the 1970s have been confronted with a never-ending demand for demonstrating "relevance" based on criteria increasingly distant from the original mandate of democratic responsibility. The co-optation of the open democratic university by the dogmas of neoliberal globalization theory and the local pressures of budgetary constraints have increasingly alienated the popular and social democratic forces that once supported making the ivory tower "more relevant." One of the contributions of this volume is providing a variety of cases in North America and Latin America that illustrate various implications of the privatization and commercialization of higher education and its betrayal of both "the idea of the university" and its potential contribution to public life.

Yet the resulting analyses of this book also need to be situated in the broader context of the politics of higher education that have contributed to the erosion of autonomy and constrained the ability of universities to contribute to their traditional mandate as institutions. Although only rarely alluded to in this volume, the so-called cultural turn in the human sciences—most notably in the United States—has inadvertently contributed to this process as part of a cannibalistic process of self-criticism of the university as a major source of social and cultural reproduction in society, a theme still ironically echoed in Latin America in more conventional Marxist terms. Although there is an important element of truth in the charge that higher education has colluded in reproducing the dominant social order, such effects have been far outweighed by contributions to envisioning alternatives and social criticism. Alongside social and cultural movements, higher education remains a primary source of cultural and social innovation in modern societies—a contribution well recognized by its right-wing and fundamentalist enemies. Partly as a consequence of these new circumstances, however, the immense constructive opportunities for higher education represented by globalization have been increasingly subverted by the kinds of processes described by the political economic analyses presented in this book.

A central theme of this foreword is that a new alliance between critical social theory and political economy represents an important step toward clarifying and dealing with the fallout from the "canon" and "science wars" in higher education. Although these issues have now been dealt with reasonably well by most institutions, the overall confrontation and lingering effects have played into the hands of the enemies of academic autonomy by calling into question the capacity of higher education to retain persuasive academic authority outside the "hard" sciences and positivist forms of social science. Postmodernist cultural critics may enounce again and again the "death" of metanarratives and the collapse of the subject-centered model of Western reason, but academic institutions remain firmly under the control of rather conventional—if now more pluralistic—conceptions of science and knowledge. At the same time, and reinforcing some of the limitations of the dominant model of science and technology, university curricula and research have increasingly opened themselves to market pressures without having taken into account necessary long-term safeguards and alternative strategies.

The cumulative failure of postmodern critiques of knowledge to have adequately addressed these issues results in a challenge for the reconciliation of critical theory and political economy in higher education. The advantage of critical theory in this context is that, unlike postmodernist critiques of knowledge, it has avoided self-contradictory relativism and retained a sense of the *reconstructive* moment of social theory based on a constructivist epistemology that views deconstructive strategies as simply a means, not an end in themselves. What critical theory calls for are new forms of cultural theory that can demystify the often invisible reproductive effects of higher education and research and yet can also suggest new strategies for renewing the autonomy of higher education based on the precarious balancing act of relating social relevance and the free pursuit of knowledge and "truth." Only in this way can the democratic mandate of the university be preserved. Only by retaining its autonomy can higher education fulfill its responsibility to the community—and humanity—as a whole and offset the apparently "rational" efforts to subordinate knowledge to the forces of the market and its shortsighted definitions of relevance.

To make the preceding argument more convincing, I need to introduce a number of issues in somewhat greater depth: Why political economy and critical theory? How has the opening up of higher education to public relevance been corrupted? How has the opening up of universities and research to market forces become a Trojan horse for eroding intellectual autonomy?

And what are the prospects for alternative models of envisioning and organizing the mission of higher education and research?

Political Economy, Critical Theory, and Democracy

Why use political economy and critical theory as strategies for studying higher education? The term *political economy* has a confusing variety of meanings. Originally it referred to an approach to economic theory associated initially with the classical economics of Adam Smith and David Ricardo and the critique of political economy found in Marx. As used in this volume, however, political economy refers primarily to an interdisciplinary social scientific approach that studies the interaction between democratic politics and market relations. The key theoretical point of departure is the assumption that, although self-regulating market mechanisms may contribute reliably to the accumulation of profit, this process has no necessary relation to collective needs and public interests. Similarly, the left has also increasingly recognized that the use of state power per se is no guarantee of public interest. The task of a *critical political economy* is thus to provide empirical evidence and theoretical arguments for showing how, when, and with what consequences the use of market mechanisms or state power can be utilized in problematic ways to guide public policies. Although it is acknowledged that market mechanisms are inevitably a crucial aspect of the democratic openness of the kind of capitalist social formation in which we appear to be destined to live in for the foreseeable future, those unregulated, self-regulating market systems are held to represent an ongoing threat to social pluralism and the democratic claims of state policy.

It is important to have some historical perspective here in recalling the rebirth of political economy in the 1970s and early 1980s, partly as a response to the reception of neo-Marxist and critical theories. Although the use of political economy was especially important in fields such as work or mass communications that were primarily market based, it also played a rather different role in the analysis of public education, as we will see shortly. In this period the emergence of the fiscal crisis of the state created possibilities for a legitimation crisis that some suggested could provide the catalyst for a renewal of democratic politics and an opening for the left.

Instead, a fundamental reorganization of capital—often described theoretically as a post-Fordist regime of production—succeeded in coordinating a downsizing of the welfare state coupled with a neoliberal strategy of globalization that made the imperatives of international competition into the new basis of social control. By using the political rhetoric of the imperatives of structural adjustment of fiscal and monetary policies to the new low-inflation era, it became increasingly possible to undermine populist and democratic pressures from below on strictly financial and "technical" grounds. The result was a kind of economic technocracy through which human needs and democratic aspirations became marginalized in the name of economic necessity and the allocation of resources became dictated by primarily technical criteria determined by international economic institutions and the international financial community. In effect, neoliberal economics, backed up by the proliferation of rational choice theories and related research, has made the contemporary economics into the new "dismal science" through which "rationality" is reduced to an economic "realism" that formally liberates human choice at the individual level but suffocates and marginalizes social and public choice (Sen 2002).

But it is important to recall that this earlier renaissance of political economy was rather prematurely eclipsed as a major orientation in the mid 1980s, although it continued to enjoy considerable support as a minority orientation in many areas of social research, including education at the primary and secondary levels. The relative decline of political economy had both internal and external sources. From within it was often acknowledged that classical political economy suffered from an excessive structuralism that did not adequately account for agency (Apple 1981). Although this weakness could in principle be corrected within a reconstructed version of political economy understood in the form of critical theory (Morrow and Torres 1995), the shift to the focus on agency took on a life of its own, especially in the form of critical pedagogy (Giroux 1983). In any case, whereas critical (social) theory in its renewed forms was in principle based on linking political economy as an analysis of structure with a theory of resistance and agency, *in practice*—especially as postmodernist critical pedagogy—this articulation tended to break down (Slott 2002).

But these internal disputes and problems were minor compared to the external developments that marked a kind of cultural shift in the "spirit of the times" (Zeitgeist) associated with the concept of postmodernism. Postmodernism as an academic phenomenon can be viewed as the last exhausted gasp of the otherwise important cultural and interpretive turn that marked the rise of cultural studies in the 1970s. Although cultural studies originated in close relation to critical theory, political economy, and Gramsci's theory of cultural hegemony, its academic popularization in the 1980s was increasingly defined by its association with postmodernism and poststructuralism. In its most popular form, as a kind of simplistic reaction against political economy (and critical theory) as totalizing "metanarratives," postmodernist theories proclaimed a radical pluralism and voluntarism oriented toward ahistorical understandings of the local and the here and now. Theoretically, social analysis was reduced to cultural theory and was understood primarily in purely discursive terms that neglected the extratextual dimensions and material aspects of institutions and social reality. Although postmodernism as a kind of cultural movement claimed to rely on poststructuralist theories as the basis of a new, postempiricist form of subversive social theory, it appropriated poststructuralist theories in selective ways—most notably those of Michel Foucault—that often distorted their innovative insights into social and cultural reality. In the process, however, critical theory, political economy, and other dimensions of poststructuralist theory were neglected in the 1990s in the name of a hypertextual form of postmodernist cultural theory. Perhaps it is now possible to envision what can now—retrospectively—be labeled the *cul-de-sac of the postmodernist version of the cultural turn*—the dead end that signaled the point of departure for new beginnings. To be sure, there were numerous eloquent calls for a critical postmodernism or a postmodern critical theory, but they were largely marginalized by the whirlwind of academic postmodernism that marked the humanities above all in the 1990s (Agger 2002; Best and Kellner 2001). Against the excesses of postmodernism, it can be argued that critical theory without political economy retreats into a free-floating cultural space that loses contact with the historical specificity necessary for its insights as a form of social analysis and critique. Similarly, political economy without critical theory remains a structuralist methodology that cannot ground itself in a broader conception of the state, society, the subject, and cultural change.

It is in this context that it is important to stress the strategic importance of forms of political economy informed by critical theory that have more recently drawn on a selective critical appropriation of themes from the postmodernism-poststructuralism debates (e.g., Foucault's contributions to a theory of power). The version of the debate presented here under the heading of political economy, however, presupposes a broad conception of critical theory (or critical social theory) that—despite occasional impressions— does not ground itself in a series of dogmatic claims about higher education and public policy or any naïve leftist faith in the state. What it does do is use empirically grounded theoretical arguments to justify pragmatic policy options that are attuned to regional and national variations as well as to the global context. An aspect of the general approach that links the essays of the present volume is that they represent—even if they do not explicitly theorize—a renewal of a political economy of education that has learned from these past lessons without succumbing to the wish fulfillments of the postmodernist spirit of the times. A major policy assumption is that public sector education should define the basic agenda of national policies that are responsive to global change but should not be dictated by international agencies intent on imposing a problematic model of economic development. Matters are complicated by the often misleading use of the "American model" of higher education and research (e.g., the role of private research universities) that may lead to imitating some of its most problematic aspects (e.g., academic capitalism) and ignoring its best aspects (e.g., the leadership role of major research-oriented state universities and multiple levels of entry and opportunities for upward movement).

Political Economy, Higher Education, and the Lure of "Relevance"

Against its good intentions the left contributed to the current situation by originally joining the call for public relevance, only to later see representatives of the postmodernist cultural left turn on the university itself, even if intending to use it as a bastion of radical cultural change. Although this possibility was anticipated in the New Left attacks on universities in the generation of 1968, this antipathy abated with the subsequent pluralistic opening up of scholarship in the humanities and social sciences. A more recent attack on academic authority in the name of postmodernism, however, threatens to have more enduring and problematic effects in the wake of the post-1989 generation.

Historically the relationship between political economy and higher education has been limited because of the long-standing autonomy of colleges and universities relative to the K–12 levels of education. As well, political economic studies of primary and secondary education focused on the social and cultural reproduction of workers rather than on economic determinants of actual educational systems and policies. Because political economy as a theoretical and methodological strategy is oriented toward the interplay between state policies and market-driven institutional spheres, higher education appeared to be relatively immune—at least in North America—to political economic analysis, given its apparent autonomy. In Latin America, on the other hand, public universities never enjoyed such a period of extended expansion and relative affluence. Although modernization theories advocated the expansion and funding of public higher education in Latin America, political economic realities and state incompetence contributed to a chronic failure with respect to access, quality, and levels of research funding.

During this period of apparently endless expansion in North America, public higher education enjoyed universal support and generous funding until the emerging fiscal crisis of the state in the 1970s. In the general theory of Talcott Parson's structural functionalism, this expansion of higher education could be understood as the preordained outcome of the evolutionary differentiation of society toward a "knowledge society" (Parsons 1973). On the one hand, curriculum decisions were autonomous beyond general guidelines for accreditation based on principles of technical quality. On the other hand, financing could be understood as the outcome of either state policies in the case of public education or endowment and philanthropic activities in the case of private institutions. Even in the exceptional case of the United States, which has the largest privately based higher education sector, private colleges and universities were not typically for-profit enterprises but rather voluntary associations based on various religious or cultural goals. Most obviously, the elite private and public institutions were guided by a kind of universalistic competition for "distinction" in research and undergraduate training in the sense of the French sociologist Pierre Bourdieu. Such competition greatly restricted political restrictions on autonomy, and there was no significant difference between public and elite private higher education with respect to political orientations, aside from more traditional denominational religious schools in some fields. To be sure, these private colleges served to reinforce the cultural capital of the children of elites, but multicultural policies in the 1970s began to significantly widen the range of entrants and so-lidified to some extent meritocratic claims to equality of opportunity. In this context the notion of a political economy of higher education was similar to that of a political economy of religious institutions in that it was relatively peripheral for understanding the origins and changes of such institutions.

On the other hand, a form of political economy did come to play a sig-nificant role in the study of primary and secondary education in the 1970s in the form of structuralist or correspondence theories of educational repro-duction. In the widely influential research of Samuel Bowles and Herbert Gintis (1976), Michael Apple (1982), and many others in various countries, it was argued that public school autonomy was illusory because of its latent function in preparing docile workers for the capitalist economy. Another line of research focused more on the fiscal crisis of research and the effect of the lack of revenues on the deterioration of public schooling, again focusing more on primary and secondary education, as for example, in the work of Carlos Alberto Torres (Morrow and Torres 1995).

Although this is not the place to recount the gradual breakdown of the public model of higher education expansion, which has taken rather differ-ent forms in the United States and Canada, it is important to stress that an important factor in the erosion of autonomy has been the corruption of the model of "public relevance" as a result of the pressures of both fiscal con-straint and demands for market relevance. Although originally envisioned in terms of a balance between autonomy and broader social concerns, the cu-mulative result has been an exposure to a classic version of the "slippery slope" dilemma through which the ultimate outcome looks little like the intended point of departure. To the extent that many on the left became enamored with projects of immediate political relevance, however, the left contributed to this process by acquiescing to short-term appeals to political efficacy. In this earlier context the institutionalization of science and higher education policy could be viewed as a way of coordinating research for the public good. The subsequent emergence of neoliberal models of globaliza-tion, however, has provided a theoretical basis for undermining the original intentions of science and research policy by subordinating them to the rhet-oric of privatization and global competitiveness. Unfortunately, appeals to a political activist conception of the public good can rarely compete with the "practical" imperatives defined by market-based agendas, thus opening the way for private interests to dominate the space opened up by declining university autonomy.

Yet the current conjecture of cultural politics has made it extremely difficult to imagine how an effective rearticulation of the justification of the forms of autonomy is necessary for the contemporary research university. The crucial problem is recognizing that defending the principle of academic autonomy is not by itself a specifically "conservative" stance in the ideological sense but part of the liberal spirit of mind that links various ideological tendencies around the post-Enlightenment project of higher education as an institution with unique origins and responsibilities that need to be protected from within and without (Burke 2000). What might be called the *disenchantment of academic authority*—carried about in different ways by the right and cultural left—has culminated in a tragic polarization between epistemological relativism and a dominant positivism that undermines new alternatives.

The Left, Higher Education, and the State:
Cultural Critique and the Postmodernist Cultural Turn

The corruption of the public relevance argument in the face of fiscal constraints and neoliberal ideology was not the only setback for advocates of public higher education. The cultural politics of the 1980s contributed to a crisis of confidence in the social sciences and humanities that has raised major questions about the knowledge claims of these disciplines. However intellectually important and necessary the cultural turn in the human sciences has been, it has also unwittingly contributed—most evidently in the wake of postmodernism—to weakening the cultural basis for legitimating the autonomy of higher education and research. The great benefactor of the desacralization of the university as a cultural institution has been the increasing penetration of market forces into higher education and the reorganization of university governance around "playing the game" of academic capitalism. In this context it has become increasingly difficult to generate any public support for abstract ideas such as "academic freedom," given that the new process is sufficiently insidious to usually avoid charges of direct political interference of a more traditional kind. In this context the market becomes the Trojan horse for undermining academic autonomy by ostensibly nonideological and noncoercive means based on the interests of the "consumers" of education and research.

Although the present discussion focuses on some of the particular effects of postmodernist cultural theory on this process, it should be noted that the critical modernist sociological theory of Pierre Bourdieu also has unwittingly contributed. Such effects are especially ironic in the case of Bourdieu because his sociology of education originated as a critique of inequality and educational reproduction and a defense of the autonomy of academic disciplines. His analysis of the role of "distinction" in higher education was intended to provide a reflexive basis for a defense of the autonomy of academic disciplines, but it has indirectly served—even on the left—to unmask and to delegitimize the "sacral" origins of the autonomy of higher education (Bourdieu 1984). So long as higher education could retain a faith in its higher mission inherited from religious institutions, partly in the name of a vision of "liberal education" and the rituals of higher education that consecrated it as a unique cultural space, it could provide a justification for seemingly "irrelevant" forms of instruction and research whose value could be demonstrated only in the long run.

The more influential and immediate sources of the undermining of academic authority, however, are closely associated with postmodernist cultural theory and related questioning of the conventional canons of Western humanities scholarship and the effects of positivism in the human sciences in general. This point should not be read as a condemnation of these tendencies per se, which on the whole—despite obvious excesses of "political correctness"—represent important and necessary forms of self-criticism and intellectual renewal. The issue is rather that of confronting the perplexing fact—the unintended consequence—that such internal disputes *have been used* by the cultural and neoliberal right as bases for undermining the intellectual authority of the resulting forms of scholarship. In particular, relativist forms of radical constructivism and militant standpoint theories of the politicization of scholarship become easy targets for those advocating a return to traditional cultural canons and the authority of a positivist social science. Given the vacuum created by the resulting polarization in the academy, neoliberal policy makers have pounced on the confusion by calling for market forces to provide the criteria for supporting and distributing social knowledge, because the academy no longer knows how to conceptualize its demands for autonomy coherently. Indeed, if radical constructivists were right and all aspirations to autonomy are an illusion, there is little to be lost in any case.

Consequently, it is possible to direct specific criticism—at least from the perspective of critical theory—against what might be called certain postmodernist abuses of poststructuralism. Although often articulated on behalf of new forms of political subversion through cultural politics, such efforts have become increasingly self-referential islands of contestation within elite sectors of the academy. To illustrate the limitations of the postmodern hijacking of poststructuralism, the case of Michel Foucault is instructive. At least three kinds of uses of Foucault's ideas in educational theory can be identified. The first involves a kind of reductionist view of Foucault's theory of disciplines, knowledge, and the state that inadvertently plays into the hands of the right by identifying autonomous academic expertise and state power with oppression. Although Foucault's general point was that power/ knowledge relations affect even the most autonomous of scientific institutions, it was far from his intention to denounce research autonomy as a fraud. A second strategy uses Foucault's ideas in a more responsible way, as a kind of corrective to the oversimplifications of both reformist liberalism and the utopian aspirations of some forms of critical theory with respect to the possibilities of educational reform (Popkewitz and Fendler 1999). A third strategy exemplified in this volume is to use Foucault as a resource for a new form of political economy in which regimes of knowledge become subordinate to market processes—a novel development and also a central theme of classical critical theory in the Frankfurt School tradition.

The Free Market as the Ideological Trojan Horse for Eroding Autonomy: Taking Advantage of the Desacralization of Universities

Given the confusion generated by academic discussions of culture and knowledge, it has been easy for neoliberal policy makers to offer a "nonideological" solution to policy in higher education: *Let the market decide.* This strategy has had incremental effects in educational systems with well-established research universities (i.e., the United States and Canada), but it has had disastrous consequences in Latin America, as reflected in generally abysmal public (and private) expenditures on research and development and higher education. In accommodating the "free market" doctrine of why "create" knowledge when it can be imported, political leaders have cynically sold out future generations of an entire region.

The great intellectual coup of neoliberal ideology (although often labeling itself as a form of social theory) was to successfully equate—at least in key segments of the popular imagination and the more powerful policy circles dominated by economists—the simplistic thesis that everything to do with the state is *bad* (inefficient, paternalistic, undemocratic, oppressive, etc.) and everything to do with unregulated markets is *good* (efficient, empowering, democratic, liberating, etc.). A certain lip service was also given to creative potentials of voluntary associations (partly because they are defined as independent of the state), despite their nonprofit altruism. Indeed, neoliberal ideology imagines off-loading state responsibilities to such voluntary associations, most notably religious ones.

This is not the place to detail the theoretical and empirical vacuity of such dogmas. More significant has been the increasing capacity of social liberal and social democratic alternatives to use new forms of social theory to rethink many of the dogmatic assumptions of the old left, most notably an uncritical reliance on the state as the all-purpose solution to social problems, the recognition of the importance of voluntary associations in civil society, and the useful social functions performed by competition, although the concept is understood more broadly than merely market-based competition. But self-reflexive critiques of "seeing like a state" should not be confused with a rejection of the crucial importance of the state for the very idea of democracy (Scott 1998).

The great significance of neoliberal attacks on the autonomy of higher education is that they use a mystifying strategy for undermining academic and scientific autonomy in the name of freedom and competition. This serves as a kind of Trojan horse that undermines academic autonomy as a means of realizing individual liberty. As a close look at the literature on scientific communities suggests, the spirit underlying scientific competition and distinction is grounded in a kind of socialism of knowledge as a cooperative enterprise. Truth cannot be patented and sold off to the highest bidders— the competitive process underlying science is quite distinct from that of private enterprise. By strangling academic autonomy, the defenders of liberty could one day realize the worst forebodings of Herbert Marcuse's conception of a "one-dimensional society."

The ultimate enemy of the right is this very autonomy, which is not only the organizational foundation of scientific communities but also the basis of independent forms of criticism necessary for democracy itself. By letting individual, client-driven, competitive anxiety drive the organization of educational institutions, the whole basis of reasoned collective intelligence is undermined—foresight is eroded in the name of an abstract and ideological conception of individual freedom. When students become increasingly obsessed with a cost-benefit analysis of the "returns" of alternative educational strategies, it is a sign of bizarre constraints on choice. Reducing education and research to a commodity relation has the paradoxical effect of undermining individual freedom in the long run, reinforcing inequalities and distorting the allocation of talent. Not only are such overtly "rational" individual choices difficult and risky to make, given rapid change and uncertainty, they presume forms of equality of opportunity that remain formal and unrealized for marginalized groups. At the same time the erosion of the capacity of political communities to democratically monitor and regulate the protections necessary for an inclusive notion of the public good undermines the framework of equity that is the necessary foundation of authentic individual choice. Such individualism is pseudodemocratic because it does not recognize the bonds of community and civic solidarity that have made modern democracy—for all its current limitations—possible.

Political Economy, Globalization, and Critical Theory

Finally, it can be suggested that even though the chapters in this volume do not fully develop the question, they set the stage for a new articulation between critical theory and higher education research. In short, questions relating to higher education and globalization need to be informed by new forms of research that integrate critical theory, political economy, and democratic theory within the context of a global understanding of democracy and higher education. From this perspective the traditions of critical social theory represent a critique of knowledge and epistemology that calls for a more reflexive and pluralist understanding of inquiry, which entails a dialogue between the universal and the local, of the general and the particular, not the repudiation of the knowledge claims of the social sciences and hu manities in the name of antifoundationalist language games, local knowledge, or self-indulgent personal expression.

Although globalization has created new opportunities for higher education, these are viewed in completely different ways from the perspectives of the neoliberal model of globalization and the alternative modernities envisioned by various forms of critical theory oriented toward "shaping globalization" (Nederveen Pieterse 2000). In the neoliberal model higher education is ideally integrated into the system of production and accumulation in which knowledge is reduced to its economic functions and contributes to the realization of individual economic utilities. This strategy has direct ideological effects in that the cultural legacy of higher education as a form of "humanization" is marginalized as wasteful and unproductive, thus leaving it to the commercial mass media to form the postmodern consumer subject without unsettling questions from educational systems.

In contrast, political economic approaches informed by critical theory seek to defend the autonomy of public higher education, a position that can also accommodate socially conscious private institutions that encourage autonomous research. This stance does not involve a traditional elitist, ivory tower model that resists all links with society or the economy. The democratic multiversity has long recognized the importance of such responsibilities so long as they do not become a rationale for undermining the core functions of teaching and research. Indeed, in certain national contexts a critical policy stance might entail demands for increasing linkages between higher education and industry where appropriate. For example, given the highly defensive posture of Latin American universities (which has understandable historical origins in a long struggle for autonomy), the left has tended to reject all university-industry associations as a capitulation to the private interests of capital. Yet, given the realities of economic life, such connections are essential ingredients for sustaining economic growth and innovation. The crucial question is the terms of reference of such contracts (e.g., ensuring the primacy of retaining sufficient autonomy) and the limitation of private-public alliances to appropriate spheres of activity, not their endless expansion as part of an indiscriminate ideological mantra. In this connection globalization creates new opportunities for cross-national linkages between emergent but impoverished centers of scholarship and better funded and developed research traditions. However, in all spheres of knowledge—cultural, economic, social—public institutions have a fundamental responsibility to encourage research on alternative strategies for realizing human needs and purposes—irrespective of the market demands of the moment.

Nevertheless, as those who speak of "the university in ruins" suggest, the deterioration of the "idea of the university" may have passed beyond the point of no return (Readings 1996). Even if the option of a return to some previous, somewhat idealized state can be set aside as impractical, that leaves open the question of the alternatives. A crucial problem here is that the autonomous university is an increasingly vulnerable institution and that organizing and coordinating resistance to creeping commercialization and privatization is extremely difficult to sustain. The situations in North America and Latin American are dramatically different with respect to the specific challenges and opportunities. In the relatively privileged context of the United States and Canada, it is virtually impossible to rally attention around such slowly working processes that undermine the broader mission of higher learning. As in the case of the loss of cultural legacies or some forms of environmental deterioration, sufficient numbers wake up only when it is too late. Although one can point to significant increases in faculty and graduate student unionization, it is difficult to imagine how to mobilize larger publics of support, at least without a political regime whose leadership makes this a major priority. In Latin America students and faculty are wide awake to the problems, as is evident in a long history of student strikes, culminating in the closure of the National Autonomous University of Mexico for a year in 1999. Yet such confrontations have been largely without meaningful effects, given fiscal constraints and the pressures of international banking institutions to reduce state functions and give other areas of public policy higher priority. As this book eloquently attests, however, new forms of research on higher education are emerging to confront the challenge of a *reenchantment* of academic life as a quasisacred place of independent learning dedicated—to invoke post-Enlightenment images—to a plural (but not relativistic) conception of "truth" and an inclusive sensitivity to the well-being of humanity and nature.

References

Agger, B. 2002. *Postponing the Postmodern: Sociological Practices, Selves, and Theories.* Lanham, MD: Rowman & Littlefield.

Apple, M. W. 1981. "Reproduction, Contestations, and Curriculum: An Essay in Self-Criticism." *Interchange* 12: 27–47.

Apple, M. W., ed. 1982. *Cultural and Economic Reproduction in Education: Essays on Class, Ideology, and the State*. London: Routledge & Kegan Paul.

Best, S., and D. Kellner. 2001. *The Postmodern Adventure: Science, Technology, and Cultural Studies in the Third Millennium*. New York: Guilford Press.

Bourdieu, P. 1984. *Distinction: A Social Critique of the Judgment of Taste*. Cambridge, MA: Cambridge University Press.

Bowles, S., and H. Gintis. 1976. *Schooling in Capitalist America: Educational Reform and the Contradictions of Economic Life*. New York: Basic Books.

Burke, P. 2000. *A Social History of Knowledge: From Gutenberg to Diderot*. Cambridge, UK: Polity Press.

Giroux, H. 1983. *Theory and Resistance in Education: A Pedagogy for the Opposition*. Amherst, MA: Bergin & Garvey.

Morrow, R. A., and C. A. Torres. 1995. *Social Theory and Education: A Critique of Theories of Social and Cultural Reproduction*. Albany: State University of New York Press.

Nederveen Pieterse, J., ed. 2000. *Global Futures: Shaping Globalization*. London: Zed Books.

Parsons, T. 1973. *The American University*. Cambridge, MA: Harvard University Press.

Popkewitz, T., and L. Fendler, eds. 1999. *Critical Theories in Education: Changing Terrains of Knowledge and Politics*. New York: Routledge.

Readings, B. 1996. *The University in Ruins*. Cambridge, MA: Harvard University Press.

Scott, J. C. 1998. *Seeing Like a State: How Certain Schemes to Improve the Human Condition Have Failed*. New Haven, CT: Yale University Press.

Sen, A. 2002. *Rationality and Freedom*. Cambridge, MA: Belknap Press and Harvard University Press.

Slott, M. 2002. "Does Critical Postmodernism Help Us 'Name the System'?" *British Journal of Sociology of Education* 23: 413–425.

Stein, D. G., ed. 2004. *Buying In or Selling Out? The Commercialization of the American Research University*. Piscataway, NJ: Rutgers University Press.

THE UNIVERSITY, STATE, AND MARKET

PART ONE

Theoretical and Conceptual Underpinnings

CHAPTER ONE

Introduction: Globalization and Higher Education in the Americas

Carlos Alberto Torres
Robert A. Rhoads

The Global Context

Globalization is the buzzword of the day. Whether we like it or not, globalization is affecting our lives and the lives of most of the people on earth in complex ways. From the growing diversity of our urban centers to the many ways in which technology touches our lives, to the long arms of international economic organizations and transnational corporations, to the far-reaching power of weapons of mass destruction, to the violent and tragic responses of the disenfranchised, global processes abound. As with most social phenomena, globalization is contradictory and difficult to define. What cannot be disputed, however, is that globalization is playing a major role in reshaping culture, politics, and education.

Globalization provides the backdrop for this book as we seek to make sense of the dynamic relationships among universities, states, and markets throughout the Americas. Of course, the challenge is that there are many definitions of globalization, or perhaps more accurately, there are many globalizations. For example, globalization has been defined as "the intensification of worldwide social relations which link distant localities in such a way that local happenings are shaped by events occurring many miles away and vice versa" (Held 1991, p. 9). Another view sees globalization as "a feature of late capitalism, or the condition of postmodernity, and, more important, . . . the emergence of a world system driven in large part by a global capitalist economy" (Luke and Luke 2000, p. 287). Others see globalization as the transformation of time and space in which complex interactions and exchanges once impossible become everyday activities (Urry 1998). And still others see globalization as an assault on traditional notions of society and nation-state, whereby the very nature of citizenship and social change are dramatically altered (Castells 1997; Touraine 1988).

Images also suggest certain definitions of globalization. For some, the site of a Burger King in Merida, Mexico, or a Starbucks in Guangzhou, China, is telling. For others, the incredible cultural complexity of major urban centers produced by migration and the flow of peoples between countries and continents brings to mind the global nature of today's world. Some may ponder the realities of globalization when they see the presence of US and British soldiers engaged in the construction and bolstering of an Iraqi government or when they see an airplane flying overhead and for an instant think of September 11, when similar planes were turned into missiles and the reality of terrorism instantly became global.

For the two editors of this book few images offer more profound insights into globalization than the trip we took to Argentina to conduct research for this project. In the spring of 2002 we flew from Los Angeles to Buenos Aires to interview faculty and policy makers at the University of Buenos Aires. After arriving at the Buenos Aires airport, we took a taxi to our hotel near the center of the city. Along the way, however, our driver encountered a crowd of maybe 200 people marching in the streets, banging on pots and pans. They chanted phrases condemning Argentine leaders and global financial agencies such as the International Monetary Fund (IMF). We had read about the nightly *cacerolazos* in the newspapers back in the states. In fact, one of us already had experienced the scores of unemployed protesters marching in the streets of Buenos Aires during a previous trip to his homeland and birthplace. For one of us the profound nature of the economic calamity that had become the Argentine economy touched home most profoundly. But what brings the two of us together in this book—and what brings us together with the other contributors who have decided to join our project—is an attempt to make sense of the hegemony of a particular strain of globalization and the potentially devastating effects global economic policies continue to have throughout the Americas. And given that we are all educators and intellectuals who value the democratic possibilities of higher education, we have chosen to turn our critical lens on the university. Thus at the heart of this book is a grave concern about the ways in which relationships among universities, states, and markets increasingly are being shaped by forces that are at times antidemocratic. These issues matter to us because we are deeply concerned about the nature of democratic life in an age of globalization.

A Critical Perspective

This book is framed by an intellectual tradition associated with critical social science (Fay 1987). By critical social science we refer to a variety of theoretical frameworks that center social analysis on advancing democratic possibilities. Many critical social theorists see education as a key site for their work, given the role that schools, colleges, and universities play in preparing citizens for participation in the broader society (Giroux 1983; Rhoads and Valadez 1996; Tierney 1993; Torres 1998, 2002). Whether or not educational institutions actually embrace democratic values and also seek to instill such values in students is a major point of concern for critical theorists. From the perspective of the contributors gathered for this book, a central point of contention is the degree to which democratic values are brought to bear on the complex global processes that affect universities throughout the Americas.

Critical theorists tend to believe that all research is politically based and that it is incumbent upon investigators to clarify their basic theoretical positions (Tierney and Rhoads 1993). Consequently, we use the next few pages to identify the theoretical assumptions we bring to this work. And although each of the writers contributing to this book takes a slightly different direction in offering a critical analysis of globalization, all of them embrace the basic assumptions outlined here.

Critical theorists use inquiry as a means for challenging forms of oppression and marginality that limit full and equitable participation in public life (Habermas 1973; Horkheimer 1972; Marcuse 1972). Thus a key contribution of critical theory is the belief that research ought to serve an emancipatory goal. That is, and we paraphrase Karl Marx here, social scientists should not simply interpret the world but should use their inquiry as a vehicle for improving, reforming, or revolutionizing social life. Furthermore, from a critical perspective the changes that social scientists seek ought to advance democratic ideals and practices.

In thinking about democratic possibilities, we take the work of John Dewey and Paulo Freire as starting points for advancing a critical analysis of higher education in a global age. Dewey had a particular vision of democratic life that entailed much more than simply the right to vote. He saw democracy as people actively engaging in meaningful social relations and participating in decisions that affect their lives. Dewey's vision has a strong relational tone, meaning that democracy is dependent on the quality of social relations forged among individuals and groups. A passage from his classic work *Democracy and Education* is relevant: "A democracy is more than a form of government; it is primarily a mode of associated living, of conjoint communicated experience. The extension in space of the number of individuals who participate in an interest so that each has to refer his own action to that of others, and to consider the action of others to give point and direction to his own" (1916, p. 93). In simple terms, no woman or man is an island. Our experiences, our decisions, our actions all influence and shape the lives of others.

Dewey's vision of democracy challenges all citizens to take part in a variety of decisions that balance one's own interests with the interests of others. An important point relative to this book and to issues linked to globalization is Dewey's vision of citizens participating in everyday decisions that affect their lives. Given the role that economic policies play in the lives of citizens, Dewey's democratic vision calls for citizen input at the local, national, and global levels. But where is the democratic space within the context of corporate-driven forms of globalization, when public spheres are increasingly distanced from the nexus of decision making and global trade organizations and multinational enterprises (MNEs) define the terms of world economic affairs? Indeed, a fundamental criticism coming from a variety of social movements, including those who gathered in the streets of Seattle in 1999 to protest the meetings of the World Trade Organization (WTO), is the lack of representation and the use of open and democratic processes in the construction of global relations. How can average citizens and workers influence global processes when they and their representatives are absent from the table?

Similar to Dewey, Paulo Freire's work in education focused on advancing democratic opportunities. Freire was deeply touched by the lives of quiet desperation that so many lower- and working-class citizens throughout his native homeland of Brazil experienced. He saw education at a grassroots level and believed that engaging people in their communities was key to elevating literacy and raising consciousness. Self-empowerment was vital to the pedagogical project spelled out in Freire's (1970) *Pedagogy of the Oppressed*, and he believed that average citizens could take charge of their own lives and ultimately develop the critical skills necessary to write their own histories.

Developing literacy programs was a major component of Freire's early work in Brazil, but literacy was much more than simply the ability to read and write. For Freire literacy also involved reading culture and comprehending social structure; every citizen ought to have the opportunity to develop skills and dispositions that will be helpful to making sense of one's own life and for understanding the complex forces that shape the nature of society. The goal for Freire was to develop critical consciousness, or *conscientização*, whereby citizens develop the capacity to offer their own critical analysis of society. But simply critiquing society was insufficient for Freire; he also compelled citizens to act in order to change the course of events that contribute to lives of desperation. The action component of Freire's pedagogy is in part why his work is seen as revolutionary—its basis rests with the Marxist tradition of seeking to understand the world in order to change it. This is the essence of a critical treatment of education.

The Many Faces of Globalization

In seeking to convey a somewhat unified understanding of globalization, we found ourselves spinning in circles. In the end we came to the conclusion that globalization is far too complex to present in a simple formulaic manner. What became rather obvious to us is that globalization has many manifestations that interact simultaneously in a fairly convoluted fashion (or multiple "globalizations"). Yet the many forms of globalization are all deeply affected by the dynamics of international relations of the past few years and, by implication, influence the role that higher education and reform play in the improvement of people's lives and the societies in which they exist. Consequently, instead of presenting one notion of globalization, we have identified five primary manifestations that stand out in today's context. Certainly, globalization takes other forms, but the following five provide a solid foundation for framing our book.

One form of globalization, often seen as "globalization from above," is framed by an ideology that we describe as *neoliberalism*. Neoliberals call for an opening of national borders for the purpose of increased commodity and capital exchange, the creation of multiple regional markets, the elevation of free markets over state-controlled markets and interventions, the proliferation of fast-paced economic and financial transactions, and the presence of governing systems other than nation-states. Neoliberalism seeks to privatize virtually every process or service that can possibly be turned over to private capital. "Selective deregulation" is the motto of this version of globalization.

Another form of globalization is the antithesis of the first. This form of globalization is often described as "globalization from below," or "anti-globalization," which we see as a misnomer because various groups and movements whose aim is to challenge neoliberal versions of globalization are not opposed to increased international integration in general. Globalization from below is largely manifested in individuals, institutions, and social movements that are actively opposed to what is perceived as corporate globalism. For these individuals and groups, "no globalization without representation" is the motto.

A third form of globalization is represented by the movement and exchange of people and ideas and the subsequent influence on culture. Now, it is certainly true that the globalization of people and ideas dates back to the Colonial Period and the emergence of the first great navies and shipping industries. But, in the last part of the 20th century we have seen an escalation of international exchange such that now it is quite common to speak of the internationalization of cultures and societies. There is a "creolization" of the world to some extent, and technology is playing a central role in such processes, because transportation and communication technologies—the computing industry and the Internet come to mind especially—increasingly are reshaping the world. Clearly, the international integration of culture is the theme of this manifestation of globalization.

A fourth form emerges from increased international integration and pertains more to rights than to markets: the globalization of human rights. With the growing ideology of human rights taking hold of the international system and international law, many traditional practices endemic to the fabric of particular societies or cultures (from religious practices to esoteric practices) are now being called into question, challenged, forbidden, or even outlawed. Advancement of cosmopolitan democracies and plural citizenship is the theme of this version of globalization.

Finally, there is a fifth manifestation of globalization that we consider. This form extends beyond markets and to some extent is against human rights. Here we speak of the globalization of the international war against terrorism. This new form of globalization has been prompted in large part by the events of September 11, 2001—which were interpreted as the globalization of the terrorist threat—and the reaction of the United States. The antiterrorist response has been militaristic in nature, resulting in two coalition wars led by the United States against Muslim regimes in Afghanistan and Iraq. Yet the overall theme of this process is not only its military flavor but also the emphasis on security and control of borders, people, capital, and commodities—that is, the reverse of open markets and high-paced commodity exchanges. Security as a precondition of freedom is the theme of this form of globalization. Not surprisingly, its nemesis, terrorism, endorses the motto that only chaos will bring about freedom.

Clearly, globalization can be characterized by multiplicity and contradictions, with deep-rooted historical causes. And, if one thinks of the tenets of human rights, for instance, globalization is a historical process that is difficult to reverse or even confront. Let us now explore in some detail these five possible forms of globalization vis-à-vis their implications for higher education.

The Impact on Higher Education

The impact of globalization on colleges and universities is both direct and indirect. An example of a direct effect is the way in which national economies are restructuring their systems of support for higher education as a consequence of shifting economic priorities and structural adjustment policies mandated from above. Examples of indirect effects include the manner by which the war against terrorism has come to limit academic freedom and the transnational flow of scholars and students and the way in which academic culture at some Latin American universities is shifting from a collectivist orientation to ideals associated with individualism. What is clear is that the various manifestations of globalization have the potential to produce different kinds of effects, although disentangling cause and effect can be quite problematic.

GLOBALIZATION FROM ABOVE

Multilateral or bilateral agencies, such as the World Bank, the IMF, some agencies of the United Nations, and perhaps the Organization for Economic Cooperation and Development (OECD) have promoted a model of neoliberal globalization (Teodoro 2003). This agenda includes a push toward privatization and decentralization of public forms of education, a movement toward educational standards, a strong emphasis on testing, and a focus on accountability. Specific to higher education, neoliberal versions of globalization suggest four primary reforms for universities related to efficiency and accountability, accreditation and universalization, international competitiveness, and privatization.

Concerns about efficiency and accountability are manifested in the effort of legislatures, governing boards, and policy makers to increase the productivity of faculty while decreasing university and college expenditures. The classic example is the effort to increase faculty teaching loads without raising salaries. The proliferation of large classes in which one professor can reach hundreds of students is another example, as were early efforts to promote distance and Internet-based education, at least until universities discovered how costly such efforts can be.

With regard to accreditation and universalization, major efforts are underway throughout the world to reform academic programs through accreditation processes and various strategies that produce increased homogeneity across national boundaries. For example, in Mexico efforts are under way to reform various professional preparation programs in a manner consistent with those operating in the United States. Proponents argue that such efforts will enable increased exchange between the United States and Mexico. Opponents see such programs as potentially increasing brain drain as part of the south to north flight of intellectuals and the highly skilled. Another example was the recent push by the Japanese government to open law schools mirroring American-style graduate-level legal education (Brender 2003), as was the plan by UNESCO to develop an international quality-assurance agency to monitor global higher education ventures (Lin-Liu 2001).

Reforms associated with international competitiveness are akin to what Martin Carnoy (2001) described in the K–12 sector as "competition-based reforms." These reforms are characterized by efforts to create measurable performance standards through extensive standardized testing (the new standards and accountability movement), the introduction of new teaching and learning methods leading to the expectation of better performance at low cost (e.g., the universalization of textbooks), and improvements in the selection and training of teachers. Competition-based reforms in higher education tend to adopt a vocational orientation and reflect the point of view that colleges and universities exist largely to serve the economic well-being of a society.

Privatization, of course, is the final major reform effort linked to neoliberalism and is perhaps the most dominant. Neoliberal economic supporters view the marketplace as the ideal regulator of services, products, and costs. Consequently, if we think of higher education as a product or service, then from a neoliberal perspective the best way to regulate colleges and universities is to allow the market to do so. Nation-states need not fund or concern themselves with tuition costs; the market can take on such responsibilities quite handily. If institutions of higher education price themselves too high, prospective students will inform them by selecting other less pricey colleges. Alternatively, if a prospective student cannot afford to participate in higher education, then there are other options that societies offer for the less fortunate, including military service and work within the service sector of the economy. The rationality of such a system is purely economic. Furthermore, from the perspective of neoliberalism the system is entirely just, given that subjective individuals do not open and close doors, but a system of costs and payments dictates nearly every outcome.

The privatization of higher education in debt-riddled countries such as Mexico, Brazil, and Argentina typically is advanced by the IMF and the

World Bank as a precondition to further borrowing by these countries. A central precondition of such lending involves the transference of educational financing from higher education to lower levels of education—under the premise that subsidizing higher education is subsidizing the wealthiest members of society, because most of the students enrolled in higher education are from the middle and upper classes. This was one of the key premises of the failed Education for All Initiative sponsored in Jomtien, Thailand, in 1990 by UNESCO, the UN Development Program (UNDP), UNICEF, and the World Bank. The meeting attracted the participation of government representatives from 155 countries and more than 150 nongovernmental organizations (NGOs). The pledge was to provide education for all by the year 2000. As the argument goes, investments in lower levels of education, namely primary and secondary schooling, will result in higher rates of return and a better equity-investment ratio than investments in higher education. This strategy increasingly has come under attack in Latin America, in part because of long-standing social contracts between governments and citizens that include expectations of accessible, if not free, forms of higher education.

Privatization also has advanced hand in hand with increased entrepreneurialism, especially in the most developed countries, as universities have sought to expand their revenue through a variety of profit-seeking endeavors, including satellite campuses and extension programs around the world. In addition, many universities in the wealthiest countries are actively involved in shaping the nature of higher education in less developed countries, as is the case with a program funded by the United States Agency for International Development (USAID) in which US colleges and universities received funds to assist in the development of Iraqi higher education (Del Castillo 2003b). Similarly, US officials are actively involved in developing a stronger private higher education sector in Afghanistan (Del Castillo 2003a). In these two instances we see clear connections between neoliberalism and the US-led war on terrorism, with two countries identified by US officials as breeding grounds for terrorism on the receiving end of heavy doses of "American-style" higher education. Of course, privatization is also driving research and development agendas at universities, especially in the United States. The quest by US colleges and universities to acquire funds for research and development activities is discussed in much detail by Slaughter and Rhoades (2004), who highlight the "academic capitalist knowledge/learning/consumption regime."

In closing this section, we think it is important to emphasize that privatization policies are crucial elements of the reforms oriented toward promoting open markets, and, as such, they are important policy tools of neoliberalism. Two key benefits are seen by neoliberals: (1) The pressure of fiscal spending is reduced by the privatization of public sector enterprises, and (2) privatization is a powerful instrument for depoliticizing the regulatory practices of the state in the area of public policy formation. However, as has been clear throughout the last two decades, the implications of privatization and the push for market policies to limit the state's role in social sectors pose serious problems: "In the context of the market forces, the state's interventionist role is likely to decline. This will have implications for all categories of people who, by virtue of their already weak position in spheres of knowledge, skills, access to goods and services and control over resources, need some protective legislations and provisions. Left to themselves in the open market, their situation is likely to get further deteriorated" (Kaur 1999, p. 126).

GLOBALIZATION FROM BELOW

Of course, the forces opposing neoliberal forms of globalization see a system that is based entirely on costs and payments as harsh and cruel. Individuals are not born into the same economic or class standing, and, consequently, governments acting in the name of the public good must intervene to create systems and processes that extend beyond the arbitrary rationality of economic determinism. The challenge that antineoliberalist forces are confronted with is the degree to which global economic systems—and, in effect, social relations—are being constructed almost entirely by corporations and a select group of extremely rich and powerful individuals.

Diverse groups have been brought together under the banner of anti-globalization (which should be understood as antineoliberal globalization), including groups opposed to corporate capitalism but also environmentalists, unions, and even nationalistic isolationists, such as Pat Buchanan's followers in the United States. The isolationists are worried about intergovernmental organizations (IGOs) and NGOs replacing national governments, and they fear, in the United States, that their own country will lose its global dominance and that their citizens will lose their economic privilege. But the primary theme of "globalization and its discontents" concerns establishing a set of rules governing a global economy and defining whose interests those rules ultimately serve (Stiglitz 2002).

The social movements opposed to corporate globalism argue from positions focused on social justice and democracy for workers and citizens. These movements have had a variety of important dissident voices. For example, world summits such as the September 2000 IMF–World Bank summit in Prague and the July 2001 G-8 meeting in Genoa took place amid a chorus of critics reacting to the closed nature of global decision making. Outspoken individuals and groups have included the likes of the late Pope John Paul II and the Catholic Church, various Protestant churches, feminist groups, environmental groups such as Green Peace, indigenous rights groups, and communist, socialist, anarchist, and libertarian groups. In short, the oppositional groups are vast and growing in number and degree of discontent (Rhoads 2003; Stiglitz 2002).

The rich array of worldwide anticorporate globalization views and actions have found sources of support within academe in part because colleges and universities also have come under the influence of global processes and at times seem just as disempowered as those groups and individuals who took to the streets in Seattle, Prague, and Genoa. Let us look to Latin America for an example.

Throughout Latin America universities have a distinguished and long tradition of academic work based on the notion of autonomy and financial autarchy. For example, the Autonomous University of Santo Domingo was founded in 1538, less than 50 years after the historic voyage of Christopher Columbus to America, and the Autonomous University of Córdoba, Argentina, was founded in 1613. Despite this long tradition, for the last two decades these institutions and many others throughout the region have faced the hammering of the neoliberal agenda of privatization, decentralization, and accountability based on entrepreneurial models, including productivity incentives that are leading professors in countries such as Mexico to mirror those in the United States. As a consequence of such forces challenging the very nature of academic life and the values that many academics hold dear, including the value of academic freedom, leading intellectuals such as Noam Chomsky (1998) have struck back with virulent criticism of neoliberalism, adding fuel to the movements opposed to corporate-driven forms of globalization.

In addition, colleges and universities throughout the world have been sites of student resistance to a variety of forms of globalization. As privatization spreads to the realm of higher education funding, increasingly colleges and universities are either implementing fees or raising tuition, the results of which have been large-scale student protests. Over the past few years we have witnessed a year-long fee-related strike at the National Autonomous University of Mexico (Rhoads and Mina 2001), nationwide protests by Canadian students over tuition hikes (Birchard 2002), university occupations by German students in protest of the privatization of education, and massive protests by students in Great Britain after higher education officials broke with tradition and implemented annual fees for first-year full-time students (Rhoads 2003).

Students also have been actively engaged in protests at the meetings of global trade organizations and world economic leaders. Students were well represented in the massive WTO protests in Seattle in December 1999. Furthermore, campus organizations with global concerns, such as the Free Burma Coalition and the Environmental Action Coalition, have been effective in forging worldwide Internet-based movements. And students have been actively involved in organizations such as the Citizens Trade Campaign (CTC), Mobilization for Global Justice, and the Poor People's Campaign for Economic Human Rights in the Americas. These groups reject the notion that neoliberal globalization is the natural outcome of contemporary economic relations and instead believe that powerful economic organizations create the climate and context for an oppressive version of globalization.

GLOBALIZATION OF CULTURE

A variety of arguments circulate around globalization and culture. One perspective suggests that the increasing exchange of peoples and ideas is producing a "creolization" effect as societies more and more resemble a complex mix of East and West, North and South. Another argument sees the globalization of culture as the "Americanization" of the world (or the "McDonaldization," as some like to say) and focuses on the ways in which central nation-states affect the semiperiphery and the periphery. Here, the flow of peoples and ideas is seen as mostly one directional, from west to east and north to south. Hence nation-states such as the United States impose their values, norms, and beliefs on other parts of the world and for the most part are not mutually influenced, at least not to the same degree. In seeking to reconcile these alternative views, we think it is probably safe to say that some nation-states disproportionately influence other parts of the world, culturally speaking, but nonetheless also are influenced by remote regions and countries. In addition, although powerful nation-states with colonial and imperial histories have no doubt shaped the cultural landscape of remote parts of the world, clearly such influence has met with much resistance, and in many cases local cultures have adapted impositions to form a variety of cultural hybrids (Said 1993).

Of course, universities play a central role in advancing increased cultural exchange. For example, the Internet has made transnational scholarly collaboration a common endeavor. Some of the most significant intellectual innovations of the past 20 years have been the result of international collaboration. In addition, improved transportation technologies make travel more affordable, and international conferences and forums flourish in today's environment, despite the restrictions of the post-9/11 era. And the movement of students from country to country for the purpose of studying abroad continues to be a major source of international exchange for nation-states around the world.

But elements of imperialism also exist within the context of universities and cultural globalization, particularly in the area of higher education reform. For example, US universities and their scholars have the ability to shape a variety of discourses associated with university reform; this influence is clearly evident in the Americas as well as throughout vast regions of the world. Interestingly, here we see "globalization from above" intersecting with cultural globalization; elements of the US system of higher education are transmitted to other nation-states, both through the growing power and influence of neoliberalism and through cultural exchanges, which reflects the strength of US universities.

GLOBALIZATION OF HUMAN RIGHTS

The presence of another form of globalization that is centered on advancing human rights poses, by itself, yet another round of issues to be addressed. The movement toward universal human rights is a powerful force that pushes us beyond conversations about certain rights being "a good idea to that which ought to be the birthright of every person" (Bunch 2001, pp. 138–139). Furthermore, the idea of global human rights has become a central issue in considering citizenship and democracy. Nuhoglu Soysal's (1994) analysis of the limits of citizenship in the era of globalization highlighted some of the issues. She argued that "the logic of personhood supersedes the logic of national citizenship [and] individual rights and obligations, which were historically located in the nation state, have increasingly moved to a universalistic plane, transcending the boundaries of particular nation-states" (pp. 164–165). Soysal went on to discuss the idea of "cosmopolitan democracies," or transnational political systems relatively divorced in their origin and constitute dynamics from nation-states.

If the agenda for human rights is reconfiguring the boundaries of nations and individual rights of national citizens and if they are seen as preconditions to attain basic equality worldwide, then educational systems will need to confront more and more the tension between human rights as a globalized project of cosmopolitan democracies and the long-standing influence of nationalism. This tension also is projected in questions of identity and whether the particular rights of cultural and religious groups will be upheld in the face of an ideology of global human rights (Torres 1998).

The interests of global human rights advocates largely center on the universal rights to food, water, and health care. But other issues also arise within the context of global rights discussions, including equality for all women, indigenous peoples, and ethnic minorities. Others suggest that the right to participate in a society's governance structure and the right to a quality education also ought to be universal. In terms of the last two rights, schools and universities become key sites of struggle, because concerns about what constitutes "quality" and the role that educational institutions play in shaping expectations and dispositions relative to civic participation come to the forefront.

A key concern specifically tied to higher education is the question of whether a college or university education is a privilege or a right. This has become a major point of contention in countries such as Mexico and Argentina, where structural adjustments clearly situate participation in higher education as a privilege but long-standing social contracts within these two countries suggest otherwise. Here we see a clear clash of two oppositional agendas, one focused on privatization and advancing a competition-based social structure and the other focused on social intervention and advancing a spirit of collectivism (Torres and Puiggrós 1996).

GLOBALIZATION OF THE INTERNATIONAL WAR AGAINST TERRORISM

The most obvious change in the process of globalization in the last few years is the terrorist attack of September 11, 2001, which undermined the invincibility of the United States. In waging a relentless counterassault against the Taliban and Al-Qaeda, and a second war against Iraq, the United States has produced massive change at a global level. In combination with the continuing reverberations of September 11, US-led antiterrorist initiatives continue to transform global relations, including significant changes within the spheres of economics, politics, culture, and education (Apple 2002).

The reverberations of the September 11 attacks and the ensuing global war against terrorism have important consequences for an increasingly interconnected world. Our concern here is with the effect on higher education. One consequence is the restrictive climate for scholars and students seeking transnational mobility. This phenomenon, of course, is most notable in the United States, where political and social pressure to ensure domestic security has led to more highly regulated and monitored borders and points of entry. A concern for many universities is the availability of international education for foreign students—not a minor source of income for countries heavily involved in international education. The United States, for example, is the biggest exporter of international education. Ravinder Sidhu (2003) pointed out that the United States had 547,867 foreign students studying at American institutions during the 2000–2001 academic year. Second to the United States is the United Kingdom, which during the 1999–2000 academic year had 277,000 international students (129,180 were at the postsecondary level). According to Sidhu, the US economy benefited in the billions (US dollars), and the United Kingdom brought in roughly £8 billion. The fear, of course, is that September 11 and the responses to it, such as those enacted by the US Office of Homeland Security (OHS) and stricter policies with regard to visas, will curtail international students seeking to study at US universities.

In addition to possible financial reverberations associated with international education, there are concerns about limitations placed on scholarly exchange and the general assault on academic freedom. Here, we focus our analysis on the United States, but we note that the effect extends to the global intellectual arena. A key threat to academic freedom centers on the US government's demand on colleges and universities to track foreign students and some professors through a computerized system known as the Student and Exchange Visitor Information System, or SEVIS. The US government requires that colleges and universities keep track of who is admitted and hired from a foreign country and when they enter and leave the country. This requirement creates a situation in which members of a particular academic community are expected to monitor the movement of members of their own community, contributing to an environment of mistrust; we must keep in mind that foreign students and professors are full members of the same academic community that is now expected to monitor their coming and going. The responsibility for managing SEVIS is more likely than not to fall on staff at campus international centers. Consequently, instead of providing academic and cultural support, staff members may be just as likely to be engaged in information management for the US government, all in the name of the "new militarism" aimed at fighting global terrorism.

Threats to academic freedom come in many forms under the new militarism. Burton Bollag (2003) described the case of Professor Carlos Alzugaray Treto, a leading expert on US-Cuban relations. Professor Alzugaray and more than 30 other Cuban scholars were denied visas when they sought to participate in the Latin American Studies Association (LASA) International Congress in Dallas in March 2003. Homeland-security policies deemed them potential risks, and so instead of participating in three panels on Latin American issues and "giving American scholars and students a Cuban perspective, Mr. Alzugaray [was] driving his blue 1979 Soviet Lada each day down Havana's palm-tree lined roads to his job as professor at the Advanced Institute for International Relations" (Bollag 2003, p. A16). In addition, Professor Alzugaray was scheduled to visit Ohio's Miami University for six days in April 2003, but this trip also had to be canceled because his visa request was rejected. One Miami University professor described it as a "deeply disturbing sign of the many impacts of the 'war on terror'" (p. A17). One year later, similar events took place when LASA met in Las Vegas and all the visa requests from Cuban scholars were rejected by the US Department of State (Lipka 2004).

Although all the forms of globalization outlined in the preceding pages contribute in complex ways to transformation within higher education, in this book we primarily center on "globalization from above"—the form of globalization that we have come to associate with neoliberalism. However, the reality is that the other manifestations of globalization, relating to the spread of culture, oppositional social movements, human rights, and the global war on terrorism, cannot easily be separated from concerns linked to the political economy of globalization. Consequently, although we focus primarily on neoliberal globalization and its relationship to universities throughout the Americas, we also bring the other forms of globalization to bear on our analysis.

Why the Americas?

One major consequence of globalization is increased regionalization. As pressure to participate in global markets increases, nation-states seek economic partnerships and arrangements that better enable their own industries to compete. One response has been to strengthen ties to neighboring and proximal countries as well as among countries sharing a common geographic identity. By increasing the strength of regional relationships, nation-states hope to enhance their ability to compete in globalized markets. We see this phenomenon in a variety of geographic contexts. Countries in Europe have forged the European Union (EU). Asian countries have enhanced trade opportunities through the Asia Pacific Economic Cooperation (APEC) agreement, and a variety of sub-regional trade arrangements (RTAs) have flourished over the past decade or so in eastern and southern Africa.

Given the context of globalization and the role that regionalization plays as an economic buffer, one might expect that countries in the Americas also would forge formal trade relations and seek to take advantage of regional connections among nations in the Western Hemisphere. And this is precisely what is taking place; nation-states in the Americas increasingly are becoming economically and politically interdependent. Countless examples support such a conclusion. The North American Free Trade Agreement (NAFTA) has brought the economies of the United States, Canada, and Mexico into greater interdependence. Following NAFTA, the Central America Free Trade Agreement (CAFTA) has sought to increase economic interaction among the countries of Central America and the United States through various regulations favoring free trade. In South America, Mercosur has achieved similar interdependence among the economies of Argentina, Brazil, Paraguay, and Uruguay. And, of course, US-led efforts have attempted to increase unrestricted trade throughout the Americas through establishment of the Free Trade Area of the Americas, which, in essence, would bring all the countries of the Americas under the regulations and service agreements authorized by the World Trade Organization. Clearly, more interconnected economic structures are emerging in the Americas, and analysis of the implications for public policy is sorely needed, most specifically in the area of higher education and the role of universities.

As harmonization—the effort to develop uniform standards for products and trade—is advanced throughout the Americas, not only are political and economic interests brought into greater contact but also culture itself is influenced by such connections. Harmonization is dependent on transnational working groups and committees to monitor trade and to ensure that trade agreements are followed. Such working groups represent new forms of global or transnational governing systems and as such play a significant role in advancing certain norms and values for particular regions (in this case, the Americas). What is evident in the evolution of NAFTA, CAFTA, Mercosur, and the WTO is that the interests of business and industry take precedence over most other concerns. What is often absent from key governing bodies that decide and monitor global trade relations are groups and individuals concerned with the environment, labor, and human rights. Clearly, the key priority of the emerging global governing bodies is capital, not labor. This poses a serious challenge to the socialist, communitarian, progressive, and labor-oriented interests that are deeply embedded in the cultures of many countries throughout the Americas. Indeed, the alienation of groups associated with such traditions is a major factor in fueling grassroots movements that challenge corporate-led versions of globalization.

Despite powerful efforts to create regional and global trade alliances throughout the Americas, there are dramatic countermovements to resist increased economic and political interdependence. One of the most significant countermovements has been the Zapatista uprising in southern Mexico; this group first came into public view at almost the precise time that NAFTA was being adopted by Mexico, Canada, and the United States. The Zapatista localist movement highlights the serious contradictions in the Americas that accompany neoliberal globalization. Of importance is the fact that global trade processes often elicit harsh responses. It is more than symbolic that the indigenous population of southern Mexico emerged from the bushes precariously armed yet defiant of the Mexican army and political system and in large numbers sought to challenge NAFTA as part of a project to redress social and economic inequities.

The strains of resistance also have been evident in governmental sectors throughout the Americas, most notably in South America. Although highly developed countries such as the United States are the leading proponents of capital-driven forms of globalization, less developed countries such as Argentina and Brazil are more skeptical. Consequently, the governments of these countries are not as quick to jump on the procapital globalist project. For example, Argentina's Nestor Kirchner refused to follow the dictates of the IMF during the early months of his presidency and successfully negotiated a restructuring of his country's debt so that Argentina could invest in antipoverty and public works programs. Similarly, President Luis Ignácio Lula da Silva of Brazil has been a major proponent of models of globalization that advance workers' rights.

The Americas as a unified economic force are part of an emerging vision embedded in the consciousness of powerful individuals and groups operating in the Western Hemisphere. With the United States as the epicenter of such an economic groundswell, powerful corporations and industries increase their chances for economic survival in the increasingly competitive global market. But free trade initiatives and privatization increasingly meet resistance throughout the Americas, and so the push and pull of multiple forms of globalization may be most obvious within this dynamic region. The strains of globalization within the Americas as much as anything else reinforce this region's significance. Hence, given the relevance of the Americas as a regionalized entity, what countries should we address as part of our analysis of globalization and the role of universities?

We have clear reasons for selecting four particular countries—Argentina, Brazil, Mexico, and the United States—as the primary focus of our analysis. The United States is an obvious choice because it is the world's largest economy and its political and cultural systems have influenced nearly every corner of the world, most notably countries throughout the Americas. The

United States has been a major force in promoting free trade at a global level, and its support of the WTO has enabled the organization to assume a regulatory function relative to global trade. In addition, US industries have helped to set the tone for global competitiveness. For example, US-based companies are some of the leading firms in outsourcing and the general push toward casualization of workforces. Companies close in the United States and then move southward to Mexico or elsewhere as they seek to take advantage of lower wages and a less regulated manufacturing environment. Citizens in the United States lose jobs, but Mexican citizens see the *possibility* for improved wages. (Indeed, these may be only possibilities because growing evidence of post-NAFTA Mexico increasingly points to economic decline.) Of course, such trends come with significant price tags. More to the point, one of the Mexican scholars we interviewed as part of a study we conducted of the national university in Mexico City suggested that his country rapidly is becoming a *maquiladora* society—giving up any chance of contributing to the global technology boom and instead making a home for low-level, highly dangerous, and environmentally costly manufacturing industries. Clearly, these are concerns that must be brought to bear on US-led global economic policies.

The US system of higher education plays a major role in advancing the nation's economic interests, and, in fact, universities themselves are caught up in the same global economy and trends affecting other industries. So, as greater expectations are placed on the US university to prepare citizens for a global economy, academic capitalism becomes deeply embedded within the culture of academe and universities are increasingly expected to contribute to the economic development of a global economy (Slaughter and Leslie 1997; Slaughter and Rhoades 2004). And given the success of the US university, it should surprise no one that key nations throughout the Americas have turned to the US model as a possible basis for higher educational reform. Consequently, the role of the United States and the relevance of the US university are central facets of our analysis of the political economy of globalization throughout the Americas.

Mexico is another obvious choice for our focus. It has the world's 11th largest economy, based on gross national product (among nation-states). Mexico also has been and continues to be a major player in Latin American culture and politics and the push toward globalization. Only a decade ago

Daniel Levy noted that Mexico is considered "a leader in the Latin American movement toward greater privatization, market competition, and US-oriented internationalization" (1994, p. 25). But by comparison to major economic powers such as the United States, Japan, and Germany, Mexico has a great distance to go to achieve an advanced level of technological and economic development. In its efforts to modernize and improve its position in a global marketplace, Mexico's system of higher education must play a critical role. However, with limited tax revenue and pressure from international organizations such as the IMF to target lower and intermediate levels of education, universities in Mexico face serious challenges in their efforts to strengthen the Mexican economy. Among these challenges is developing adequate support for scholarly careers and academic-based science. These are just a few of the Mexican higher education concerns to be addressed in this book, but clearly no analysis of globalization and its effect on the Americas would be complete without a serious focus on this key country.

Brazil and Argentina make up a major portion of South America's Southern Cone and constitute the world's 8th and 15th largest economies, respectively. Both countries also have been heavily guided by IMF and World Bank policies and are at the heart of regional and global economic activity originating in South America. Both countries also face massive debt and major political change and are home to some of the most powerful grassroots globalization movements in the world. Such movements actively oppose versions of globalization advanced by the IMF, the World Bank, and the WTO and are quite global themselves.

In Argentina the economic crisis of the early years of the 21st century establishes the context for an analysis of globalization and higher education. Under the direction of the IMF and in combination with government corruption, the Argentine economy collapsed in the fall of 2001. The result was massive unemployment and violent protests in the streets of Buenos Aires; the citizens of Argentina saw a steady flow of five different presidents in a matter of days. From Argentina's devastating economic conditions emerged significant citizen-led anti-IMF and antineoliberalism movements. The "pot bangers" of Buenos Aires provided vital energy to calls for globalization from the bottom up and led to democratically organized neighborhood assemblies throughout Argentina. The Argentine People's Rebellion, as it is sometimes called, has fueled a growing movement that is especially strong in developing nations in the Americas, particularly in South America. A central objective of the movement from below is to challenge corporate-driven forms of globalization and introduce more democratic methods of economic policy making. Advancing worker and human rights is also a key objective.

Like Argentina, Brazil too has seen devastating economic times. The election of Lula da Silva (simply known as Lula throughout Brazil) in the fall of 2002 was as much a condemnation of neoliberal globalization as it was a statement about the centrality of labor (he is a member of Brazil's labor party, Partido dos Trabalhadores). Brazil also has seen the emergence of powerful grassroots movements to challenge neoliberalism. Movimento dos Sem-Terra, the Brazilian landless movement, has been at the forefront of the growing assault on what movement leaders describe as unchecked corporate globalism. The growing verve of bottom-up globalization was evident at the World Social Forum in January 2002, hosted in Porto Alegre, where anti-neoliberal organizations and groups listened to Noam Chomsky condemn the exploitation of September 11 by powerful economic leaders simultaneously meeting at the World Economic Forum in New York. Chomsky argued that September 11, and the threat of terrorism in general, essentially was being used to wage an assault on citizen- and worker-led globalization movements (Sullivan 2002).

Caught in the struggle between bottom-up and top-down global movements, universities in Argentina and Brazil face the challenge of reform in a context that has become highly contentious and politicized. Consequently, university reform faces a period of turmoil and transition with competing pulls, some favoring privatization and neoliberalism and others favoring governmental support and long-standing social contracts.

At a cultural level, as the push for open markets and privatization initiatives advance throughout the Americas, these initiatives come face to face with diverse cultures and traditions. Relevant to this book, significant problems arise when developing countries in the Americas seek to advance more privatized forms of higher education in a manner similar to the heavily privatized US university. First and foremost is a lack of recognition of a multi-layered system of higher education in the United States; too often reformers turn to the US research university and ignore the fact that the US system also includes private liberal arts colleges, comprehensive state colleges and universities, and community colleges, with the last two institutional types serving a critical function by providing high levels of educational access. What we suggest in this book is that efforts to advance universities in less developed countries (relative to the United States), such as Argentina and Mexico, cannot simply mimic US research universities because such universities and their service to the broader public are mitigated by the contributions of state-supported comprehensive colleges and community colleges. Obviously, the social context and the broader systems of education must be considered as developing countries throughout the Americas face pressure to mirror privatized forms in the United States. And efforts by international organizations to push public and national universities toward more privatized models must recognize the differential educational support systems at work throughout the Americas. For example, although it may make sense for elite research universities in the United States to be somewhat restrictive in terms of access, given the role of comprehensive colleges and community colleges (the California Master Plan offers an excellent example of the relationships among such institutions), the same cannot be said of Mexico's top research university, the National Autonomous University of Mexico (UNAM), which historically also serves the masses through high levels of access. Consequently, it is not surprising that efforts by international organizations to alter the historic role of UNAM, and in essence to redefine its social contract, are met with high levels of student and public resistance (Rhoads 2003; Rhoads and Mina 2001). Clearly, efforts to transform universities and enhance their contribution to global economies must take into account the social and cultural context. And what works in the United States cannot be assumed to work elsewhere. Hence issues such as these are at the heart of the analysis in this book.

Layout of the Book

This book is divided into three parts. In Part I some of the key theoretical and conceptual underpinnings of the book are delineated in contributions from Noam Chomsky, Robert Rhoads, Boaventura de Sousa Santos, and Carlos Alberto Torres. In Part II specific findings and points of discussion centered on particular countries or regions in the Americas are offered in chapters written by Estela Mara Bensimon, Atilio Boron, Andrea Brewster,

Ana Loureiro Jurema, Ken Kempner, Marcela Mollis, Imanol Ordorika, Gary Rhoades, Robert Rhoads, Sheila Slaughter, and Carlos Alberto Torres. Finally, in Part III concluding analyses are offered by Robert Rhoads, Daniel Schugurensky, and Carlos Alberto Torres.

In Chapter 2, "A World Without War," Noam Chomsky, of the Massachusetts Institute of Technology, outlines the significant role that the United States takes in promoting neoliberalism and war at global levels. Chomsky provides conceptual insight into the nature of today's globalism and the role that neoliberalism plays in supporting structures of oppression. He describes a world in which the battle lines have been clearly drawn between the concentrated power centers, both state and private, and the general population worldwide. The United States, of course, sits at the center of the world's power base and gives leadership and incentives to economic and militaristic endeavors waged around the world.

Chomsky argues that those at the center of power, defined to a large degree by wealth, pursue war endlessly because they realize that the system of global domination is fragile and that their hold on power requires disciplining the population by one means or another. The pretexts change as the world shifts. But pretexts must be advanced to maintain power. At one time it was the cold war and the Soviet threat. September 11 offered another rationale for renewed pursuit of favored programs and a deepening of neoliberal policies, the core of which is militarism, environmental destruction, and a far-reaching assault on democracy and freedom.

Chomsky highlights the importance of resistance movements and makes it clear that opposition to neoliberalism, as evidenced by those gathering at the World Social Forum, is anything but antiglobalization. He astutely points out that labor parties, workers' movements, and the left in general have long favored international integration of workers' rights (as well as human rights) and consequently are clearly in support of globalization.

In examining the role of militarism in propping up an exploitative economic system, Chomsky turns his attention to the global war on terrorism and notes that the centers of power have defined "terror" as what "they" carry out against "us." Meanwhile, the United States continues its long history of military intervention in weak, underdeveloped countries throughout the world, threatening global stability and annihilation, as the goal of "hegemony" is placed above the goal of "survival." But given the growing gap that planners anticipate between the haves and the have-nots, increased militarization and disciplinary tactics by the United States are deemed necessary, lest the "great beast" of the world—the have-nots—revolt and disrupt the neoliberal quest for increased capital and dominance. Above all else, the world capitalist system must be protected and the United States must be in the lead.

Part I closes with Chapter 3, "The University in the 21st Century: Toward a Democratic and Emancipatory University Reform," written by Boaventura de Sousa Santos of Coimbra University. Santos analyzes the impact of neoliberal globalization on the university by embracing a truly global perspective. He offers a critique of present-day conditions and offers constructive ideas for a project to rescue the university from its present mercantilist path. He sees the university as facing three pressing crises: the crisis of hegemony, the crisis of legitimacy, and the institutional crisis. The crisis of hegemony is the result of the growing intellectual deprivation of the university as it is increasingly called on to produce commercial knowledge at the expense of all other forms of knowledge. The crisis of legitimacy is the result of the increasing segmentation of the university system and the growing devaluation of university diplomas. The institutional crisis of the university is the result of decreased support by the state and the erasure of the public benefit mission that universities, especially public ones, traditionally served. Concentrating on the institutional crisis served only to exacerbate the problems of hegemony and legitimacy.

A key point of Santos's argument is that the nature of university knowledge has been transformed from scientific knowledge to what he terms "pluriversity knowledge." Pluriversity knowledge is application oriented and extramurally driven. Consequently, the initiative for formulating the concerns to be addressed and for evaluating the criteria of relevance is the result of interactive processes among researchers (scientists) and users situated outside the university. Pluriversity knowledge fundamentally calls into question the relationship between science and society; society ceases to be an object of science, and instead becomes a subject questioning and challenging university science. Although a transition from scientific knowledge to pluriversity knowledge has many positive elements—including a university that is potentially more responsive to social concerns—problems arise when the "users" who are able to interact with science in order to fashion knowledge are selected on the basis of capital made available to the university. In other words, the users who are able to utilize university science for their benefit are those who are able to assist the university in solving its institutional crisis—the lack of support from the state for its social mission.

Given the crises confronting today's universities throughout the world, Santos presents a strategy for rescuing the institution. He calls for democratic and emancipative tactics that embrace elements of today's university—including service to the public, but service that is not bound by the revenue-generating potential of users—and he delineates several important points. A key element of his strategy is "confronting the new with the new." Santos implores universities to embrace institutional innovation and avoid the tendency for resistance to neoliberal globalization to turn back to some mythical university of the past that had significant democratic shortcomings already. He also calls for a "new institutionalization," in which he argues that universities must build connections across institutions at the national level. He suggests that the university's public benefit may be best produced through university networks. Furthermore, universities must implement more democratic strategies, both internally and externally. And finally, Santos argues for a more participative system of university evaluation.

In the opening chapter of Part II, Gary Rhoades, of the University of Arizona, and Sheila Slaughter, of the University of Georgia, examine governmental and institutional policies in US higher education over the past two decades as they explore universities in the context of the new economy. In Chapter 4, "Academic Capitalism in the New Economy: Privatization as Shifting the Target of Public Subsidy in Higher Education," they argue that a pattern of increasing "academic capitalism" is evident in US higher education. Such a pattern goes beyond the technology transfer activities focused on by Slaughter and Leslie (1997) in their book *Academic Capitalism* and extends to the fundamental educational functions of colleges and universities. The emerging pattern, Rhoades and Slaughter argue, is rooted in increasing pressures and opportunities for colleges and universities to generate revenue through various partnerships with the private sector.

Drawing on the theoretical contributions of Michel Foucault's (1972) "archaeology of knowledge" and his conceptualization of "power" and "regimes of truth" (Foucault 1980), Rhoades and Slaughter delineate the academic capitalist knowledge/learning/consumption regime. Their conception of academic capitalism as a regime of power is supported through analyses of federal patent and copyright policies and of federal policies and programs that support academic research. The academic capitalist knowledge/learning/consumption regime also is evident to varying degrees in the policies of states across the country. Furthermore, it plays out in the policies and practices of colleges and universities. With regard to the political economy, these patterns do not simply consist of public entities being taken over or manipulated by private enterprise. Instead, governments and states are facilitating a fundamental change in the nature of not-for-profit colleges and universities, which themselves are increasingly engaged in a broad range of profit-making enterprises. With the rise of academic capitalism in US higher education, we witness a reduced commitment to, support of, and emphasis on the "publicness" of higher education.

In Chapter 5, "Reforming the Reforms: Transformation and Crisis in Latin American and Caribbean Universities," Atilio Alberto Boron, of the University of Buenos Aires and executive secretary of the Latin American Council of Social Sciences (CLACSO), explores global trade initiatives and mandates derived from transnational organizations and their effect on the economy of Latin America and the Caribbean. From a comparative perspective Boron argues that a central problem of the model of structural adjustment imposed on higher education is the negative effect on the financing of public universities and the related impact on social structure. More specifically, Boron examines the regressive transformation of class structure within Latin American society and the corresponding weakened support for public higher education as a general assault on democracy and the social good. Boron contends that the effects of neoliberal globalization have profoundly and dangerously weakened the autonomy and self-determination of Latin American and Caribbean nations and consequently has damaged their ability to sustain and strengthen publicly supported universities. In essence, the costs of economic stabilization and structural adjustments have fallen on the popular sectors, affecting most negatively the poorest Latin Americans and significantly reducing their educational opportunities.

Given that higher education has a key role to play during times of economic transition and restructuring, public universities face major shortfalls and cuts when in fact new educational programs are needed to support the development of a highly skilled workforce. Hence structural adjustment policies of global financial institutions that seek cuts to higher education actually are limiting the ability of many Latin American countries to compete in the global marketplace. Boron suggests that equity and rapid economic growth must go hand in hand and that policy makers need to act to ensure broadened educational access during times of economic turmoil and transition. Furthermore, in the much celebrated "knowledge society," universities play a critical role. Promotion of education at all levels is necessary, and so too is a serious commitment to science and technological development. Clearly, this is not a time to be reducing support for public universities in Latin America, but just the opposite.

Robert Rhoads, Carlos Alberto Torres, and Andrea Brewster, of the University of California, Los Angeles, examine the growing problems faced by national universities in Chapter 6, "Globalization and the Challenge to National Universities in Argentina and Mexico." The writers give serious consideration to North-South relations between the United States and Latin American countries, as they explore the growing challenges and opportunities confronting national universities. More specifically, findings from case studies conducted at the University of Buenos Aires (UBA) and the National Autonomous University of Mexico (UNAM) are presented.

Interestingly, both Argentina and Mexico can be seen politically and economically as being in a state of transition. For example, both countries face massive debt, and during the early part of the 20th century both experienced major regime shifts. As in other Latin American countries, Argentina and Mexico increasingly have tried to participate in the global marketplace, mostly following the lead of free-market entrepreneurialism largely fashioned by the United States. Given the political and economic challenges faced by the broader society, UBA and UNAM face major barriers as they seek to reform in light of global pressures and opportunities.

Some telling issues raised by Rhoads and colleagues include concerns among academics that key aspects of academic culture at UBA and UNAM may in fact be eroding as a consequence of global economic pressures. One example is the manner in which notions of the "public" and the "public good" are being reconfigured by growing pressure to privatize. Some analysts affiliated with UBA and UNAM blame structural adjustment policies advanced by the IMF. Others look to the general pressure to compete in a global marketplace and the important role of universities and academic sci-

ence. Key issues related to the development of university-industry partnerships are raised, with some faculty and policy makers in both countries voic-
ing concern about the need to remain autonomous. Others, however, see
university-industry partnerships as inevitable, given the growing influence
of the US model of the research university and growing economic pressure
to increase academic science and development.

In Chapter 7, "Latin American Identities in Transition: A Diagnosis of
Argentine and Brazilian Universities," Marcela Mollis, of the University of
Buenos Aires, examines recent policy changes that have sought to transform
the identity of public universities throughout Argentina and Brazil. Mollis
contends that the historic and valued role of universities as centers of
knowledge is being eroded and displaced by the notion of the university as a
"supermarket," whereby students acting as "clients" consume knowledge as
merchandise and professors are simply wage earners who teach. This alteration of the fundamental identity of the Argentine and Brazilian public university continues under the banner of globalization, as influences from the
North continue to reshape higher education in the South.

Nowadays, Argentine and Brazilian public universities—influenced by
neoliberal policies, budget reductions, fiscal challenges, and an erosion of the
social contract between the state and the civil society—have altered "university knowledge" and turned it into "mercantilist learning." Knowledge is
now evaluated with the language of finance, and universities are measured by
their efficiency in awarding degrees and certificates. Academic leaders are replaced by managers with business backgrounds, and the university shifts
from an educational institution to just another business with a bottom line.

Of particular concern to Mollis is the shift from the roots of the Latin
American university invested in the preparation of professionals committed
to serving the public ethos, to the production of graduates committed to
serving the corporate ethos. Such a shift is evident in various curricular reforms in which programs and courses once aimed at preparing graduates for
public service now seek to produce entrepreneurs capable of competing in
private markets. As a consequence of the growing strength of the corporate
ethos, the identity of the Argentine and Brazilian public university is fundamentally altered. The far-reaching effect is that the political identity of the
people's representatives is also changed; many politicians now govern with
private interests in mind and no longer express a strong commitment to the
broader public ethos.

Ken Kempner, of Southern Oregon University, and Ana Loureiro Jurema, of the Federal University of Pernambuco, argue in Chapter 8 that the path to economic development for nations on the periphery is not a linear process. In "Brazil's Local Solutions to Global Problems," they contend that creating solutions for an individual nation's development should not be based on the same cultural assumptions used in other nations. However, international economic agencies, guided by neoclassical economic theory (neoliberalism), predominantly assume developing countries to be merely cultural variations of the same problems that require the same solutions. Consequently, Kempner and Jurema consider the effect of supposed culturally neutral modernization policies imposed by international agencies on the political economy of developing nations.

Specifically, Kempner and Jurema address the case of Brazil and the role that structural adjustment policies have had on mediating the influence of the state on higher educational policy. Of particular interest are the effects of the World Bank's policies on Brazil's political economy and the resistance to these policies by several of Brazil's educational institutions, specifically the Brazilian Service of Support to Micro and Small Enterprises (SEBRAE). SEBRAE offers a unique case study of internal resistance to globalization and privatization for other developing countries. By focusing on points of tension between SEBRAE and the dictates of the World Bank, Kempner and Jurema are able to conceptualize ways in which North-South relations might be reconfigured around more egalitarian values and interests. They conclude the chapter by discussing the role of maintaining national sovereignty in the face of globalization and externally imposed solutions to local problems.

The importance of the Brazilian context cannot be underestimated. By any political and theoretical account, the new experience with the democratic socialist administration of Luis Ignácio Lula de Silva, known universally as Lula, now is being watched internationally. Brazil, with the largest external debt of any country, excluding the United States, is at the same time fiercely independent in terms of funding its higher education institutions. Some government agencies, such as CAPES (Coordenação de Aperfeiçoamento de Passoal de Nível Superior), command a budget that cannot be equaled in the region and have been able to fund scientific and technological research of a magnitude similar to the work of the National Science Foundation in the United States. With a system of federal universities supported by the nation's tax base, Brazil reveals an interesting reversal-of-fortune model in which high-achieving wealthier students attend public universities and lower achieving students (also wealthy) are more likely to attend second-tier private universities. Consequently, Brazil makes for fascinating comparisons with other Latin American countries and its neighbors to the north.

In Chapter 9, "Mexico's *Estímulos*: Faculty Compensation Based on Piecework," Estela Mara Bensimon, of the University of Southern California, and Imanol Ordorika, of the National Autonomous University of Mexico, offer a critical analysis of Mexico's extreme form of variable faculty compensation known as *estímulos* (merit pay or incentives). Under this system, which has been in place for more than a decade, more than 50 percent of a professor's annual salary may be based on a combination of *estímulos*. The system, which has been portrayed as a "Darwinian nightmare," "perverse," and "savage," encourages faculty members to be ultraconscious of producing the required number of "pieces" in order to qualify for monetary rewards and earn a minimum salary. The race to accumulate "pieces" as fast as possible turns faculty members into *maquiladoras* of papers and demonstrates neoliberal economic principles at work in the day-to-day lives of professors.

The *estímulos* program has the potential to transform in dramatic ways the very nature of academic culture throughout Mexico. A country whose academics once embraced a strong sense of collectivism and saw themselves as serving the larger social good now is being transformed into a culture of individualism as universities increasingly turn to more competition-based programs and structures. In the end Bensimon and Ordorika contend that the implementation of the monetary *estímulos* system is consistent with the growing commodification of faculty work under the privatization model advanced by hegemonic economic views. Such a system is likely to have a devastating effect on the quality of academic life and may in fact reduce the contribution of Mexico's faculty to economic and social development.

Part II closes with Chapter 10, "Graduate Student Unionization as a Postindustrial Social Movement: Identity, Ideology, and the Contested US Academy," by Robert Rhoads and Gary Rhoades. The writers examine the growing movement among graduate student employees in the United States to pursue collective bargaining. As Rhoads and Rhoades point out, the unionization of graduate student employees has met with fairly stiff resistance from university administrations, which have argued that graduate students more or less serve as apprentices and that the work they perform is part of their academic experience. Under these conditions graduate student employees should not be allowed to unionize. Graduate student organizers have rejected such claims and instead have pointed to the quantity of work that graduate students perform in delivering undergraduate education to countless students. Although administrators have argued that the university as a "collegial community" looks out for the interests of graduate students, organizers reject such claims and point instead to corporate-oriented practices that have come to dominate research universities in the United States. In the eyes of graduate student organizers, academe is less a "collegium" and more a "corporation." As low-level wage earners in a corporate enterprise, graduate student organizers see collective bargaining as the logical extension of an organization firmly entrenched in a business model of operation.

Rhoads and Rhoades present and analyze findings from qualitative case studies conducted at four universities where graduate student unionizing has been relatively significant: the University of Michigan, Michigan State University, New York University, and the University of California, Los Angeles. They argue that, as a consequence of a shift from an industrial society characterized by manufacturing processes to a postindustrial society driven by the creation of new technologies and the management and communication of information, the US research university takes on great importance in a global economic system. The battle over control of the university thus is a key feature of what many see as a political struggle to insert corporate capitalism into the center of the academic enterprise. Hence it is in the context of the growing influence of corporate capitalism and postindustrialization that Rhoads and Rhoades examine the identity and ideologies of graduate student organizers seeking to forge collective lines of action. Of central importance is the emergence of working-class sensibilities among groups of graduate student employees who define themselves as postindustrial line workers engaged in the production of knowledge.

Part III begins with Chapter 11, "The Political Economy of Higher Education in the Time of Global Markets: Whither the Social Responsibility of the University?" by Daniel Schugurensky, of the University of Toronto. In this chapter Schugurensky analyzes the degree to which universities can continue to meet their historic social responsibilities in light of neoliberalism's emphasis on global markets. Schugurensky explores competing visions of the university over time and discusses the eventual rise of the "service university," which he argues is rooted in entrepreneurialism and academic capitalism and elevates the market over all other externally driven interests. Unlike the community orientation of the service model typical of the land grant movement, the current service model subsumes the ideal of a socially responsible university into a corporate model that aligns the university to market demands. Schugurensky contends that a more comprehensive account of the present-day university may be found in examining the transition from an autonomous university to one that is best characterized as "heteronomous." Whereas autonomy is the quality of being independent and self-directed, heteronomy describes the condition in which the university is subjected to external controls and impositions. On the basis of the heteronomous model, the university is increasingly conditioned by market demands and state imperatives. The consequence is a university that is both "commercial" and "controlled" and that lacks the wherewithal to pursue ends that serve the broader social good.

Finally, in Chapter 12, "The Global Economy, the State, Social Movements, and the University: Concluding Remarks and an Agenda for Action," we seek to synthesize the complex lines of argumentation advanced throughout this book by forging clear connections across the global economy, the state, social movements, and the university. We close the book by calling on the revolutionary pedagogy of Paulo Freire of Brazil and point to generative themes around which to build an agenda for action. We argue that thoughtful action must center on the following: building a powerful movement to challenge the hegemony of neoliberal globalization; recognizing that freedom involves emancipation and not tutelage; defending public higher education in the face of the neoliberal free-market onslaught; defending the democratic state in the face of the growing power and influence of global capital; and forging a planetarian multicultural citizenship.

References

Apple, M. 2002. "Patriotism, Pedagogy, and Freedom: On the Educational Meanings of September 11th." *Teachers College Record* 104(8): 1760–1772.

Birchard, K. 2002. "Canadian Students Hold Nationwide Protests over Tuition Increases." *Chronicle of Higher Education*, February 8. Available at http://chronicle.com/daily/2002/02/2002020805n.htm

Bollag, B. 2003. "A Cuban Scholar Shut Out." *Chronicle of Higher Education*, April 11, A16–A18.

Brender, A. 2003. "74 Universities in Japan Hope to Open Graduate Level Law Schools." *Chronicle of Higher Education*, June 4. Available at http://chronicle.com/daily/2003/06/2003060404n.htm

Bunch, C. 2001. "Women's Human Rights: The Challenges of Global Feminism and Diversity." In *Feminist Locations: Global and Local, Theory and Practice* (pp. 129–146), M. Dekoven, ed. New Brunswick, NJ: Rutgers University Press.

Carnoy, M. 2001. "El Impacto de la Mundialización en las Estrategias de Reforma Educativc." *Revista de Educación* (special issue): 101–110.

Castells, M. 1997. *The Power of Identity*. Boston: Blackwell.

Chomsky, N. 1998. *Profit over People: Neoliberalism and Global Order*. New York: Seven Stories Press.

Del Castillo, D. 2003a. "Afghan Government Backs Plan for an American-Style University in Afghanistan." *Chronicle of Higher Education*, May 6. Available at http://chronicle.com/daily/2003/05/2003050604n.htm

Del Castillo, D. 2003b. "American Colleges Are Offered Grants to Aid in Revival of Iraqi Higher Education." *Chronicle of Higher Education*, June 2. Available at http://chronicle.com/daily/2003/06/2003060203n.htm

Dewey, J. 1916. *Democracy and Education*. Carbondale: Southern Illinois University.

Fay, B. 1987. *Critical Social Science*. Ithaca, NY: Cornell University Press.

Foucault, M. 1972. *The Archaeology of Knowledge and the Discourse on Language*, A. M. Sheridan Smith, trans. New York: Pantheon Books.

Foucault, M. 1980. *Power/Knowledge*, C. Gordan, trans. New York: Pantheon Books.

Freire, P. 1970. *Pedagogy of the Oppressed*, M. B. Ramos, trans. New York: Continuum.

Giroux, H. A. 1983. *Theory and Resistance in Education*. South Hadley, MA: Bergin & Garvey.

Habermas, J. 1973. *Theory and Practice*, J. Vietel, trans. Boston: Beacon Press.

Held, D., ed. 1991. *Political Theory Today*. Stanford, CA: Stanford University Press.

Horkheimer, M. 1972. *Critical Theory*, M. J. O'Connell, trans. New York: Herder and Herder.

Kaur, M. 1999. "Globalization and Women: Some Likely Consequences." In *Globalization, Culture, and Women's Development* (pp. 119–128), R. Mohini Sethi, ed. Jaipur and New Delhi: Rawat.

Levy, D. 1994. "Mexico's Changing Higher Education and US Universities." *Planning for Higher Education* 22(4): 24–30.

Lin-Liu, J. 2001. "Unesco Plans Transnational Quality-Assurance Agency for Academe." *Chronicle of Higher Education*, December 21. Available at http://chronicle.com/daily/2001/12/2001122109n.htm

Lipka, S. 2004. "U.S. Denies Visas to 65 Cuban Scholars Planning to Attend an Academic Conference." *Chronicle of Higher Education*, October 1. Available at http://chronicle.com/prm/daily/2004/10/2004100104n.htm

Luke, A., and C. Luke. 2000. "A Situated Perspective on Cultural Globalization." In *Globalization and Education: Critical Perspectives* (pp. 275–297), N. C. Burbules and C. A. Torres, eds. New York: Routledge.

Marcuse, H. 1972. *Studies in Critical Philosophy*, J. De Bres, trans. Boston: Beacon Press.

Rhoads, R. A. 2003. "Globalization and Resistance in the United States and Mexico: The Global Potemkin Village." *Higher Education* 45(2): 223–250.

Rhoads, R. A., and L. Mina. 2001. "The Student Strike at the National Autonomous University of Mexico: A Political Analysis." *Comparative Education Review* 45(3): 334–353.

Rhoads, R. A., and J. R. Valadez. 1996. *Democracy, Multiculturalism, and the Community College: A Critical Perspective.* New York: Garland.

Said, E. 1993. *Culture and Imperialism.* New York: Random House.

Sidhu, R. 2003. "Selling Futures to Foreign Students: Global Education Markets." University of Queensland, Australia (unpublished manuscript).

Slaughter, S., and L. L. Leslie. 1997. *Academic Capitalism: Politics, Policies, and the Entrepreneurial University.* Baltimore: Johns Hopkins University Press.

Slaughter, S., and G. Rhoades. 2004. *Academic Capitalism and the New Economy: Markets, State, and Higher Education.* Baltimore: Johns Hopkins University Press.

Soysal, N. 1994. *Limits of Citizenship: Migrants and Postnational Membership in Europe.* Chicago: University of Chicago Press.

Stiglitz, J. E. 2002. *Globalization and Its Discontents.* New York: Norton.

Sullivan, R. E. 2002. "Chomsky Blasts Forum from Brazil." *Earth Times*, January 31. Available at http://www.globalpolicy.org/globaliz/econ/2002/0131chomsky.htm

Teodoro, A. 2003. "Educational Policies and New Ways of Governance in a Transnationalization Period." In *The International Handbook on the Sociology of Education* (pp. 183–210), C. A. Torres and A. Antikainen, eds. Lanham, MD: Rowman & Littlefield.

Tierney, W. G. 1993. *Building Communities of Difference: Higher Education in the 21st Century.* Westport, CT: Bergin & Garvey.

Tierney, W. G., and R. A. Rhoads. 1993. "Postmodernism and Critical Theory in Higher Education: Implications for Research and Practice. In *Higher Education: Handbook of Theory and Research* (pp. 308–343), J. C. Smart, ed. New York: Agathon Press.

Torres, C. A. 1998. *Democracy, Education, and Multiculturalism: Dilemmas of Citizenship in a Global World.* Lanham, MD: Rowman & Littlefield.

Torres, C. A. 2002. "Globalization, Education, and Citizenship: Solidarity Versus Markets?" *American Educational Research Journal* 39(2): 363–378.

Torres, C. A., and A. Puiggrós, eds. 1996. *Education in Latin America: Comparative Perspectives.* Boulder, CO: Westview Press.

Touraine, A. 1988. *Return of the Actor: Social Theory in Postindustrial Society.* Minneapolis: University of Minnesota Press.

Urry, J. 1998. "Contemporary Transformations of Time and Space." In *The Globalization of Higher Education* (pp. 1–17), P. Scott, ed. Buckingham, UK: Open University.

CHAPTER TWO

A World Without War[1]

Noam Chomsky

I want to set the stage with a few truisms. It is hardly exciting news that we live in a world of conflict and confrontation. There are lots of dimensions and complexities, but in recent years, lines have been drawn fairly sharply. To oversimplify, but not too much, one of the participants in the conflict is concentrated power centers, state and private, closely interlinked. The other is the general population, worldwide. In old-fashioned terms, it would have been called "class war."

Concentrated power pursues war relentlessly, and very self-consciously. Government documents and publications of the business world reveal that they are mostly vulgar Marxists, with values reversed of course. They are also frightened—back to 17th century England in fact. They realize that the system of domination is fragile, that it relies on disciplining the population by one or another means. There is a desperate search for such means: in recent years, communism, crime, drugs, terrorism, and others. Pretexts change, policies remain rather stable. Sometimes the shift of pretext along with continuity of policy is dramatic and takes real effort to miss: immediately after the collapse of the USSR, for example (see Chomsky 1991, 1994). They naturally grasp every opportunity to press their agenda forward: 9/11 is a typical case. Crises make it possible to exploit fear and concern to demand that the adversary be submissive, obedient, silent, distracted, while the powerful use the window of opportunity to pursue their own favored programs with even greater intensity. These programs vary, depending on the society: in the more brutal states, escalation of repression and terror; in societies where the population has won more freedom, measures to impose discipline while shifting wealth and power even more to their own hands. It is easy to list examples around the world in the past few months.

Their victims should certainly resist the predictable exploitation of crisis, and should focus their own efforts, no less relentlessly, on the primary issues that remain much as they were before: among them, increasing militarism, destruction of the environment, and a far-reaching assault against democracy and freedom, the core of "neoliberal" programs.

The ongoing conflict is symbolized by meetings of the World Social Forum [WSF] in Porto Alegre, Brazil, and the World Economic Forum [WEF] in New York in 2002. The WEF—to quote the national US press—is a gathering of "movers and shakers," the "rich and famous," "wizards from around the world," "government leaders and corporate executives, ministers of state and of God, politicians and pundits" who are going to "think deep thoughts" and address "the big problems confronting humankind." A few examples are given, for example, "How do you inject moral values into what we do?" Or a panel entitled "Tell Me What You Eat," led by the "reigning prince of the New York gastronomic scene," whose elegant restaurants will be "mobbed by forum participants." There is also mention of an "anti-forum" in Brazil, where 50,000 people are expected. These are "the freaks who assemble to protest the meetings of the World Trade Organization." One can learn more about the freaks from a photo of a scruffy-looking guy, with face concealed, writing "world killers" on a wall.

At their "carnival," as it is described, the freaks are throwing stones, writing graffiti, dancing and singing about a variety of boring topics that are unmentionable, at least in the US: investment, trade, financial architecture, human rights, democracy, sustainable development, Brazilian-African relations, GATS, and other marginal issues. They are not "thinking deep thoughts" about "big problems"; that is left to the wizards of Davos in New York.

The infantile rhetoric, I presume, is a sign of well-deserved insecurity.

The freaks at the "anti-forum" in Porto Alegre are defined as being "opposed to globalization," a propaganda weapon we should reject with scorn. "Globalization" just means international integration. No sane person is "anti-globalization." That should be particularly obvious for the labor movement and the left; the term "international" is not exactly unknown in their history. In fact, the WSF is the most exciting and promising realization of the hopes of the left and popular movements, from their modern origins, for a true international, which will pursue a program of globalization concerned with the needs and interests of people, rather than of illegitimate concentrations of power. These, of course, want to appropriate the term "globalization," and to restrict it to *their* peculiar version of international integration, concerned with their own interests, those of people being incidental. With this ridiculous terminology in place, those who seek a sane and just form of globalization can be labeled "anti-globalization," derided as primitivists who want to return to the Stone Age, to harm the poor, and subjected to other terms of abuse with which we are familiar.

The wizards of Davos modestly call themselves the "international community," but perhaps we should adopt the term used by the world's leading business journal: "the masters of the universe" (de Jonquières 2001). Since the masters profess to be admirers of Adam Smith, we might expect them to abide by his account of their behavior, though he only called them "the masters of mankind"—that was before the space age.

Smith was referring to the "principal architects of policy" of his day, the merchants and manufacturers of England, who made sure that their own interests are "most peculiarly attended to," however "grievous" the impact on others, including the people of England. At home and abroad, they pursue "the vile maxim of the masters of mankind": "all for ourselves and nothing for other people." It should hardly surprise us that today's masters honor the same "vile maxim." At least they try, though they are sometimes impeded by the freaks—the "great beast," to borrow a term used by the Founding Fathers of American democracy to refer to the unruly population that did not comprehend that the primary goal of government is "to protect the minority of the opulent from the majority," as the leading framer of the Constitution explained in the debates of the Constitutional Convention.

I will return to these matters, but first a few words about the immediate topic of this essay, which is closely related: "a world without war." We cannot say much about human affairs with any confidence, but sometimes it is possible. We can, for example, be fairly confident that either there will be a world without war or there won't be a world—at least, a world inhabited by creatures other than bacteria and beetles, with some scattering of others. The reason is familiar: Humans have developed means of destroying themselves, and much else, and have come dangerously close to using them for half a century. Furthermore, the leaders of the civilized world are now dedicated to enhancing these dangers to survival, in full awareness of what they are doing, at least if they read the reports of their own intelligence agencies and respected strategic analysts, including many who strongly favor the race to destruction. Still more ominous, the plans are developed and implemented on grounds that are rational within the dominant framework of ideology and values, which ranks survival well below "hegemony," the goal pursued by advocates of these programs, as they often state quite frankly.

Wars over water, energy, and other resources are not unlikely in the future, with consequences that could be devastating. In substantial measure, however, wars have had to do with the imposition of the system of nation-states, an unnatural social formation that typically has to be instituted by violence. That is a primary reason why Europe was the most savage and brutal part of the world for many centuries, meanwhile conquering most of the world. European efforts to impose state systems in conquered territories are the source of most conflicts under way right now, after the collapse of the formal colonial system. Europe's own favorite sport of mutual slaughter had to be called off in 1945, when it was realized that the next time the game was played would be the last. Another prediction that we can make with fair confidence is that there will be no war among great powers; the reason is that if the prediction turns out to be wrong, there will be no one around to care to tell us.

Furthermore, popular activism within the rich and powerful societies has had a civilizing effect. The "movers and shakers" can no longer undertake the kinds of long-term aggression that were options before, as when the US attacked South Vietnam 40 years ago, smashing much of it to pieces before significant popular protest developed. Among the many civilizing effects of the ferment of the 1960s was broad opposition to large-scale aggression and massacre, reframed in the ideological system as unwillingness to accept casualties among the armed forces ("the Vietnam syndrome"). The Reaganites had to resort to international terrorism instead of invading Central America directly, on the Kennedy-Johnson model. The same changes explain the intelligence review of the incoming Bush-I administration in 1989, warning that in conflicts against "much weaker enemies"—the only kind it makes sense to confront—the US must "defeat them decisively and rapidly," or the campaign will lose "political support," understood to be thin. Wars since have kept to that pattern, and the scale of protest and dissent have steadily increased. So there are changes, of a mixed nature.

When pretexts vanish, new ones have to be concocted to control the great beast while traditional policies are continued, adapted to new circumstances. That was already becoming clear 20 years ago. It was hard not to recognize that the Soviet enemy was facing internal problems and might not be a credible threat much longer. That is, presumably, part of the reason why the Reagan administration, 20 years ago, declared that the "war on terror" would be the focus of US foreign policy, particularly in Central America and the Middle East, the main source of the plague spread by "depraved opponents of civilization itself" in a "return to barbarism in the modern age," as administration moderate George Shultz explained, also warning that the solution is violence, avoiding "utopian, legalistic means like outside mediation, the World Court, and the United Nations." We need not tarry on how the war was waged in those two regions, and elsewhere, by the extraordinary network of proxy states and mercenaries—an "axis of evil," to borrow a more up-to-date term.

It is of some interest that in the months since the war was re-declared, with much the same rhetoric, after 9/11, all of this has been entirely effaced, even the fact that the US was condemned for international terrorism (technically, "unlawful use of force") by the World Court and Security Council (in two resolutions vetoed by the US), and that Washington responded by sharply escalating the terrorist attack it was ordered to terminate; or the fact that the very people who are directing the military and diplomatic components of the re-declared war on terror, or their mentors, were leading figures in implementing terrorist atrocities in Central America and the Middle East—and elsewhere—during the first phase of the war. Silence about these matters is a real tribute to the discipline and obedience of the educated classes in the free and democratic societies.

It is a fair guess that the "war on terror" will again serve as a pretext for intervention and atrocities in coming years, not just by the US; Chechnya is only one of a number of examples. In Latin America, there is no need to linger on what that portends; certainly not in Brazil, the first target of the wave of repression that swept Latin America after the Kennedy administration, in a decision of historic importance, which shifted the mission of the Latin American military from "hemispheric defense" to "internal security"—a euphemism for state terror directed against the domestic population. That still continues, on a huge scale, particularly in Colombia, well in the lead for human rights violations in the hemisphere in the 1990s and by far the leading recipient of US arms and military training, in accord with a consistent pattern documented even in mainstream scholarship.

The "war on terror" has, of course, been the focus of a huge literature, during the first phase in the '80s and since it was redeclared in the past few months. One interesting feature of the flood of commentary, then and now, is that we are not told what "terror" is. What we hear, rather, is that this is a vexing and complex question. That is curious: There are straightforward definitions in official US documents. A simple one takes terror to be the "calculated use of violence or threat of violence to attain goals that are political, religious, or ideological in nature." That seems appropriate enough, but it cannot be used, for two good reasons. One is that it also defines official policy, called "counterinsurgency" or "low-intensity conflict." Another is that it yields all the wrong answers, facts too obvious to review though suppressed with remarkable efficiency.

The problem of finding a definition of "terror" that will exclude the most prominent cases is indeed vexing and complex. But fortunately, there is an easy solution: Define "terror" as terror that *they* carry out against *us*. A review of the scholarly literature on terror, the media, and intellectual journals will show that this usage is close to exceptionless, and that any departure from it elicits impressive tantrums. Furthermore, the practice is probably universal: The generals in South America were protecting the population from terror directed from outside, just as the Japanese were in Manchuria and the Nazis in occupied Europe. If there is an exception, I haven't found it.

Let us return to "globalization," and the linkage between it and the threat of war, perhaps terminal war.

The version of "globalization" designed by the masters of the universe has very broad elite support, not surprisingly, as do the so-called "free trade agreements"—what the business press, more honestly, sometimes calls "free investment agreements." Very little is reported about these issues, and crucial information is simply suppressed. For example, after a decade, the position of the US labor movement on NAFTA, and the conforming conclusions of Congress's own research bureau (the Office of Technology Assessment, OTA), have yet to be reported outside of dissident sources (Chomsky 1994). And the issues are off the agenda in electoral politics. There are good reasons. The masters know well that the public will be opposed if information becomes available. They are fairly open when addressing one another, however. Thus a few years ago, under enormous public pressure, Congress rejected the "fast track" legislation that grants the president authority to enact international economic arrangements with Congress permitted to vote yes (or, theoretically, no) with no discussion, and the public uninformed. Like other sectors of elite opinion, the *Wall Street Journal* was distraught over the failure to undermine democracy. But it explained the problem: Opponents of these Stalinist-style measures have an "ultimate weapon," the general population, which must therefore be kept in the dark (Burkins 1997). That is very important, particularly in the more democratic societies, where dissidents can't simply be jailed or assassinated, as in the leading recipients of US military aid, such as El Salvador, Turkey, and Colombia, to list the recent and current world champions (Israel-Egypt aside).

One might ask why public opposition to "globalization" has been so high for many years. That seems strange, in an era when it has led to unprecedented prosperity, so we are constantly informed, particularly in the US, with its "fairy tale economy." Through the 1990s, the US has enjoyed "the greatest economic boom in America's history—and the world's," Anthony Lewis (2001) wrote in the *New York Times*, repeating the standard refrain from the left end of the admissible spectrum. It is conceded that there are flaws: Some have been left behind in the economic miracle, and we good-hearted folk must do something about that. The flaws reflect a profound and troubling dilemma: The rapid growth and prosperity brought by "globalization" has as a concomitant growing inequality, as some lack the skills to enjoy the wondrous gifts and opportunities.

The picture is so conventional that it may be hard to realize how little resemblance it has to reality, facts that have been well known right through the miracle. Until the brief late '90s boomlet (which scarcely compensated for earlier stagnation or decline for most people), per capita growth in the US in the "roaring '90s" was about the same as the rest of the industrial world, lower than in the first 25 postwar years before so-called "globalization," and vastly lower than the war years, the greatest economic boom in American history, under a semi-command economy. How then can the conventional picture be so radically different from uncontroversial facts? The answer is simplicity itself. For a small sector of the society, the '90s really were a grand economic boom. That sector happens to include those who tell others the joyous news. And they cannot be accused of dishonesty. They have no reason to doubt what they are saying. They read it all the time in the journals for which they write, and it accords with their personal experience: It is true of the people they meet in editorial offices, faculty clubs, elite conferences, and the elegant restaurants where they dine. It is only the world that is different.

Let's have a quick look at the record over a longer stretch. International economic integration—one facet of "globalization," in a neutral sense of the term—increased rapidly before World War I, stagnated or declined during the interwar years, and resumed after World War II, now reaching levels of a century ago by gross measures; the fine structure is much more complex. By some measures, globalization was greater before World War I: One illustration is "free circulation of labor," the foundation of free trade for Adam Smith, though not his contemporary admirers. By other measures, globalization is far greater now: One dramatic example—not the only one—is the flow of short-term speculative capital, far beyond any precedent. The distinction reflects some central features of the version of globalization preferred by the masters of the universe: To an extent even beyond the norm, capital has priority, people are incidental.

The Mexican border is an interesting example. It is artificial, the result of conquest, like most borders, and has been porous in both directions for a variety of socioeconomic reasons. It was militarized after NAFTA by Clinton (Nevins 2002), thus erecting barriers to "free circulation of labor." That was necessary because of the anticipated effects of NAFTA in Mexico: an "economic miracle," which would be a disaster for much of the population, who would seek to escape. In the same years, the flow of capital, already very free, was expedited further, along with what is called "trade," mostly centrally managed within private tyrannies, increasingly so post-NAFTA. For example,

Quinlan and Chandler (2001) report that nearly two-thirds of US imports from Mexico are between MNEs [multinational enterprises] and affiliates. Pre-NAFTA estimates were about 50 percent. That is "trade" only by doctrinal decision. The effects of NAFTA on trade in some meaningful sense of the term have not been examined, to my knowledge.

A more technical measure of globalization is convergence to a global market, with a single price and wage. That plainly has not happened. With respect to incomes at least, the opposite is more likely true, insofar as the rules of the game have been followed. Though much depends on exactly how it is measured, there is good reason to believe that inequality has increased within and across countries that have kept to the rules. That is expected to continue. US intelligence agencies, with the participation of specialists from the academic professions and the private sector, recently released a report on expectations for 2015 (National Intelligence Council 2000). They expect "globalization" to proceed on course: "Its evolution will be rocky, marked by chronic financial volatility and a widening economic divide." That means less convergence, less globalization in the technical sense, but more globalization in the doctrinally preferred sense. Financial volatility implies still slower growth and more crises and poverty.

It is at this point that a clear connection is established between "globalization" in the sense of the masters of the universe and the increasing likelihood of war. Military planners adopt the same projections, and have explained, forthrightly, that these expectations lie behind the vast expansion of military power. Even pre–September 11, US military expenditures far surpassed those of any potential combination of adversaries. The terror attacks have been exploited to increase the funding sharply, delighting key elements of the private economy. The most ominous program is militarization of space, also being expanded under the pretext of "fighting terror."

The reasoning behind these programs is explained publicly in Clinton-era documents. A prime reason is the gap between the "haves" and the "have-nots," which planners expect to grow, contrary to economic theory but consistent with reality. The "have-nots"—the "great beast" of the world—may become disruptive, and must be controlled, in the interests of what is called "stability" in technical jargon, meaning in practice subordination to the dictates of the masters. That requires means of violence, and having "assumed, out of self-interest, responsibility for the welfare of the world capitalist system" (Haines 1989), the US must be far in the lead. Overwhelming dominance in conventional forces and weapons of mass destruction is not sufficient. It is necessary to move on to the new frontier: militarization of space, undermining the Outer Space Treaty of 1967, so far observed. Recognizing the intent, the UN General Assembly has reaffirmed the treaty several times; the US has refused to join, in virtual isolation. And Washington has blocked negotiations at the UN Conference on Disarmament for the past year over this issue—all scarcely reported, for the usual reasons. It is not wise to allow citizens to know of plans that may bring to an end biology's only experiment with "higher intelligence."

As widely observed, these programs benefit military industry, but we should bear in mind that the term is misleading. Throughout modern history, but with a dramatic increase after World War II, the military system has been used as a device to socialize cost and risk while privatizing profit. The "new economy" is to a substantial extent an outgrowth of the dynamic and innovative state sector of the US economy. The main reason why public spending in biological sciences has been rapidly increasing is that intelligent right-wingers understand that the cutting edge of the economy is shifting from electronics-based to biology-based, and must continue to rely on these public initiatives. A huge increase is scheduled under the pretext of bioterror, just as the public was deluded into paying for the new economy under the pretext that the Russians are coming—or after they collapsed, by the threat of the "technological sophistication" of third world countries as the party line shifted in 1990, instantly, without missing a beat and with scarcely a word of comment (Chomsky 1991, 1994). That is also a reason why national security exceptions have to be part of international economic agreements: It doesn't help Haiti, but it allows the US economy to grow under the traditional principle of harsh market discipline for the poor and a nanny state for the rich—what's called "neoliberalism," though it is not a very good term: The doctrine is centuries old, and would scandalize classical liberals.

One might argue that these public expenditures were often worthwhile. Perhaps, perhaps not. Perhaps if there had been a democratic choice, the population would have preferred to spend public funds for health care, education, decent living and work conditions, sustainable development, and a livable environment for their grandchildren, and other such choices, rather than the glories of the "new economy." But it is clear that the masters were unwilling to allow democratic choice. All of this is concealed from the general public, though the participants understand it very well.

Plans to cross the last frontier of violence by militarization of space are sometimes disguised as "missile defense," but anyone who pays attention to history knows that when we hear the word "defense," we should think "offense." The present case is no exception. The goal is quite frankly stated: to ensure "global dominance," "hegemony." Official documents stress prominently that the goal is "to protect US interests and investment," and control the "have-nots." Today that requires domination of space, just as in earlier times the most powerful states created armies and navies "to protect and enhance their commercial interests" (US Space Command 1997). It is recognized that these new initiatives, in which the US is far in the lead, pose a serious threat to survival. And it is also understood that they could be prevented by international treaties. But as I've already mentioned, hegemony is a higher value than survival, a moral calculus that has prevailed among the powerful throughout history. What has changed is that the stakes are much higher, awesomely so.

The relevant point here is that the expected success of "globalization" in the doctrinal sense is a primary reason given for the programs of using space for offensive weapons of instant mass destruction.

Let us return to "globalization," and "the greatest economic boom in America's history—and the world's"—in the 1990s.

Since World War II, the international economy has passed through two major phases: the Bretton Woods phase to the early '70s, and the period since, with the dismantling of the Bretton Woods system of regulated exchange rates and controls on capital movement. It is the second phase that is commonly called "globalization," associated with the neoliberal policies of the "Washington consensus." The two phases are quite different. The first is often called the "golden age" of (state) capitalism. The second phase has been accompanied by marked deterioration in standard macroeconomic measures: rate of growth of the economy and capital investment, higher interest rates (harming economies), vast accumulation of unproductive reserves to protect currencies, increased financial volatility, and other harmful consequences (Felix 1998; Weisbrot, Naiman, and Kim 2000). There were exceptions, notably the East Asian countries that did not follow the rules: They did not worship the "religion" that "markets know best," as Joseph Stiglitz

(1996) wrote in a World Bank research publication shortly before he was appointed chief economist, later removed (and winning the Nobel Prize). In contrast, the worst results were found where the rules were rigorously applied, as in Latin America, facts widely acknowledged, among others, by José Antonio Ocampo (2001), Executive Secretary of the Economic Commission for Latin America and the Caribbean (ECLAC), in an address before the American Economic Association in 2001. The "promised land is a mirage," he observed; growth in the 1990s was far below that of the three decades of "state-led development" in Phase I. He too noted that the correlation between following the rules and poor economic outcomes holds worldwide.

Let us return, then, to the profound and troubling dilemma: The rapid growth and great prosperity brought by globalization has brought inequality because some lack skills. There is no dilemma, because the rapid growth and prosperity are a myth.

Many international economists regard liberalization of capital as a substantial factor in the poorer outcomes of Phase II (Baker, Epstein, and Pollin 1998; Eatwell and Taylor 2000; Felix 1998). But the economy is a complex affair, so that one has to be cautious about causal connections. One consequence of liberalization of capital, however, is rather clear: It undercuts democracy. That was understood by the framers of Bretton Woods; one reason why these agreements were founded on regulation of capital was to allow governments to carry out social democratic policies, which had enormous popular support. Free capital movement creates what has been called a "virtual Senate" with "veto power" over government decisions, sharply restricting policy options. Governments face a "dual constituency": voters, and speculators, who "conduct moment-by-moment referendums" on government policies (Canova 1995, 1999; Mahon 1996). Even in the rich countries, the private constituency tends to prevail.

Other components of the investor-rights version of "globalization" have similar consequences. Socioeconomic decisions are increasingly shifted to unaccountable concentrations of power, an essential feature of neoliberal "reforms" (a term of propaganda, not description). Extension of the attack on democracy is presumably being planned, without public discussion, in the negotiations for a General Agreement on Trade in Services (GATS). The term "services" refers to just about anything that might fall within the arena of democratic choice: health, education, welfare, postal and other communications, water and other resources, and so forth. There is no meaningful sense in which transferring such services to private hands is "trade," but the term has been so deprived of meaning that it might as well be extended to this travesty as well.

The huge public protests in Quebec in April 2001 at the Summit of the Americas, set in motion by the freaks in Porto Alegre, were in part directed against the attempt to impose the GATS principles in secret within the planned Free Trade Area of the Americas (FTAA). Those protests brought together a very broad constituency, North and South, all strongly opposed to what is apparently being planned by trade ministers and corporate executives behind closed doors.

The protests did receive coverage, of the usual kind: The freaks are throwing rocks and disrupting the wizards thinking about the big problems. The invisibility of their actual concerns is quite remarkable. For example, *New York Times* economics correspondent Anthony DePalma (2002) writes that the GATS agreement "has generated none of the public controversy that has swirled around [WTO] attempts to promote merchandise trade," even after Seattle. In fact, it has been a prime concern for years. As in other cases, this is not deceit. DePalma's knowledge about the freaks is presumably based on what passes through the media filter, and it is an iron law of journalism that the serious concerns of activists must be rigidly barred, in favor of someone throwing a rock, perhaps a police provocateur.

The importance of protecting the public from information was revealed dramatically at the April 2001 Summit. Every editorial office in the United States had on its desk two important studies, timed for release just before the Summit. One was from Human Rights Watch [HRW] (2001), the second from the Economic Policy Institute [EPI] (2001) in Washington; neither organization is exactly obscure. Both studies investigated in depth the effects of NAFTA, which was hailed at the Summit as a grand triumph and a model for the FTAA, with headlines trumpeting its praises by George Bush and other leaders, all accepted as Gospel Truth. Both studies were suppressed in the US with near-total unanimity. It's easy to see why. HRW analyzed the effects of NAFTA on labor rights, which, it found, were harmed in all three participating countries. The EPI report was more comprehensive: It consisted of detailed analyses of the effects of NAFTA on working people, written by specialists on the three countries. The conclusion is that this is one of the rare agreements that has harmed the majority of the population in all of the participating countries.

The effects on Mexico were particularly severe, and particularly significant for the South. Wages declined sharply with the imposition of neoliberal programs in the 1980s. That continued after NAFTA, with a reported 24 percent decline in incomes for salaried workers, and 40 percent for the self-employed, an effect magnified by the rapid increase in unsalaried workers. Though foreign investment grew, total investment declined, as the economy was transferred to the hands of foreign multinationals. Manufacturing declined, and development stagnated or may have reversed. A small sector became extremely wealthy, and foreign investors prospered.

These inquiries confirm what had been reported in the business press and academic studies. "By 2000 the real minimum wage had fallen to 50 percent of its 1980 value," Mexico business correspondent Lucy Conger (2001) reported, while "a *Wall Street Journal* poll taken in 1999 found that 43 percent of Mexicans say their parents' standard of living 30 years ago was better than theirs today." The *Journal* reported further that although the Mexican economy was growing rapidly in the late '90s after a sharp post-NAFTA decline, consumers suffered a 40 percent drop in purchasing power, the number of people living in extreme poverty grew twice as fast as the population, and even those working in foreign-owned assembly plants lost purchasing power. Similar conclusions were drawn in a study of the Latin American section of the Woodrow Wilson Center, which also found that economic power had greatly concentrated, as small Mexican companies cannot obtain financing, traditional farming sheds workers, and labor-intensive sectors (agriculture, light industry) cannot compete internationally with what is called "free enterprise" in the doctrinal system. Agriculture suffered for the usual reasons: Peasant farmers cannot compete with highly subsidized US agribusiness, with effects familiar throughout the world (Millman 1999).

Most of this was predicted by critics of NAFTA, including the ignored OTA [Office of Technology Assessment] and labor movement studies. Critics were wrong in one respect, however: Most anticipated a sharp increase in the urban-rural ratio, as hundreds of thousands of peasants were driven off the land. That didn't happen. The reason, it seems, is that conditions deteriorated so badly in the cities that there was a huge flight from them as well to the US. Those who survive the crossing—many do not—work for very low wages, with no benefits, under awful conditions. The effect is to destroy lives and communities in Mexico and to improve the US economy, where "consumption of the urban middle class continues to be subsidized by the impoverishment of farm laborers both in the United States and Mexico," the Woodrow Wilson Center study points out.

These are among the costs of NAFTA, and neoliberal globalization generally, that economists generally choose not to measure. But even by the highly ideological standard measures, the costs have been severe.

None of this was allowed to sully the celebration of NAFTA and the FTAA at the 2001 Summit. Unless they are connected to activist organizations, most people know about these matters only from their own lives. And carefully protected from reality by the Free Press, many regard themselves as somehow failures, unable to take part in the celebration of the greatest economic boom in history.

Protests at the Summit were too visible to ignore, however, and were widely reported, in the usual fashion: anarchists throwing rocks, etc. The Summit rhetoric did take some notice of the concerns of the protestors, placing great emphasis not only on the heralded performance of the NAFTA model, but also on democracy and transparency (DePalma 2001). Its character was described by the *Financial Times*, departing from the celebratory norm in the US:

> In an effort to show that they were listening to dissenting voices, the Canadian hosts organised a get-together between a group of ministers and representatives of "civil society." The event turned out to be a turgid public relations exercise at which a string of exquisitely well-mannered speakers—many of them university academics—trotted out their viewpoints in presentations limited to a maximum of three minutes. But when the organisers spotted that some journalists—who might have asked a few hard-hitting questions—were in the audience, they ejected them. . . . So much for all those pious ministerial commitments to transparency in global policymaking. ["Breathless at the Summit," 2001]

Data from the richest country in the world are enlightening, but I will skip the details.[2] The picture generalizes, with some variation of course, and exceptions of the kind already noted. The picture is much worse when we depart from standard economic measures. One cost is the threat to survival implicit in the reasoning of military planners, already described. There are many others. To take one, the International Labor Organization reported a rising worldwide epidemic of serious mental health disorders, often linked to stress in the workplace, with very substantial fiscal costs in the industrial countries. A large factor, they conclude, is "globalization," which brings loss of job security, pressure on workers, and a higher workload, particularly in the US. Is this a cost of "globalization"? From one point of view, it is one of its most attractive features. When he lauds the performance of the US economy over which he presides, Alan Greenspan often stresses that an important factor in the success is "atypical restraint on compensation increases [which] appears to be mainly the consequence of greater worker insecurity," which leads to reduced costs for employers. The World Bank agrees. It recognizes that "labor market flexibility" has acquired "a bad name . . . as a euphemism for pushing wages down and workers out," but nevertheless, "is essential in all the regions of the world. . . . The most important reforms involve lifting constraints on labor mobility and wage flexibility, as well as breaking the ties between social services and labor contracts."[3] In brief, pushing workers out, pushing wages down, undermining benefits are all crucial contributions to economic health, according to prevailing ideology.

Unregulated trade has further benefits for corporations. Much, probably most, "trade" is centrally managed through a variety of devices: intrafirm transfers, strategic alliances, outsourcing, and others. Broad trading areas benefit corporations by making them less answerable to local and national communities. This enhances the effects of neoliberal programs, which regularly have reduced labor share of income. In the US, the '90s were the first postwar period when division of income shifted strongly to owners of capital, away from labor. Trade has a wide range of unmeasured costs: subsidizing energy, resource depletion, and other externalities not counted. It also brings advantages, though here too some caution is necessary. The most widely hailed is that trade increases specialization—which reduces choices, including the choice to modify comparative advantage, otherwise known as "development." Choice and development are values in themselves: Undermining them is a substantial cost. If the American colonies had been compelled to accept the WTO regime 200 years ago, New England would be pursuing its comparative advantage in exporting fish, surely not producing textiles, which survived only by exorbitant tariffs to bar British products (mirroring Britain's treatment of India). The same was true of steel and other industries, right to the present, particularly in the highly protectionist Reagan years, which broke postwar records—even putting aside the state sector of the economy. There is a great deal to say about all of this. Much of the story is masked in selective modes of economic measurement, though it is well known to economic historians and historians of technology.

The rules of the game are likely to enhance deleterious effects for the poor. The rules of the WTO bar the mechanisms used by every rich country to reach its current state of development, while also providing unprecedented levels of protectionism for the rich, including a patent regime that bars innovation and growth in novel ways, and allows corporate entities to amass huge profits by monopolistic pricing of products often developed with substantial public contribution.

Under contemporary versions of traditional mechanisms, half the people in the world are effectively in receivership, their economic policies managed by experts in Washington. But even in the rich countries democracy is under attack by virtue of the shift of decision-making power from governments, which may be partially responsive to the public, to private tyrannies, which have no such defects. Cynical slogans such as "trust the people" or "minimize the state" do not, under current circumstances, call for increasing popular control. They shift decisions from governments to other hands, but not "the people": rather, the management of collectivist legal entities, largely unaccountable to the public, and effectively totalitarian in internal structure, much as conservatives charged a century ago when opposing "the corporatization of America."

Latin American specialists and polling organizations have observed for some years that extension of formal democracy in Latin America has been accompanied by increasing disillusionment about democracy, "alarming trends," which continue, analysts have observed, noting the link between "declining economic fortunes" and "lack of faith" in democratic institutions. As Argentine political scientist Atilio Boron (1995, 1996) pointed out some years ago, the new wave of democratization in Latin America coincided with neoliberal economic "reforms," which undermine effective democracy, a phenomenon that extends worldwide, in various forms.

To the US as well, there has been much public clamor about the "stolen election" of November 2000, and surprise that the public does not seem to care. Likely reasons are suggested by public opinion studies, which reveal that on the eve of the election, three-fourths of the population regarded the process as largely a farce: a game played by financial contributors, party leaders, and the public relations industry, which crafted candidates to say "almost anything to get themselves elected" so that one could believe little they said even when it was intelligible. On most issues, citizens could not identify the stands of the candidates, not because they are stupid or not trying, but because of the conscious efforts of the PR industry. A Harvard University project that monitors political attitudes found that the "feeling of powerlessness has reached an alarming high," with more than half saying that people like them have little or no influence on what government does, a sharp rise through the neoliberal period (Patterson 2000a, 2000b, 2001).

Issues on which the public differs from elites (economic, political, intellectual) are pretty much off the agenda, notably questions of economic policy. The business world, not surprisingly, is overwhelmingly in favor of corporate-led "globalization," the "free investment agreements" called "free trade agreements," NAFTA and the FTAA, GATS, and other devices that concentrate wealth and power in hands unaccountable to the public. Also not surprisingly, the great beast is generally opposed, almost instinctively, even without knowing crucial facts from which they are carefully shielded. It follows that such issues are not appropriate for political campaigns, and did not arise in the mainstream for the November 2000 elections. One would have been hard-pressed, for example, to find discussion of the Summit of the Americas and the FTAA, and other topics that involve issues of prime concern for the public. Voters were directed to what the PR industry calls "personal qualities," not "issues." Among the half of the population that votes, heavily skewed towards the wealthy as usual, those who recognize their class interests to be at stake tend to vote for those interests: overwhelmingly, for the more reactionary of the two business parties. But the general public splits its vote in other ways, leading in 2000 to a statistical tie. Among working people, noneconomic issues such as gun ownership and "religiosity" were primary factors, so that people often voted against their own primary interests—perhaps assuming that they had little choice (Jacobson 2001).

What remains of democracy is to be construed as the right to choose among commodities. Business leaders have long explained the need to impose on the population a "philosophy of futility" and "lack of purpose in life," to "concentrate human attention on the more superficial things that comprise much of fashionable consumption." Deluged by such propaganda from infancy, people may then accept their meaningless and subordinate lives and forget ridiculous ideas about managing their own affairs. They may abandon their fate to the wizards, and in the political realm, to the self-described "intelligent minorities" who serve and administer power.

From this perspective, conventional in elite opinion particularly through the last century, the November 2000 elections do not reveal a flaw of US democracy, but rather its triumph. And generalizing, it is fair to hail the triumph of democracy throughout the hemisphere, and elsewhere, even though the populations somehow do not see it that way.

The struggle to impose that regime takes many forms, but never ends, and never will as long as high concentrations of effective decision-making power remain in place. It is only reasonable to expect the masters to exploit any opportunity that comes along—at the moment, the fear and anguish of the population in the face of terrorist attacks, a serious matter for the West now that, with new technologies available, it has lost its virtual monopoly of violence, retaining only a huge preponderance.

But there is no need to accept these rules, and those who are concerned with the fate of the world and its people will surely follow a very different course. The popular struggles against investor-rights "globalization," mostly in the South, have influenced the rhetoric, and to some extent the practices, of the masters of the universe, who are concerned and defensive. These popular movements are unprecedented in scale, in range of constituency, and in international solidarity; the meetings at the 2002 World Social Forum were a critically important illustration. The future to a large extent lies in the hands of these popular movements. It is hard to overestimate what is at stake.

Notes

1. This is an edited version of a talk given at the World Social Forum in Porto Alegre, Brazil, on February 1, 2002. An earlier version appeared in *Radical Priorities*, Carlos Otero, ed. (AK Press, 2003; http://www.akpress.org).

2. See the regular biennial studies of the Economic Policy Institute, *The State of Working America*.

3. See Alan Greenspan's testimony before the Senate Banking Committee, February 1997, cited in "Editorial" (*Multinational Monitor*, March 1997), by the World Bank (*World Development Report 1995: Workers in an Integrated World*), and in "The International Financial System: A Flawed Architecture" (*Fletcher Forum*, winter/spring 1999).

References

Baker, D., G. Epstein, and R. Pollin. 1998. *Globalization and Progressive Economic Policy*. Cambridge, UK: Cambridge University Press.

Boron, A. 1995. *State, Capitalism, and Democracy in Latin America*. Boulder, CO: Lynne Rienner.

Boron, A. 1996. "Democracy or Neoliberalism?" *Boston Review*, October/November.

"Breathless at the Summit." 2001. *Financial Times*, April 23.

Burkins, G. 1997. "Labor Fights Against Fast-Track Trade Measure," *Wall Street Journal*, September 16.

Canova, T. 1995. "The Transformation of U.S. Banking and Finance." *Brooklyn Law Review* 60(4): 1330–1336.

Canova, T. 1999. "Banking and Financial Reform at the Crossroads of the Neoliberal Contagion." *American University International Law Review* 14(6): 1571–1645.

Chomsky, N. 1991. *Deterring Democracy*. London: Verso.

Chomsky, N. 1994. *World Orders Old and New*. New York: Columbia University Press.

Conger, L. 2001. "Mexico's Long March to Democracy." *Current History*, February, 58–64.

DePalma, A. 2001. "Talks Tie Trade in the Americas to Democracy." *New York Times*, April 23, p. 1.

DePalma, A. 2002. "W.T.O. Pact Would Set Global Accounting Rules." *New York Times*, March 1.

Eatwell, J., and L. Taylor. 2000. *Global Finance at Risk*. New York: New Press.

Economic Policy Institute. 2001. *NAFTA at Seven*. April.

"Editorial." 1997. *Multinational Monitor*, March.

Felix, D. 1998. "Asia and the Crisis of Financial Globalization." In *Globalization and Progressive Economic Policy*, D. Baker, G. Epstein, and R. Pollin, eds. Cambridge, UK: Cambridge University Press.

Haines, G. K. 1989. *Americanization of Brazil*. Wilmington, DE: Scholarly Resources.

Human Rights Watch. 2001. "Trading Away Rights." *Human Rights Watch*, April.

"The International Financial System: A Flawed Architecture." 1999. *Fletcher Forum,* winter/spring.

Jacobson, G. 2001. "A House and Senate Divided." *Political Science Quarterly* 116(1): 5–28.

de Jonquières, G. 2001. "Power Elite at Davos May be Eclipsed by Protesters." *Financial Times,* January 24.

Lewis, A. 2001. "The Golden Eggs." *New York Times,* March 10.

Mahon, J. 1996. *Mobile Capital and Latin American Development.* University Park: Pennsylvania State University Press.

Millman, J. 1999. "Is the Mexican Model Worth the Pain?" *Wall Street Journal,* March 8. (Cited by Greenfield, G. 2001. "The Toxicity of NAFTA's Ruling." *Against the Current* [January/February].)

National Intelligence Council. 2000. *Global Trends 2015.* Washington, DC: National Intelligence Council.

Nevins, J. 2002. *Operation Gatekeeper.* New York: Routledge.

Ocampo, J. A. 2001. "Rethinking the Development Agenda." Paper presented at the Annual Meeting of the American Economic Association, January.

Patterson, T. 2000a. "Point of Agreement: We're Glad It's Over." *New York Times,* November 8.

Patterson, T. 2000b. "Will Democrats Find Victory in the Ruins?" *Boston Globe,* December 15.

Patterson, T. 2001. *The Vanishing Voter.* New York: Knopf.

Quinlan, J., and M. Chandler. 2001. "The U.S. Trade Deficit: A Dangerous Obsession." *Foreign Affairs,* May–June.

Stiglitz, J. 1996. "Some Lessons from the East Asian Miracle." *World Bank Research Observer* (August), 11(2): 151–177.

US Space Command. 1997. *Vision for 2020.* Washington, DC: US Space Command.

Weisbrot, M., R. Naiman, and J. Kim. 2000. *Declining Economic Growth Rates in the Era of Globalization.* Washington, DC: Center for Economic and Policy Research (November).

World Bank. 1995. *World Development Report 1995: Workers in an Integrated World.* New York: Oxford University Press.

CHAPTER THREE

The University in the 21st Century:
Toward a Democratic and Emancipatory University Reform [1]

Boaventura de Sousa Santos

More than a decade ago, I published a brief essay about the university, its crises, and the challenges that it faced at the end of the 20th century (Santos 1994). The essay was titled "From the Idea of the University to the University of Ideas," and it was published in my book *Pela Mão de Alice: O Social e o Político na Pós-Modernidade*. In this essay I identified three crises facing the university. First, the crisis of hegemony was the result of contradictions between the traditional functions of the university and those that had come to be attributed to it throughout the 20th century. On the one hand, the production of high culture, critical thinking, and exemplary scientific and humanistic knowledge, necessary for the training of elites, had been the concern of the university since the European Middle Ages. On the other hand, the production of average cultural standards and instrumental knowledge was seen as useful for training the qualified labor force demanded by capitalist development. The university's inability to fully carry out contradictory functions led the state and its economic agents to look beyond it for alternative means to attain these objectives. When it stopped being the only institution of higher education and research production, the university entered a crisis of hegemony. The second crisis was a crisis of legitimacy, provoked by the fact that the university ceased to be a consensual institution in view of the contradiction between the elevation of specialized knowledge through restrictions of access and credentialing of competencies on the one hand and the social and political demands for a democratized university and equal opportunity for the children of the working class on the other hand. Finally, the institutional crisis was the result of the contradiction between the demand for autonomy in the definition of the university's values and objectives and the growing pressure to hold it to the same criteria of efficiency, productivity, and social responsibility that private enterprises face.

In that essay I analyzed in some detail each one of the three crises and the way that they were managed by the university, especially in the central countries. My analysis was centered on public universities. I showed that the university, unable to solve its crises and relying on its long institutional memory and the ambiguities of its administrative profile, tended to manage crises formulaically to avoid their growing out of control. This pattern of action depended on external pressures (it was reactive), incorporated more or less acritically external social and institutional logics (it was dependent), and was blind to medium- or long-range perspectives (it was immediatist).

What has happened in the past decade? How can we characterize the situation in which we find ourselves? What are possible responses to the problems that the university faces today? In this chapter I try to provide answers to these three questions. In the first part I undertake an analysis of recent transformations in the system of higher education and their impact on the public university. In the second part I identify and justify the basic principles of democratic and emancipatory reform of the public university, that is, a reform that allows the public university to respond creatively and efficiently to the challenges it faces at the outset of the 21st century.

Part 1: Recent Transformations

THE LAST DECADE

The predictions I made more than a decade ago have come to pass, beyond my expectations. Despite the fact that the three crises were intimately connected and could only be confronted jointly and by means of vast reform programs generated both inside and outside the university, I predicted (and feared) that the institutional crisis would come to monopolize reformist agendas and proposals. This is in fact what has happened. I also predicted that concentrating on the institutional crisis would lead to the false resolution of the two other crises, a resolution by default: the crisis of hegemony, by the university's increasing loss of specificity; and the crisis of legitimacy, by the growing segmentation of the university system and the growing devaluation of university diplomas, in general. This has also happened.

Concentrating on the institutional crisis was fatal for the university and was due to a number of factors, some already evident at the beginning of the 1990s and others gaining enormous weight as the decade advanced. The institutional crisis is and has been, for at least two centuries, the weakest link of the public university, because the scientific and pedagogical autonomy of the university is based on its financial dependency on the state. Although the university and its services were an unequivocal public good that was up to the state to ensure, this dependency was not problematic, any more than that of the judicial system, for example, in which the independence of the courts is not lessened by the fact they are being financed by the state. However, contrary to the judicial system, the moment the state decided to reduce its political commitment to the universities and to education in general, converting education into a collective good that, however public, does not have to be exclusively supported by the state, an institutional crisis of the public university automatically followed. If it already existed, it deepened. It can be said that for the last 30 years the university's institutional crisis in many countries was provoked or induced by the loss of priority of the university as a public good and by the consequent financial drought and disinvestment in public universities. The causes and their sequence vary from country to country. In countries that lived under dictatorships for the previous four decades, there were two reasons for the onset of the institutional crisis: (1) to reduce the university's autonomy to the level necessary for the elimination of the free production and diffusion of critical knowledge and (2) to put the university at the service of modernizing authoritarian projects, opening the production of the university-as-public-good to the private sector and forcing the public university to compete under conditions of unfair competition in the emerging market for university services.

In the democratic countries the onset of the crisis was related to this second reason, especially beginning in the 1980s, when neoliberalism was imposed as the global model of capitalism. In countries that made the transition from dictatorship to democracy in this period, the elimination of the first reason (political control of autonomy) was frequently invoked to justify the goodness of the second reason (creation of a market for university services). In these countries the affirmation of the universities' autonomy was on a par with the privatization of higher education and the deepening of the public universities' financial crisis. It was a precarious and deceiving autonomy because it forced the universities to seek new dependencies that were much more burdensome than dependence on the state and because the concession of autonomy was subject to remote controls finely calibrated by the Ministries of Finance and Education. Consequently, in the passage from dictatorship to democracy, unsuspected continuities ran beneath the evident ruptures.

The onset of the institutional crisis by way of the financial crisis, accentuated in the last 20 years, is a structural phenomenon accompanying the public university's loss of priority among the public goods produced by the state. The fact that the financial crisis was the immediate impetus for the institutional crisis does not mean that the causes of the institutional crisis can be reduced to the financial crisis. The analysis of the structural causes will reveal that the prevalence of the institutional crisis was the result of the effects of the two other unsolved crises, the crises of hegemony and of legitimacy. And in this domain there have been new developments in relation to the picture I described at the beginning of the 1990s.

The public university's loss of priority in the state's public policies was, first of all, the result of the general loss of priority of social policies (education, health, social security) induced by the model of economic development known as neoliberalism or neoliberal globalization, which was internationally imposed beginning in the 1980s. In the public university it meant that the university's identified institutional weaknesses—and they were many—instead of serving as justification for a vast politico-pedagogical reform program, were declared insurmountable and were used to justify the generalized opening of the university-as-public-good to commercial exploitation. Despite political declarations to the contrary and some reformist gestures, underlying this first collision of the university with neoliberalism are the ideas that the public university is not reformable (any more than the state is) and that the true alternative lies in the creation of the university market. The savage and deregulated way in which this market emerged and was developed is proof that there was a deep option in its favor. And the same option explained the disinvestment in the public university and massive transferences of human resources that, at times, looked like a "primitive accumulation" on the part of the private university sector at the cost of the public sector.

I identify two phases in the process of mercantilization of the public university. In the first phase, which began in the early 1980s and ended in the mid 1990s, the national university market expanded and consolidated. In the second phase, along with the national market, the transnational market of higher and university education emerged with great vitality, so much so that, by the end of the 1990s, it was transformed by the World Bank and the World Trade Organization into a global solution for the problems of education. In other words, the neoliberal globalization of the university was under way. This transformation of the university is a new phenomenon. Certainly, the transnationalization of university exchanges is an ancient process, dating back to the medieval European universities (not to mention the early Islamic universities in Africa). After World War II, transnationalization was translated into the training, at the postgraduate level, of students from peripheral or semiperipheral countries in the universities of the central countries and into partnerships between universities from different countries. In recent years, however, such transnational relations have advanced to a new level. The new transnationalization is much vaster than the former one, and its logic is, unlike its predecessor's, exclusively mercantile.

The two defining processes of the decade—the state's disinvestment in the public university and the mercantile globalization of the university—are two sides of the same coin. They are the two pillars of a huge global project of university politics destined to profoundly change the way the university-as-public-good has been produced, transforming it into a vast and vastly profitable ground for educational capitalism. This middle- to long-range project includes different levels and forms of the mercantilization of the university. I deal with the forms later. As for the levels, it is possible to distinguish two. The primary level consists of inducing the public university to overcome the financial crisis by generating its own resources, namely, through partnerships with industrial capital. On this level the public university maintains its autonomy and its institutional specificity, privatizing part of the services it renders. The second level consists of the biased elimination of the distinction between public and private universities, transforming the university as a whole into a business, an entity that not only produces for the market but which is itself produced as a market—a market of university services as diverse as administration, teaching programs and materials, certification of degrees, teacher training, and teacher and student evaluation. Whether or not it will still make sense to speak of the university as a public good when this second level is attained is a rhetorical question.

THE DISINVESTMENT OF THE PUBLIC UNIVERSITY

The crisis of the public university as a consequence of disinvestment is a global phenomenon, although its consequences are significantly different at the core, the periphery, and the semiperiphery of the world system. In the central countries the situation is differentiated. In Europe where, with the exception of England, the university system is almost totally public, the public university has had the power to reduce the extent of disinvestment while developing the ability to generate its own income through the market. The success of this strategy depends in good measure on the power of the public university and its political allies to block the significant emergence of the private university market. For instance, in Spain this strategy has so far been more successful than in Portugal. However, it is important to bear in mind that, throughout the 1990s, a private, nonuniversity sector, aimed at the professional job market, emerged in almost every European country. This fact led the universities to respond by structurally modifying their programs and by increasing their variety. In the United States, where private universities occupy the top of the hierarchy, public universities were motivated to seek alternative funding from foundations, in the market, and by raising tuition fees. Today, in some North American public universities, state funding is less than 20 percent of the total budget.

On the periphery, where the search for alternative income in the market is virtually impossible, the crisis attains catastrophic proportions. Obviously, the ills are long-standing, but they have been seriously aggravated in the past decade by the state's financial crisis and the structural adjustment programs. A UNESCO report from 1997 about African universities drew a dramatic

picture of all sorts of shortages: the collapse of infrastructures; an almost total lack of equipment; miserably remunerated, unmotivated, and easily cor-
ruptible teaching personnel; and little or no research investment. The World
Bank diagnosed the situation in a similar way and, characteristically, declared it irreparable. Unable to include in its calculations the importance of
the university in the building of national projects and the creation of long-
term critical thinking, the World Bank concluded that African universities
do not generate sufficient "return" on their investment. As a consequence,
the African countries were asked to stop investing in universities and to concentrate their few resources on primary and secondary education, thus allowing the global market of higher education to resolve the problem of the
university for them. This decision had a devastating effect on the universities of the African countries.

The Brazilian case is representative of the attempt to apply the same logic
in the semiperiphery (see Chauí 2003). The World Bank's 2002 report on
higher education assumes that Brazil is not going to (i.e., it should not) increase the university's public resources and that therefore the solution is in
the expansion of the university market combined with the reduction of the
cost per student (which, among other things, serves to maintain the pressure
on teachers' salaries) and the elimination of free public instruction, as is now
beginning to happen in Portugal.

This marketization (or "commercialization") is a global process, and it is
on this scale that it should be analyzed. The development of university instruction in the central countries, in the 30 or 40 years after World War II,
was based, on the one hand, on the successes of the social struggles for the
right to education, which translated into the demand for more democratic
access to the university; on the other hand, the development of university instruction was based on the imperatives of an economy that required a more
highly qualified workforce in key industrial sectors. The situation changed
significantly with the economic crisis that peaked in the mid 1970s. Since
then, there has been a growing contradiction between the reduction of public investment in higher education and the intensification of the international
economic competition based on the search for technological innovation and
hence on the technological and scientific knowledge that makes it possible,
as well as on the training of a highly qualified workforce.

As for the demand for a qualified workforce, the 1990s revealed another

contradiction: The growth of the qualified workforce required by an economy based on knowledge coexisted with the explosive growth of very low
skilled jobs. The neoliberal globalization of the economy has deepened the
segmentation of the labor markets between countries and within countries.
At the same time it has allowed both the qualified worker and the unqualified
worker *pools* to be recruited globally—the qualified workers predominantly
through *brain drain* and *outsourcing* of technically advanced services and the
unqualified workers predominantly through businesses delocalizing across
the globe and (often clandestine) immigration. The global availability of
skilled labor permits the central countries to lower the priority of their investment in public universities, making funding more dependent on market
needs. Actually, there is another contradiction in this domain between the
rigidity of university training and the volatility of the qualifications required
by the market. This contradiction was shaped, on the one hand, by the creation of modular nonuniversity tertiary training systems and, on the other
hand, by shortening the periods of university training and making it more
flexible. Despite ad hoc solutions, these contradictions became enormously
acute in the 1990s and had a disconcerting effect on higher education: The
university was gradually transformed from a generator of conditions for competition and success in the market into an object of competition, that is, into
a market of university services.

THE TRANSNATIONALIZATION OF THE UNIVERSITY MARKET

The other pillar of the neoliberal project for the university is the transnationalization of the market for university services. As I said, this project
is linked but not limited to the reduction in public financing. Other equally
decisive factors are the deregulation of commercial exchanges in general,
the imposition of the mercantile solution by multilateral financial agencies,
and the revolution in information and communication technologies, especially the enormous growth of the Internet, even if a crushing percentage
of the electronic flows are concentrated in the North. Because it is a global
development, it affects the university-as-public-good in the North as
much as in the South, but with different consequences. The inequalities between universities in the North and those in the South are thus enormously
exacerbated.

World expenditure on education has grown to $2 trillion, more than double the world market for automobiles. It is therefore an alluring area with great potential for capital and new areas of valorization. Since the beginning of the 1990s, financial analysts have called attention to education as potentially one of the hottest markets of the 21st century. Merrill Lynch analysts think that the educational sector possesses characteristics similar to those displayed by the health field in the 1970s: a gigantic market, fragmented and unproductive, looking to improve its low technological level, with a tremendous deficiency of professional administration and a low rate of capitalization. The growth of educational capital has been exponential and the rates of return are very high: £1,000 invested in 1996 was worth £3,405 in 2000, a gain of 240 percent, vastly superior to the general growth rate of the London stock market, the FTSE: 65 percent (Hirtt 2003, p. 20). In 2002 the USA-OECD Forum concluded that the global market for education was being transformed into a significant part of the world services market.

With the growing dominance of neoliberal globalization in mind, the following ideas are likely to guide the future expansion of the educational market:

1. We live in an information society. The administration, quality, and speed of information are essential to economic competition. Information and communication technologies, which depend on a qualified workforce, share the characteristic of not only contributing to increased productivity but also serving as incubators of new services, particularly in the field of education.

2. The economy based on knowledge demands more human capital as a condition for informational creativity and the efficient growth of the service economy. The higher the skills level of human capital employed, the greater the ability to transfer cognitive capacities and aptitudes in the constant processes of recycling and innovation expected by the new economy.

3. To survive, universities have to be at the service of these two master ideas: information society and knowledge-based economy. For that, they must undergo internal transformation, by means of information and communication technologies and the new kinds of institutional

management and by means of relations among knowledge workers and between suppliers and users or consumers of technological knowledge.

4. None of this is possible if the present institutional and politico-pedagogical paradigm dominating public universities remains in place. This paradigm does not allow for relations between the relevant publics to be mercantile relations; for efficiency, quality, and educational responsibility to be defined in terms of the market; for technological mediation (based on the production and consumption of material and immaterial objects) to become commonplace in professor-student relations; for the university to be open and vulnerable to pressure from its "clients"; for competition between "instructional operators" to be the stimulus for flexibility and adaptability to the expectations of employers; or for selectivity in the search for niches of consumption (i.e., student recruitment) to be the highest return on the capital invested.

5. To confront this, the university's current institutional paradigm must be replaced by an entrepreneurial paradigm to which both public and private universities would be subjected, and the educational market in which they are involved must be designed globally to maximize profitability. The favoritism bestowed on the private universities stems from their being able to adapt much more easily to the new conditions and imperatives.

The preceding items are the ideas that govern the educational reforms proposed by the World Bank and, more recently, the idea of its conversion into a knowledge bank (Mehta 2001). They are also the ideas that structure the General Agreement on Trade in Services (GATS) in the area of education currently under negotiation in the World Trade Organization, which I will discuss later. The World Bank's position in the area of education is perhaps one of the most ideological that it has assumed in the last decade (and there have been many), because, being an area in which nonmercantile interactions are still dominant, investments cannot be based merely on technical language, as can those imposed by structural adjustment. Ideological inculcation is served by analyses that are systematically twisted against public education to demonstrate that education is potentially a commodity like any other and that its conversion into an educational commodity is evidence of the superiority of capitalism as an organizer of social relations and of the superiority of neoliberal economic principles as the driving force of capitalism through mercantilization, privatization, deregulation, liberalization, and globalization.

The reformist zeal of the World Bank reverberates wherever it identifies the weaknesses of the public university, the power held by the faculty being one of its main targets. Academic freedom is seen as an obstacle to the responsibility of the entrepreneurial university vis-à-vis firms that wish to enlist its services. The power of the university must be wrested from the faculty and given to administrators trained to promote partnerships with private agents. What is more, the World Bank foresees that the power of the faculty and the centrality of the classroom will inexorably decline as the use of pedagogical technologies *online* becomes more prevalent. In accordance with this, the peripheral and semiperipheral countries can count on World Bank financial aid directed toward private higher education, provided that they reduce public investment in the university and create legal frameworks that facilitate the expansion of private higher education as an essential complement of public higher education. For example, in Brazil, during the government of Fernando Henrique Cardoso, the Ministry of Education, through the Program for the Recuperation and Expansion of the Physical Infrastructures of Institutions of Higher Instruction and in partnership with the National Bank for Economic and Social Development (BNDES), established a line of credit of about R$750 million (US$250 million) for institutions of higher learning, with resources originating from a World Bank loan. These resources were in large part channeled to private universities. Since 1999 the BNDES has loaned R$310 million (US$103 million) to private universities and only R$33 million (US$11 million) to public universities.

The transformation of higher education into an educational commodity is a long-term goal, and this horizon is essential for understanding the intensification of transnationalization currently under way in this market. Since 2000 the university's neoliberal transnationalization has been under the aegis of the World Trade Organization and GATS (Knight 2003). Education is one of the 12 services covered by this agreement, the goal of which is to promote the liberalization of commercial services through the progressive and systematic elimination of commercial barriers. Recently, GATS has become one of the most controversial topics in higher education, involving politicians, professors, and entrepreneurs. Its defenders see it as an opportunity for broadening and diversifying the educational supply in such a way that combining economic gain with greater access to the university becomes possible. This opportunity is based on the following conditions: the strong growth of the educational market in recent years, a growth only obstructed by national frontiers; the diffusion of electronic means of teaching and learning; needs for a qualified workforce that are not being met; the growing mobility of students, professors, and programs; and the financial inability of governments to meet the growing need for higher education. This is the market potential that GATS hopes to achieve through the elimination of trade barriers in this area.

GATS distinguishes four major ways of offering the transnational mercantilization of educational services: transborder offerings, foreign consumption, commercial presence, and presence of natural persons.

Transborder offerings are represented by transnational provisions of service without the need for physical movement on the consumers' part. Included are distance learning, online learning, and "virtual" universities. It is still a small market but one with strong growth potential. One-fourth of the foreign students who are taking courses offered by Australian universities do so through the Internet. Three great North American universities (Columbia, Stanford, and Chicago) and one in the United Kingdom (London School of Economics) formed a consortium to create Cardean University, which offers Internet courses to the world at large.

Foreign consumption consists of the provision of services through the transnational movement of the consumer. This is currently the big slice of the university's mercantile transnationalization. A recent study by the Organization for Economic Cooperation and Development (OECD) calculates that this commerce was worth US$30 billion in 1999. At the beginning of 2000, 514,000 foreigners were studying in the United States, more than 54 percent of them from Asia. India alone contributed 42,000 students. By contrast, during the 1998–1999 academic year, only 707 US students were studying in India. This area, like so many others, demonstrates the North-South (as well as West-East) asymmetries.

The third area has to do with commercial presence and consists of private producers of higher education establishing branches in foreign countries to sell their services. These are usually local branches or satellite campuses of

large global universities or local institutions operating under franchise contracts with such universities. It is an area of great potential and the one most
directly on a collision course with national educational policies, because it
implies that local centers or satellite campuses submit to international rules
agreed on by foreign investors.

Finally, the presence of natural persons is represented by the temporary
dislocation of suppliers of services, professors, or researchers, established
in one country and offering service to another (foreign) country. This is an
area that appears to have great development potential, given the growing
mobility of professional people.

South Africa should be cited in this context because it effectively illustrates the risks of GATS. South Africa has come to assume a position of total reserve in relation to GATS. It refuses to subscribe to international commercial commitments in the area of education and incites other countries to
do the same. This is a significant position, given the fact that South Africa
exports educational services to the rest of Africa. However, it does so through
bilateral agreements and within a framework of mutual benefit for the countries involved in and outside the regime of international trade policies. This
conditionality of mutual benefit and mutual respect is absent from the logic
of GATS. South Africa's rejection of GATS is based on the experience of
foreign offerings of higher education providers and of World Bank financial
aid that supports them, which, according to those responsible for South African education, has had devastating effects on higher education in Africa.
The refusal of GATS is based on the idea that any noncommercial considerations are strange to it and that this invalidates any national educational
policy that considers education a public good and a major component of the
national project. An example given by the then South African minister of
education, Kader Asmal, in a March 4, 2004, communiqué to the South African Portfolio Committee on Trade and Industry illustrates this point. It is
known that, with the end of apartheid, South Africa launched an enormous
program to combat racism in educational institutions that had, among its
principal targets, the so-called historically white universities; it was a program involving a multiplicity of actions—among them, affirmative action
regarding access. The antiracist struggle is thus a central part of the national
project underlying educational policies. It is against this backdrop that the
minister of education gives as an example of unacceptable conduct the fact

that a foreign institution intended to operate in South Africa by selectively recruiting students from the upper classes and, in particular, white students. The minister commented: "As you can imagine, the impact of these agendas on our efforts to construct a non-racist higher education in South Africa can be very profound" (Asmal 2003, p. 51).

FROM UNIVERSITY KNOWLEDGE TO PLURIVERSITY KNOWLEDGE

The developments of the past decade presented the university, especially the public university, with demanding challenges. The situation is near collapse in many countries on the periphery, and it is difficult in the semiperipheral countries. Although the expansion and transnationalization of the market for university services has contributed decisively to this situation in recent years, they are not the only cause. Something more profound occurred, and only this occurrence explains why the university, although still the institution par excellence of scientific knowledge, has lost its hegemony and has been transformed into an easy target for social criticism. I think that in the past decade the relations between knowledge and society began to change significantly, and these alterations promised to be profound to the point of transforming the way we conceive of knowledge and of society. As I said, the commercialization of scientific knowledge is the most visible side of these alterations. However, and despite their enormity, they are the tip of the iceberg, and the transformations now in progress have contradictory meanings and multiple implications, some of them epistemological.

University knowledge—that is, the scientific knowledge produced in universities or institutions separate from the universities but that retains a similar university ethos—was, for the entire 20th century, a predominantly disciplinary knowledge whose autonomy imposed a relatively decontextualized process of production in relation to the day-to-day pressures of the societies. According to the logic of this process, the researchers are the ones who determine what scientific problems to solve, define their relevance, and establish the methodologies and rhythms of research. It is a homogeneous and hierarchically organized knowledge insofar as the agents who participate in its production share the same goals of producing knowledge, have the same training and the same scientific culture, and do what they do according to well-defined organizational hierarchies. It is a knowledge based on the distinction between scientific research and technological development, and the autonomy of the researcher is translated as a kind of social irresponsibility as far as the results of the application of knowledge are concerned. Moreover, in the logic of this process of the production of university knowledge, the distinction between scientific knowledge and other kinds of knowledge is absolute, as is the relation between science and society. The university produces knowledge that the society does or does not apply, an alternative that, although socially relevant, is indifferent or irrelevant to the knowledge produced.

The university's organization and ethos were created by this kind of knowledge. It happens that, throughout the past decade, there were alterations that destabilized this model of knowledge and pointed to the emergence of another model. I designate this transition, which Gibbons et al. (1994) described as a transition from "type 1 knowledge" to "type 2 knowledge," as the passage from *university knowledge* to *pluriversity knowledge*.

Contrary to the university knowledge described in the preceding paragraph, pluriversity knowledge is a contextual knowledge insofar as the organizing principle of its construction is its application. Because this application is extramural, the initiative for formulating the problems to be solved and the determination of their criteria of relevance are the result of sharing among researchers and users. It is a transdisciplinary knowledge that, by its very contextualization, demands a dialogue or confrontation with other kinds of knowledge. Thus pluriversity knowledge is more heterogeneous internally and is more adequately produced in less perennial and more open systems that are organized less rigidly and hierarchically. All the distinctions on which university knowledge is based are put in question by pluriversity knowledge, but, most basically, it is the relation between science and society that is in question. Society ceases to be an object of scientific questioning and becomes itself a subject that questions science.

The tension between these two models of knowledge highlights the extremes of two ideal types. In reality, the kinds of knowledge produced occupy different places along the *continuum* between the two poles, some closer to the university model and others closer to the pluriversity model. This heterogeneity not only destabilizes the current institutional specificity of the university but also questions its hegemony and legitimacy in such a way as to force it to evaluate itself by self-contradictory criteria.

Pluriversity knowledge has had its most consistent realization in university-industry partnerships in the form of mercantile knowledge. But, especially in the central and semiperipheral countries, the context of application has been nonmercantile as well—cooperative and dependent on the solidarity created by partnerships between researchers on the one hand and labor unions, nongovernmental organizations (NGOs), social movements, particularly vulnerable social groups (women, illegal immigrants, the unemployed, people with chronic illnesses, senior citizens, those afflicted with HIV/AIDS, etc.), working-class communities, and groups of critical and active citizens on the other. There is a growing sector of civil society developing a new and more intense relationship with science and technology, demanding greater participation in their production and in the evaluation of their impact. In multiethnic and multinational countries, pluriversity knowledge begins to emerge from inside the university itself when incoming students from ethnic and other minority groups understand that their inclusion is a form of exclusion. They are confronted with the tabula rasa that is made of their cultures and of the traditional knowledge of their communities. All of this leads scientific knowledge to confront other kinds of knowledge and demands a higher level of social responsibility from the institutions that produce it and, consequently, from the universities. As science becomes more ingrained in the society, the society becomes more a part of science. The university was created according to a model of unilateral relations with society, and it is this model that underlies its current institutionalism. Pluriversity knowledge supplants this unilateral notion with interactivity and interdependence, processes enormously invigorated by the technological revolution of information and communication.

In light of these transformations, we can conclude that the university finds itself in the presence of opposing demands, which have the convergent effect of destabilizing its current institutionalism. On the one hand, the ultraprivate pressure to commodify knowledge displaces the social responsibility of the university with a focus on producing economically useful and commercially viable knowledge. On the other hand, an ultrapublic social pressure shatters the restricted public sphere of the university in the name of a much broader public sphere traversed by much more heterogeneous confrontations and by much more demanding concepts of social responsibility. This contrast between ultraprivate and ultrapublic pressures has not only begun to destabilize the university's institutionalism but also has created a profound fracture in the university's social and cultural identity, a fracture translated as disorientation and defensive tactics and, above all, as a kind of paralysis covered up by a defensive attitude, resistant to change in the name of university autonomy and academic freedom. The instability caused by the effects of these contrasting pressures creates impasses in which it becomes evident that demands for larger changes often accompany equally large forms of resistance to change.

THE END OF THE COUNTRY PROJECT?

The passage from university knowledge to pluriversity knowledge is thus a much more ample process than the commodification of the university and of the knowledge it produces. It is a process most visible today in the central countries, although it is also present in semiperipheral and peripheral countries. But in both semiperipheral and peripheral countries another transformation has been occurring for the last two decades, one that is linked to neoliberal globalization and that is not limited to economic dimensions or reducible to the commodification of the university. It is, moreover, an eminently political transformation. In these countries, the public university—and the educational system as a whole—was always tied to the construction of a national project. This was as evident in Latin American universities in the 19th century or, in Brazil's case, in the 20th century as it was in African and various Asian countries, as was the case of India after it became independent in the mid 20th century. I am referring to projects of national development or modernization led by the state and aimed at generating and consolidating the country's coherence and cohesion as an economically, socially, and culturally well-defined geopolitical territory for which it was frequently necessary to wage border-defining wars. The study of liberal arts and social sciences (and frequently of the natural sciences as well) was aimed at lending consistency to the national project, creating knowledge and shaping the personnel necessary for its realization. In the best of times, academic freedom and university autonomy were an integral part of such projects, even when they criticized them severely. This involvement was so profound that in many cases it became the second nature of the university: To question the national political project was to question the public university. The reactive defensiveness that has dominated the university, namely, in its responses to the financial crisis, derives from the fact that the university—endowed with reflexive and critical capacity like no other social institution—is lucidly coming to the conclusion that it is no longer tied to a national project and that, without one, there can be no public university.

In the last 20 years, neoliberal globalization has launched a devastating attack on the idea of national projects, which are conceived as obstacles to the expansion of global capitalism. From the standpoint of neoliberal capitalism, national projects legitimize logics of national social production and reproduction that are embedded in heterogeneous national spaces and geared to intensifying such heterogeneity. Moreover, the operation of these logics is guaranteed by a political entity that is endowed with sovereign power over the territory, the nation-state, whose submission to global economic impositions is problematic from the start with regard to its own interests and those of the national capitalism on which it has been politically dependent.

The neoliberal attack has as its special target the nation-state and particularly the economic and social policies in which education has played a major role. In the case of the public university the effects of this attack are not limited to the financial crisis. They have direct or indirect repercussions on the definition of research and training priorities, not only in the areas of social science and liberal arts but also in the natural sciences, especially in those areas most closely connected to technological development projects. The political disempowerment of the state and of the national project was reflected in the quasi-epistemological disempowerment of the university and its consequent disorientation as far as its social functions were concerned. University policies of administrative autonomy and decentralization, when adopted, have had the effect of dislocating the fulcrum of these national project functions toward local and regional problems. The identity crisis affected the university's critical thinking itself and, more broadly, the university's public sphere. The university was faced with two equally self-destructive options: an isolationist nationalism from which it has always distanced itself and that has now become totally anachronistic, or a hegemonic globalization that reduces nationally based critical thinking and the public sphere to the condition of a defenseless or indefensible local idiosyncrasy in the path of an unstoppable global flood.

This lack of a country project does not know how to affirm itself except through uneasiness, defensiveness, and paralysis. Meanwhile, I think that the university will not escape from the tunnel between the past and the future in which it finds itself, so long as the country project is not reconstructed. Actually, this is exactly what is happening in the central countries. The global universities of the United States, Australia, and New Zealand act within national scenarios that have the world as their playing field. Otherwise, it is difficult to justify the support that the diplomacy of these countries gives to such projects. We are foreseeing a third-generation colonialism that has the colonies of second-generation colonialism as its protagonists. From the perspective of the peripheral and semiperipheral countries the new global context demands a total reinvention of the national project without which there can be no reinvention of the university. There is nothing nationalistic about this demand. There is only the need to invent a critical cosmopolitanism in a context of aggressive and exclusive globalization.

Part 2: Democratic and Emancipatory Reform

WHAT IS TO BE DONE?

Here, I try to identify some of the master ideas that should preside over a creative, democratic, and emancipatory reform of the public university. Perhaps the first step is to identify the subjects of the actions that need to be undertaken efficiently to confront the challenges that face the public university. In the meantime, to identify the subjects, it is first necessary to define the political meaning of the response to such challenges. In light of the precedent, it becomes clear that, despite the multiple and sometimes long-standing causes of the university crisis, the subjects are currently being reconfigured by neoliberal globalization, and the way they affect today's university reflects that project's intentions. As I have suggested for other areas of social life (Santos 2000, 2002a, 2002b, 2002c, 2003), I think that the only efficient and emancipatory way to confront neoliberal globalization is to oppose it with an alternative, counterhegemonic globalization. Counterhegemonic globalization of the university-as-public-good means that the national reforms of the public university must reflect a country project that is centered on policy choices that take into account the country's insertion into increasingly transnational contexts of knowledge production and distribution. These policy choices will become increasingly polarized between two contradictory processes of globalization: neoliberal globalization and counterhegemonic globalization. This country project has to be the result of a broad political and social pact consisting of different sectoral pacts, among them an educational pact in which the public university is conceived of as a collective good. The reform must be focused on responding positively to the social demands for the radical democratizing of the university, putting an end to the history of exclusion of social groups and their knowledge for which the university has been responsible for a long time, starting well before the current phase of capitalist globalization. From now on, the national and transnational scales of the reform interpenetrate. Without global articulation a national solution is impossible.

The current global context is strongly dominated by neoliberal globalization but is not reduced to it. There is space for national and global articulations based on reciprocity and on the mutual benefit that, in the case of the university, will reconstitute and broaden long-lasting forms of internationalism. Such articulations should be cooperative, even when they contain mercantile components; that is, they should be constructed outside the regimes of international trade policy. This alternative transnationalization is made possible by new information and communication technologies and is based on the establishment of national and global networks, within which new pedagogies, new processes of construction and diffusion of scientific and other knowledge, and new social (local, national, and global) commitments circulate. The goal is to resituate the role of the public university in the collective definition and resolution of social problems, which are now insoluble unless considered globally. The new university pact starts from the premise that the university has a crucial role in the construction of its country's place in a world polarized by contradictory globalizations.

Neoliberal globalization is based on the systematic destruction of national projects and, because these projects were often designed with the active collaboration of university professors and students, the public university will be targeted for destruction until it is fine-tuned to neoliberal objectives. This does not mean that the public university should be isolated from the pressures of neoliberal globalization, which, apart from being impossible, might give the false impression that the university has been relatively protected from such pressures. Actually, it could be said that part of the university's crisis is the result of its passive incorporation of and co-optation by the forces of hegemonic globalization. What is called for is an active response to this co-optation, in the name of a counterhegemonic globalization.

The counterhegemonic globalization of the university-as-public-good that I am proposing here maintains the idea of a national project but conceives it in a nonnationalistic way. In the 21st century nations exist only to the extent that their national projects are qualified for a relatively autonomous insertion into the global society. For peripheral and semiperipheral countries the only way to qualify is to resist neoliberal globalization with strategies for another kind of globalization. The difficulty and, often, the drama of university reform in many countries reside in the fact that reform involves revisiting and reexamining the idea of the national project, something that the politicians of the last 20 years have hoped to avoid, either because they see such an idea as throwing sand in the gears of their surrender to neoliberalism or because they truly believe nationhood is outmoded as an instrument of resistance. The public university knows that, without a national project, there are only global contexts, and these are too powerful to be seriously confronted by the university's resistance. The university's excess lucidity allows it to declare that the emperor has no clothes, and for this reason university reform will always be different from the rest.

The counterhegemonic globalization of the university-as-public-good is thus a demanding political project that, to be credible, must overcome two contradictory but equally rooted prejudices: that the university can be reformed only by the university community and that the university will never reform itself. These are powerful prejudices. A brief examination of the social forces potentially committed to confront them is in place. The first social force is the public university community itself, that is, those within it interested in an alternative globalization of the university. The public university today is a fractured social field within which contradictory sectors and interests fight each other. In many countries, especially peripheral and semiperipheral ones, such contradictions are still latent. Defensive positions that maintain the status quo and reject globalization, whether neoliberal or alternative, predominate. This is a conservative position, not just because it advocates hewing to the status quo but mainly because, deprived of realistic alternatives, it will sooner or later surrender to plans for the neoliberal glob-

alization of the university. University personnel who denounce this conservative position while rejecting the idea that there is no alternative to neoliberal globalization will be the protagonists of the progressive reform that
I am proposing.

The second social force of such reform is the state itself, whenever it
is successfully pressed to opt for the university's alternative globalization.
Without this option the national state ends up adopting more or less un-
conditionally or succumbing more or less reluctantly to the pressures of neoliberal globalization and, in either case, transforming itself into the enemy of
the public university, regardless of any proclamation to the contrary. Given
the close love-hate relationship that the state carried on with the university
for the whole of the 20th century, the options tend to be dramatized.

Finally, the third social force to carry out the reform are citizens who
are collectively organized in social groups, labor unions, social movements,
nongovernmental organizations and their networks, and local progressive
governments interested in forming cooperative relationships between the
university and the social interests they represent. In contrast to the state, this
third social force has had a historically distant and, at times, even hostile relationship with the university, precisely because of the university's elitism
and the distance it cultivated for a long time in relation to the so-called un-
cultured sectors of society. This is a social force that has to be won through
a response to the question of legitimacy, that is, by means of nonclassist,
nonracist, nonsexist, and nonethnocentric access to the university and by a
whole set of initiatives that deepen the university's social responsibility in
line with the pluriversity knowledge mentioned earlier (more on this later).

Beyond these three social forces there is, in the semiperipheral and peripheral countries, a fourth entity that may be loosely called national capitalism. Certainly, the most dynamic sectors of national capital are transnationalized, and consequently they become part of the neoliberal globalization that
is hostile to the emancipatory reform of the university. However, in peripheral and semiperipheral countries the process of transnational integration of
these sectors is filled with tensions. Under certain conditions such tensions
may lead these sectors to see an interest in defending the project of the public university as a public good, especially when there are no realistic alternatives to the public university for the production of the kind of technological
knowledge needed to strengthen their insertion into the global economy.

With the preceding in mind, I identify key principles that should guide the emancipatory reform of the public university.

Confront the New with the New

The transformations of the past decade were profound and, despite having been dominated by the mercantilization of higher education, they were not reduced to only mercantile interests. There were also transformations in the processes and social contexts of knowledge production and diffusion, and the changes are irreversible. Under such conditions the new cannot be viewed as the problem and the old as the solution. Besides, what existed before was not a golden age and, if it was, it was just for the university and not for the rest of society, and, within the bosom of the university itself, it was for some and not for others.

Resistance has to involve the promotion of alternatives that address the specific contribution of the university-as-public-good to the collective definition and solution of new national and global social problems.

Fight for the Definition of the Crisis

To abandon its defensive position, the university has to be sure that the reform is not designed against it. The idea of an educational pact is crucial here because there can be no pact when there are nonnegotiable impositions and resistances. The question is, Under what conditions and why should the university abandon its defensive position? To answer this question, it is necessary to review the concepts of the crises of hegemony and of legitimacy.

The attack against the university on the part of the states that have yielded to neoliberalism was so massive that it is now difficult to define the terms of the crisis in any but neoliberal terms. This is the first manifestation of the university's loss of hegemony. The university lost the capacity to define the crisis in a hegemonic way, autonomously but in a way that society could identify. Herein lies the preponderance of defensive positions. However difficult, it is crucial (now more than ever) to define and sustain a counterhegemonic definition of the crisis.

For the last 20 years the university has suffered a seemingly irreparable erosion of its hegemony, originating in part in the current transition from conventional university knowledge to pluriversity knowledge, that is, to transdisciplinary, contextualized, interactively produced and distributed knowledge. Thanks to the new communication and information technologies, this pluriversity knowledge has altered the relations among knowledge, information, and citizenship. The university has been unable, until now, to take full advantage of these transformations.

Fight for the Definition of the University

There is a question of hegemony that, although seemingly residual, is central to enabling the university to fight successfully for its legitimacy. This is the question of the definition of the university. The big problem of the university in this domain has been the fact that what easily passes for a university is anything but. This problem was made possible because of the indiscriminate accumulation of functions attributed to the university throughout the 20th century. Because the functions were added without logical articulation, the market for higher instruction was able to self-designate its product as a university without having to assume all the functions of a university, concentrating only on those functions that made it profitable.

Reform should start from the assumption that a university must have graduate and postgraduate training, research, and socially responsible extension. Without any one of these, what you have is higher instruction, not a university. In terms of this definition, in many countries the overwhelming majority of private universities and even some of the public ones are not universities at all.

Thus reform must distinguish more clearly than it has up until now between university and tertiary education. With respect to public universities that are really not universities, the problem ought to be solved by creating a public university network (proposed later) so that universities without autonomous research or postgraduate courses can offer them in partnership with other universities in national or even transnational networks. A university system in which postgraduate programs and research are concentrated in a small number of universities cannot guarantee the sustainability of a national educational project in a cultural and political context pulled apart by contradictory forms of globalization.

As far as private universities are concerned—in case they wish to maintain the status and designation of universities—their licensing ought to be subject to the existence of postgraduate, research, and socially responsible extension programs that are subjected to frequent and demanding reviews.

As with public universities, if private universities cannot autonomously sustain such programs, they must do so through partnerships, either with other private universities or with public ones.

The definition of what constitutes a university is crucial to protect the university from predatory competition and society from fraudulent consumer practices. A successful struggle for the definition will allow the public university a minimal playing field in which to conduct the most encompassing and demanding struggle, the struggle for legitimacy.

Reclaim Legitimacy

In a situation in which hegemony is irremediably affected, legitimacy is simultaneously more urgent and more difficult. Thus the battle for legitimacy is going to be ever more demanding, and university reform must be centered on it. There are five areas of action in this domain: access, extension, action-research, ecology of knowledge, and university/public school partnerships. The first two are the most conventional, but they will have to be profoundly revised; the third has been practiced in some Latin American and African universities during periods of greater social responsibility on the part of the university; the fourth constitutes a decisive innovation in the construction of a postcolonial university; the fifth is an area of action that had a great presence in the past but that now has to be totally reinvented.

Access.   In the area of access the greatest frustration of the past two decades was that the goal of democratic access was not attained. In most countries, factors of discrimination, whether of class, race, gender, or ethnicity, continued to make access a mixture of merit and privilege. Instead of democratization, there was "massification," and afterward, in the alleged postmassification period, a strong segmentation of higher education involving practices of authentic "social dumping" of diplomas and degree recipients. The most elitist universities took few initiatives, other than defending their access criteria, invoking the fact, often true, that the most persistent discrimination occurs on the way to the university, in primary and secondary education. It is foreseeable that the transnationalization of higher education services will aggravate the segmentation phenomenon by transnationalizing it. Some foreign providers direct their offers to the best students coming from the best (often, most elitist) secondary schools or having graduated from the best national universities. In a transnationalized system the best universities, occupying the top national rungs in peripheral and semiperipheral countries, will become the bottom rungs of the global ladder. Of the four kinds of transnationalized services, foreign consumption is one of those most responsible for the new brain drain, particularly evident in India but also present in some African countries, such as Kenya and Ghana.

Among the master ideas that should guide the matter of access, I discern the following four. First, in countries where discrimination of university access is largely based on blockages at the primary and secondary instructional levels, progressive university reform, in contrast to the World Bank's recipes, must give incentives to the university to promote active partnerships with public schools in the areas of science and technology.

Second, the public university must be made accessible for students from subaltern classes through scholarships rather than loans. If it is not controlled, the indebtedness of university students will become a time bomb: A population encumbered by the certainty of a debt that can take 20 years to repay is being thrown into an increasingly uncertain labor market. Scholarships that include the possibility of student jobs in university activities both on and off campus should be granted to students—a rare practice especially in peripheral and semiperipheral countries. For example, undergraduate and graduate students could volunteer some hours each week as tutors in public schools, helping pupils and, if necessary, teachers.

Third, in multinational and multicultural societies racial and ethnic discrimination should be confronted with programs of affirmative action focused both on access and retention, especially during the first years when attrition rates are often high. Needless to say, racial and ethnic discrimination occurs in conjunction with class discrimination but cannot be reduced to the latter; it must be the object of specific measures. In India caste discrimination is the object of affirmative action, despite acting in conjunction with class and gender discrimination. In South Africa racial discrimination is the object of affirmative action, despite acting in conjunction with class discrimination. As happens in these two countries, antidiscrimination action in the university must be carried out in conjunction with antidiscrimination measures in other spheres, such as access to public employment and to the labor market in general. In this way the university will be linked to a progressive national project and bear witness to it.[2]

Fourth, the critical evaluation of access and its obstacles—like the rest of the discussion on the areas of extension and ecology of knowledge—must explicitly confront the colonial character of the modern university. In the past the university not only participated in the social exclusion of so-called inferior races and ethnicities but also theorized about their inferiority, an inferiority extended to the knowledge produced by the excluded groups in the name of the epistemological priority conferred on science. The task to democratize access is thus particularly demanding because it questions the university as a whole, not just who attends it but what kind of knowledge is transmitted to those who attend it.

Extension. The area of extension is going to have a special meaning in the near future. At a moment when global capitalism intends to functionalize the university and, in fact, transform it into a vast extension agency at its service, an emancipatory reform of the public university must confer a new centrality to the activities of extension and conceive of them as an alternative to global capitalism. Universities must become active participants in the construction of social cohesion, the deepening of the democracy, the struggle against social exclusion and environmental degradation, and the defense of cultural diversity. The extension involves a vast area of service provision for a variety of recipients: working-class social groups and organizations, social movements, local or regional communities, local governments, the public sector, and the private sector. Apart from providing services to well-defined recipients, an entirely different area of service provision has the society in general as its recipient: the promotion of scientific and technical culture and the study of the arts and literature as tools to empower citizenship and deepen democracy.

For extension to fulfill this role, it must avoid being directed toward moneymaking activities for the sole purpose of gathering nonstate resources. In this case we are faced with a discrete (or not so discrete) privatization of the public university. On the contrary, the extension activities I have in mind are designed to address the problems of social exclusion and discrimination in such a way as to give voice to the excluded and discriminated social groups.

Action-Research. Action-research and the ecology of knowledge are areas of university legitimacy that transcend extension because they act both at the level of extension and at the level of research and training. Action-research consists of the participative definition and execution of research projects involving working-class and, in general, subaltern communities and social organizations who are grappling with problems and who can benefit from the results of the research, that is, the solution to the problem. The social interests are tied to the scientific interests of the researchers, and so the production of scientific knowledge is directly linked to the satisfaction of the needs of social groups who lack the resources to have access to specialized technical knowledge through the market. Action-research has a long tradition in Latin America, but it has never been a university priority. Just as with extension activities, the new centrality of action-research is due to the fact that the neoliberal transnationalization of higher education is transforming the university into a global institution of action-research at the service of global capitalism. Here, too, the battle against this functionalism is made possible only by constructing a social alternative that focuses on the university's social utility and defines it in a counterhegemonic way.

Ecology of Knowledge. The ecology of knowledge is a more advanced form of action-research. It implies an epistemological revolution in the ways that research and training have been conventionally carried out at the university.[3] The ecology of knowledge is a kind of counterextension or extension in reverse, that is, from outside to inside the university. It consists of the promotion of dialogues between, on the one hand, scientific and humanistic knowledge produced by the university and, on the other hand, the lay or popular knowledge that circulates in society and that is produced by common people, both in urban and rural settings, originating in Western and non-Western cultures (indigenous, African, Asian, etc.). Along with the technological euphoria, today there is also a lack of epistemological confidence in science that derives from the growing visibility of the perverse consequences of some kinds of scientific progress and the fact that many of modern science's social promises have not been fulfilled. It is beginning to be socially perceptible that the university, by specializing in scientific knowledge and considering it the only kind of valid knowledge, has actively contributed to the disqualification and destruction of much potentially invaluable nonscientific knowledge; thus social groups to whom these kinds of knowledge are the only ones available are marginalized and, more generally, human experience and diversity become impoverished. Hence social injustice contains cognitive injustice at its core. This is particularly obvious on the global scale, where peripheral countries, rich in nonscientific wisdom but poor in scientific knowledge, have seen scientific knowledge, in the form of economic science, destroy their ways of sociability, their economies, their indigenous and rural communities, and their environments.

University and Public School. Here, I want to stress the relevance of "pedagogical knowledge," which comprises three subthemes: production and diffusion of pedagogical knowledge, educational research, and the training of public school teachers. It is a theme of growing importance, avidly coveted by the educational market. The public university once performed a hegemonic role in this area, but it has withdrawn or been pushed aside from it in recent decades. This fact is now responsible for the university distancing itself from the public school—the separation between the academic world and the world of the school—a distancing that, if maintained, will destroy any serious effort to relegitimize the public university as a collective good.

Under the aegis of neoliberal globalization, international agencies, nongovernmental organizations, and a number of foundations and private institutes have taken over some of the public university's functions in the development of public education, especially in the field of applied educational research. This change in functional entitlement reflects on the content of its practice. The change is manifest in the primacy of quantitative methodologies, in the emphasis on evaluative and diagnostic studies informed by an economistic rationality, which is based on narrowly conceived cost-benefit analyses, and, finally, in an obsessive concern with measuring the results of learning through the periodic application of standardized tests. Themes such as efficiency, competition, performance, choice, and accountability have become central to the educational agenda. The studies produced outside the universities, sponsored and financed by international organizations and private foundations, have had enormous influence on public educational policy, determining issues as diverse as the curriculum and the selection of public school system directors. The university—excluded from the debate and frequently accused of defending the status quo of corporate public instruction—has retreated to the role of questioning the dominant discourse about the public school crisis and has not bothered to formulate alternatives. Not surprisingly, educators and school administrators committed to progressive and counterhegemonic projects often complain about the public university's lack of involvement and support.

The university's marginalization goes along with the demand for tertiary qualification of teachers at all instructional levels, resulting in the progressive privatization of teacher training. The "training and empowerment of teachers" has become one of the most prosperous segments of the emerging educational market, confirmed by the proliferation of private institutions offering teacher-empowerment courses for school systems.

The wide gap between the public university and pedagogical knowledge is prejudicial both for the public school and the public university. The public university's resistance to the new educational prescriptions cannot be reduced to a critique, especially because criticism, in the context of the university's crisis of legitimacy, ends up increasing the social isolation of the public university. The critique produced in the schools of education has reinforced the perception that the university is completely obsessed with the defense of the status quo. Doing away with this perception ought to be one of the main goals of a progressive and democratic university reform. The principle to be affirmed is the university's commitment to the public school. Among other directives, the reform defended here proposes (1) valuing the initial training and linking it to programs of ongoing training, (2) restructuring degree-awarding courses to ensure curricular integration between professional and academic training, (3) collaboration between university researchers and public school teachers in the production and diffusion of pedagogical knowledge through the recognition and stimulation of action-research, and (4) creation of regional and national networks of public universities for the development of programs of ongoing training in partnership with the public instructional systems.

Rethink University and Industry Connections

As we have seen, the industrial sector is growing rapidly as a producer of educational and university services. I mention it here in a consumer role. The current popularity of the concepts of a knowledge society and a knowledge-based economy, especially in the central countries, is indicative of the pressure that has been put on the university to produce the kind of knowledge needed to increase business productivity and competitiveness. The entrepreneurial pressure is so strong that it goes far beyond the sphere of extension, trying to define according to its own image and interests what counts as relevant research. This redefinition does away with both the distinction between extension and research and the distinction between fundamental and applied research. In the central states, especially the United States, the relation between state and university has begun to be dominated by the central imperative in this domain: the university's contribution to economic competitiveness and to military supremacy. Research policies have been directed to privilege studies in areas of interest to businesses and to the commercialization of research results. Cuts in the public funding of universities are seen as "incentives" for universities to procure private investments, enter into partnerships with industry, patent their results, and develop commercial activities, including the commercialization of their own brand names.

The response to this pressure becomes quite dramatic, and it raises the most serious challenges to the survival of the public university as we know it. There are four main reasons for this: (1) This is the area in which there is the biggest disconnection between the university's traditional institutional model and the new model that is implicit in the performances demanded; (2) this is the area in which the university enters into direct competition with other institutions and actors that emerged from the new demands; (3) it is here that the university's models of public administration are most directly exposed and negatively compared with the prevalent models of private management; and (4) more than in any other area, it becomes evident here that the university's legitimacy and responsibility in relation to dominant interests and social groups can signify its illegitimacy and irresponsibility in relation to subaltern interests and social groups.

In this area the progressive reform of the university as a public good should be oriented by the following ideas. First, it is crucial that the scientific community and the social groups it chooses to associate itself with not lose control of the scientific research agenda. For this to happen, it is necessary to prevent the financial asphyxia from compelling the public university to privatize its functions to compensate for budget cuts. It is crucial that "opening to the outside" not be limited to opening to the market. On the contrary, the university must develop spaces of intervention that somehow balance the multiple, often contradictory. and at times conflicting interests that circulate in the society and that are endowed with the power to summon and interrogate the university. Even in the United States, where the knowledge business is most advanced, the country's technological leadership is based on a kind of equilibrium in the universities between the basic research undertaken, without direct commercial interest, and applied research, which is subject to entrepreneurial rhythms and risk.

Second, the public research-funding agencies should act on behalf of emergent research topics considered socially relevant but without any foreseeable commercial value. The growing appeal of competition for so-called targeted research must be moderated by general competition in which the younger scientific community has a chance to creatively and freely develop new areas of research that, for the time being, do not arouse the interest of capital.

The usefulness to the university of interacting with the entrepreneurial milieu to identify new themes for research, develop applied technology, and carry out impact analyses cannot be ignored. Indeed, it is important that the university be granted the ability to explore this potential and, in so doing, not be placed in a dependent position, especially on the level of survival, with regard to commercial contracts.

The most polemic theme in this area is the patenting of knowledge. In the central countries the fight for patents, especially in the most commercially attractive areas, such as biotechnology, is completely transforming the processes of research and relations within the scientific community and is threatening the collegiality of research processes and free and open discussion of findings. According to many, patenting puts the advance of science at risk and provokes a fatal distortion of research priorities. The patent problem is one of those that best reveals the global segmentation of knowledge production. It is relevant only in the few countries where there is a great capacity for commercial absorption of the knowledge produced.

TOWARD A NEW INSTITUTIONALISM

The institutional domain is a key area of the public university's democratic and emancipatory reform. I previously noted that the virulence and salience of the institutional crisis reside in its being a condensation of the deepening crises of hegemony and legitimacy. This is why I have focused up to now on these two crises. It is my opinion that university reform must be centered on the matter of legitimacy. In fact, the loss of hegemony seems irremediable, not only because of the emergence of many alternative institutions but also because of the growing internal segmentation in the university network, both at the national and the global levels. The university today is not the unique organization it was, and its heterogeneity makes it even more difficult to identify the uniqueness of its character. The processes of globalization make this heterogeneity more visible and intensify it. What remains of the university's hegemony is the existence of a public space where the debate and the criticism of society can, in the long run, happen with fewer restrictions than in the rest of society. This core of hegemony is too irrelevant in today's capitalist societies to sustain the university's legitimacy. This is why institutional reform has to be centered on the crisis of legitimacy.

The institutional reform I propose here intends to strengthen the public university's legitimacy in the context of the neoliberal globalization of education and envisions supporting the possibility of an alternative globalization. Its principal areas can be summed up in the following ideas: networking, internal and external democratizing, and participative evaluation.

Networking

The first idea is that of a national network of public universities on which a global network can be developed. In almost every country there are university associations, but such associations do not come close to constituting a network. In most cases they are merely pressure groups collectively demanding benefits that are appropriated individually. In another direction entirely, I propose that the university's public good begin to be produced in networks, meaning that none of the nodes in the network can ensure by itself all the functions into which this public good is translated, be it knowledge production, undergraduate and graduate training, extension, action-research, or the ecology of knowledge. This implies an institutional revolution. Universities were institutionally designed to function as autonomous and self-sufficient entities. The culture of university autonomy and of academic freedom, although defended publicly in the name of the university against outside forces, has been frequently used inside the university system to pit university against university. Competition for ranking exacerbates separation, and, because it takes place without any compensatory measures, it deepens the existing inequalities, making the slope of the pyramid even steeper and the overall segmentation and heterogeneity more profound. Building a public network implies the sharing of resources and equipment, the internal mobility of teachers and students, and minimal standardization of course plans, of school year organization, of systems of evaluation. None of this has to eliminate the specificities of each university's response to the local or regional context in which it is located. On the contrary, maintaining such specificity gives each individual university more value within the network.[4] The network, while creating more polyvalence and decentralization, strengthens the public university network as a whole. It is not about making excellent universities share their resources in such a way that their excellence would be put at risk. Rather, it is about multiplying the number of excellent universities, offering each the possibility of developing its niche potential with the help of the rest.

Once the network is created, its development is subject to three basic action principles: Make it dense, make it democratic, and qualify it. Network theory provides precious organizational leads. They can be multilevel and multiscale; they should stimulate the formation of clusters and promote the growth of multiconnectivity among universities, research and extension centers, and programs that deal with publicizing and publishing knowledge. I think it is useful to keep the example of the European Union in mind when building a network. European university policy envisions the creation of a university network that will prepare European universities for the globalization of higher education. Although I do not agree with the excessive emphasis on the mercantile aspects, I think the strategy is correct in acknowledging that, until recently, relations among European universities were characterized by institutional heterogeneity, enormous segmentation, and reciprocal isolation—that is, a set of features that weakened the opportunities for inclusion of the European universities in the global context of higher education. What the European Union is trying to do at an international level, among its member countries, is certainly more difficult to achieve than at the national level. And if a central region of the world system concludes that it is vulnerable in this domain on the global scale and decides to prepare itself to remedy this through the creation of a European-wide university network, then it appears that with better reasons the same should be done through associations among semiperipheral and peripheral countries.

The organization of universities within the network must be directed toward promoting internal articulation in the four areas of legitimacy: access, extension, action-research, and ecology of knowledge.

Internal and External Democratizing

Apart from the creation of the network, the new institutionalism must work toward the deepening of the university's internal and external democracy. When we discuss university democratization, we are usually thinking about ending forms of discrimination that limit access. But there are other dimensions. Recently, the university's external democratization has become a highly debated theme. The idea of external democratization gets conflated with the idea of the university's social responsibility, because what is being discussed is the creation of an organic political link between the university and society that ends the isolation that has demonized the university in recent years as a corporative manifestation of elitism, an ivory tower, and so forth. The appeal for external democracy is ambiguous because it is made by social groups with contradictory interests. On the one hand, the call comes from an educational market that invokes the university's democratic deficit to justify the market's need for greater access to it, something that is possible only if the university is privatized. External democratization implies the university's new relation with the world of business and its ultimate transformation into a business. On the other hand, the call for external democratization comes from progressive social forces that are behind the transformations occurring in the passage from the university model to the pluriversity model; it comes especially from the allies of historically excluded groups that today demand that the public university become responsive to their long-neglected interests. The pluriversity model, in assuming the contextualization of knowledge and the participation of citizens or communities as users or even coproducers of knowledge, requires that such contextualization and participation be subject to rules that will guarantee the transparency of the relations between the university and its social environment and will legitimatize the decisions made in the ambit of such relations.

This second appeal for external democracy aims to neutralize the first, the call for privatizing the university. The appeal for privatization has had an enormous impact on the universities of many countries in the last decade, to the point where university researchers have lost much of the control they had over research agendas. The most obvious case is the way research priorities are defined today in the field of health, where diseases that affect the majority of the world's population (e.g., malaria, tuberculosis, HIV/AIDS) are not given research priority. From the moment the regulatory mechanisms of the scientific community begin to be dependent on the centers of economic power, only external bottom-up democratic pressure can ensure that matters with little commercial interest but great social impact make their way into research agendas.

The need for a new institutionalism of external democracy—a new university-society public sphere—is fundamental to making the social pressures on university functions transparent, measurable, and susceptible to reasonable regulation. This is one of the paths of participative democracy that lead to a new platform of public university legitimacy.

Internal democracy is to be articulated with external democracy. This is a theme that acquired great visibility in the central countries during the 1960s; all the countries that went through periods of dictatorship during the second half of the 20th century introduced forms of democratic university governance as soon as the dictatorship was toppled. The entrepreneurial pressure on the university has launched a systematic attack on this internal democracy. The reason is obvious: Putting the university at the service of capital entails the proletarianization of professors and researchers, and this cannot occur while the mechanisms of internal democracy are in place, precisely because they sustain the academic freedom that bars the way to proletarianization. Proletarianization can be attained only when an entrepreneurial model of administration and organization is established, professionalizing university functions and maintaining a strict separation between administration, and faculty and researchers.

The external democracy proposed by capital is thus strongly hostile to internal democracy. The same is not true of community and solidarity-based external democracy that can stimulate internal democracy and vice versa. Therefore the reform of the public university as a collective good must defend internal democracy for its own sake and also avoid external democracy being reduced to university-industry relations. External democracy can be made concrete through socially and culturally diverse social councils, with participation based on social relevance rather than on financial contributions, defined on local or regional, class, racial, and gender bases. The participation in internally democratic organs will thus be informed by the principles of affirmative action, bringing social groups and interests to the councils that are now quite distanced from the university. It is important that the councils be more than a mere façade so that, apart from their consultative functions, they can participate in the internal processes of the university's participative democracy.

Participative Evaluation

Finally, the new institutionalism entails a new system of evaluation that includes each of the universities and the university network as a whole. Mechanisms of self-evaluation and hetero-evaluation should be adopted for both cases. Evaluation criteria should be congruent with the aforementioned goals of the reform and should be applied through technodemocratic or participative tools rather than through technocratic tools. Today technocratic tools are strongly recommended by transnational educational capital. They entail quantitative external evaluations, both of teaching and research, and leave out the fulfillment of any other functions, namely, extension and, of course, action-research and ecology of knowledge. In research, evaluation is focused on what is most easily accounted for by bibliometric techniques that differentiate publication types and locations and measure the impact of the publications by the number of citations. Little evaluation has been done of the less easily quantifiable areas of extension, and, when it occurs, it tends to privilege university-industry relations and to center on quantitative criteria, such as the number of patents.

The fixation of criteria through mechanisms of internal and external democracy is fundamental because these criteria define the social value of the different university activities. The university should not promote single models of professorial activity but rather differentiated models that value the specific competencies of different groups of professors. This allows the university to increase its social returns and to introduce internal incentives for new activities that serve as a shield against the unilateral pressure of the mercantile incentives. The participative evaluation models facilitate the emergence of sufficiently robust internal evaluation criteria to measure up to the external criteria. The principles of self-management, self-regulation, and self-discipline allow the evaluative processes to serve as processes of political apprenticeship. These principles are the only guarantee that participative

self-evaluation will not turn into narcissistic self-contemplation or an exchange of evaluative favors.

Conclusion

The university in the 21st century will certainly be less hegemonic but no
less necessary than it was in previous centuries. Its specificity as a public
good resides in its being the institution that links the present to the medium
and long term through the kinds of knowledge and training it produces and
through the privileged public space it establishes, dedicated to open and critical discussion. For these two reasons the university is a collective good without strong allies. Many people are not interested in the long term, and others have sufficient power to be wary of those who dare to suspect them or
criticize their interests.

The public university is thus a permanently threatened public good,
which is not to say that the threat comes only from the outside; it comes
from the inside as well. It is possible that in this chapter I have emphasized
the external threat more than the internal one. But in my previous work
about the university—"From the Idea of the University to the University
of Ideas," published in my book *Pela Mão de Alice: O Social e o Político na Pós-
Modernidade* (Santos 1994)—I paid more attention to the internal threat.
The reason for this change of emphasis is that, today, the factors of the internal threat are stimulated by a perverse interaction, unknown to many,
with factors of the external threat. I am more than ever aware that a university that is socially ostracized for its elitism and corporate tendencies and
paralyzed by the inability to question itself in the same way it questions society is easy prey for the proselytes of neoliberal globalization. This is why
the emergence of a university market—first, a national market and now a
global one—by making the public university's vulnerabilities more evident,
constitutes such a profound threat to the public good it produces or ought
to produce.

The conjunction between factors of internal threat and factors of external threat is quite obvious in evaluating the university's capacity for long-
term thinking, perhaps its most distinctive characteristic. Those who work
in today's university know that university tasks are predominantly short

term, dictated by budget emergencies, interdepartmental competition, professorial tenure, and so forth. The management of such emergencies allows for the flourishing of types of professionals and conduct that would have little merit or relevance were it possible and urgent to focus on long-term questions. This emergency-ridden state of affairs, which is surely due to several factors, must also be seen as a sign that powerful outside social actors are influencing the university. What is the social return on long-term thinking, on using the public spaces for critical thinking, or even on the production of knowledge apart from what the market demands? In the World Bank's way of thinking, the answer is obvious: None. If long-term thinking existed, it would be dangerous and, if not dangerous, unsustainable in semiperipheral and peripheral countries, because it would have to compete with the central countries that have supposedly unequivocal comparative advantages in this domain. If this global and external logic did not find such fertile ground for local and internal appropriation, it would certainly not be so dangerous. The proposal I have presented in this chapter is antipodal to this global and external logic and seeks to create conditions to prevent it from finding a welcoming plot for its local and internal appropriation.

The university is a public good intimately connected to the country's project. The political and cultural meaning of this project and its viability depend on a nation's ability to negotiate, in a qualified way, its universities' insertion into the new transnational fields. For the university, and education in general, this qualification is the condition necessary for not making the negotiation an act of surrender and thus marking the end of the university as we know it. The only way to avoid surrender is to create conditions for a cooperative university in solidarity with its own global role.

Notes

1. This chapter has been translated by Peter Lownds of the University of California, Los Angeles (UCLA). The first version of this text was presented in Brasilia, on April 5, 2004, in the context of the official calendar of debates about university reform organized by Dr. Tarso Genro, the minister of education.

2. In Brazil today, affirmative action politics are playing a leading role and merit special mention. In response to growing pressure from social movements for democratic access to higher learning, especially from the black movement, Lula's govern-

ment launched the University for All program (PROUNI) in the first semester of 2004. The program proclaims affirmative action based on racial and socioeconomic criteria and is based on two main measures. The first measure provides access and full scholarships to low-income students to attend private universities in exchange for the fiscal and social security exemptions granted them by the state. The institutions that adhere to the program earmark at least 10 percent of their seats for low-income students and public school basic education teachers. The second measure requires that the public federal universities earmark at least 50 percent of the enrollment for students coming from public schools (in Brazil the best secondary schools are private and the best universities are public). These vacancies will be distributed so that they reflect the ethnic composition of each state of Brazil, leaving it up to the universities to fix the percentages of vacancies to be filled by low-income students and racial or ethnic groups underrepresented in higher education. This program is a worthwhile effort that goes against the traditional social elitism of the public university, and it has met with much resistance. The debate has touched on the conventional theme of the contradiction between democratic access and meritocracy and also on some new themes, such as the difficulty of applying racial or ethnic criteria in a highly miscegenated society.

3. I have analyzed this epistemological revolution in greater detail in my other writings (Santos 1995, 2000).

4. For example, in Brazil, I have become aware of extremely rich experiences in the extension services of northern and northeastern universities that are totally unknown or undervalued in the central and southern universities. And I am certain that the reverse happens too.

References

Asmal, K. 2003. "Implications of the General Agreement on Trade in Services (GATS) on Higher Education." *Kagisano* 3: 47–53.

Chauí, M. 2003. "A Universidade Pública Sob Nova Perspectiva." Opening conference of the 26th annual meeting of ANPED, Poço de Caldas, Minas Gerais, Brazil, October 5.

Gibbons, M., C. Limoges, H. Nowotny, S. Schwartzman, P. Scott, and M. Trow. 1994. *The New Production of Knowledge*. London: Sage.

Hirtt, N. 2003. "Au Nord Comme au Sud, L'Offensive des Marches sur L'Université." *Alternatives Sud* 10(3): 9–31.

Knight, J. 2003. "Trade in Higher Education Services: The Implications of GATS." *Kagisano* 3: 5–37.

Mehta, L. 2001. "The World Bank and Its Emerging Knowledge Empire." *Human Organization* 60(2): 189–196.

Santos, B. S. 1994. *Pela Mão de Alice: O Social e o Político na Pós-Modernidade.* Oporto, Portugal: Afrontamento.

Santos, B. S. 1995. *Toward a New Common Sense: Law, Science, and Politics in the Paradigmatic Transition.* New York: Routledge.

Santos, B. S. 2000. *A Critica da Razão Indolente: Contra o Desperdício da Experiência.* Oporto, Portugal: Afrontamento.

Santos, B. S., ed. 2002a. *Coleção Reinventar a Emancipação Social,* v. 1, *Democratizar a Democracia: Os Caminhos da Democracia Participativa.* Rio de Janeiro: Civilização Brasileira.

Santos, B. S., ed. 2002b. *A Globalização e as Ciências Sociais.* São Paulo: Cortez.

Santos, B. S., ed. 2002c. *Coleção Reinventar a Emancipação Social,* v. 2, *Produzir para Viver: Os Caminhos da Produção Não Capitalista.* Rio de Janeiro: Civilização Brasileira.

Santos, B. S., ed. 2003. *Coleção Reinventar a Emancipação Social,* v. 3, *Reconhecer para Libertar: Os Caminhos do Cosmopolitismo Multicultural.* Rio de Janeiro: Civilização Brasileira.

World Bank. 2002. *World Bank Higher Education in Brazil: Challenges and Options.* New York: World Bank.

Findings from Particular Countries and Regions in the Americas

Academic Capitalism and the New Economy: Privatization as Shifting the Target of Public Subsidy in Higher Education

Gary Rhoades
Sheila Slaughter

The rise of industrialization in the United States shaped American higher education as we know it, giving birth to public (and some private) research universities and two-year colleges. The interpretations of the relationship between higher education and the political economy in that era vary from one scholar to another—defining the connection as undesirable or desirable and as serving narrow interests or broad societal interests (Geiger 1986; Scott 1983; Silva and Slaughter 1984; Trow 1973; Veblen 1918; Veysey 1965). But there is general agreement that higher education was affected by and benefited from the emerging corporate economy and the nation-state. With the rise of a postindustrial economy we suggest that US higher education has experienced the growth of "academic capitalism and the new economy" (Slaughter and Rhoades 2004). By that we mean the increasing engagement of higher education institutions and participants in marketlike and market behaviors in creating and taking to the marketplace (1) research and education products and services that commodify higher education's basic work and (2) nonacademic products and services that feature higher education as a nonacademic consumption item (dimensions of the new economy). In short, there has been a shift in the nature of higher education and its relationship to the political economy.

In contrast to many scholars, we do not see higher education as being taken over by or subject to external entities, whether of the private sector economy or the neoliberal state (Bok 2003; Gould 2003; Readings 1996). Although we recognize the powerful influence of external economic and political entities, we also see entrepreneurial higher education as being driven by internal cultural, economic, and political forces and actors. And we see it as being central to the new information-based economy. More so than in the rise of the industrial economy, higher education in the postindustrial United States is a central economic player and realm of market activity, framing and directly engaging in the private marketplace. That role is expressed in governmental and institutional policies; in interconnections among state, higher education, and market organizations; and in the practices of multiple players—academic managers, faculty, and various types of nonfaculty support professionals (whom we call managerial professionals). In the policies, interconnections, and practices of higher education, we see the emergence of an academic capitalist knowledge/learning/consumption regime.

Yet US higher education not only is central to the nation's political economy but also helps to define regional and global political economies. It does so because the US higher education model is preeminent internationally. It also does so by virtue of the physical presence of US higher education institutions and participants in other countries. Thus, after mapping key aspects of academic capitalism in the new economy in the United States, we draw out the implications of this knowledge/learning/consumption regime for higher education policies and practices in the Americas (and beyond).

A further theme of our chapter is that the privatization embedded in academic capitalism shifts the target of public subsidy. We unpack the meaning of privatization. Rather than conflating it with a reduction of public monies for higher education, we explore how privatization shifts public subsidy toward particular private interests in the postindustrial economy. And rather than decrying privatization as turning away from an idealized past in which higher education was devoted to the public interest, we explore ways in which it redefines how the public interest is served and to what effects.

Most colleges and universities are experiencing fiscal pressure, and there is an apparent political unwillingness to enhance government investment in higher education. In this context there appear to be few alternatives to the entrepreneurial direction of academic capitalism in the new economy. Thus we offer some thoughts about alternatives to the current path being pursued by higher education institutions, and we pose questions that should be explored about the choice of and balance between different entrepreneurial efforts and investments that colleges and universities might undertake.

Expressions of Academic Capitalism in the New Economy

In our book *Academic Capitalism and the New Economy* (Slaughter and Rhoades 2004), we detailed expressions of an "academic capitalist knowledge/learning/consumption regime." For us that means in a Foucauldian sense (Foucault 1977, 1980) a set of policies and practices that are not simply external to institutions and actors in higher education but that are also inscribed internally in their consciousness and practices. We see this regime as applying to the production (research) and transmission (education) of knowledge. We also see it as applying to nonacademic aspects of higher education that are consumed, particularly by students. In this regime, research, education, and the nonacademic experience of higher education become commodities, consumption items. In this chapter we outline three expressions of this regime, sketching its character in governmental and institutional policies, in interconnections between state, higher education, and market organizations, and in practices of faculty, managers, nonfaculty professionals, and students.

GOVERNMENTAL AND INSTITUTIONAL POLICIES

The last quarter of the 20th century witnessed major shifts in federal public policy in higher education with respect to student financial aid, research, and copyright. Neoliberal conceptions of market competition and of the need to marketize not-for-profit entities were inscribed in legislation. Colleges and universities, and participants in them, came to be disciplined, in a Foucauldian sense, by the logic of the private marketplace. One mechanism by which such discipline has been expressed and exercised is through a revised external policy regime. In the case of student financial aid, higher education institutions lobbied against the new regime, although some scholars and many economists lobbied for it. In research policy, higher education institutions and many groups of scholars lobbied for the new regime, although some lobbied against it. In copyright protection legislation, higher education institutions and academics were conflicted about the new regime. In any event the emergent policy regime at the federal and state levels instantiated a more central, involved role in the political economy for higher education.

That policy regime is evident and expressed in the institutional policies of public and private colleges and universities. As with federal policy, institutional intellectual property policies have changed significantly over the past quarter-century. Institutions have become more aggressive in pursuing the commercial potential of intellectual products created by their employees. Moreover, institutions are extending their academic capitalist efforts beyond research to include ventures in the realm of education.

The initial point of marketization with regard to student aid came with the Higher Education Amendments of 1972. Policy makers were deliberating how to channel new federal monies into higher education to promote access. The question was whether monies should be allocated to higher education institutions in block grants or to students through financial aid. Most higher education institutional associations lobbied for institutional grants (Gladieux and Wolanin 1976). But the Carnegie Commission on Higher Education, many economists, and the Committee on Economic Development (CED), consisting largely of CEOs of large corporations, including financial institutions (Domhoff 1967), articulated a market discourse of student choice. Casting students as consumers, their idea was to enhance access and quality through the efficiencies of the market: Give consumers the money, and the competition for them among institutions would yield improvements. They argued that a government policy of low tuition in state institutions unfairly disadvantaged private higher education; they advocated instead a high tuition/high aid policy, with students paying more of the costs of higher education but receiving grants and loans to enable them to choose among institutions in a competitive higher education marketplace (Leslie and Johnson 1974).

The 1972 higher education legislation adopted a market model of students and institutions. Over time the logic of the private marketplace came to be even more embedded in federal policy. Whereas initially most federal student aid was in the form of grants instead of loans, by 2000–2001 the balance between the two had been reversed, with 58 percent of the total aid being in loans, largely channeled through banks. Students and families were being asked to bear more of the costs of a higher education through a mechanism of low-interest loans subsidized by the government but largely run through for-profit financial institutions, to their benefit. A similar policy pattern has played out at the state level. Over time large increases in tuition have not been matched by increases in financial aid—a high tuition/low aid public policy (Griswold and Marine 1996; Hearn 1998).

Subsequent pieces of federal legislation have further embedded the logic of the market in higher education. The 1997 Taxpayer Relief Act constructed the higher education marketplace in ways that benefited particular student populations. Just as the increased emphasis on loans worked to the detriment of lower income and underserved populations (McPherson and Shapiro 1998), so the Taxpayer Relief Act provided the greatest relief to those who had money to be protected. Middle and upper-middle income families of traditional-aged students benefited from the Hope Scholarship, tax-sheltered college savings accounts, and penalty-free IRA withdrawals for college expenses. In short, the "user pays" model has favored those prospective students who can pay.

The 1998 Higher Education Act took the market model a step further, supporting the expansion and greater public subsidy of for-profit postsecondary schools. Rather than treating for-profit schools as a separate category, the act redefined them as institutions of higher education, making it easier for them to share in federal student financial aid, which is critical to their profitability. The law also created a special liaison in the Department of Education for proprietary schools. By 2000, then, federal policy was encouraging and subsidizing profit taking in higher education by proprietary colleges and universities.

Marketization in federal research policy came somewhat later. Most scholars identify the starting point as the Bayh-Dole Act of 1980, which facilitated university ownership of patents from federally funded research. Universities were now in the business of creating products with public monies and taking profit from them. This practice fundamentally challenged prevailing conceptions of conflict of interest, which worked to keep public entities and their employees separate from direct involvement in the market. This Mertonian conception of the public interest and of the basic norms of science was replaced by a more market based conception, which suggested that the public interest was best served by public sector involvement in the private sector marketplace (Rhoades and Slaughter 1991). That shift has been evidenced in state statutes and in university policies (Slaughter and Rhoades 1993), which most recently allow for public universities to own equity in companies that have been spun off by their faculty.

In the years since Bayh-Dole various pieces of federal legislation have promoted the transfer of technology from universities and federal laboratories to private industry. Despite bitter relations between Democrats and Republicans on other matters, bipartisan support for this legislation in the 1980s and 1990s coalesced into a "competitiveness coalition" (Slaughter and Rhoades 1996), which coexists with a "cold war coalition" in academic science and technology policy. It has promoted legislation aimed at enhancing the global competitiveness of new-economy industries in the United States by more effectively harnessing the creative strength of academic science. For example, the 1984 National Cooperative Research Act afforded antitrust status to joint ventures and consortia in research and development. It facilitated collaborative research endeavors that mingled federal and university monies with financial support from the private sector and enabled firms in the same industry to be cooperative partners in these ventures. Shortly thereafter, the Federal Technology Transfer Act of 1986 (and Executive Order 12591 in 1987) required federal agencies that support research in biotechnology to establish collaborations with industry.

The passing of such laws in Congress was mirrored by a policy shift within federal agencies that promoted and funded various forms of cooperative activity between universities and industry. Even the agency identified with supporting basic science, the National Science Foundation (NSF), came to emphasize interconnections between academe and industry by funding engineering research centers and other organizational forms designed to pump prime public and private sector partnerships. A 1989 NSF study, *Industrial Participation in NSF Programs and Activities*, found more than 100 examples of cooperative ventures made possible by the 1984 act. Moreover, the boundaries between the public and the private sector have collapsed even in evaluating the research projects of individual academic investigators. Many research programs at NSF now include business representatives, whose explicit role is to ensure attention to research's relevance.

Just as the marketization of student aid policy has meant privileging some student markets over others, so too in the privatization of research policy, some fields of research and some industries are privileged over others. In the cold war coalition, with its defense economy focus, physics has clearly been the favored and most funded science. By contrast, the competitiveness coalition shifts funding priorities toward new-economy fields in the biomedical and life sciences, such as biotechnology and information sciences (in both coalitions, social sciences, humanities, and the fine arts are largely left out).

The service- and information-based economy focus of the competitiveness coalition is evident as well in federal legislation related to copyright. In the new economy copyrighted educational materials are a prime site of commercialization. Most scholars who address entrepreneurial activity in higher education concentrate on research, patents, and technology transfer (Anderson 2001; Slaughter and Leslie 1997). However, our analysis takes us into the realm of copyright, which has more recently seen the passage of legislation that promotes and makes preeminent the logic of the market. Such legislation was a response partly to technological changes in telecommunications and digital industries that presented new possibilities for creating valuable intellectual property and for "pirating" copyrighted material. Thus major business interests pushed for legislation that would protect their intellectual property claims, extend their economic power beyond current industrial boundaries, and foster the growth of new businesses in the realm of educational materials. For example, in 1995 the Digital Performance Right in Sound Recording Act made illegal the use of new technologies and the Internet to bypass existing industrial monopolies, outlawing the downloading of copyrighted music recordings and extending protections to this sort of copyrighted material. One year later the Telecommunications Act deregulated a long-standing framework that authorized monopolies in separate technological and business realms, such as broadcast, cable, wire, wireless, and satellite, stimulating the growth of various forms of what has come to be called e-business. It also facilitated more aggressive academic capitalism by colleges and universities in distance education and the provision of courseware packages and educational materials. Just as federal research policy fostered cooperation between academe and business and between businesses in the same industry, so too federal legislation regarding copyright enabled and promoted such cooperative and commercializing activities. A final example of copyright legislation is the Technology, Education, and Copyright Harmonization (TEACH) Act of 2002, which addresses distance education. Because the legislation is so new, we cannot track its full effects. However, it modifies some restrictions on distance education that were embedded in the Digital Millennium Copyright Act of 1998. Moreover, as with Bayh-Dole, the TEACH Act may lead higher education institutions to develop internal capacity to manage the commercial responsibilities surrounding copyrighted materials and distance education. Institutions are responsible for monitoring and policing these activities in a variety of ways. And they are encouraged to develop and distribute copyright policies.

We now turn to institutional policies regarding patents and copyright. In both realms of intellectual property, universities and colleges have become more aggressive over time in pursuing the potential profits from employees' intellectual products. In both realms the logic of the private sector marketplace has come to redefine the policy parameters and public purposes established and pursued by academic institutions.

In the case of patenting the Bayh-Dole Act precipitated a rapid expansion of institutional activity in the development and revision of patent policies and in the internal managerial capacity to pursue technology transfer. Several facts point to the aggressiveness of universities' efforts. One has to do with when such policies were created. Although some universities in the United States had patent policies before 1980, most institutions developed these policies in the 1980s (Slaughter and Rhoades 2004). Another fact has to do with the internal managerial capacity for pursuing technology transfer. Historically, universities tended to work through outside patent management firms for managing such activity; Research Corporation and University Patents managed most of the patents of US universities until the 1970s. After that point and particularly after Bayh-Dole, more universities developed the capacity to manage patenting internally; there was an explosion of activity in the 1980s—the number of university technology transfer offices expanded dramatically, as did the number of technology transfer professionals working in those offices. The Association of University Technology Managers (AUTM) was founded in 1974. In 1984, when the membership was 381, a professional staff was hired. By 1990 the AUTM had 709 members, increasing to 1,600 by the late 1990s (Rhoades 1998b). Over time universities were running more patents through their own offices, decreasing the proportion of patents assigned to foundations from 46 percent in 1985 to 22 percent in 1995 (Owen-Smith 2001, p. 37).

The increased aggressiveness of institutions is also evident in the content of patent policies, in at least five ways. First is the policies' coverage. Early on, most policies covered faculty. Over time other categories of employees and employed students were increasingly covered; in some policies undergraduates are treated as employees even when they are not working for the institution. A second pattern is that over time institutions claimed greater shares of the proceeds from the intellectual property. Third, policies increasingly reduced the range of exceptions to the institutions claiming ownership of the property—in the early years more policies afforded an exception to faculty who created property "on their own time." Fourth, in later years some universities instituted policies that required employees to sign patent policy agreements as a part of their employment contract. Finally, recent policies afford institutions new claims in companies that are spun off by faculty. The provision for universities to own equity in the companies started up by their employees carries to a new level the reversal of past formulations and laws regarding the public interest and conflict of interest. At one time, the public interest was served by keeping public and private sectors separate, and it was a conflict of interest for professionals and not-for-profit institutions to have a material interest in other entities. But in the academic capitalist knowledge/learning regime, the public interest is served by knocking down those firewalls and enabling not-for-profit institutions and professionals to directly engage the private sector marketplace.

Institutional policies have changed over time with regard to copyrighted materials as well. However, the aggressive entry of universities and colleges into the marketplace for educational materials came later. A national study of research universities in the 1980s found that most had patent policies but not copyright policies (Lape 1992). Subsequent research on the same sample of universities found that by 2001 almost all had copyright policies (Packard 2002). Part of the reason that universities pursued property claims in this arena at a later point in time probably had to do with faculty's long-standing ownership of property rights to copyrighted intellectual products such as books and articles. Nevertheless, if the institutional claim came later in the realm of copyright than of patents, it eventually extended to a much wider range of institutions. The contest over ownership and royalty shares of copyrighted materials extends far beyond research universities to encompass all of higher education (Rhoades 1998a). In community colleges, most of which have faculty unions, the ownership of copyrighted educational materials developed by faculty for distance education, particularly for technology-mediated instruction, is a hotly contested issue between management and faculty (Rhoades 1999; Rhoades and Maitland 2000). Copyrighted educational materials are prominent in the political economy of essentially all of American higher education.

The increasing aggressiveness of higher education institutions' pursuit of claims to and proceeds from copyrighted educational materials is evident in the content of the policies. Over time policies extend coverage of who and what materials are covered; if there is more variation in who is covered by the copyright policies than in the case of patents (there is also less aggressive pursuit of property created by students), there is no evidence of coverage becoming less restrictive (Slaughter and Rhoades 2004). Policies increasingly utilize terminology of "work for hire" or "within the scope of employment" (language drawn from the 1976 Copyright Act), giving institutions greater property claims. Furthermore, the policies increasingly specify ownership of materials produced with new information technologies. Over time there is more language referring to the "use of institutional resources" and grounding institutions' claims to ownership and royalties to such use (with more exceptions to institutional ownership than found for patents). By the 1990s three-fourths of collective bargaining agreements with intellectual property clauses had provisions related to the use of institutional resources (Rhoades 1998a).

For copyrighted materials the political economy does not appear to be as one-sided and as single-minded as in the case of patents. There is even organized resistance in unionized higher education to protect faculty property rights. However, what is featured in this struggle is more the interests of creators/professors than some consideration of the public interest (Rhoades 2002). As with patents, the pursuit of revenues has become a prominent part of institutions' efforts in relation to educational materials. That is evident in the policies' content and in their reference to institutions' investment in and capacity to produce such materials. That is what the phrase "use of institutional resources" is about. Colleges and universities are building the capacity to produce copyrightable educational materials that can be sold in the private marketplace.

In sum, public policy at the federal and state levels and institutional policies of public and private universities have ushered in an academic capitalist knowledge/learning regime. The logic of the private marketplace has come to be inscribed in the formal legal parameters of higher education. The redefinition of the boundaries between public and private sectors has not simply been imposed by political and economic actors outside higher education; it also expresses the initiative and commitments of many actors within the academy. Not surprisingly, then, the emergent regime is being codified not only in formal public policy but also in academic practices.

INTERCONNECTIONS BETWEEN STATE, HIGHER EDUCATION,
AND MARKET ORGANIZATIONS

Another mechanism by which the discipline of a marketplace logic has been expressed in colleges and universities is through interconnections among state entities, higher education institutions, and private sector markets. Some of these interconnections have been promoted and supported by the changing policy regime at the federal and state levels of government. Other interconnections stem more from the internal policies and initiatives of colleges and universities and their managers. For the most part the policy shift relates to the pursuit of revenues from the marketing of academic products in the realm of research or educational materials. However, other interconnections are linked to the pursuit of revenues from the marketing of nonacademic products and services. Colleges and universities are becoming more directly involved in marketlike and market behaviors and activities in the pursuit of revenues. That is a central feature of the new political economy of US higher education.

Particularly in research and technology transfer and increasingly in education and copyrighted materials, partnerships between the public and private sectors have taken various forms. As noted in our discussion of federal agencies, the promotion and support of consortium arrangements between universities and private sector business has led to the establishment of hundreds of cooperative ventures in centers, institutes, consortia, and contracts.

The aim of these efforts in technology transfer has been to facilitate the translation of research discoveries in universities into commercial products that can be taken into the marketplace, with monies accruing to businesses and to universities and their faculty. The assumption is now that if science stays in the laboratory, it is of no use; it must be more rapidly moved into the market, and academic scientists and institutions increasingly have a direct hand in effecting and benefiting financially from such movement.

A similar set of efforts can be found in education, with a similar assumption. Through various organizational arrangements, from for-profit arms of colleges and universities to contracts with private business, institutions have sought to develop commercial educational products that can be marketed externally to tap into new student markets and generate revenues. Federal legislation has facilitated and promoted such enterprising efforts. And the assumption underlying the regime of policy and practice is that if education and educational materials stay on campus, the extent to which society will benefit will be unduly restricted; education should be moved beyond the walls of the academy, and colleges and universities should benefit financially from that movement.

The institutional policies we examined reveal that colleges and universities are translating the policy push into practice by establishing, managing, and monitoring interconnections among state, higher education, and private sector organizations. The effect of these efforts has been to restructure professional employment in US higher education. The growth category of professional employment over the past two decades has been support professionals, or "managerial professionals" (Rhoades 1998b). During this time period, the proportion of faculty in the professional workforce has declined (to a little more than 50 percent) and the proportion of part-time faculty has doubled. One of the three major areas in which these professionals are employed is in entrepreneurial activity (Rhoades and Sporn 2002a). They are personnel working in technology transfer offices, distance education centers, revenue-generating auxiliary units, and in development (fund-raising) offices; such offices have become increasingly common in public universities (Tolbert 1985) and in various colleges within these universities, which develop their own fund-raising capacities. In short, as academic institutions and units seek to connect more closely with and directly enter the private sector marketplace, this entrepreneurial activity requires a management and support infrastructure.

Interconnections between the not-for-profit and for-profit sectors are also evident in various sorts of boards that universities are developing. To tap into private sector support, academic colleges are establishing advisory boards that consist of moneyed people, often connected to or representative of corporate enterprise. Although the primary point of these boards is to facilitate fund-raising, they also often represent a link to the employers of the college's students and can be a source of feedback, advice, and influence with regard to academic programs. Most common in business and engineering schools, on many university campuses such boards are also now found in the colleges of education, fine arts, humanities, and social and behavioral sciences.

In addition to this newer form of interconnection, there are forms of board interlock at the central institutional level, between corporate CEOs and boards of directors on the one hand and university presidents and boards of trustees on the other. A significant minority of public and private university presidents serve on one to five corporate boards (Goldschmidt and Finkelstein 2001). A more long-standing interlock has been evident in university boards of trustees, on which large numbers of businesspeople sit. Studies of business leaders' control of higher education through board membership date back to Veblen (1918) and Upton Sinclair (1923). However, the types of corporations represented reflect the changing political economy. Our analysis of the 20 leading public and private universities in federal grant monies found that the most represented sectors of industry on university boards were information and electronics, and medical substances and devices, the cutting edge of the new economy. The interlock among companies and individual universities was evident in private universities, not in public universities, in which connections to new-economy business lie elsewhere.

We focus on one major example to highlight both the centrality of colleges and universities in the new political economy of US higher education and the concentration of many such interconnections in new-economy business realms. The case is that of Internet2, the next generation of the Internet, which is being created by a consortium partly in response to the increased congestion of the Internet as a result of its commercialization in 1995. Although there are important similarities between this iteration of the Internet and the original, there are some important differences as well, which point to what we call administrative capitalism (Slaughter and Rhoades 2004).

Both iterations of the Internet exhibit a coalition of state, higher education, and market organizations. However, the government took the lead in the early construction of the Internet in the 1960s and 1970s. The Department of Defense was particularly central; the industrial partners were a small number of defense contractors. By contrast, in the current iteration university presidents are taking the lead organizationally and financially. Members of the University Corporation for Advanced Internet Development (UCAID) have committed $50 million per year, whereas the corporate members have committed $20 million per year. The industrial sector from which members are drawn has changed, reflecting the shift from a cold war academic science and technology policy coalition to a competitiveness one. They are high-tech companies such as IBM, Lucent Technologies, Microsoft, Nortel, Sun Microsystems, and Cisco Systems. The major federal agency contributing to the effort has changed as well; it is now the National Science Foundation that is organizing the infrastructure for the knowledge economy.

Moreover, the purposes of the Internet have shifted, expressing the values of academic capitalism and the new economy. Commercialization was not on the agenda in the first phase of the Internet. The focus was defense, research, and education. Yet the designers of Internet2 are clear that they are developing a high-tech infrastructure for the new economy, with the commercial function of diffusing new technologies to the market and the goal of stimulating an economic boom. Internet2, then, is an archetype of the heightened interconnections between state, higher education, and market organizations.

In sum, academic capitalism in the new economy goes well beyond a shift in the policy parameters confronted (and negotiated and implemented) by academic institutions and personnel. In practice, the forms of interconnection between public and private sector organizations vary. The logic of the marketplace is increasingly evident in points of contact that are housed within long-standing academic structures, such as federal agencies that support academic research and academic colleges that organize academic work. Changes in practice are such that we see a shift in professional employment, with the hiring of more managerial professionals who represent a growing internal capacity that academic institutions are developing in order to intersect with and enter into market activity. Changes in practice are also evident in heightened CEO and board interactions across the sectors. And the permeating logic of the marketplace is evidenced in the central involvement of universities in developing a more commercially oriented Internet infrastructure. As we discuss in the next section, the pervasiveness of the marketplace logic is also evident in the efforts and activities of various personnel in the academy.

PRACTICES OF FACULTY, MANAGERIAL PROFESSIONALS, MANAGERS, AND STUDENTS

Yet another mechanism by which the discipline of a marketplace logic has been expressed and enacted in colleges and universities is through the internal initiative and practices of faculty, academic managers, and managerial professionals who are pursuing the commercial potential of academic and nonacademic products. For faculty that has meant seeking to profit from academic products they have created; for academic managers and managerial professionals that has meant seeking revenues for the institution and seeking to indirectly profit through the establishment and advancement of their careers, individually and collectively. In either case a private sector logic has increasingly come to shape human agency in and the political economy of the academy.

As individuals many faculty members have engaged in activities that point to increasingly closer connections with business and that express the logic of the private sector. The Bayh-Dole Act and the 1980s serve as important markers of this pattern. For example, "the number of articles co-authored by academic and industrial scientists rose from 22 percent of all articles written by scientists in industry in 1981 to 35 percent in 1991" (Slaughter and Rhoades 1996, p. 329). More than just co-authoring articles that cut across the public-private sector divide, academic scientists became more deeply involved in technology transfer activities. For example, in a study of 38 faculty members involved with industry, Slaughter and colleagues (2002) found that although they give voice to the values of a public good research regime, these faculty members enacted complex and contested academic capitalist values and practices. Thus professors still prioritized publications over patents but also believed that patenting was an increasingly important role of academic scientists. And in their "heroic" stories of starting up companies, professors glossed over conflicts of interest or public subsidization of private profit issues and instead valorized these activities.

The extent of faculty involvement with the private sector shows up in national surveys, particularly in the life sciences, where large proportions of faculty are engaged in entrepreneurial activity (Blumenthal et al. 1986; Louis et al. 1989). It also is expressed in national data on the increasing percentage of patents that are assigned to universities and industry, a figure that rose from less than 1 percent in 1985 to almost 7 percent in 1995 (Owen-Smith 2001, p. 37). In each of the realms of entrepreneurial activity, academic managers have encouraged such faculty efforts—rewriting conflict of interest policies, allowing for equity ownership, and working to partner academics with corporate enterprise. Similarly, such activity has been promoted by managerial professionals aiming to expand their universities' patent portfolios and licensing revenues. What has resulted is a "renorming of the social relations of academic science" (Slaughter and Rhoades 1990, p. 341). Beyond the changing policy parameters that facilitate academic capitalism in the new economy, academics are renegotiating, in ambivalent, contradictory patterns, their daily relations with administrators, corporate sponsors, peers, and graduate students in ways that commercialize the values informing academic research.

The logic of the marketplace increasingly characterizes more than individual academics; it can also be found in the "academic heartland" (Clark 1998) of basic academic departments. As academic units increasingly get treated as cost centers that must generate revenue, there is evidence of various collective entrepreneurial activities in these settings. A large proportion of these center on educational initiatives; the research initiatives tend to come more from the central administration or from individual academics (Rhoades 2000; Slaughter and Rhoades 2004). Departmental educational initiatives include (1) setting up and marketing to business employees thesis-free "professional" master's degree programs, aimed at generating tuition monies; (2) fund-raising for operations, equipment, and student support; (3) developing undergraduate programs linked to new-economy enterprise; and (4) setting up placement services for companies seeking to hire department graduates. And there has been investment at the central administrative level in distance education that seeks to tap into new student markets.

Collectively, faculty have also articulated positions that express the logic of the private sector marketplace. In the realm of copyrighted educational materials, including courseware and distance education courses, the three major faculty unions, the American Association of University Professors (AAUP), the American Federation of Teachers (AFT), and the National Education Association (NEA), have taken a strong position that faculty creators own such materials, although most institutions now claim ownership of materials produced with institutional resources. As the commercial possibilities of copyrighted educational materials become more evident, faculty contract negotiators increasingly are bargaining for faculty shares in the proceeds generated by the property they have created (Rhoades and Maitland 2000). Without arguing that faculty should leave the proceeds to the colleges and universities that employ them, it is telling that faculty have not negotiated in ways that speak to the public interest, apart from the notion that if faculty do not control the property, quality will suffer (Rhoades 2002). They are complicit in the logic of academic capitalism in the new economy.

Finally, we offer a brief note on the increased commodification of colleges and universities in nonacademic products. Academic managers and managerial professionals have increasingly exploited the commercial potential of captive student markets and the branding potential of their institutions' logos. Consider the example of the development of all-school contracts that institutions have signed with sports apparel companies such as Nike and Adidas. Such contracts are a phenomenon of the 1990s, following an explosion of corporate sponsorship spending and expanding on contracts signed with coaches, starting with Jerry Tarkanian at the University of Nevada, Las Vegas, in the 1970s. Another example is the establishment of trademark offices in many universities in the 1990s. Before then, most institutions used licensing agents, much as they had used nonprofit patent firms. Both of these phenomena are quintessentially new-economy branding strategies—the selling of images and identities; the university itself is situated as commodity, as a product.

In sum, then, the marketplace logic is evident in the practices of actors in higher education. In various ways faculty are complicit in the pursuit of academic capitalism in the new economy in education and research. Managerial professionals are facilitators of and liaisons in this process of developing and taking intellectual products to the marketplace. Academic managers have worked across institutions in ventures of administrative capitalism, and they have worked within their own institutions to capitalize on the market potential of their student bodies and the brand potential of their institutions' identities. New-economy academic capitalism is not something being done to those within the academy. They are major players in and initiators of the process.

The US Knowledge/Learning/Consumption Regime and the Americas

US higher education has a significant influence on the political economy of higher education in the Americas and beyond. Partly such influence derives from the position of the United States as the world's economic and military superpower. The presumed connection between that national dominance and the strength of US higher education makes the United States a model for other nations to enhance their economic and political vitality. Also, the wealth of the United States translates into resources and opportunities in higher education, making the United States an attractive destination for international students and professionals (and becoming a model that these global flows of human resources take back home).

Another source of US higher education's transnational influence derives from the international preeminence of US scholarship and science. For some that makes the US system a model of how to improve the quality of academic work in a country. For others it simply means that the academy in the United States in some sense defines and "gatekeeps" quality in higher education. The intellectual infrastructure of academic work globally is largely produced and controlled by academics and institutions in the United States—for example, professional journals and the basic texts and technology of academic work. Even the language (English) in professional publications and at professional conferences globally models the discourse of US higher education. As Altbach and Selvaratnam (1989) detailed for Asian universities, the impact of the English language is extensive, shaping and stratifying academic activity and networks through various mechanisms. Whether it is through reward structures that essentially require publication in English-language (read "global," read "quality") journals or through the education of large numbers of Asian academics and administrators in the United States (and Australia and the United Kingdom), the influence of English—and the set of understandings about education that go with it—is enormous.

Layered on top of this intellectual preeminence are two other sources of influence particular to US academic capitalism. First, the entrepreneurial market-oriented higher education model is identified with the United States and has been marketed by US actors and organizations and by international agencies. Second, with the emergence, intensification, and expansive pursuit of academic capitalism in the United States, universities have come to conceive of other parts of the world as markets to be exploited for revenue. Thus the policies and practices of academic capitalism in the United States are inscribed in the policies and practices and in the political economy of higher education of national systems in the Americas and beyond. As with the film, music, and media industries, higher education is a new-economy service enterprise that benefits from and promotes the global economic position of the United States and of English. It is part of a larger knowledge/learning/consumption regime.

THE US HIGHER EDUCATION MODEL

Central to the global influence of US higher education is the market model of higher education. That model has been a key component of policy discourse about higher education internationally for at least two decades. More recently, the general conception of a market model of higher education has been specified in neoliberal conceptions of government policy (expressed in the new managerialism) and in economic-centered conceptions of academic institutions (expressed in the idea of entrepreneurial universities).

The mechanisms through which the force of these models are effected vary. In the advanced industrial world, regional and global agencies contribute to the articulation and implementation of neoliberal higher education policies through a normative process of comparing national systems of higher education to US-connected benchmarks. In the developing world, in addition to these normative processes, other international agencies undertake a more coercive leveraging of national higher education policies with the conditional provision of financial support. In both cases agencies draw on a community of consultants that is disproportionately US based in people and ideas.

The idea of the US higher education system being market driven relative to other systems has been clearly articulated in Burton Clark's (1983) triangle model. Building on liberal theory that defines the state and market as separate entities and focusing on patterns of governance and control in higher education, Clark identified a new point in the schema: professional-collegial control. Comparisons of national systems focused on whether they were defined more by state control, professional-collegial control, or market control. The US system is consistently characterized as one in which various markets shape higher education organization and policy. The most obvious example is student markets, which have contributed to the growth of new institutions and new structures and academic programs within existing institutions. Part of the market model stressed in the United States and abroad is the idea that institutions should be responsive to student markets, attending to student needs with services and academic structures, down to the level of how assessment is done (within classes with multiple assignments and exams versus leaving the assessment to the end of the entire year, as has been done in many European systems). Over time policy discourse globally has focused on making institutions more responsive to student markets and needs and has increasingly identified greater access for the "masses" as a desirable goal that requires some restructuring of the national higher education system. Similarly, part of the market model has been the relative closeness historically of US colleges and universities to the private sector marketplace—to business and industry. Again, over time there has been a clear tendency for other national systems to encourage more of a connection between the academy and industry.

Recent decades have also seen the rise and proliferation of so-called neoliberal policies at the national level, with direct implications for higher education systems. Part of these neoliberal policies involve encouraging universities to reduce their financial dependency on the state and to generate more of their own revenues. In short, neoliberalism has encouraged the development of policies, connections between state, higher education, and the private sector market, and higher education practices that are modeled after developments in the United States. And international agencies serve as one of the key mechanisms through which this US model is promoted globally.

The neoliberal policies are straightforward. A major thrust is to reduce state subsidies and shift costs to user-consumers, to marketize a range of public services. In higher education that means reducing state-subsidized low- or no-tuition policies and raising tuition, shifting costs to students. At the same time the role of higher education in serving and stimulating the economy is emphasized; in educational programs and research activities the push is to increase the connection between higher education and the economy. That means developing courses and degree programs at traditional institutions linked directly to private sector employment as well as the expansion of short-cycle and vocational institutions and programs. It also means formulating academic science and technology policies at the state and institutional levels that expand the academy's role in transferring technology to the private sector and developing and marketing new products within the academy. From one country to the next we can see the emergence of these policies: reduced state subsidy, increased tuition, vocationally linked programs, and an expanded technology transfer role in the academy (Marginson and Rhoades 2002).

The upshot of these neoliberal policies has been to encourage universities to generate more of their own revenues, again with US institutions as the model. The idea of an entrepreneurial university, which contributes to the global competitiveness of national economies, has become prominent in higher education policy throughout the world. Reduced dependence on the state and increased connections to and involvement in the private sector economy are valorized (Clark 1998; Slaughter and Leslie 1997).

In different parts of the world there are different mechanisms through which the US model is promoted. In the advanced industrial world key international agencies and associations through which such influence flows are the Organization for Economic Cooperation and Development (OECD) and international professional associations. Much has been written about the ways in which the OECD establishes parameters by which national systems are compared, setting up a norming process in which nations seek to model themselves after countries that are higher in the hierarchy (Lingard 2000; Lingard and Rizvi 1998). Similarly, through various professional networks Anglo-American models of quality assurance and assessment have percolated across the globe, in some cases relatively directly and in other cases mediated by the "translation" of other model countries within regions (e.g., the United Kingdom and the Netherlands in Europe) (see Rhoades and Sporn 2002b; Vidovich 2002). In both cases the role of consultants, emerging in a global policy network (Lingard 2000) centered in the United States, is prominent.

In the developing world and throughout Latin America these agencies and mechanisms are also important (e.g., Mexico is part of the OECD). However, other agencies are more coercive, leveraging adoption of neoliberal models through the provision of large loans. In Latin America the World Bank and the Inter-American Development Bank (IDB) have profoundly influenced the adjustment of national higher education policies to fit the neoliberal model (Kempner and Jurema 2002; Mollis and Marginson 2002).

Again, the influence of a global policy network of experts and consultants plays a role in this process, as do various internal elites and intelligentsia within the countries, who benefit from their connection to the global neo-liberal network.

Yet, for all the power of the neoliberal policies and the entrepreneurial models of universities, there has been considerable resistance, and we can identify alternatives that are being articulated in some settings. In Mexico a dramatic example of resistance was the student strike at the National Auton-omous University of Mexico (UNAM) in Mexico City. Student and faculty resistance can be identified throughout Latin America, and even in the core setting of the United States (Rhoads 2003) and Canada (on the York Univer-sity strike, for example, see Newson [1998]). Several examples of alternatives can be identified: a community-service-oriented university in South Africa focused on community development (Subotzky 1999); a "socially committed university" in Latin America focused on redressing inequalities and improv-ing local working and living environments (Sutz 2003); and models of insti-tutions committed to community economic development in Canada (New-son 1998). In each case the idea is not to reject the global but to intersect it in ways that do not subsume local communities to the prevailing economi-cally entrepreneurial model of universities.

POLICY PARAMETERS AND PHYSICAL PRESENCE OF US ACADEMIC CAPITALISTS

Another source of US influence internationally is negotiations in interna-tional law regarding trade and intellectual property and the physical pres-ence of US academic capitalists seeking to exploit international markets. More than just the fact that national higher education policy in Latin Amer-ican systems is increasingly incorporating features of the US-based neolib-eral model, these systems are subject to international agreements and law that increasingly advance the principles of free trade and private profit in higher education. Moreover, academic capitalist institutions, units, and in-dividuals in the United States are seeking to capitalize on international mar-kets in educational services. Thus the enterprising efforts of US entities and individuals are working to influence the higher education political economy and to provide services in the Americas and beyond.

In the 1980s, with the increased export activity and commercial potential of copyrighted products and services, the United States pursued a more aggressive negotiation of international policy surrounding copyright protection and trades and services. One example is the Trade-Related Aspects of Intellectual Property Rights (TRIPS), initiated during the Uruguay round of talks regarding the General Agreement on Tariffs and Trade (GATT) in 1986. The US contingent took the lead in enhancing copyright protection—for example, extending copyright from the life of the author to another 50 years. TRIPS also extended copyright protection to computer software and data compilations.

Such international negotiations directly affect the political economies of national higher education systems. Indeed, they contributed to a greater commercialization of this political economy in the United States. Having negotiated extended copyright protection globally, US representatives then turned to revising US copyright policy accordingly. One leverage point for doing so was that US law had to be changed to meet TRIP mandates.

Similar to the realm of copyright, trademark protection was extended in the 1990s. One example particularly relevant to academically capitalist US universities was the 1999 Anticybersquatting Consumer Protection Act, which extended protection into cyberspace. This was significant for the enhanced commodification of trademarks and logos, because universities used this and other legislation to protect their commercial interests in university names, mascots, and logos (Bearby and Siegal 2002).

More recently, as the World Trade Organization negotiates a General Agreement on Trade in Services (GATS), the United States is again aggressively pursuing free trade provisions and protection of private property rights. Key areas of negotiation are distance education, virtual education, educational software, and Internet-based corporate training on the one hand and direct foreign investment in higher education on the other. The Department of Commerce has been seeking to remove various barriers to free trade in educational services, such as restrictions on foreign entities' training services and the electronic transmission of course material, establishment of educational entities, requirements for local partners, and fees and taxes on foreign providers.

In this context it is not surprising that we find increased exports from the United States of commercialized intellectual products and increased efforts of US institutions to enter into foreign higher education markets. In some cases these are for-profit institutions, such as the University of Phoenix, which has extended its activities to Latin America, and Sylvan Learning Systems, which has acquired universities and business schools in Mexico and Chile as well as in Europe (Larsen and Vincent-Lacrin 2002). In other cases they are public and private not-for-profit universities, many of which have established overseas activities and campuses. Or they are the for-profit distance education arms of these not-for-profit universities. Even community colleges have entered the game, marketing themselves abroad to international students, seeking to attract students with claims in their brochures that stretch the truth, claiming, for example, that their graduates matriculate to top US universities such as Harvard and Stanford (Golden 2002). The incentive for these colleges' recruiting efforts is that they can charge international students up to 10 times as much in tuition as their local students.

The US academic capitalist knowledge/learning/consumption regime, then, has extended its influence beyond the political economy of the United States to that of the Americas and beyond. More than just through international law or even the physical presence of US entrepreneurial academic institutions and individual academic entrepreneurs, that influence is evident in the infrastructure through which information, resources, and technology flow. As noted earlier, the fact that English is the international language of choice in the academy (and in the economy) has a profound influence on the higher education systems of other countries. Layered on top of that is the mechanism through which so much global communication and information travels—the Internet. Again, the fact that this medium is overwhelmingly in English has a major effect on the political economies and higher education practices of other countries. The case of Internet2 even more explicitly connects the influence of such a medium of academic exchange to the realm of the global economy. Internet2 is a global infrastructure (the network is national, but through partnerships that intersect with international members' networks the reach of this network is global), developed by a consortium of state, higher education, and market organizations to facilitate the flow of new technologies from the academy in the United States to higher education systems and the private sector economies of other nations. Therein lies a new level of US influence and of political economic dependency in other political economies. US higher education has created and is at the center of the network of circuits through which much new-economy commerce and technology will flow.

In sum, the nature of the knowledge/learning/consumption regime of academic capitalism, like capitalism itself, is global in nature. As with capitalism, the knowledge/learning/consumption regime is embedded in a rationalized legal structure of free trade, opening up international markets to the US academic capitalist. It is expressed in the active pursuit of global markets by US-based academic institutions and academics. And it operates through an information and commercial infrastructure that was created by US academic institutions. In these complex and interconnected ways, the US knowledge/learning/consumption regime shapes higher education policies and practices in the Americas (and beyond).

Shifting the Targets and Purposes of Public Subsidy in Higher Education

Most higher education scholars point to the privatization of US higher education as a major trend of the past quarter-century. Privatization is generally defined as colleges and universities generating greater shares of their own revenues and interacting with and responding to the needs of customers and employers. We offer a different interpretation, one that is embedded in new-economy academic capitalism. Privatization is shifting the targets and purposes of public subsidy. It involves redefining how public entities should behave and how public monies should be allocated. It also involves redefining which student populations should gain access, and how institutions can best serve them and society.

SERVING PRIVATE NEW-ECONOMY INTERESTS OF LARGE CORPORATE ENTERPRISES

Various private interests might be served by higher education. In our view the private interests that are featured and most served by academic capitalism in the postindustrial economy are those of new-economy multinational corporate enterprises. These include the organizational interests, particularly the short-term economic ones, of not-for-profit (and for-profit) universities and colleges.

As detailed in previous sections of this chapter, the boundaries between the public and the private sector are becoming more permeable. Over the past quarter-century public policy has systematically contributed to blurring those boundaries, both in the allocation of public monies and in the use of those monies to leverage closer interactions and interconnections between colleges and universities and private enterprise. The public interest is being redefined. At one time the public interest was served by preventing situations in which individuals in public institutions might be compromised in their professional activity by having a direct economic interest in the outcome of their work. Similarly, there were restrictions regarding the activities of public institutions and their direct involvement in the market. That is changing, dramatically. Public policy now enables and encourages public employees and entities to interact with and become directly involved in the private sector economy.

Yet, if the academic capitalist knowledge/learning/consumption regime foregrounds connections to and features values of private sector markets, the student aid and academic research markets continue to be largely subsidized by public sector monies. Even as the policy discourse proclaims the need for public entities to generate more of their revenues, most of these revenues continue to be provided through public subsidy. Moreover, the government now provides a new source of public subsidy for private industries that intersects with and benefits from higher education. There is a shift in the beneficiaries of public subsidy, from not-for-profit to for-profit entities.

Consider students and tuition. In an earlier era low tuition in public institutions was subsidized by state government. Now, these institutions generate more of their own revenues through higher tuition. Such tuition is partly subsidized by state-supported financial aid (and by institutionally provided aid). And there is a new layer of public subsidy in the form of federal-government-supported financial aid. Moreover, private sector financial institutions, banks, receive a new form of public subsidy, in revenues they generate from handling these publicly provided and guaranteed loans.

Now consider the realm of academic research. In an earlier era the expansion of basic academic research was largely underwritten by federal monies. Now, academics and universities seek to generate more of their own revenues and to connect more closely with private industry, competing for more private support of research and engaging in more applied research and product development. Yet the overwhelming proportion of academic research and development in the academy continues to be subsidized by the federal government. And new layers of public subsidy are directed to private industry, as publicly supported colleges and universities connect more closely with and provide more services and benefits to business and as federal monies

are allocated to support such a redirection of services through various centers, institutes, and research grants.

In short, an academic capitalist policy regime makes higher education institutions more capitalistic even as they sustain large public subsidies. It also
provides new public subsidy to capitalist business enterprises in realms that
intersect with higher education. That is the irony of academic capitalism
in the new economy. It seems to emphasize privatization but actually involves public subsidy of private sector activity in not-for-profit entities and
in business. As in the industrial economy, which emerged with the assistance
of enormous public subsidy, so it is with the postindustrial economy. And
as we reduce the old welfare state, we provide a new layer of welfare to
corporations.

Academic capitalism and the new economy also produce a shift in the purposes of public entities. Increasingly, these entities pursue their short-term
economic interests, focusing more on revenue generation than on broad societal interests. The organizational interests of public sector enterprises become conflated with the public interest: In a variation of the saying, "What's
good for General Motors is good for the country," the idea is that what's
good for a not-for-profit college or university is good for the public.

More than that, the sorts of activities that receive public subsidy have
shifted. Ironically, as colleges and universities pursue revenue generation
and intersection with the private marketplace, they are reallocating public
monies to support these ventures, shifting the balance of public support
from fields and activities that are not seen as having revenue-generating potential to those that do. Research parks, economic development, and technology transfer activities are cases in point. Moreover, it is clear that the
public monies available for work that involves the use of new information
and instructional technologies are considerable, whether in federal agency
funding for research grants or in allocations from state legislatures. The
point is that there is ongoing public subsidy, but more for activities that are
linked to new-economy revenue-generating efforts.

SHIFTING THE TARGET AND PURPOSE OF ACCESS

Academic capitalism and the new economy also involve a shift in the meaning and purpose of access. For most of the 20th century governmental policies targeted potential populations that had been underserved by virtue of

characteristics other than merit. In the last quarter-century the federal government has worked to expand access to higher education for women, students of color, and working- or lower-class students with limited funds. For 25 years (until the Bush administration's reversal of this bipartisan focus) that purpose has been a central part of federal public policy in civil rights, desegregation, and financial aid. A large part of that policy has been the sense not only that higher education is important in an economic sense for individual students but that it also benefits society in various ways. For example, the federal government's first major direct investment in supporting students' education, the GI Bill, benefited the individual recipients and also served the interests of society by helping to expand and strengthen the American middle class, which many scholars see as a key to a healthy democracy.

Dating even further back to the first half of the 20th century, in various regards public policy has centered on opening up access to a larger proportion of the population with the broader purposes of serving democracy and benefiting society at large. The City University of New York (CUNY) is a classic case of an urban municipal university that took on as its major function the provision of educational opportunity for immigrant populations, particularly Jewish immigrants in the early 20th century and then other immigrant populations, minorities, and the poor in the 1970s (Lavin 1996). In the same spirit, community colleges, although they have fallen short of ensuring equal educational opportunity in higher education (Brint and Karabel 1989; Dougherty 1994; Levin 2001), are nevertheless the principal point of access for many students who would not otherwise be able to pursue a higher education, most particularly Latino students. So, too, the function of comprehensive (master's degree granting) public universities has been to expand access. Indeed, this has been a central function of public US higher education.

However, academic capitalism in the new economy is changing that, shifting the target and purposes of access. The new-economy focus is more on physical accessibility (and convenience) that overcomes physical obstacles of distance and time than it is on access that overcomes social and cultural barriers to educational opportunity. In an era of academic capitalism institutions seek out students who can pay. Technology-mediated delivery of instruction enables colleges and universities to tap into new student markets, but not markets that have been underserved in the traditional sense. For instance, many institutions are targeting students who have already been served (who have already attended higher education and may even have degrees), providing continuing and contract education services to students employed in business. Such services generate more revenue than does targeting historically underserved populations of poor, minority, traditional-age students. Similarly, community colleges are increasingly investing in serving students at a distance, enabling the colleges to raise their fees and tuition at the expense of serving local populations of underserved potential students. In both cases institutions move to student populations that will serve the economic interests of the colleges and universities, as enterprises, but in the process they are reducing their commitment to and investment in providing access to historically underserved populations. Ironically, those are precisely the populations that are currently expanding significantly.

Thus in some significant ways public investment in expanding access is shifting to high-tech servicing of more privileged populations. There is less public policy support for subsidizing widespread access to public colleges and universities. There is more support and subsidization of access to private not-for-profit and for-profit higher education. And public institutions themselves are moving away from their historical focus on expanding access for underprivileged populations.

In sum, public policy and the practices of higher education institutions are shifting. There is a shift in the targets of public subsidy toward the private new-economy interests of large corporate enterprises in education and financial aid and in research. Within institutions there is also a shift in the targets of subsidy toward units that are perceived by academic managers to have connections to new-economy markets and to have the potential to generate external revenues. Further, part of the institutional strategy to link up more closely to the new economy and generate new revenues is a shift in the target and purposes of access. Colleges and universities are turning toward more privileged, moneyed student markets (just as they are toward more privileged research and service markets) and turning away from the public responsibility of expanding access for historically underserved markets. That movement reflects a shift in purpose: Decisions about access are increasingly calculated in terms of cost, efficiency, and revenue yield and in terms of the short-term economic interests of the higher education enterprise.

Conclusion: Unexamined Premises and Possibilities

The growth of academic capitalism in the new economy may seem inevitable. The current economic situation in the United States and the related fiscal pressure experienced by colleges and universities are said by many to be the new reality of higher education in the United States and elsewhere. We cannot count on a return to previous days when new public monies were invested in higher education. Moreover, the current political situation in the United States and the related policy pressure for accountability and productivity in higher education institutions are said by many to also be the new reality. We cannot count on a return to days when policy makers were willing and able to invest in higher education as a matter of public commitment to and trust in the value of the academy. And if that is true in the United States, it is even more true throughout the rest of the Americas—at least that is the line being adopted by international agencies and articulated by local elites as well.

Yet such views are based on problematic premises. Speaking of new fiscal realities and championing the need for entrepreneurial academic capitalism presume that most such efforts generate net profits. They do not. For example, in a national study of technology transfer in the United Kingdom, Packer and Webster (1996, p. 429) found that "60 percent of respondents said that patenting activity was not self-financing." It is also clear from the licensing revenues and legal fees listed in the annual AUTM survey that many universities are losing money. And this is in the United States, in which there is much private sector wealth to support technology transfer, far more than in the rest of the Americas. Views about the new realities also presume that entrepreneurial efforts reduce public monies devoted to higher education. Again, they do not. In fact, entrepreneurial efforts generally involve leveraging of new public monies to support the activity. What is declining is the share of institutional revenues that come from government (Hearn 2003); in absolute terms state and federal allocations to higher education continue to rise.

Moreover, current economic and political constraints hold many possibilities. The choice is not between maintaining current patterns of dependence on public monies (a path presumed to ensure fiscal scarcity and mediocrity) and becoming entrepreneurial and diversifying revenues (a path presumed to ensure fiscal independence and quality). Entrepreneurial efforts can involve a range of activities and target a range of markets, not all of them economic. Colleges and universities might pursue political entrepreneurial activity, aimed, like the political action committees of some private sector organizations, at securing political favor. Indeed, many are doing that: maintaining offices in Washington to secure federal monies through a set-aside (pork barrel) process. To what extent does this strategy yield revenues compared to technology transfer or online education? Another path might lie in institutions investing more heavily in entrepreneurial promotional efforts (analogous to the philanthropic and advertising activities of many corporations) aimed at increasing general political and public support for greater allocations of public monies to higher education. Still another path might be to engage in social entrepreneurial activities that address major social problems in local communities, states, and regions, again with possible spillover effects in terms of public support and funding. Such a focus on social entrepreneurialism is increasingly found in business schools, addressing the not-for-profit sector. Finally, various economic entrepreneurial paths could be chosen, and these paths could be geared not primarily to the global economy but more to local, state, and regional economies.

To flesh out a few of the possibilities, we discuss a particular university setting—the University of Arizona, a public research university that is in the top 20 nationally in federal research monies. Although state allocations have increased in absolute terms over the past decade, they have decreased as a share of institutional revenues. Despite a relatively strong state economy during the 1990s, in general, conservative state legislators did not reinvest public monies in higher education. And the University of Arizona, the flagship university, suffered relative to the other two public universities in the state. (Arizona State University, also a research university, has larger student numbers and benefits from its location in the state's capital and largest city; Northern Arizona University, a doctorate-granting university, has gained legislative favor by expanding distance and online programs.)

Like many other public research universities, the University of Arizona is pursuing an academic capitalist path that involves raising tuition significantly, expanding the proportion of out-of-state and graduate students, emphasizing fund-raising, and prioritizing the potentially commercially lucrative area of biotechnology, a key sector of the global economy. But the institution has not been very successful in technology transfer, and it lacks academic strength in relative terms in key fields of biomedical science and engineering. We understand the attraction of biotechnology and realize that a university that does not play in this realm is opting out of a major area of academic research and entrepreneurial activity. Yet for all the external revenue they generate, most academic health centers are hemorrhaging and are in trouble fiscally. It takes money to generate grant monies. In general, the balance between investment and yield is a wash at best, although like bad accountants we still talk about fields "bringing in" monies. And although biotechnology promises great profit for a few investors and companies, it does not promise a great yield in educational access or employment.

We offer two alternatives, which we believe should receive a greater balance of investment, because they are more connected to public purposes and interests than the current path. Both alternatives play to existing academic strengths and are areas in which the university has competitive advantage nationally, by virtue of its geographic location. One alternative stems from the niche strength that the university has gained in small programs, centers, and institutes in ecological natural-resource-related sciences, from hydrology and arid lands science to environmental science to meteorological sciences and optics. Such fields have great promise (and have had much success) in obtaining federal and state research funding, in tapping into international student and government markets, and making connections with environmentally sensitive industries. They also hold much promise in positively affecting local, regional, and state environments and economies in visible ways. Despite such promise, strength, and success in these realms, several programs in these areas were targeted for reduction or amalgamation in the university's recent exercise in "focused excellence." Essentially, this process is reallocating monies away from areas of demonstrated academic excellence to more costly areas of relative academic weakness (such as biotechnology), gambling on their potential to generate future revenues. We are incurring an opportunity cost of not capitalizing on academic strengths distinctive to the natural environment in which the university is located and which could generate external monies. The university is betting on a volatile new-economy industry (biotechnology) that promises improvements on Mother Nature at the expense of a strategy focused on fostering sustainable development that is sensitive to maintaining distinctive ecosystems. Yet the latter strategy is consistent with the needs and more predictable yield of the successful service- (and public sector–) based new economy that currently characterizes the state.

A second alternative stems from the university's strength in various social and behavioral science, humanities, and education units related to language, border, and international issues. If these fields do not generate tens of millions of dollars in research grants, they nevertheless generate considerable external research support and have much potential in securing foundation support (e.g., the Udall Foundation has donated millions of dollars to support work on border and Native American issues). They also are fields with relatively low capital and labor costs, high student numbers, and high student to faculty ratios (translating into tuition monies); thus they are net generators of revenues (many are the so-called cash cows of universities). Moreover, they make direct and significant social and cultural contributions to the quality of life in the city, state, and region, with spillover economic effects. They are connected to and build on the cultural and geographic location of the university. Furthermore, they serve diverse and historically underserved student populations, and they are connected to large employment markets in the public sector and in various private sector services, addressing various social needs in the region. As a result, they can positively affect educational equity and public and political goodwill and support for the university. Despite such promise and demonstrated academic strength, few of these fields were targeted as foci of excellence.

We are not the only ones who see such alternative possibilities for entrepreneurial activity. The current dean of science at the University of Arizona has an initiative that combines elements of the two alternatives just described. The strategy is to set up a series of binational (University of Arizona and Mexico) institutes in key areas of university strength and socioeconomic need. The first two areas are in science, but in fields that relate to the university's long-standing strengths in optics and environmental sciences. Subsequent institutes will draw on strengths in other fields (we have undertaken one in higher education). Some of the features of these institutes will be to leverage new research monies, to address human resource needs in the region, and to provide outreach and knowledge transfer that involves translating academic knowledge into social and economic impact. As with so many entrepreneurial ventures, the dean of science aims to secure public monies from various sources—local, state, and federal (in both countries)—to support the venture. We see this dean's strategy as a much less expensive, less risky, and more viable entrepreneurial initiative than biotechnology, and the strategy builds on a range of university strengths and promises a wider range of benefits to partner institutions and local communities. It also offers promise and potential yields for Mexican (and Latin American) universities, different from the prevailing entrepreneurial model of exploiting international markets.

Entrepreneurial choices, then, are connected to conceptions of the role of higher education and the public interest. They also are connected to conceptions of global flows of people and resources. The prevailing model of entrepreneurial universities channels increased public subsidy to more privileged private organizations and individuals even as it restricts and reduces public subsidy to not-for-profit and less privileged organizations and individuals. This, we think, is the real meaning of "privatization": Neoliberals seek to privatize not-for-profit higher education and redirect public subsidy to private entities.

By contrast, the alternatives we offer involve "re-publicizing" (i.e., making more public) academically capitalist higher education, ensuring that a greater share of institutional public monies and privately generated revenues are redirected to historically underserved and less privileged social groups, sectors, programs, services, and purposes. This does not mean turning away from entrepreneurialism; it means engaging in and redirecting more entrepreneurial programs and proceeds to public purposes. Ironically, one model for how to do that lies in traditional conceptions of socially committed and responsible universities that are found in many Latin American systems— valuable models that are imperiled by the current push for and pull of academic capitalism in the new economy that emanates from the US higher education system and global political economy.

References

Altbach, P. G., and V. Selvaratnam, eds. 1989. *From Dependence to Autonomy: The Development of Asian Universities.* Dordrecht, The Netherlands: Kluwer Academic.

Anderson, M. 2001. "The Complex Relations Between the Academy and Industry: Views from the Literature." *Journal of Higher Education* 72(2): 226–246.

Bearby, S., and B. Siegal. 2002. "From the Stadium Parking Lot to the Information Superhighway: How to Protect Your Trademark from Infringement." *Journal of College and University Law* 28: 633–662.

Blumenthal, D., M. Gluck, K. S. Louis, M. Soto, and D. Wise. 1986. "University Industry Research Relationships in Biotechnology: Implications for the University." *Science* 232: 1361–1366.

Bok, D. 2003. *Universities in the Marketplace: The Commercialization of Higher Education.* Princeton, NJ: Princeton University Press.

Brint, S., and J. Karabel. 1989. *The Diverted Dream: Community Colleges and the Promise of Educational Opportunity in America, 1980–1985.* New York: Oxford University Press.

Clark, B. R. 1983. *The Higher Education System: Academic Organization in Cross National Perspective.* Los Angeles: University of California Press.

Clark, B. R. 1998. *Creating Entrepreneurial Universities: Organizational Pathways of Transformation.* Oxford, UK: IAU Press and Pergamon.

Domhoff, G. W. 1967. *Who Rules America?* Englewood Cliffs, NJ: Prentice-Hall.

Dougherty, K. 1994. *The Contradictory College: The Conflicting Origins, Impacts, and Futures of the Community College.* Albany: State University of New York Press.

Foucault, M. 1977. *Discipline and Punish: The Birth of the Prison*, A. Sheridan, trans. New York: Vintage Books.

Foucault, M. 1980. *Power/Knowledge: Selected Interviews and Other Writings 1972– 1977*, C. Gordon, trans., ed. New York: Pantheon Books.

Geiger, R. 1986. *To Advance Knowledge: The Growth of American Research Universities.* New York: Oxford University Press.

Gladieux, L. E., and T. R. Wolanin. 1976. *Congress and the Colleges: The National Politics of Higher Education.* Lexington, MA: Lexington Books.

Golden, D. 2002. "Foreign Students' High Tuition Spurs Eager Junior Colleges to Fudge Facts." *International Higher Education* 29: 7–8. Reprinted from the *Wall Street Journal.*

Goldschmidt, N. P., and J. H. Finkelstein. 2001. "Academics on Board: University Presidents as Corporate Directors." *Academe* 87(5): 33–37.

Gould, E. 2003. *The University in a Corporate Culture.* New Haven, CT: Yale University Press.

Griswold, C. P., and G. M. Marine. 1996. "Political Influences on State Policy: Higher Tuition, Higher Aid, and the Real World." *Review of Higher Education* 19(4): 361–390.

Hearn, J. C. 1998. "The Growing Loan Orientation in Federal Financial Aid Policy: A Historical Perspective." In *Condemning Students to Debt: College Loans and Public Policy*, R. Fossey and M. Bateman, eds. New York: Teachers College Press.

Hearn, J. C. 2003. *Diversifying Campus Revenue Streams: Opportunities and Risks.* Washington, DC: American Council on Education.

Kempner, K., and A. L. Jurema. 2002. "The Global Politics of Education: Brazil and the World Bank." *Higher Education* 43(3): 331–354.

Lape, L. 1992. "Ownership of Copyrightable Works of University Professors: The Interplay Between the Copyright Act and University Copyright Policies." *Villanova Law Review* 37: 223–271.

Larsen, K., and S. Vincent-Lacrin. 2002. "International Trade in Educational Services: Good or Bad." *Higher Education Management and Policy* 14(3): 9–46.

Lavin, D. E. 1996. *Changing the Odds: Open Admissions and the Life Changes of the Disadvantaged.* New Haven, CT: Yale University Press.

Leslie, L. L., and G. Johnson. 1974. "The Market Model and Higher Education." *Journal of Higher Education* 45: 1–20.

Levin, J. S. 2001. *Globalizing the Community College: Strategies for Change in the Twenty-First Century.* New York: Palgrave.

Lingard, B. 2000. "It Is and It Isn't': Vernacular Globalization, Educational Policy, and Restructuring." In *Globalization and Education: Critical Perspectives*, N. C. Burbules and C. A. Torres, eds. New York: Routledge.

Lingard, B., and F. Rizvi. 1998. "Globalization, the OECD, and Australian Higher Education." In *Universities and Globalization: Critical Perspectives*, J. Currie and J. Newson, eds. Thousand Oaks, CA: Sage.

Louis, K. S., D. Blumenthal, M. Gluck, and M. Soto. 1989. "Entrepreneurs in Academe: An Exploration of Behaviors Among Life Scientists." *Administrative Science Quarterly* 34: 110–131.

Marginson, S., and G. Rhoades. 2002. "Beyond National States, Markets, and Systems of Higher Education: A Glonacal Agency Heuristic." *Higher Education* 43(3): 281–309.

McPherson, M. S., and M. O. Shapiro. 1998. *The Student Aid Game: Meeting Need and Rewarding Talent in American Higher Education.* Princeton, NJ: Princeton University Press.

Mollis, M., and S. Marginson. 2002. "The Assessment of Universities in Argentina and Australia: Between Autonomy and Heteronomy." *Higher Education* 43(3): 311–330.

National Science Foundation. 1989. *Industrial Participation in NSF Programs and Activities.* Washington, DC: National Science Foundation.

Newson, J. 1998. "Repositioning the Local Through Alternative Responses to Globalization." In *Universities and Globalization: Critical Perspectives*, J. Currie and J. Newson, eds. Thousand Oaks, CA: Sage.

Owen-Smith, J. 2001. "New Arenas for University Competition: Accumulative Advantage in Academic Patenting." In *Degrees of Compromise: Industrial Interests and Academic Values*, J. Croissant and S. Restivo, eds. Albany: State University of New York Press.

Packard, A. 2002. "Copyright or Copy Wrong: An Analysis of University Claims to Faculty Work." *Communication Law and Policy* 7: 275–315.

Packer, K., and A. Webster. 1996. "Patenting Culture in Science: Reinventing the Scientific Wheel of Credibility." *Science, Technology, and Human Values* 21(4): 427–453.

Readings, B. 1996. *The University in Ruins*. Cambridge, MA: Harvard University Press.

Rhoades, G. 1998a. *Managed Professionals: Unionized Faculty and the Restructuring of Academic Labor*. Albany: State University of New York Press.

Rhoades, G. 1998b. "Reviewing and Rethinking Administrative Costs." In *Higher Education: Handbook of Theory and Research, Volume 13*, J. C. Smart, ed. New York: Agathon Press.

Rhoades, G. 1999. "Technology and the Changing Campus Workforce." *Thought and Action* 15(1): 127–138.

Rhoades, G. 2000. "Who's Doing It Right? Strategic Activity in Public Research Universities." *Review of Higher Education* 24(1): 41–66.

Rhoades, G. 2002. "Whose Property Is It?" *Academe* 87(5): 38–43.

Rhoades, G., and C. Maitland. 2000. "Innovative Approaches to Bargaining." In *The NEA 2000 Almanac of Higher Education* (pp. 27–42). Washington, DC: National Education Association.

Rhoades, G., and S. Slaughter. 1991. "The Public Interest and Professional Labor: Research Universities." In *Culture and Ideology in Higher Education: Advancing a Critical Agenda*, W. G. Tierney, ed. New York: Praeger.

Rhoades, G., and B. Sporn. 2002a. "New Models of Management and Shifting Modes and Costs of Production: Europe and the United States." *Tertiary Education and Management* 8: 3–28.

Rhoades, G., and B. Sporn. 2002b. "Quality Assurance in Europe and the U.S.: Professional and Political Economic Framing of Higher Education Policy." *Higher Education* 43(3): 355–390.

Rhoads, R. 2003. "Globalization and Resistance in the United States and Mexico: The Global Potemkin Village." *Higher Education* 45(2): 223–250.

Scott, B. A. 1983. *Crisis Management in American Higher Education*. New York: Praeger.

Silva, E. T., and S. Slaughter. 1984. *Serving Power: The Making of a Social Science Expert, 1865–1921*. Westport, CT: Greenwood Press.

Sinclair, U. 1923. *The Goosestep: A Study of American Education*. Pasadena, CA: Author.

Slaughter, S., T. Campbell, P. Holleman, and E. Morgan. 2002. "The Traffic in Students: Graduate Students as Tokens of Exchange Between Industry and Academe." *Science, Technology, and Human Values* 27(2): 283–313.

Slaughter, S., and L. L. Leslie. 1997. *Academic Capitalism: Politics, Policies, and the Entrepreneurial University*. Baltimore: Johns Hopkins University Press.

Slaughter, S., and G. Rhoades. 1990. "Renorming the Social Relations of Academic Science: Technology Transfer." *Educational Policy* 4(4): 341–361.

Slaughter, S., and G. Rhoades. 1993. "Changes in Intellectual Property Statutes and Policies at a Public University: Revising the Terms of Professional Labor." *Higher Education* 26: 287–312.

Slaughter, S., and G. Rhoades. 1996. "The Emergence of a Competitiveness Research and Development Policy Coalition and the Commercialization of Academic Science and Technology." *Science, Technology, and Human Values* 21(3): 303–339.

Slaughter, S., and G. Rhoades. 2004. *Academic Capitalism and the New Economy: Markets, State, and Higher Education*. Baltimore: Johns Hopkins University Press.

Subotzky, G. 1999. "Alternatives to the Entrepreneurial University: New Modes of Knowledge Production in Community Service Programs." *Higher Education* 38(4): 401–440.

Sutz, J. 2003. "Inequality and University Research Agendas in Latin America." *Science, Technology, and Human Values* 28(1): 52–68.

Tolbert, P. S. 1985. "Institutional Environments and Resource Dependence: Sources of Administrative Structure in Institutions of Higher Education." *Administrative Science Quarterly* 30(1): 1–13.

Trow, M. 1973. *Problems in the Transition from Elite to Mass Education*. Princeton, NJ: Carnegie Commission on Higher Education (reprint).

Veblen, T. 1918. *The Higher Learning in America: A Memorandum on the Conduct of Universities by Business Men*. New York: Viking Press.

Veysey, L. 1965. *The Emergence of the American University*. Chicago: University of Chicago Press.

Vidovich, L. 2002. "Quality Assurance in Australian Higher Education: Globalisation and 'Steering at a Distance.'" *Higher Education* 43(3): 391–408.

CHAPTER FIVE

Reforming the Reforms: Transformation and Crisis in Latin American and Caribbean Universities [1]

Atilio A. Boron

Universities have played a key role throughout the entire history of Latin America and the Caribbean, from early colonial times to the present. A few of them were founded immediately after the Conquest, in the first half of the 16th century, long before the creation of some of the most renowned European and American universities. In Santo Domingo, Dominican Republic, the first university in the Americas was established well before John Harvard had even been born. Shortly afterward, universities were created in Mexico City, Guatemala City, and Lima. As a result of this long-standing heritage, public universities are an integral part of our history. It is highly unlikely to find a major event in Latin America without finding in it the trace of the university, its faculty, and its students. Charged with the duty of training the priests, lawyers, bureaucrats, accountants, doctors, and engineers needed to administer the vast Spanish and Portuguese empires in this region, university professors and authorities and, more generally, intellectuals, linked in different ways to the university environment, played a critical role during the colonial wars and the independence at the beginning of the 19th century and in the ensuing national governments. Of course, significant variations were evident: If the Spanish crown took pains—for selfish or whatever reasons—to dot the map of its empire with many universities, the Portuguese crown found such initiative completely redundant, given that the natives could always reach the cloisters of Coimbra and Lisbon to receive the education they deserved. The superseding republican governments took some time to correct this little problem, to the point that the Universidade do Estado de Rio de Janeiro (UERJ), the first university in Brazil, was created only after World War I.

Early in the 20th century the rebellion against the old oligarchic order—sparked by the 1918 uprising of university students at the University of Córdoba, Argentina, a reactionary bulwark of obscurantism and all sorts of Catholic archaisms—was not at all surprising. The so-called university reform inflamed the minds and consciousness of the rising middle classes and popular sectors throughout Latin America, provoking major social, economic, and political changes in almost every country of the region. The domino effect of the university reform was felt with extraordinary intensity in Mexico, not to mention Perú, where the foundation of APRA (Alianza Popular Revolucionaria Americana) by Víctor Manuel Haya de la Torre was noticeably influenced by the Córdoba events.

Despite their outstanding role played in the past, which of course varied according to the conditions prevailing in different countries, Latin American and Caribbean (LAC) universities face renewed challenges and are in the midst of a severe crisis. In the last two decades major changes have shaken them to their foundations. These changes relate to major transformations taking place both in their extramural environment and inside, affecting their internal structure, organization, and patterns of functioning. With regard to the external front, universities were rudely challenged by the wave of so-called market-friendly reforms that reshaped the very structure of our societies in socially, economically, and politically regressive terms. To these reforms should be added the mortal threat nested in the likely institutionalization of the General Agreement on Trade in Services (GATS), an initiative steadily promoted by the US government and aimed at the "commodification" of higher education and the constitution of an international deregulated market of university programs. Internally, universities had to respond to the rapid and radical changes unleashed by these policies and by the major transformations occurring in science and technology during the third industrial revolution, which started in the second half of the 20th century. To what extent, one could ask, have our universities been "reformed or simply altered," as suggested by a fairly recent book dealing with this subject (Mollis 2002)? Have our universities been able to internally reform in order to improve their capacities to respond to the renewed challenges of our time? We are afraid that many of the so-called reforms carried out under the uncontested inspiration of neoliberalism—with the clear aim of privatizing the universities and introducing in them World Bank–sponsored policies of "structural adjustment"—have further weakened the few capacities that our universities may have had to positively respond to the challenges of our time. Thus the so-called reforms only made things worse.

In the Western political tradition the word *reform* has a clear progressive meaning. The *American Heritage Dictionary*, for instance, gives as one of the meanings of *reform* the following: "Correction of evils, abuses, or errors. Action to improve social or economic conditions without a radical or revolutionary change." Of course, the meaning of the word is intimately associated in its historical genesis to the Protestant Reformation and its struggle against the outrageous privileges of the clergy, the exaltation of the capacity of individuals to relate to their God without the mediation of the priests, its rejection of the infamous pomp and riches of the Vatican, and so on. Later, *reform* would acquire an even wider connotation during the Enlightenment (Immanuel Kant's ethics being perhaps the most shining example) and during the 19th century, when some variants of liberalism, from Jeremy Bentham to John Stuart Mill, came to resolutely sponsor a reformist *aggiornamento* of the old doctrine. These reforms led Mill to reconsider the situation of women in late Victorian England. If all the connotations and definitions are taken into account, then it can be easily understood that what in the 1980s and 1990s we have known as "reforms" in our universities have in fact been extreme "counterreforms," skillfully sold by the neoliberal propaganda as if they were exactly the contrary.

In this chapter we intend to portray a general picture of the major problems facing LAC universities. In a region of the world where there are more than 800 universities any generalization runs the risk of being unfair to some concrete unit. Yet in its broad terms this general overview is accurate—and disconcerting. Much needs to be done if our universities are to survive the formidable challenges of our time. But what has to be done has little connection with both the direction and the contents of the "reforms" introduced in recent years. In the much celebrated (and equally exaggerated!) "knowledge society" and in an era in which the critical variables for international competitiveness in the global economy are science, technology, and knowledge and the key raw material is intelligence, the role of education in general and of universities in particular can hardly be overestimated. Promotion of education at all levels and of scientific research and technological developments should be at the top of the governmental agenda of our countries. Nevertheless, the nice words and eloquent statements pronounced by presidents, ministers, and high-ranking officials in the region have rarely been followed by corresponding actions and policies. Quite to the contrary, the depressing conclusion is that despite all these statements, the resources allocated to higher education fall far below their words. Cuba is the only exception in this matter, despite the economic blockade and the implacable harassment imposed by the White House. Even more, when the Soviet Union collapsed and Cuban integration into the world economy was subjected to unheard-of hardships and restrictions, the voice of order in Havana was "save our culture first," and the investments in education and science were preserved. If the Cuban case is brought to our attention here, it is because there can hardly be any other country in the region in which economic restrictions and international hostility could be more negative. If Cuba did it, why couldn't other countries? Why haven't other countries in the region, countries much more favorably located and endowed with all kind of resources, tried to set up a vigorous program of university upgrading?

After more than 20 years of democratic reconstruction the social and educational debt of the governments of Latin America and the Caribbean is as impressive as unforgivable. Time is running out, and immediate actions have to be taken. If our countries fail to make a major effort to improve the quality of our universities and to dramatically expand access to higher education for a larger proportion of our youth, the future of our countries will be bleak: A huge continent unable to compete in the international economy and barely kept afloat by the beauty of its beaches, the exotic ways and mores of its culture, its gastronomy, and its popular music and dances, and the wonderful biodiversity of its rain forests, rivers, and mountains risks decimation. But all that will hardly be enough to survive in the turbulent waters of the international economy of the 21st century, when "brain-intensive" industries will become much more important than raw materials and when the collective intelligence of the populations will be the dividing line that separates the winners and the losers of the international economy. The continuation of the current economic and educational policies will accentuate our deplorable dependency on foreign capital, which is attracted to our countries by governmental authorities transformed into white-collar international beggars who proclaim, as if it were a good thing, the virtues of our "cheap labor" ("cheap" because it relies on the uneducated, unhealthy, and unsheltered!) and the total readiness of our countries to accept without restrictions and limitations of any sort the conditions imposed by the capitalists. At a time when brain-intensive industries lead the economic race, brains need to be more cultivated than ever, and this requires governments to put money and actions behind their words.

Having said all this, let us now quickly review some of the more important trends in higher education in Latin America and the Caribbean and outline some of the major problems besieging our universities at the beginning of the 21st century.

Major Trends

The widespread consensus among scholars is that the situation of universities in Latin America and the Caribbean can be characterized, in rough terms, by the presence of three major trends: massification, privatization, and a decline in quality. Let's look at each trend separately.

MASSIFICATION

In accordance with worldwide tendencies, Latin America and the Caribbean experienced a rapid expansion of university enrollment in the second half of the 20th century. The number of university students rose from 270,000 in 1950 to almost 9 million at the beginning of the 21st century. Impressive as they are, these figures are far from being a major achievement of our countries. They only reflect a universal trend that has asserted itself in even stronger terms in the advanced capitalist nations and in Southeast Asia, where the quantitative expansion of university enrollment increased at a faster pace than in Latin America and the Caribbean.

PRIVATIZATION

In line with the major recommendations of the Washington consensus, the educational system was redefined as an "educational market" in which private providers were not only welcomed but also enticed and in which rules and regulations aimed at providing a quality university education to the student body were kept at low levels. Privatization and deregulation of higher education became the rallying cries from the 1980s onward. Until the mid 20th century public universities prevailed without counterweight in the region, but in the last 25 years the situation has been radically modified. Today enrollment in private universities accounts for 40 percent of the total student body, but as far as the institutions are concerned, almost 60 percent of all the universities in Latin America and the Caribbean are private. A closer look at national cases shows that in countries such as Brazil, Chile, Colombia, Dominican Republic, and El Salvador the majority of students are enrolled in private universities, whereas in Argentina, Guatemala, Mexico, Paraguay, Perú, and Venezuela the opposite is true. In Brazil three out of the five bigger universities are private, and the biggest university is private as well. On the opposite side, in Argentina and Mexico the huge enrollment at the University of Buenos Aires and at the National Autonomous University of Mexico (UNAM), among other large public universities, is a brake to the disproportionate influence that private universities have acquired in other countries of the region.

DECLINE IN QUALITY

The quality of university education has declined worldwide, including developed and underdeveloped countries. Many factors—among them the crisis at the secondary level, the effect of television on the learning habits of youth, the disrepute of academia and learning in general compared with the prestige of money-making professions—explain this regrettable performance, which is visible even in the elite institutions of the United States and Europe. But the fact is that, again, as a general trend, in Latin America and the Caribbean the situation has acquired extremely distressing features. Despite efforts, only 7 percent of the faculty of our universities hold doctoral degrees, and another 20 percent have only a few years of graduate studies. The overwhelming majority of our university professors, therefore, scarcely hold a BA degree. In addition, full-time dedication is far from widespread, except in some elite programs at the graduate level. At the University of Buenos Aires, to cite just an example of the trend prevailing in the area, full-time faculty do not even reach the 10 percent mark. In short, the quantitative expansion of the system and the increased massification of the student body were not accompanied by the reaffirmation of the preexisting levels of educational quality, not to mention by the improvement in quality of a university education. The illusory expectations placed on the contribution that the vigorous surge of the private universities might have to the improvement of educational quality proved unrealistic. Although there exists in our region a small number of good private universities, the overwhelming majority of them have been opportunistic commercial enterprises that profit from the continuing expansion of educational demand and take advantage of decreased state capacities to establish and enforce stringent standards of academic quality. Contrary to what happened with the handful of good private institutions, the overwhelming majority of the rest specialized in the creation of "chalk and blackboard" careers, or, in short, courses that supposedly ensure an untroubled insertion into the labor market (e.g., tourism, public relations, marketing, social communication). From an entrepreneurial point of view the commercial advantage of these careers is that they require little, if any, investment in infrastructure, libraries, and laboratories and that the professorial staff can be easily recruited and poorly paid. The problem is not so much these sorts of careers, which, if taken seriously, may respond to some concrete societal needs. But under the prevailing conditions of educational neoliberalism, their contribution to the educational and scientific development of the country is equal to zero (even today the natural and biological sciences as well as the engineering sciences, of course, are almost exclusively taught in public universities). As profit-making enterprises these private institutions have been extraordinarily successful in many cases, and this is the reason that they have flourished so strongly in this part of the world.

The Educational Reforms of the 1990s

Today the main challenges that besiege LAC universities have prompted a variety of initiatives, not all of them felicitous or constructive. Let us begin by saying that the unspoken assumptions presiding over if not all then at least most of the changes introduced in university life reflect the ideological ascendancy of neoliberalism in our region. As will be seen later, it is unnecessary to insist on the crucial role played in this process by the World Bank, which provided the rationale for reform and, with its conditionalities, forced governments to adopt proposed reforms even if they were not totally willing to do so.

According to the prevailing ideological orientations, the educational system has come to be increasingly regarded by so-called prominent experts and policy makers as a marketplace, and education—principally higher education—is regarded as an immaterial commodity and therefore as something that should not be considered separate from mercantile logic. Subtle changes in the lexicon used in the working papers, research reports, and articles and books written by World Bank experts in the last 20 years—or by researchers and ministerial staff financed by the World Bank—show how the pseudoscientific language of economics gradually but steadily came to replace the discourse originating traditionally in the humanities. This orientation consecrated the triumph of the barbarous notion that education is a commodity and the educational system a market, that is, a space in which isolated individuals—not citizens but clients or consumers—endowed with equal economic capacities, perfectly well informed, and acting rationally, "buy" educational services freely sold in the marketplace by a heterogeneous group of providers such as the state, the churches, or private businessmen of any sort. The consequence of all this was a socially regressive redefinition of education, which was hitherto conceived of as an inalienable citizen right and which nowadays, especially in the case of higher education, is regarded as a service that, like any other service, must be purchased in the market at a given price by those who can afford to do so. As happens with any commodity or service traded in the markets, nobody can claim to have a "right" to own a Ferrari or to wear an Armani suit if he or she does not have the money to afford it. Much more nonsensical would be to request the government to deliver those goods for free. Education should not be an exception to this rule, and this explains the strong pressures exerted by Washington to include higher education as one more service whose international transactions should be placed under the norms and regulations established by the World Trade Organization.

One of the consequences of the neoliberal dominance in framing the so-called educational reforms of the 1980s and 1990s has been the generalized

acceptance gained by the hitherto bizarre idea that universities should be regarded as profitable, money-making institutions able to live on their own incomes. It is regrettable to acknowledge that this absurdity has become a sort
of conventional wisdom of the times, shared with varying degrees of enthusi-
asm by university professors and administrators, educational experts, relevant
policy makers, and, more generally, public opinion manipulated by a bour-
geois press. No wonder then that some of the innovations put into effect by
the "reformed" universities have little relation to the quality of academic standards. On the one hand, the paramount concern of these reforms was to ensure that universities would be able to function with the financial resources
generated by them, thus reproducing in the educational sphere the more
general trend toward privatization and commodification of all kinds of goods
and services required by society to sustain its own existence. On the other
hand, with this policy the central governments of the region sought to free
themselves from part of their financial responsibilities in the area of higher
education and to reap some savings that situated them in a better position to
obtain the huge fiscal *superávits* (surplus) required for the payment of foreign
debt. As the Brazilian political philosopher Marilena Chauí (2003) recently
argued, the university passed from being regarded as a social institution—
autonomous, republican, laicized, and democratic—to being considered a
"social organization" ruled by utilitarian principles, functional to the preservation of the existing social order and deprived of all critical intention.

Among the most important transformations that occurred in recent years
are the following:

- The steady privatization of higher education by means of the subtle but
  pervasive introduction of fees into hitherto tuition-free public universities or through the inordinate and deregulated expansion of "chalk and
  blackboard" private institutions.
- The diversification of courses and careers, most of them requiring shorter
  terms, to make room for a growing mass of students requiring postsecondary training and to better respond to the whims of the market.
- The decentralization taking place in large universities, both along regional lines and within the university itself, that grants increased levels of
  academic and financial autonomy to internal schools, departments, and
  institutes.

- The development of graduate courses, more than 8,000 in the region, almost exclusively offered by public universities and highly concentrated in Brazil and Mexico, while Argentina, Chile, Colombia, Cuba, Peru, and Venezuela rank in an intermediate position.

- The growth of distance education and the role of the new information technologies to foster the enlarged impact of tertiary education throughout society.

- The introduction of accreditation and evaluation criteria and agencies, more often than not motivated by purely budgetary considerations derived from the need to slash governmental expenditures, to take charge of the Sisyphean tasks of assessing "faculty performance and productivity," something that is exceedingly difficult to do, especially when everything is measured with the rude and improper yardstick of "cost-benefit analysis" sponsored by the evaluating agencies.

- The increasing presence of foreign universities, especially US universities, which opened branches in our countries thanks to the loopholes and gaps in our legislation that, while reinforcing to unprecedented levels the mechanisms of control and surveillance of the public universities, left the door wide open for the establishment of private universities, with little control, if any, by the educational authorities.

- Finally, as a sort of countercurrent, the positive role played by regional associations of universities, such as UDUAL (Unión de Universidades de América Latina) and CSUCA (Consejo Superior Universitario de Centroamérica), and the universities belonging to the Montevideo Group, all of which have taken pains to point out the catastrophic consequences that the neoliberal project has on university life in Latin America and the Caribbean.

A Triple Crisis of the University in Latin America and the Caribbean

The combination of old problems arising even before the 1980s and the radical regressiveness of the neoliberal reforms carried out in more recent years has plunged LAC universities into a series of major problems. Let us quickly summarize the most important of them.

FINANCIAL CRISIS

The financial situation is absolutely critical because without adequate financial support universities can neither function properly nor reform themselves. Nothing could be more mistaken than the naïve belief that reforms
can be carried out when universities are in the stranglehold of rampant
financial crisis. What often has been pretentiously announced as university
reform in our countries has been little more than a collection of wild budgetary cuts tied to massive faculty layoffs, the introduction of fees and the
abolition of gratuity, the shutting down of departments or research institutes, and so forth. But these are not reforms at all, at least if the term *reform*
is to keep the progressive, egalitarian, and libertarian meaning it used to
have in the Western political tradition. As in any other policy area, true reformers require additional resources of all sorts to carry out their plans. This
is the reason that the chronic financial weakness is the Achilles' heel of LAC
universities and a major obstacle to the introduction of necessary reforms,
which of course have no connection to the program being promoted by the
World Bank and its local mouthpieces. The financial situation of our public
universities radically worsened in the last two decades, especially after the
outbreak of the 1982 debt crisis and the ensuing programs of economic stabilization and structural adjustment implemented under the dual guidance
of the International Monetary Fund (IMF) and the World Bank. Thus Latin
America and the Caribbean is the region of the world with the smallest
amount of money invested for each student in the tertiary level per year:
about US$650 against a figure almost 4 times as large in Asia; in the United
States and Canada the annual investment per university student is about
US$9,500, or 14 times bigger than in Latin America and the Caribbean.
Furthermore, it is not by chance that Latin America and the Caribbean is
also the region of the world with the most unequal distribution of income
and wealth. The seriousness of the problem is only compounded when one
is reminded that in this region the governmental investment in higher education is by far the single most important contribution to the global university budgets of our countries. Private universities cannot even remotely compensate for the financial desertion of the state.

Comparisons of university budgets render scandalous results. For instance, the University of California, a state institution, has a student body on

all its campuses of 250,000, whereas UNAM, the largest university in Latin America, has 280,000 students. The two universities are relatively equal in terms of size of enrollment, but the disparity in the budgets is considerable. The University of California has a total budget of US$7 billion, whereas UNAM has to make ends meet with US$1.4 billion, that is, one-fifth of the California amount. And we should bear in mind that UNAM is a privileged institution with the largest university budget in the region. Dramatic examples of the financial crisis facing our universities could be provided for hours. Let us simply remember that student and faculty protests and strikes caused by financial troubles in LAC universities have become a common feature of our countries in recent times.

The origin of the financial crisis that affects higher education in our countries is crystal clear: the gradual but steady desertion of the governments from some of their essential responsibilities in the area of higher education. The cause of this deplorable situation is the adoption of neoliberal fundamentalism sponsored by the governments of the G-7 and led by the United States and the increasing role that organizations such as the World Bank, the IMF, the Inter-American Development Bank (IDB), and other similar institutions play in the region. The international financial institutions have imposed on our governments and societies a couple of wrong and absurd ideas: first, that governments in the third world should end the infamous "subsidy to the rich" implicit in the public financing of higher education; and second, that the virtuous dynamism of higher education systems rests on the impulse derived from private universities. These assertions purposely conceal several facts: (1) that most countries that are in a leading position worldwide in teaching and research do not have private universities, for example, most European countries and Canada (Sweden, France, the United Kingdom, and Germany do not have private universities, although in Germany there are some marginal universities left in the system for political and religious reasons, as in Bavaria); (2) that the rapidly developing Southeast Asian countries are noteworthy for the high quality of their public universities; and (3) that there is a decisive role played by the huge transfer of federal and state funds in the financing of "private" US universities.

A special paragraph must be devoted to the increasingly significant role played by the World Bank in educational, health, nutrition, social security, and all matters related to the welfare of the population. This institution—in fact, an extension of the US government, as Zbigniew Brzezinski has admitted—has become in recent times the most authoritative organization regarding the "correct policy line" to apply in a wide variety of areas, among them education at all its levels as well as science and culture. It is a serious matter of concern that the World Bank succeeded in replacing UNESCO in the critical role it performed, under the umbrella of the United Nations system, for over half a century. Needless to say, a bank, no matter how it names itself or how its president likes it to be seen, is always a bank, and the natural tendency of any bank official is to consider all things, and certainly all social institutions and social practices, as simple items in a cost-benefit calculation grid. "When you only have a hammer," the old saying goes, "all your problems start to look like nails."

Needless to say, this mercantile ethos creates an insurmountable barrier for the adequate consideration of all educational matters. The commercial logic of the World Bank implies that education should no longer be regarded as the supreme task of the polis. Plato's vision of education as the cultivation of the spirit leading to the formation of an enlightened citizenry is replaced by the meticulous reading of the Dow Jones Index of the New York Stock Exchange or by the Country Risk Scoreboard published daily by the financial wizards and gamblers who run the international financial system to their advantage. In this light, education is a commodity not different from soybeans, car transmissions, or tuna fish and deserves no special treatment. Little wonder that hand in hand with the World Bank's ideological and political ascendancy in Latin America and the Caribbean came pressures in favor of educational privatization, deregulation, governmental retreat, and so on. It has proved difficult for the governments of the region to resist these pressures. Their economies are in bad shape, razed by prolonged economic recession, orthodox economic policies, and the hemorrhaging caused by external debt, all of which made these countries extremely vulnerable to foreign pressures and the "conditionalities" of international financial institutions in all policy areas, including education. Of course, strong social resistance opposed these interferences, and large popular mobilizations succeeded, in some cases, in stopping the predominant drive. But the situation has not been reversed yet.

The last chapter of this depressing story is the outrageous decision, which we must oppose resolutely, of the World Trade Organization (WTO) to incorporate higher education as one of the "services" to be included within the area of competence of the WTO. If this initiative finally succeeds, all the "barriers" to the free flow of "educational services" will be removed by the signatories of the agreement, and noncompliance with this "free trade regulation" would entail the application of severe commercial and financial penalties for the governments that dare to break the rule. Thus, in this liberalized educational environment, LAC universities will have to "compete" fairly in the provision of higher education (and in the production of diplomas and certificates) with some of the richest and strongest universities of the North. Some initial estimates indicate that in Brazil alone this new "educational business" would produce benefits in the vicinity of US$2 billion in the first five years of "university liberalization." It does not take a genius to predict the final outcome of this unequal battle. Public universities in our region will face no better a future in their competition with the academic giants of the North than local capital does at the hands of the transnational corporations.

Obsessed with fiscal *superávits* and subjected to permanent blackmail by the lords of the world and the international financial institutions, the governments of the regions have slashed "unproductive" expenses, cut all sorts of social programs, and decentralized functions (such as education and health services) without providing adequate financial resources to the subnational units now in charge of delivering these public goods. All these initiatives were blessed by the established powers and their ideological agents as a beneficial "devolution" of prerogatives to lower levels of the governmental structure, which were supposedly more in touch with the real people, and as a noble "empowerment" of civil society. Needless to say, both arguments are unable to pass the empirical test: The motivating force behind this story is the need to produce the budgetary surplus destined to repay external debt. Hard times like these require major financial adjustments, and education (and health, social security, etc.) has to be sacrificed to the financial markets.

QUALITY CRISIS

As mentioned, there is a widespread crisis in the quality of higher education, and not only in Latin America and the Caribbean. By and large, universities seem to have been unable to adequately respond to the formidable challenges posed by the combination of rapid social changes, accelerated scientific and technological innovations, paradigmatic revolutions, massiveness, skyrocketing costs, and financial restrictions. Complaints and laments are heard worldwide, and although a small number of universities seem to have been able to respond more or less adequately to the new challenges of the time, for the overwhelming majority of higher education institutions the situation is exactly the opposite.

As usual, the factors at work are many. On the one hand, the educational crisis affects the system at all levels. If primary education is besieged by severe problems and the secondary level is regarded as a sort of "disaster zone," even in highly advanced countries, it would be a miracle of sorts if universities could remain untouched and aloof in light of such a situation. As a matter of fact, this is not the case. Save for a few exceptions, the students who enter the university bring with them all the problems accumulated in their previous passage through the primary and secondary levels. Such problems, compounded as time passes, explode in the university.

The irresistible massification of the university only added to the quality problem, despite the fact that massification is a healthy trend, because it is egalitarian and democratic and must be welcomed. Massification largely reflects the strength of the democratic impulse and the growing integration of women into higher education. And in this regard the worst is still to come in Latin America and the Caribbean, because even today the proportion of the university-age population enrolled in higher education institutions is much lower than in the advanced capitalist countries and in certain countries of Southeast Asia. This means that, other things being equal—certainly, an optimistic hypothesis!—and despite the economic crisis affecting the region in the last 30 years, the numbers of young people that will be knocking at the doors of our universities is likely to double in less than 20 years. Are our institutions prepared to receive such a huge wave of new entrants? Do they have the material, personnel, organizational skills, and strategic plans to cope with this formidable challenge? As of today, the answer is no. Moreover, if our universities continue to be "reformed" along the neoliberal lines, their chances of survival are weakened, and a major educational disaster will be waiting for us at the end of the day. Sensible reform is needed, but the blueprint is not likely to be found in the headquarters of the World Bank or the World Trade Organization, global institutions that so far have provided the rationale and the money for the regressive transformations carried out in the last 20 years. To face the new challenges, we need something different from the neoliberal recipe.

Quality also has been affected by major scientific and technological revolutions resulting from the spectacular advances in science and engineering. This progress brought about a new cycle of scientific advancements that prompted the crisis of the old theoretical paradigms. Changes that previously had taken place over several centuries now occur in the life span of a single generation. It is only natural that these transformations blurred the boundaries of traditional scientific disciplines and led them to lose some of their time-honored identity. This situation is not only valid for the so-called hard sciences but also prevalent in the social sciences and the humanities, where, as shown in the Gulbenkian Report, the traditional separation between sociology, economics, political science, history, and anthropology has become completely untenable these days. Shortly after the passage of 100 years since Marx's death, his pioneering call to build a unified social science has become an unavoidable need, even for his most bitter critics.

Of course, a situation like the one we describe is fraught with unheard-of challenges and circumstances that have a direct effect on the organization of university life. The Napoleonic-Humboldtian model of the university, organized along the lines of the *grand ecoles* or faculties, lasted a century and a half, only to collapse by the mid 20th century, but the American university, organized along narrow departmental lines and now extremely fragmented, survived even less. But is the new organizational format likely to respond adequately to the unprecedented challenges posed to the university in our epoch? Nobody seems to have a satisfactory answer. The only thing we know is that the financial restrictions affecting university life today cannot but compound the problem.

Many other issues are involved in the discussion of the quality crisis of higher education institutions. The growing heterogeneity of the university system, eased by the policies of deregulation and liberalization, has as a result produced a system in which some outstanding institutions survive along with others that are mere commercial undertakings completely indifferent to issues of intellectual excellence and academic quality. Another factor is the low level of training of an important part of the faculty, explained by causes as diverse as a lack of adequate policies to upgrade the qualifications of university professors, the absence of material and intellectual stimuli to undertake a process of academic improvement by professors, and the protracted military rule that devastated LAC universities. In this regard we should be reminded that, in accordance with the basic tenets of the National Security Doctrine elaborated and propagated by the US government, in Latin America the military rulers perceived the universities as "nests of the subversive" that should be annihilated. The policies used to this effect varied from strict ideological persecution and control to the introduction of exclusionist fees, as in Pinochet's Chile, to the sheer kidnapping and disappearance of university professors, as happened in a good deal of Latin America and the Caribbean, to the outright bombardment of the university campus, as at the National University of El Salvador in San Salvador.

Finally, a last reflection is on the issue of the quality of research and teaching. How are we supposed to evaluate the quality of university research and teaching? Are the methodologies currently used to evaluate the quality sound enough for such a purpose? We do not believe so. The mercantile criteria elaborated by World Bank experts, who preside over most, if not all, of the evaluation processes taking place today in Latin America and the Caribbean, do not seem adequate to really assess the quality of education offered to students. The economic reductionism of this approach makes it ill-suited to genuinely appraise the quality of the educational process, which requires the ability to transcend the coarse indexes of "academic productivity" measured by quantitative criteria or by the magic of "cost-benefit" analysis. Against the prevailing inordinate focus on quantitative techniques of assessment and evaluation, it is helpful to recall what Albert Einstein once said: "Not all that can be counted counts, and not all that counts can be counted." To produce useful and realistic evaluations of the quality of education, it is necessary to recover an integral humanistic approach, abandoning for good the barbarous economic reductionism. To evaluate the educational systems and processes, we should heed the words of Rousseau, Piaget, Vygotsky, and Freire rather than the likes of Milton Friedman and the evaluation manuals of the World Bank and the IMF.

On the "Mission" of the University

The question of the purpose of the university, its paramount "mission," is a critical problem. Yet it is totally neglected these days. In the 1960s discussion of this issue inflamed the Latin American public debate. By that time many of us ardently defended the idea that the university should be the "critical consciousness of the society." To perform this crucial role, the university had to guarantee a rather unique combination of scientific excellence and an outstanding humanistic foundation—refined analytical skills juxtaposed with a vision of the good society. This thesis, rooted in the seminal theories of great Latin American educators such as Paulo Freire and Darcy Ribeiro in Brazil, Risieri Frondizi and Rodolfo Mondolfo in Argentina, Justo Barros Sierra and Pablo González Casanova in Mexico, and many others, provided the theoretical and doctrinal foundations for the progressive reforms experienced by LAC universities in the 1960s. However, with the advent of the dictatorships in the 1970s, the discussion was suddenly wiped from the public scene, and the idea of the university as a critical consciousness of its epoch became a dangerous subversive slogan. As such it was banned and its spokespeople were persecuted, jailed, and, many times, killed. Unfortunately, the new "ideological climate," which surrounded the democratic reconstruction that started in the region at the beginning of the 1980s, prevented us from reintroducing the theme of critical consciousness, and the question of the role of the university remained largely in the shadows.

With the changes that took place in the 1990s, the urgency of the question reappeared: What should be, in this era of globalized capital, the purpose and "mission" of the university? According to neoliberal theorists and practitioners in the field, the response is quite clear: The university must train the young in the kind of professional skills and dispositions required by the market. According to the Washington consensus theorists, the satisfaction of market needs is the only "realistic and responsible" approach to the matter. Any other answer to the question is an unhealthy tribute to sheer idealism or infantile nostalgia for a bygone past that will never return. Like it or not, the market has become the crucial institution in global capitalism, a truth not only confirmed in the economy but also in all aspects and dimensions of social life. It is the market that provides the material incentives for the development of different professional careers and the promise of good jobs. If university authorities are able to adequately "read" market signals, their wisdom will surely be rewarded by the market with the creation of a wide variety of jobs ready to accommodate their graduates. To reach such a felicitous outcome, both the teaching programs and the research agenda of the universities should be framed in response to the dynamics of market forces. Once again, the theoretical assumption of perfect market equilibrium is introduced as if it were an empirical conclusion, which, of course, it is not.

There has been a lot of demagoguery during the inception of the neoliberal reforms in higher education in Latin America and the Caribbean. Neoliberal advocates tirelessly announced that with the prevailing changes the students would succeed in their job search activities once they graduated. Once again, reality did not match the rosy promises. Impervious to this outcome, the neoliberal reformers and their disciples in the region insisted that the market should decide what to teach and what to investigate, leaving aside extravagant courses, disciplines, and research agenda. After all, who cares for a philosopher? What is the market value of her wisdom? Do we really need astronomers? Should we waste our scarce resources training the youth in ancient history or political theory? Do Latin American societies need people to study nuclear physics?

Obviously, this attitude is completely unacceptable for any sensible person, not to mention one with a strong humanist foundation. First, the real history of science and knowledge in general reveals that the role played by the markets was always marginal and that the growth in the humanities and sciences was alien to the commercial imperatives. Plato, Aristotle, Servetus, Linnaeus, Copernicus, Newton, Einstein, and many others made substantial additions to human knowledge without any kind of mercantile consideration and, in many cases, precisely against such considerations. Despite the fact that in some advanced countries large firms have developed significant research and development programs, there are no compelling reasons to expect that business enterprises will advance the frontiers of knowledge in a broad range of disciplines, from the humanities to astronomy to mathematics. Second, even if this were the case, the intrusion of market imperatives is also unacceptable because the progress of human knowledge must not be impaired, guided, or controlled by business-minded profit-making calculations. Surrendering to the despotism of market forces may well end up in a new type of technological barbarism and as a likely source of all sorts of misfortunes for humankind. The discovery and universal distribution of a vaccine against AIDS, for instance, must not be impaired by commercial considerations.

Of course, other responses can be given to the question of the mission of the university. If the first argument advances market adaptability, a second, rather conventional one asserts that the university's mission is to reproduce and disseminate knowledge. This is one step forward, but it is still insufficient. The emphasis here is placed on the reproductive aspects of the university rather than on its capacity to produce new knowledge and theories. In this case our universities simply become reproducers of knowledge, theories, and methodological approaches developed elsewhere and not necessarily relevant to our problems and more or less sophisticated according to the circumstances. Examples of this distortion have been typical in LAC universities. For instance, in our schools medicine has played a marginal role in the study of Chagas' disease (which affects millions of people in the region) compared to the inordinate attention paid to the study of physical illnesses common to affluent societies, or in our schools we train our medical students in the use of highly sophisticated electronic instruments and disregard the basic tools of clinics needed to serve the overwhelming majority of the population. Similar examples of academic distortion can be drawn from the exact sciences and, last but not least, the social sciences. In terms of the social sciences the propensity to fit within the limits of the dominant paradigm and the apparently irresistible tendency to imitate the intellectual fashions of the North have led to a regrettable situation in which the outstanding contributions made by LAC social scientists in the second half of the 20th century are nowadays almost completely ignored by the younger generations, who, on the other side, are quite familiar with the latest papers produced in the barren field of "rational choice" or in the rambling meanders of postmodern social theory. Incidentally, it has to be noted that this professional disease— the uncritical imitation of anything produced in the North, especially if it is written in English—has become particularly acute among economists, with the consequences that our countries know all too well.

Of course, the critical financial situation of our universities helps to explain the disjunction between university and society. Given that in Latin America and the Caribbean the salaries of professors and researchers have been kept at low levels or straightforwardly frozen for years, the role of foreign influences has become more and more crucial in determining the research agenda of our universities. With the prevailing criteria used to assess the "productivity" of our professors and researchers, they are forced, in order to improve their salaries, to publish more, and more quickly. Because the local evaluators tend to dismiss or underestimate journals or publishing houses based in Latin America, the rush to publish in some journals or in some university or commercial presses of the North has become an almost irresistible force. If their production is "acceptable" to colleagues in the United States or Europe and if their work is considered publishable by journals and publishing houses in the North, then the evaluating agencies at home, possessed by a strong, albeit unconscious, racist or colonialist bias, reward our scholars accordingly and grade their academic performance in more positive terms, and consequently their salaries will be raised accordingly.

It is important to underline the existence and depth of this colonialist bias over determining the economic bent because, as a social scientist, I can testify that although some North American or European social science journals are excellent, others are terrible; and in Latin America and the Caribbean some journals are as good as the best in the North, whereas others are definitively as bad as the worst. But this kind of reasoning is not very popular among the evaluating agencies, and as a result, they place a high premium (which is translated into the salary of the professor) on any paper published in the North while giving almost no credit at all for a book, not to mention an article, published in a country on the periphery of the capitalist system. The unfortunate result of this operation is that the research agenda and the curricula of our universities have become increasingly dependent on the theoretical and practical priorities established by our colleagues on the editorial boards of the journals and by the editors of the commercial or university presses of the United States or Europe, who decide what is and what is not publishable. Their priorities, it should be remembered, do not always coincide with ours or are not necessarily the most productive for our societies.

Second, the dependence on foreign sources of financing can also work in an indirect manner. Given that LAC university budgets have little money to finance scientific research, it has become a common practice in the social sciences to compete for grants related to so-called applied social research demanded by governmental agencies and, in many cases, by international financial institutions that provide funds for neoliberal reforms. But because our states are bankrupt, the money needed for this policy-oriented research comes also from outside sources, basically from the World Bank, the Inter-American Development Bank, and the IMF. Thus at the end of the day our social scientists are forced to give up any pretension of developing a research agenda of their own or of conducting long-range research, as was done in the 1950s and 1960s in the region, or of working with a particular theoretical and/or methodological framework that may not be agreeable to the donors. In addition, these policy-oriented forms of inquiry are *prêt a porter* and have little relationship with veritable social science. The professors are expected to produce a consulting report and not a social science research report. The theoretical and methodological framework is carefully specified in the contract and cannot be modified by the consultant, and the findings are largely built in to the basic premises of the theory and methods. The result is predictable: bad social science, despite the millions of dollars spent on this peculiar kind of "social research," whose real aim is to legitimize, with the assistance of pseudoscientific inquiry, the policies decided beforehand. As a result, no valuable knowledge is produced to alleviate the more critical problems faced by our peoples.

In sum, the mission of the university and its autonomy are greatly affected by financial vulnerability. In addition, most universities in the region also have to bear the distorting influence of extra-university actors who retain the upper hand in appointing rectors, presidents, and deans. Of course, this influence later penetrates all of university life, through curricula, research, and teaching. This does not happen only in Latin America and the Caribbean. The influence of governmental authorities is also felt, although to a lesser degree compared to some countries in the region, in Europe and in the public universities of the United States. In the United States, moreover, the public and especially the private universities also are subjected to the influence of corporate interests in the form of big individual donors, rich alumni, and the powerful CEOs who sit on the boards of trustees for individual universities. Thus the problem of academic autonomy is a major one that is not confined only to Latin America and the Caribbean. However, in our countries quite often the impact is exceedingly large. Too often the voice of the government is crucial in the appointment of the rectors of many public LAC universities, even against the opposition of the overwhelming majority of the faculty and students. In the countries in which the impact of the University Reform of 1918 has been strong—especially in Argentina but also in a handful of other countries—authorities are elected by the university community (professors, graduates, and students) without or with little exogenous interference. Yet this practice has been subjected to a fierce attack in recent years by advocates of the neoliberal project and their allies in the university. Unfortunately, and despite its crucial importance, the question of university autonomy still has not made its way onto the public agenda.

Notes

1. During the preparation of this chapter, I largely relied on the contributions made to the study of Latin American and Caribbean universities by such fine scholars as Pablo Gentili, Pablo González Casanova, Francisco López Segrera, Marcella Mollis, Domingo Rivarola, Carlos Alberto Torres, Helgio Trindade, Carlos Tunnerman Bernheim, and Hebe Vessuri. I want to thank them all for the insights they were able to transmit through their writings and the opportunity they gave me to benefit from their friendship and wisdom. Of course, they bear no responsibility whatsoever for the contents of this chapter.

References

Chauí, M. 2003. *Sociedade, Universidade e Estado: Autonomia, Dependencia e Compromisso Social*. Brasília, Brazil: Ministerio de Educación.

Gentili, P., ed. 2001. *A Universidade na Penumbra: Neoliberalismo e Restruturação Universitaria*. São Paulo: Cortés Editores.

López Segrera, F. 2003. "Higher Education and Research in the Latin American Region." Paper presented at the first meeting of the Forum on Higher Education, Research, and Knowledge of UNESCO, Buenos Aires, March 17 and 18.

Mollis, M., ed. 2002. *Las Universidades en América Latina: Reformadas o Alteradas?* Buenos Aires: CLACSO.

Trindade, H. 2001. *A Universidade em Ruinas na República dos Profesores*. Petrópolis, Brazil: Vozes.

Tunnerman Bernheim, C. 2003. "Educación Superior e Investigación en América Latina y el Caribe." Paper presented at the first meeting of the Forum on Higher Education, Research, and Knowledge of UNESCO, Buenos Aires, March 17 and 18.

CHAPTER SIX

Globalization and the Challenge to National Universities in Argentina and Mexico

Robert A. Rhoads
Carlos Alberto Torres
Andrea Brewster

The political and economic context in much of Latin America can be described as one of turmoil and transition. During the past few decades we have witnessed the toppling of authoritarian and antidemocratic regimes, and in the dust of destruction democratic governments have emerged (Lakoff 1996). With governmental change has come major economic restructuring, as Latin American countries increasingly have sought to participate in a global marketplace, mostly following the lead of free-market entrepreneurialism fashioned by the United States and other Western powers (Boron and Torres 1996). This changing sociopolitical and socioeconomic landscape poses major challenges to education throughout Latin America (Boron 1995; Morales-Gómez and Torres 1990; Morrow and Torres 2000; Torres and Schugurensky 2002). Of particular concern to us is the effect such changes may have on the national universities of Argentina and Mexico.

In Argentina, for example, the dawn of the 21st century saw the government and its citizens confronted with economic devastation and political chaos. Once the favorite son of the International Monetary Fund (IMF) and acting largely under its direction, the Argentine economy was devastated by global economic strategies and political corruption under the helm of former president Carlos Saúl Menem and then under the direction of Minister of Economy Domingo Cavallo and President Fernando de la Rúa (Frasca 2002). Corruption and failed economic strategies led to the government defaulting on its debt of $140 billion and a virtual freeze of Argentine assets while the ranks of the unemployed swelled to more than 20 percent of the nation's population. So devastated were the citizens of Argentina that their uprising in December 2001 toppled the de la Rúa presidency and led to a rapid transition of five presidents within days, culminating in the ascension of Eduardo Duhalde of the Partido Justicialista and runner-up to de la Rúa in the 1999 presidential race. The tumultuous political and economic context in Argentina has had serious repercussions for state-supported higher education. In particular, the economic fallout for the Universidad de Buenos Aires (UBA) has been crippling.

Like Argentina, Mexico also faces serious challenges, framed to a large degree by a rapidly changing political and economic context. For example, although Mexico has had democratic elections since 1929, one party—the Partido Revolucionario Institucional (PRI)—so completely dominated the political landscape that no serious political pundit would describe such a context as truly democratic. In fact, in 1988 much sentiment and hard evidence supported the case that the PRI manipulated election results to retain its political stranglehold over Mexico while perhaps denying Cuauhtémoc Cárdenas and the Partido de la Revolución Democrática the presidency. With the victory by Vicente Fox and the Partido Accion Nacional in July 2000, the possibility emerged that Mexico was entering a new era of realized democracy. Optimism, though, has faded, and the potential to further democratize the society has run into many barriers, including serious challenges linked to Fox's commitment to globalizing Mexico's economy. The global economic choices confronting Mexico have direct implications for state-supported higher education. Relatedly, we contend that the changing context of Mexican higher education policy and the nation's support for public universities is largely evident through the relationship between the state and the Universidad Nacional Autónoma de México (UNAM), or the National Autonomous University of Mexico. Known throughout the country as *la má-*

xima casa de estudios, UNAM is Mexico's preeminent public research university. UNAM's importance to the national context is why we select it as a site for our analysis.

Our intent in this chapter is to explore the changing political and economic context for state-supported higher education in Argentina and Mexico. In particular, we examine each country's preeminent public university in light of challenges and opportunities that we associate with globalization. From our perspective, globalization is a historical reality that imposes itself on societies but that also can be influenced by institutions and governments seeking to shape global processes for their own ends. Consequently, we are interested in the ways in which globalization is shaping UNAM and UBA and in how these institutions can play a role in advancing their own respective country's global endeavors. In addition, and consistent with the opening chapter to this book, we contend that processes associated with globalization largely are defined by neoliberal economic perspectives; hence we are concerned about the ways in which such views are limiting the ability of Latin American countries such as Argentina and Mexico to develop and support their public universities in accordance with their respective social contracts.

A Critical Discussion of Globalization

We operate within the tradition of critical theory. Accordingly, we believe that all inquiry is politically based and therefore that it is important for writers to clarify their basic theoretical positions (Habermas 1973; Horkheimer 1972; Marcuse 1972). With this said, the perspective we bring to our work seeks to challenge increasingly widespread views about the political economy of higher education. Such views tend to advance more privatized forms of higher education and have their roots in neoliberal economic beliefs and practices (Apple 2000). We believe that neoliberal assumptions underlie the dominant discourse of globalization and situate market-driven outcomes as the inevitable by-product of a rational and egalitarian process (Burbach 2001; Chomsky 1998; Morrow and Torres 2000; Went 2000). We use the cases of Argentina and Mexico—UBA and UNAM—to call such views into question and to suggest that neoliberalism is neither as rational nor as egalitarian as is often claimed.

At the heart of our argument is a belief that universities throughout Latin America exist within a complex and evolving environment shaped most forcefully by globalization. By globalization we speak of increasingly interdependent and sophisticated relationships among economies, cultures, institutions, and nation-states (Burbules and Torres 2000; Carnoy et al. 1993; Santos 2001, 2004). Such relationships challenge higher education leaders and policy makers in ways heretofore difficult to imagine, because the autonomy of the nation-state becomes compromised and the role of the university is increasingly aligned with market-driven interests (Morrow and Torres 2000; Rhoads 2003). Thus, although we see globalization taking on many forms, including the cultural, we center our analysis on the political economy of globalization and its growing influence on the Latin American university.

Most notably, universities take on increasing importance in the context of globalization (Morrow and Torres 2000). For example, universities play a key role in workforce preparation, economic development, scientific and technological innovation, and cross-cultural communication and exchange (Slaughter and Leslie 1997). Perhaps it is not coincidental, then, that as corporations increasingly globalize their operations, they too enter the business of higher education by offering their own degree and certificate programs. Thompson (2000) noted, for example, that such high-profile US corporations as Arthur Anderson, Federal Express, General Electric, and Motorola have established their own corporate universities. In addition, corporations have sought increased influence over scientific research as they create partnerships with universities to advance their own research and development interests (Slaughter and Leslie 1997). In fact, growing corporate-sponsored research ties have led some higher education analysts to raise concerns about conflicts of interest (Campbell and Slaughter 1999). In the United States, for example, the American Association of University Professors has called for faculty to play a key role in creating policies to guard against such conflicts (Lively 2001).

Global economics and higher education are intersecting in other provocative ways as well. Several Latin American countries, including Argentina and Mexico, have faced economic pressure to reduce public expenditures for higher education as part of structural adjustment policies mandated by the IMF. Structural adjustments are called for so that these countries might increase financial support for global trade initiatives while furthering a more competitive and costly university admissions policy (Rhoads and Mina 2001). Consequently, structural adjustments can be seen as running counter to other economic development needs generated by global trends—such as the need to expand access to higher education to elevate educational levels of the workforce and thereby attract foreign capital (Boron and Torres 1996; Carnoy and Rhoten 2002; Stiglitz 2002).

Understanding the political economy of globalization is vital to advancing higher education throughout Latin America. Arguably, no social or cultural force has come to shape the political economy of globalization in more forceful ways than neoliberal economic views (Chomsky 1998; Stiglitz 2002). Neoliberalism is framed by a vision of the weak state and a form of economic rationality that suggests that free markets and the transnational flow of capital ought to take precedence over national autonomy (Apple 2000; Burbules and Torres 2000). The free flow of capital and goods across national boundaries has in part limited the ability of nation-states to act as societies. As Urry noted, "The widespread flows across societal borders makes it less easy for states to mobilize clearly separate and coherent nations in pursuit of societal goals" (1998, p. 7). Consequently, in the Americas, we witness increasing interconnections between markets and capital as legislative acts such as the North American Free Trade Agreement (NAFTA), Mercosur (a transnational trade agreement between Argentina, Brazil, Paraguay, and Uruguay), Fast Track, and numerous World Trade Organization (WTO) agreements (such as TRIPS [Trade Related Aspects of Intellectual Property], GATT [General Agreement on Tariffs and Trade], and GATS [General Agreement on Trade in Services]) challenge the ability of nation-states to regulate their own trade. The push toward neoliberal globalization is tied directly to a set of ideological convictions in which privatization is held as the ideal and publicly supported enterprises face increased scrutiny. And, of course, as state-supported enterprises, public universities become targets of neoliberal scrutiny and the general advance of privatization.

At the global level neoliberal economic policies are largely advanced by multinational enterprises (MNEs) and are regulated by intergovernmental organizations (IGOs), such as the WTO, the IMF, the World Bank, and supercourts (e.g., the NAFTA Chapter 11 tribunals). As MNEs and IGOs increase in power and influence, the ability of nation-states to influence problems that affect the lives and circumstances of their own citizens is greatly diminished, because the interests of global corporate players take priority (Rhoads 2003). As Burbules and Torres pointed out, "Neoliberal restructuring is operating through the impersonal dynamic of capitalist competition in a progressively deregulated common market, enhancing the local impact of global trends. Nation-states have become increasingly internationalized, in the sense that their agencies and policies become adjusted to the rhythms of the new world order" (2000, p. 7). Similarly, Carnoy saw a fundamental conflict between the means and ends of the nation-state and private MNEs: "The existence of potential conflict means that the market mechanism is not an acceptable form of conflict resolution. If it were acceptable, the nation-state would allow international market prices to allocate resources worldwide, even if that were detrimental to its own citizens. Neither would the state attempt to subsidize various economic (or economy-enhancing) activities on national soil" (1993, p. 47).

Democratic nations thrive on the basis of a plurality of individuals, groups, and organizations contributing to publicly negotiated definitions of the social good. However, the dominant view of globalization, as framed by neoliberalism, lends itself to private companies and capital-driven interests that dominate the public sphere to such an extent that democracy itself is threatened (Chomsky 1998). This shift is evident in the increasing influence of IGOs, NGOs (nongovernmental organizations), and MNEs in setting public policy, especially as such policies pertain to economic development and international relations.

Neoliberal globalization and the politics associated with such a movement are fraught with contradictory claims. Take, for example, the United States and its role in advocating free-market policies while embracing protectionist strategies for its own key industries such as steel, lumber, and agriculture. During the early part of 2002 the United States imposed trade restrictions on both steel and lumber to protect these industries from foreign competitors. In addition, in May 2002 the US Senate passed a farm bill, later approved by President Bush, that would raise agricultural subsidies roughly 80 percent over a 10-year period to $180 billion (Hartcher 2002). Subsidies serve to keep prices down while keeping US farmers in business. Subsidies essentially have the same effect as imposing trade duties on foreign agricultural products. The consequence for smaller countries seeking to sell rice, cotton, corn, wheat, soybeans, and other commodities to US consumers is devastating. Thus, while economic power houses such as the United States push lesser developed countries to open their markets and customers to US-produced goods, the US takes full advantage of powerful structures that restrict access to its own markets, thereby propping up key industries. Consequently, US industries are far more likely to compete successfully in a global arena than those in Argentina and Mexico. None too surprisingly, representatives of both Argentina and Mexico voiced serious concerns about the 2002 US farm bill: Argentina joined Brazil in considering charges to be heard by the WTO, and the Mexican economy minister argued that the United States contradicted trade policies that its own political and economic leaders pushed on the rest of the world ("Mexico Sees" 2002; "South America" 2002). Given that agricultural commodities account for roughly 50 percent of its exports, Argentina has been especially hard hit by US protectionism ("South America" 2002).

But agriculture is merely one example. Our larger point is that the power imbalance between the United States and its Latin American neighbors has the potential to create a relationship of dependency, or worse yet, to lead to such economic blight that some Latin American countries "will not even be considered worth the trouble of exploitation; they will become inconsequential, of no interest to the developing, globalized economy" (Cardoso 1993, p. 156).

The US steel industry is another example. During the early part of 2002 the United States placed trade duties on steel. These duties eventually were challenged by the European Union (EU) and its executive body, the European Commission. The EU threatened sanctions of US goods and made a formal request to the WTO. Threats by the EU ultimately led to a relatively fair resolution in this instance, but no serious analyst would be so naïve to suggest that such trade debates typically are resolved through apolitical egalitarian processes. So, although powerhouses such as the United States and the EU may neutralize one another's political and economic influence, what is to come of trade disagreements between the United States or the EU and the likes of Argentina, Mexico, or Brazil?

Trade debates are not resolved on principle alone. Issues of power and influence clearly are shaping globalization and so-called free trade. And so it seems that free trade is not really free trade after all. As Martin Khor, founder of the Third World Network explained, "The WTO is about free trade *and* protectionism at the same time. It's about a double standard that continues to protect rich countries against products that poor countries are good at exporting" (Cooper 2002, p. 13). Chomsky made a similar point in *Profit over People*, when he criticized Lakoff's (1996) assertion that the primary barriers to advancing democracy in Latin America are efforts to protect domestic markets: "We are to understand, then, that democracy is enhanced as significant decision making shifts even more into the hands of unaccountable tyrannies, mostly foreign-based. Meanwhile the public arena is to shrink still further as the state is 'minimized' in accordance with the neoliberal political and economic principles that have emerged triumphant" (Chomsky 1998, p. 95).

Obviously, heightened global relations have been fueled by communication and technological advances that have in essence shrunk time and space and made complex social networks possible (Castells 1993, 1997; Urry 1998). The growth of transnational interconnections led Castells (1997) to use the phrase "network society" to describe the influence that computers, technology, and advanced communication systems have had on nations around the world. Castells characterized the global network society by strategic economic activities, networking forms of organization, flexible and unstable forms of work, and the individualization of labor.

From the perspective of the network society, few institutions play a more pivotal role than institutions of higher learning. We say this because of the major role universities play in technological and scientific development as well as workforce preparation. But although universities play a key role in today's global economic environment, this is not to suggest that such institutions experience increased financial support from nations and states. In fact, the trends associated with neoliberal globalization may lead to just the opposite. For example, universities throughout the Americas face declining public funding while expectations about their role in serving the larger social good may actually be increasing (Breneman 1993; Morrow and Torres 2000; Slaughter and Leslie 1997; Torres and Schugurensky 2002). This is one of the paradoxes of globalization: As societies increasingly demand a highly educated and skilled workforce to compete in a global marketplace, educational institutions must contend with diminished financial support as revenue is transferred from public services to privatized endeavors (Boron and Torres 1996).

As a consequence of declining state support, many university leaders have turned to entrepreneurial activities consistent with the ideals of neoliberalism, leaving others to wonder if the mission of the public university is endangered by corporate-driven interests and demands (Rhoads 2003). The turn toward entrepreneurial activity has brought with it a central focus on markets and the university as a highly competitive economic enterprise in what Slaughter and Leslie (1997) described as "academic capitalism." With the push toward privatization, unlikely bedfellows arise as IGOs such as the WTO and the United Nations Educational, Scientific, and Cultural Organization (UNESCO) seek to have their say in shaping higher education economic activity.

State-supported universities also face the challenge of operating in an environment in which nation-states are increasingly losing their ability to determine their own destiny as the "invisible hand of a changing global economy" takes control (Carnoy et al. 1993, p. 3). Consequently, state-supported universities, as extensions of public policy, exist in a chaotic age in which nation-states seem to lack the power and influence to adequately support such "public good" enterprises. Given the growing economic pressures on the university, what is to become of democratic notions of the public good as nation-states increasingly lose their autonomy relative to global economic initiatives driven by economic and political elites?

Significant evidence points to a turn toward entrepreneurial models as the quest for private sources of support grows (Clark 2000, 2001; Slaughter and Rhoades 2004). For example, intellectuals are increasingly pressed to contribute to economic and technological development, and those who cannot—typically faculty and graduate students operating in the social sciences and humanities—are relegated to second-class status (Rhoads and Rhoades 2005). Related to this, one also sees significant differences in resource allocation patterns across disciplines, depending on the revenue-generating potential of particular fields (Slaughter 1998). With increased partnering between universities and private sector forces, we see significant ethical questions revolving around conflicts of interest (Anderson 2001; Blumenthal et al. 1996; Campbell and Slaughter 1999). This is a likely outcome as faculty research, teaching, and service steadily become commodities for sale on the open market (Altbach 2001). Evidence of the commodification of academic work includes the sophisticated efforts of universities to monitor faculty research in science and technology fields as institutions seek lucrative patents and license agreements (Blumenstyk 2002).

From an entrepreneurial university model, students and corporations are seen in similar ways: as prospective consumers of products developed and produced by faculty working for their respective universities. A concern to be addressed by critical scholars is the degree to which market forces reflect the diverse and democratically rooted values and goals of education and the social good that publicly supported institutions traditionally have been chartered to serve (Carnoy and Levin 1985; Torres 2002). In other words, what is lost as universities increasingly turn to globally driven free-market views of higher education, and what becomes of the public good? In addition, in what manner might universities respond to a rapidly evolving economic and political environment shaped to a large degree by global corporate forces, IGOs, and NGOs?

With the preceding in mind, our argument is relatively straightforward: We have entered a new era of global higher education, and such a change requires serious economic, policy, and organizational analysis. From a comparative perspective such analysis ought to involve serious-minded discussions with key faculty, administrators, and policy makers. Consequently, in what follows we share findings derived from interviews we conducted with key personnel affiliated with the University of Buenos Aires and the National Autonomous University of Mexico.

The University of Buenos Aires

The University of Buenos Aires (UBA) was founded in 1821 and is located in the heart of Argentina's largest and most cosmopolitan city. With a student enrollment of nearly 200,000 students, UBA is by far the country's largest university. A member of the League of World Universities, UBA follows a programmatic structure that includes the following major schools: law and social sciences, economic sciences, exact and natural sciences, meteorology, architecture, philosophy and letters, engineering, medicine, agriculture, dentistry, pharmacy and biochemistry, veterinary sciences, psychology, and social sciences.

UBA is emblematic of the democratic ideals of higher education, offering a high degree of access to the poor and lower-middle classes. With its open door policy, minimal fees, and coverage of the most advanced segments of science and technology in the country, UBA is the flagship of higher education in the Southern Cone (more or less the southern half of South America). As one of the oldest universities in the region, it reflects more than most Latin American institutions the Napoleonic tradition of serving the state through the preparation and training of public servants. Ironically, the vast majority of contemporary Argentine elites who now advocate privatization were in fact educated at UBA.

We visited UBA in the spring of 2002 with one of us spending two months in the city as part of a sabbatical. Consequently, we were able to observe events in Argentina and Buenos Aires over an extended period of time. In addition, because one member of our research team is a citizen of Argentina and has numerous connections to professors and high-ranking officials affiliated with UBA and the Ministry of Education, we gained access to several key individuals. For example, we were able to interview the following people: a leading Argentine economist and professor at UBA; the secretary of academic affairs at UBA; the secretary of university policies at the Ministry of Education; the secretary of technology, science, and innovation and president of the National Council of Scientific and Technical Investigations (CONICET); a leading Argentine scholar at UBA specializing in higher education; and an engineering professor well known for his administrative expertise in higher education. Interviews with the preceding individuals were tape-recorded and transcribed verbatim and form the basis for the key themes discussed in this section (most were translated from Spanish to English).

Our discussions with key analysts centered on the changing political and economic context for public universities in Argentina with a particular focus on globalization and its implications for UBA. Of course, the economic crisis loomed large and was as inescapable as the pounding from the nightly *cacerolazos*—groups of protesters who marched through the streets of Buenos Aires beating on pots and pans. The days following the economic collapse in December 2001 saw thousands of Argentines take to the streets of the nation's capital. Demonstrations were aimed at the Argentine government's decision to place restrictions on bank accounts to avoid a run on cash withdrawals, as citizens and investors lost faith in the country's banking system. Protesters also directed their anger at the IMF, which many believed had led Argentina down a path to economic disaster by forcing debt reductions, cutbacks in social programs, the privatization of state enterprises, and the deregulation of commerce. Such strategies, although often supported by society's economic elites, tend to produce higher rates of unemployment and eliminate a variety of social support structures just when they are needed most. None too surprisingly, the result is civil unrest and increased economic turmoil.

Argentine president Nestor Kirchner, sworn into office in May 2003, pointed to more than a decade of failed policies imposed on Argentina by the IMF as the primary source of the country's monumental poverty. An internal IMF report, *Lessons from the Crisis in Argentina*, produced more than two years after the collapse of the Argentine economy, acknowledged that the organization's policies had exacerbated the crisis:

> In light of the gravity of the crisis that unfolded while the country was engaged in a succession of IMF-supported programs it is not surprising that the Fund has come under harsh criticism for its involvement in Argentina. Indeed, with hindsight, the Fund—like most other observers—erred in its assessment of the Argentine economy by overestimating its growth potential and underestimating its vulnerabilities. These misjudgments resulted in IMF-supported programs that were insufficiently ambitious and excessively accommodative of slippages, particularly through 1998 when the economy was booming. . . . The most glaring omission was in the fiscal area, where the Fund condoned repeated slippages of debt and deficit targets. . . . In retrospect, it is also clear that the Fund-supported programs had insufficient structural content and conditionality, given that the currency board arrangements, together with the relatively small share of exports in the economy, put a premium on the flexibility and resilience of the domestic economy. (International Monetary Fund 2003, pp. 63–64)

Predictably, Kirchner thought that the IMF's self-criticism was too little too late: "But I think the IMF has to bear in mind that it is publishing this mea culpa 10 to 15 years after the events and that the damage it's left us with in Argentina is 15 million people or more living in poverty" (BBC 2004). As recently as 1998, the IMF had invited then-president Carlos Menem to address its annual meeting, when, according to Kirchner, it was becoming more and more apparent that IMF-backed policies were pushing the Argentine economy closer and closer to disaster (BBC 2004).

In terms of higher education and support for UBA, the economic crisis produced drastic cuts to public institutions and services. Such cuts followed already established reductions, as the Argentine government decreased its support for higher education throughout the 1990s under the direction of the World Bank (Puiggrós 1999) and in keeping with structural adjustment programs of the IMF. Both the World Bank and the IMF have prescribed reduced spending on social programs combined with a shifting of funds from secondary and postsecondary education to primary schooling. Such a shift undermines the ability of Argentina to produce an adequate supply of educated professionals and scientists. Furthermore, funds that were available for institutions such as UBA often came attached with new mechanisms for measuring the performance of teachers, researchers, and students, as part of a cost-benefit analysis that was of questionable utility in an academic context (Puiggrós 1999). Consequently, budget cuts combined with poorly planned evaluative interventions added to morale problems at Argentine universities such as UBA.

Clearly, the economic context of Argentina and its place within a rapidly changing global economy establishes the context for an analysis of UBA. Although one might claim that the economic crisis "slanted" our findings in the spring of 2002, it could just as easily be argued that the crisis served as a powerful lens for focusing on globalization and the changing role of the public university. Given the proximal nature of the economic collapse, thoughts and passions ran high among UBA faculty and staff. No one could have expected otherwise.

THE ECONOMIC CRISIS AND THE NEED FOR REFORM

Much of our interactions centered on the role of globalization in shaping the contemporary context for the Argentine public university. In general, globalization was viewed as an imposition by outside forces mainly acting on the Argentine economy. In fact, some interviewees described globalization as a form of "economic colonialism" sanctioned by the United States. As one professor explained, "Globalization to us means economic hegemony from the North in terms of providing the sole model to be adopted by the nations of the globe." This individual went on to describe a research team that she is part of and their efforts to make sense of globalization and its impact on universities. She noted that within the research group there is a strong tendency to see "globalization as Americanization"; that is, the group believes that many of the transnational economic policies supposedly designed to open up world markets actually serve the interests of powerful policy makers located in countries such as the United States.

A key point stressed by several individuals was the fact that, although globalization may be inevitable, it does not necessarily produce homogeneous results. That is, global forces interact with local realities, and the consequences vary from one country to the next. "Globalization," explained one individual, "is a very powerful wind that will be blowing with great intensity for the foreseeable future. But the impact of globalization in Argentina, though, largely depends on domestic factors. . . . Globalization is an objective force in history, but the concrete effects are filtered by the local political, cultural, and economic situations. One effect may be felt in a country like Mexico. A different effect may be seen in Argentina or Korea or Taiwan."

Several interview participants criticized forms of globalization advanced by powerful IGOs such as the World Bank and the IMF. One expert found it more than interesting that several years ago, when he had argued that international agencies were driving Argentina's public policies, he had received a great deal of criticism, but now things have changed. As he explained, "Nowadays, no one, not even right-wing scholars, have a single doubt about the international impact on national and local productivity, because the IMF is deciding our daily lives, and there is no doubt about the impact and the consequence of this." This individual went on to add, "It's interesting to realize that all we have published, all we have said, all of a sudden is just the most cruel truth that we are dealing with, that we are totally dependent on what leaders within the IMF think of us." The irony, of course, is that former president Menem had been recognized by the IMF as one of its most faithful followers. "So, we were the model for the rest of the world. . . . We were doing exactly what they asked of us."

Others were just as skeptical of IGOs and their involvement in Argentina's economic collapse. One individual thought that the objective of the World Bank and the IMF is quite clear: to make sure that Argentina will have enough budgetary surplus to honor its foreign debt. "They are not concerned with any other thing, especially the IMF. The World Bank may have some other broader concerns, but the IMF is just a bank and it wants to have its money back. And, of course, this will increase the influence of free markets in Argentina, and when you talk about free markets, you are talking about monopolies. The term 'free market' is just a cover for the real aim—monopoly."

Directives from IGOs may add to funding problems faced by UBA. There is a strong push to decrease public support, despite the country's historical commitment to free public higher education. One expert described a movement sponsored by major financial institutions, including the World Bank, to advance the privatization of higher education: "There are powerful people saying that university education should not be public. Or, if it is public, one should have to pay for it. The idea that the university is for elites is becoming increasingly popular. . . . Structural adjustment policies imposed upon the country over the past 15 to 20 years are pushing the idea that the university is something that should be privatized and the state should not be involved. These policies suggest that we should be devoting our resources to elementary and high school education. Forget the university. This movement is growing stronger by the hour."

Despite financial problems, the dominant perception seems to be that even when economic recovery arrives, the degree to which the government will support its public universities raises major concerns. This has led to serious questions about the future of state-supported universities in Argentina. One expert explained that forces are at work to fundamentally alter the identity of the Argentine university, to "basically reflect the American model and see the market as the driving force for the university." As this individual pointed out, such a view suggests that the purpose of the university is to transform human resources to match the labor market. This perspective clashes with UBA and its European-style model, in which the university prepares "professionals to occupy the civil sector and meet broad public needs."

Nearly everyone acknowledged that major reforms may be needed at UBA and other state-supported universities. One individual suggested that Argentine universities should have been reformed in the 1970s, when universities in Mexico and Brazil were reformed. "The Argentinean university began to reform, too, but the military coup interrupted that. So, after the coup, reform did not continue. All we saw was the liberalization of the political life of the university. Thus the Argentinean university arrives at the age of globalization without having solved the preglobalization problems that it had." Given the importance that universities play in processes linked to globalization, Argentina clearly faces a difficult challenge.

The problem is a catch-22. Experts recognize the need to restructure the public university, but current economics necessitate a survival mode. University reform is unlikely when meeting the next payroll is a challenge. Consequently, economic woes are preventing UBA from addressing reforms considered important for its vitality. As one individual explained, "This emergency budget situation impedes us from attending to the university's central problems and keeps us from making the changes that we need to make, such as the rigidity of degree and course requirements, the low rate of graduation, and the high rate of dropping out, principally in the first year."

ACCESS TO HIGHER EDUCATION

In addition to conversations about globalization as a force imposed on Argentina, discussions also highlighted globalization as an opportunity. Unfortunately, most experts saw Argentine universities as ill-prepared to take advantage of global trends. For example, much of the discussion about UBA's participation in the country's global initiatives centered on structural problems that limit the university's contributions. Structural problems include lack of access to higher education, particularly among low-income Argentines, and lack of adequate support for faculty in general and scientific investigation in particular. The lack of support raised issues about connections between the university and industry.

A key aspect of a country's economic development and its ability to compete in a global environment is the development and support of a highly skilled workforce (Reich 1991). But this is a major challenge in Argentina because of the lack of a strong educational structure undergirding the development of human capital. For example, although attendance at public universities in Argentina is free, the reality is that few Argentines from low-income backgrounds are likely to attend a university. As one individual explained, "Access is a key question. I believe that the public university, although it is free, doesn't help the poor. It's very simple. The university students we have are not the children of laborers. It's hard for them to get to the university, even though it's public and free." A major part of the problem is attrition at the precollege level. A faculty member explained the problem in the following manner: "If you take 100 students at, say, first grade, what you will find is that the number of people who finally make it to a university and graduate is less than 4. So, there is very little access, because there is dramatic attrition at the very initial levels of the primary system. So, the university is essentially an elitist university, although not all of the people who are there are members of the elite. At best, it is a middle-class phenomenon. The poor do not make it to the university. The poor desert the system, and we can never recover them."

One expert suggested that a solution to the problem rests with a revision of the Argentine tax system. Argentina relies too much on indirect taxes, taxes to the consumer, he explained. Consequently, taxation does not impact people in relation to their earnings. Therefore lower-income sectors of the population pay proportionally more than higher-income sectors. And given that the higher-income sectors are more likely to receive a quality education and to go on to attend a free public university, they benefit disproportionately from public revenues. This individual suggested that the solution is to adjust the burden of taxation and provide necessary educational services and support to where they are most needed—among the poorest sectors of the society in the form of improved primary and secondary education and financial assistance for university studies.

Another individual supported a similar notion and used the phrase "democratic debt" to describe the need for Argentine society to see education as a necessity for its entire population. This individual suggested that globalization demands that a society increase, not decrease, its investment in education, including higher education. This expert thought that Argentina's democratic reforms had not been translated into educational policies: "In the last 20 years, Argentina moved from authoritarian rule to a democratic government. However, there was not a corresponding movement with regard to public policies. In other words, we have the dictatorship, a military dictatorship, which did not pay any attention to higher education. And then we have democracy in which there should be a shift in the public agenda in favor of science, scientific development, and higher education, but there was none." As part of the democratization of the university, many policies and practices need to be reformed, at least according to this individual. There is a need to build closer ties to communities, agencies, companies, and respective employers. In general, universities need to reframe their curricula to better match the needs of a democratic society.

Although the recent economic crisis has exacerbated problems, the reality is that the Argentine public university offers marginal economic support for faculty work. One individual stated the problem succinctly: "Salaries are very low, a little lower than those in Mexico and Brazil. Today, a full-time professor with seniority can be paid about 2,000 pesos a month [roughly US$670]." As a consequence, many professors have other careers; they simply cannot survive as full-time professors. There are many "taxicab professors," noted one person. "People are always traveling between jobs. They want to be exemplary professors, but they just don't have the time. They have other work to do."

Despite the lack of adequate financial support, the basic teaching functions of the university are maintained by a tradition in which teaching is viewed as a form of public service. In essence, many professors at Argentine universities see their teaching as a contribution to the larger social good. One individual said it best: "There is a cultural element that helps to sustain the function of the university system; that is, there is a long ingrained tradition which says that the university and the teaching activities in this country are akin to the work of a missionary. So, many people think that, 'Well, if I get paid, great, but if I don't, that's ok, because I have to spread the word.' The problem is that this goes against the general tendency that we see overseas and in most countries in Latin America in which you have full-time professors." It was pointed out that although the tradition of teaching as public service certainly is admirable and the sentiment worthy of preservation, running a university based on part-time professors may limit its intellectual vitality.

In the Argentine university the research and teaching functions are somewhat separate, with research often occurring in university institutes and centers and teaching taking place in academic departments. Thus, although it may be possible to support academic programs with part-time "missionary-minded" faculty, this is less likely to work with regard to the research function. Consequently, and in light of marginal economic support, the Argentine university in general and UBA in particular face serious challenges in developing and sustaining scientists and scientific investigation. One individual pointed out that Argentina lacks an internal structure to support scientists and their research. Instead, they must rely almost entirely on external funds simply to maintain an infrastructure. "Argentina cannot maintain an infrastructure for scientific development. It can't pay their salaries and fund their research. . . . We need a structure that permits a scientist to conduct his research, exchange ideas with colleagues, and pays him well enough to live decently, not wealthily, but with dignity." This individual pointed out that without such a structure Argentina loses some of its top scientists to other countries.

A point of concern is the need to look past the current economic crisis toward Argentina's long-range future. What is needed, maintained one individual, is to "give greater attention to developing intellect." He added, "The only way to export value is to cultivate intellect in the university and to support research, innovation, and put that creativity into the products that the country can sell." This individual went on to point out that Argentina presently produces about 500 doctoral graduates in all the sciences every year and that 30,000 may be needed over the next 10 years. Another expert in this area suggested that for every dollar invested, Argentina would get three back. This individual also noted that legislation recently had been passed to increase support for science and technology, but the economic crisis made it impossible to provide the funds to the universities.

Of course, several processes of political fragmentation are involved here. Perhaps we can explain it best with an anecdote. Years ago one of us was having dinner with the newly elected dean of the prestigious Faculty of Social Sciences at UBA. The dean complained about how difficult his job was. He explained, for example, that there were more than 100 courses of specialized sociology taught by many part-time professors who earn virtually no money but fight hard to keep their positions for political reasons—status, control of the curriculum, and so forth. The dean was asked why he did not undertake curriculum reform—cut the excessive courses of specialization, consolidate them by one-third, and create full-time positions for professors to devote their full effort to instruction and research. The answer was interesting: "The university is a house of cards. It is all about political alliances. If you take one card off the skeleton, the whole building collapses."

CONNECTIONS TO INDUSTRY

A final theme that yielded some contentious results concerns the role of industry in supporting scientific development at public universities such as UBA. Some of the experts we interviewed thought that building such connections is necessary, given the lack of state support for public universities. Others, however, saw university-industry partnerships as antithetical to a democratic university. A supporter of university-industry connections explained the need in this manner: "A crucial goal is to form a new alliance between scientific and technological research and industry. Globalization and the knowledge society force us to look at this fundamental connection. If not, Argentina will be in the same position it was in during the 1980s. We cannot survive as exporters of commodities and importers of technology."

Although one often hears complaints in the United States, especially from the left, that universities are too tied to corporate industry interests, the case is much different at UBA. In fact, a few of the individuals with whom we spoke complained of a lack of connection between the university and outside interests, including the interests of the business community. As one colleague noted, "While in the US one might complain about corporatization, in Argentina the opposite problem may in fact exist. In Argentina I would say that the dominant idea is that the university is an autonomous body, because we had to struggle for many years against political intrusion. Thus a strong tradition has formed in which university life is to be something entirely autonomous. The result of this is very, very low levels of connection with firms and even with the community." Perhaps the one exception here has been the serious efforts undertaken by the Faculty of Extension at UBA to connect with communities in diverse ways, to link technology transfer to different communities, to teach literacy, and so forth.

Forging university-industry partnerships is complicated in Argentina. In fact, any discussion of university-industry connections must begin with at least some mention of the historical relevance of university autonomy and the powerful beliefs about universities operating independently of external forces (the 1918 Córdoba Reform played a key role in advancing the autonomy of Latin American universities). One individual with whom we spoke was particularly disturbed by increasing connections between universities and corporations: "Nowadays, corporatization is totally overwhelming the purposes of universities. So, for students there is no possibility of demanding some kind of public specialties. Like, for instance, if you look at architecture; there is no urban architecture anymore because it is not marketable. The same thing happens if you look at lawyers and doctors; there is no public health, and it used to be really, very important. . . . The definition for me to best explain exactly what marketization is: It is the privatization of minds. You are being prepared to belong to corporate enterprises."

One expert argued that whereas in many modern societies universities have adapted and played a major role in globalization, Argentine universities have not kept pace with a changing global structure and now find themselves as relatively anachronistic. But this individual noted that there is still room for optimism: "To me, what is a wonderful indicator that our universities are still universities, even though their identities are in transit, is the fact that we are still discussing our problems in the university. We are discussing how to teach better, how to recruit students, how to get more participation in our province. So, we are dealing with our issues internally."

Our discussions with key faculty, staff, and policy makers at UBA revealed key issues linked to the economic crisis in Argentina, the need for higher education reform, access to higher education, faculty work and scientific support, and connections to industry. These issues all surfaced in the context of discussions about globalization and the challenges confronting Argentine society. Because similar sets of issues arose through our work in Mexico, we next present findings from our case study of UNAM, and then conclude with a comparison of the important issues linked to both UBA and UNAM.

The National Autonomous University of Mexico

The National Autonomous University of Mexico is centered in Mexico City, although it also maintains research sites throughout the country (UNAM also has three extension programs in the United States and Canada). UNAM is a complex array of preparatory, undergraduate, graduate, and technical schools and research institutes. It serves nearly 300,000 students and involves approximately 30,000 academic personnel. Programmatically, UNAM is composed of many *facultades* (similar to schools or large academic departments) that operate somewhat independently. Included among the *facultades* are the following: architecture, political and social sciences, administration and accounting, law, economics, philosophy and letters, engineering, medicine, sciences, veterinary and zoological medicine, psychology, and chemistry. Other disciplinary areas are centered in various *escuelas*, including the School of Music, the School of Art, and the School of Professional Studies. In addition, much of the research at UNAM, which accounts for roughly 50 percent of the country's university research, is conducted at research centers housed within institutes affiliated with the university. For example, the Institute of Scientific Investigation encompasses nearly 20 separate research centers focused on various natural science areas.

Officially founded in 1910, UNAM was granted autonomy from the government in 1929. With autonomy UNAM was to be funded by the federal government, but it was intended to operate politically independently from the state. However, autonomy from the federal government has never been fully realized. As Ordorika (1996, 2003) has pointed out in his work on reform at UNAM, federal intervention and political ties have long dominated the governance of the university. The lack of real autonomy has in part led over the years to numerous clashes among students, faculty, and administrators. In fact, major student movements have occurred at UNAM on several occasions, as students have sought to challenge institutional and societal practices through a variety of forms of resistance. These movements have not been inconsequential. For example, the 1968 student movement in Mexico City was a significant force in advancing democratic reform nationally (Ordorika 2003).

The 1999–2000 student movement at UNAM has particular relevance to this chapter. On April 20, 1999, students at UNAM claimed the campus as a response to the administration's efforts to institute significant tuition fees: The administration sought to raise undergraduate fees from less than 2 cents annually to US$120 (Maldonado-Maldonado 2002). Seizure of the campus lasted until February 6, 2000, when an estimated 2,400 federal police raided the campus and arrested some 1,000 striking students. The jailing of the students marked another bitter chapter in the history of UNAM and the ongoing efforts of students to preserve an accessible national university.

The student strike at UNAM was influenced by a complex set of circumstances, including shifting political allegiances (the dominance of the PRI was in question), difficult economic times, neoliberal restructuring, attempts to reform Mexican higher education, and a history of student insurgency (Casanova Cardiel and Rodríguez Gómez 2000; Domínguez Martínez and Pérez Cruz 2000; Rhoads and Mina 2001). Of particular interest here is the role of the IMF in pressuring the Mexican government to reduce subsidies for higher education and increase user fees (tuition fees). The administration of UNAM, many of whom were appointed or supported by the Mexican ruling party (the PRI), essentially supported the government's decision to reduce subsidies by attempting to institute higher tuition fees, a change that likely would have eliminated postsecondary educational opportunities for countless Mexican citizens. Many students reacted passionately to what they saw as an attack on Mexican sovereignty by international banking agencies and oppressive governmental policies rooted in neoliberal economics. The Consejo General de Huelga (CGH), the strike's governing body, explained its position in the Mexican political magazine, *Proceso*:

> The past two decades have represented for UNAM and the country a confrontation with the neoliberal project that in concrete terms has signified the imposition of commercialized criteria throughout the entire scope of national life, a competition to the death in a savage version of social Darwinism. . . . The imposition of this model has signified a gradual loss of rights obtained through other social movements and established in the Constitution, such as the right to education, health, housing, employment, and sustenance; in summary, the right to a dignified life. (1999, p. 17)

The CGH went on to argue, "At the international level, the defense of public education leads to student movements, principally in Latin America, although these struggles still occur in an isolated manner. But all of them have the same objective: to curb the offensive that seeks to privatize education" (1999, p. 17).

UNAM students were able to successfully resist tuition increases as a result of the 1999–2000 strike. Their struggle was one more example of how the "one size fits all" strategies of organizations such as the IMF can at times contribute to social instability in countries such as Mexico (keep in mind that the IMF was "supposedly" founded in part to contribute to global "stability"). This lesson of the student strike was not lost on many of the individuals with whom we interacted during two visits conducted in June 2002 and March 2003.

The student strike of 1999–2000 thus provides a backdrop to our visits to UNAM. As was the case with UBA, we interviewed key faculty, administrators, and policy makers who we believed could shed light on the political and economic challenges confronting UNAM in particular and state-supported higher education in general. The interviews were tape-recorded and transcribed verbatim (once again those conducted in Spanish were translated into English). Included among our interviewees are the following key individuals: the rector (president) of UNAM, the minister of education under former Mexican president Ernesto Zedillo Ponce de León, the director of the Center for Studies of the University (roughly equivalent to an institutional research office), and five highly esteemed research faculty at UNAM, all of whom specialize in the study of higher education. What follows is a discussion of the key themes that emerged from our interviews.

SUPPORT FOR PUBLIC HIGHER EDUCATION

Questions of access so prevalent in our interviews at UBA were not nearly as pressing at UNAM. In part, this reflects the reality that such issues were debated relatively recently with the attempted tuition hikes and the subsequent year-long student strike of 1999–2000. It seems fairly clear that raising tuition at UNAM is quite difficult, given the antipathy generated among students. Consequently, financial problems at UNAM were discussed primarily in terms of the degree to which the national government would support faculty at UNAM and other public universities.

For the past two decades Mexico has been wrestling with the question of how much support is needed to adequately fund public universities. In the 1980s and early 1990s cuts were made to public higher education as a response to two conditions: an economic downturn caused by drops in crude oil prices and structural adjustments advanced by the IMF and the World Bank. Such cuts were challenging, if not devastating. In the past few years, however, the government has shown a renewed commitment to public higher education and, recently, under the Fox administration, pledged no more cuts.

But no one we interviewed suggested that current funding for public higher education is close to being adequate. The challenge is quite grave for some faculty, and most see Mexico at a crossroads in terms of developing a clear project for public higher education. One expert situated the overall challenge: "We all know that the costs of higher education are increasing at a very rapid pace and it may not be feasible for the state to assume all the weight of financing. On the other hand, we also need to have a very clear social pact with regard to responsibilities. What are the responsibilities of the state? What are the responsibilities of the universities? What are the responsibilities of the legislature?" This individual went on to argue that Mexico needs to develop a national policy that defines the future of public higher education. "If this doesn't occur in the near future, I foresee public universities faltering very badly due to insufficient funds. I do not think we can follow the models of the United States where almost everything has been left up to the markets."

To understand the needs of public higher education in Mexico, one must recognize the nature of the social contract between the government and the citizens and the role of the national university. There are far-reaching expectations of UNAM compared to public universities in the United States. UNAM not only provides half the country's university research and educates well over 200,000 students but also runs the nation's seismological system, the National Library (roughly equivalent in the United States to the Library of Congress), the National Botanical Garden, and institutions comparable in scope to the Smithsonian and the National Observatory. As one individual explained, "UNAM has assumed these responsibilities as part of its role as the national university. There is no such parallel in the US." Consequently, when international banking organizations such as the IMF seek to impose financial cuts on public higher education, they fail to comprehend the fact that the Mexican model of higher education is different from that of the United States.

HIGHER EDUCATION REFORM AND NEOLIBERALISM

A major concern raised throughout most of our interviews was the imposition of a US-based neoliberal model of higher education. Imposition came as a result of structural adjustments as well as at the hands of Mexico's own leaders, some of whom seem intent on reshaping the country's social and economic relations based on a US perspective. One expert talked about

UNAM's student strike of 1999 and pointed out that the tuition increase sought by former rector Francisco Barnés would not have amounted to more than 3 percent of the university's budget. "It was not an issue about the budget of UNAM. It was not going to make a big difference. The problem was, in my opinion, the fact that the tuition increase was brought up at a difficult moment in Mexican life, at a time when many people believed that free education was a social right, and that the general policies that are set up by the international financial institutions run counter to this important social right." This individual went on to explain that in many countries, especially in Latin America, there is a long-standing tradition, a social contract, in which the state is expected to provide public services such as health and education. "But some of the international financing institutions have not been very clear about these social contracts; they haven't recognized that social contracts have a history, they have a background, they represent many things for many countries. And this has been part of the problem. To what extent can it be said, even if it comes from the World Bank, that states should not fund free higher education? Why not?" This individual further commented that international agencies need to understand the social history of a given society; they cannot blindly assume that "the nation-state is an old conception and that we have to leave everything up to the market."

Another expert explained that since the 1980s, when it became clear that Mexico did not have the capacity to pay its foreign debt to the World Bank and the IMF, the influence of globalization has increased in Mexico. "Now we are not entirely in control of our own fate but must follow neoliberal principles of economics as dictated by the international banking agencies. One of the major shifts then relates to the role of the public; within a neoliberal context there is very little sense of the public. What we see then is a very strong sense of individualism, a free-market mentality. So, the sense of public education has changed, and it is affecting public universities, since we exist within a public sphere that in fact may be disappearing."

One way that global trade organizations affect the Mexican university is through accreditation efforts. As one expert explained, "In the context of world commerce, and more specifically GATS, a liberalization of the commercial aspects of higher education is being promoted. The propositions of accreditation act to create limits such that only the programs or universities that are nationally accredited can participate. In this sense, accreditation can operate as a counterforce to economic opportunities, unless, of course, a university agrees to construct its programs and policies in ways that are compatible with the dictates of multilateral organizations such as the World Bank and the Organization for Economic Cooperation and Development (OECD). So, there is a real tension here: accreditation as a strategy to open global commerce and accreditation as a way of limiting which institutions get to participate." This individual also suggested that accreditation is interpreted by many within the Mexican academy as a threat to autonomy, given that external forces have increasing influence over a university's programs. There is significant disagreement with regard to this latter point. Some groups, such as physicians, lawyers, accountants, and veterinarians, see accreditation as a vehicle for increasing their participation in the global professional market. However, scholars in the natural sciences, social sciences, and humanities tend to be more skeptical, according to this expert. From the position of the skeptics, accreditation simply is being used to bring Mexican universities in line with a US-driven global vision.

As was the case in Argentina, some of the individuals with whom we spoke described globalization as "Americanization." That is, the analysts affiliated with UNAM saw reform efforts mirroring images of higher education in the United States. Here, individuals not only pointed to international organizations but also questioned Mexico's policy makers. As one individual noted, "Related to globalization is the idea of Americanization, and this has a major impact on Mexican higher education. You see, many of those in power in this country attended Harvard or Yale, and they have a very limited view of the US higher education system. You can ask one of them, 'How many universities are there in the US?' They will probably say Stanford, Harvard, UCLA, Chicago, maybe Princeton and Yale. They have no idea of the vastness of the US system, and so they simply want to recreate what they experienced at one of the world's most elite universities. This will not work for Mexico. Once again then we see how a model from another society not only is applied inappropriately to a different cultural context, but the model itself does not exist. The US higher education system is much more than Harvard and Yale." Additional analysts reinforced the notion that US models might be inappropriately applied to the Mexican context.

Still others noted that global processes that are supposed to help less developed countries likely benefit countries such as the United States in greater ways. An example one individual offered was the movement of scientists and scholars from the South to the North (this individual used the term "brain drain"); that is, Latin American countries are more likely to lose scholars to countries such as the United States and those in Europe than the other way around. Such a phenomenon is incredibly damaging to a country, like Mexico, that is seeking to compete in a global market.

Another concern linked to neoliberal globalization was the reality that the "public" aspect of universities such as UNAM is under siege. One expert argued that higher education is shifting from a "public"-oriented university to a more "private"-oriented university. "What I mean by this is that in the past it was understood that the university served the public, the social body. Now, there is a sense that even public universities must serve private sectors of our society. In the past, the role of the public came before the interests of private sectors. But globalization is creating common goals for all countries, whether they are similar or not." This individual went on to note that different economic traditions in the United States and in Latin America make the imposition of neoliberal policies in countries such as Mexico quite complex. "In Latin America, socialism and the notion of the government serving the social body, not simply ensuring free markets and the expansion of capital, have been influential. But what we see now are global processes acting on Latin American countries in a manner that reflects the project of the US and its free-market capitalist-oriented economic views."

FACULTY SUPPORT AND ACCOUNTABILITY

Discussions of financial issues at UNAM and other public universities eventually turned to conversations and concerns about faculty accountability. Most policy analysts recognize the need to increase support for faculty in Mexico. As it stands now, professors at public universities must find ways of supplementing their salaries in order to live a reasonably comfortable lifestyle. Recent funding measures have been passed and adopted, but such measures link an increase in faculty support to accountability measures. Performance programs such as PRIDE (Programa de Primas al Desempeño del Personal Académico de Tiempo Completo) offer faculty the opportunity to increase their salary by as much as 100 percent. PRIDE covers a three-year period, and, to participate, faculty must agree to improve certain performance measures. Such measures might include the number of students graduated, publications, grants, and so forth. Thus, instead of offering across-the-board raises to an underfunded professorate, the government has linked increased salaries to accountability measures. In addition, research faculty have the option of joining SNI (Sistema Nacional de Investigadores), through which they can receive additional financial support. But there are problems with these incentive programs. As one research professor explained, "You can get one-third of your salary from the university, one-third from PRIDE, and one-third from Sistema Nacional de Investigadores. But you have to fill out tons of paperwork just to earn a reasonable salary. With these three programs and the behaviors that they encourage, we start to resemble the professors in the US. However, there is a big difference. We have to sustain a very high level of performance simply to elevate our salary to a decent wage, whereas in the US sustaining such high levels of productivity often results in elevating one's salary above the norm."

Faculty must compete for the incentive funds or else they have to take other work. What this all means is that the current structure is inadequate for meeting the basic needs of professors; as a consequence of the limited support and the structure of incentives, faculty must compete against one another for the basic funds needed to survive. It is not like the United States where one starts with a basic level of adequate support and then the research stars compete for the major grants and rewards. A faculty member pointed out that this form of accountability and efficiency is promoting a culture of competition: "It's destroying the collective identity that Mexican intellectuals have had in the past. So, it's changing the academic culture from one defined by a social collective to a group of individuals acting for their own interests." Another professor added, "The neoliberal shift is really evident around the sense of accountability and efficiency. Programs have been implemented to increase the efficiency and accountability within the public sectors, including institutions such as UNAM. We are slowly becoming an individualist society when at one time we were a mass society."

The push toward increased accountability is not disconnected from global events. One expert suggested that with structural adjustments came pressure to reduce higher education expenses and at the same time to be more accountable. The policies implemented in Mexico to support faculty follow the general neoliberal push to increase accountability and efficiency. A second individual elaborated: "It's not that accountability and efficiency are bad, but these policies have been implemented in such a way that public universities lose some of their autonomy, some of their control. If the government ultimately controls the programs that fund faculty and that evaluate faculty performance, how can universities remain autonomous? How can they be autonomous when they have to follow particular rules implemented by the government to receive funds through these programs?"

We also pursued questions about the possibility of building connections with industry as a means to support higher education. We wanted to get a sense of the degree to which university-industry partnerships had begun to shape Mexican public universities, if at all. Along these lines, some individuals saw little market for university science and research. As one expert noted, "There is no real market for university development and research. The most dynamic corporations and firms are transnational, and so they don't need the technology that our institutions would offer to them. They have their own technology centers in their own countries and sometimes work with these very prestigious universities in the US, France, and Germany. They have their own resources. There are only a few examples where Mexican companies turn to academic science." This individual went on to ponder why the public university does not develop a more advanced system of research and technology as a means of attracting corporate and industrial interest. He then answered his own question: "The answer is that we would need help from industry to build such an expensive infrastructure. It's cheaper in the short run for Mexican companies to buy technology from foreign companies than to invest in our university researchers."

Others commented on efforts to advance university-industry partnerships. A few noted that CONICET (Consejo Nacional de Investigaciones Científicas y Técnicas) is supposed to serve this goal, but it has been a tough road. There is significant mistrust between the business and industry sector and the university. One expert put it this way: "Academics say that they don't trust the corporations for fear they will lose their autonomy. On the other hand, the corporations will say that they can't trust academics to deliver, because they work at a different pace. Academics don't understand the time constraints that corporations and industries face. They don't understand how industry works, so they distrust academics. This mutual distrust constrains these types of relationships."

Another analyst commented on the national program to build bridges between universities and industry, as led by CONICET: "The national program of science and technology has clear goals to build stronger ties, bridges between universities and industry. But this process is going to take many years, 15 years at the very least. We are very deficient in this area. We have a lack of internal structure for science and technology, and universities need to play a bigger role. This is why we are becoming a *maquiladora* society—we don't have the capacity to conduct advanced science and technological work." Without a more advanced university infrastructure, scientific research tends to be basic in nature, more academically oriented. CONICET will continue to play a role, but as one individual pointed out, "CONICET has been supporting Ph.D.'s for the purpose of strengthening university research, but many of these individuals go to work in the private sector, because of the salary differential."

Although some faculty expressed concern about the possibility of greater ties between the university and various industries, they feared that such a trend is inevitable. Their concern centered on the declining notion of the "public," and the increasing dominance of the "private." One analyst commented, "In the past the national university—UNAM—engaged in scientific investigation for the society. Research was to serve the interests of the state, of the public. But now, within the context of globalization, when the state and national interests no longer dictate, then university science must answer to and address private, global enterprises." A second added, "The public is disappearing, and so what becomes of a university that has been defined by its service to the public? As a result of these circumstances, there is much pressure on UNAM to reform, to become more accountable to private global enterprises and be less oriented to the public." One individual saw the problem as a loss of national vision: "There is no national vision; from a neoliberal perspective there are only markets, and the logic of markets dictates everything. And so in Mexico, national culture, national identity, the role of the national university are all in transition. What will become of the university? Who knows. Can we generate a national project within an increasingly neoliberal society?"

Discussion

We do not dispute the historical reality of globalization. With dramatic changes in communication technology, information management, and transportation, international integration is inevitable. Consequently, we do not adopt an antiglobalization stance as much as we seek to challenge a particular strain of globalization that has come to dominate social and economic policies, including policies that shape public universities. Of course, we describe this strain as neoliberalism, or neoliberal globalization. More specifically, we take issue with the presumption that processes associated with US-led definitions of free markets and privatization are necessarily more rational and egalitarian than strategies linked to strong nation-states and self-determined public interests. In addition, we see public universities in countries such as Argentina and Mexico playing a key role in challenging the hegemony of neoliberalism and forging alternative visions of global affairs that are more compatible with long-standing social contracts. In this regard we support the idea conveyed by Burbules and Torres, who argued that as global changes occur, "they can change in different, more equitable, and more just ways" (2000, p. 2).

A telling point of our study is the fact that the critique of neoliberal globalization has clearly moved from the political left to the mainstream in both Argentina and Mexico. This is not an insignificant finding. For example, although a handful of our interview subjects are positioned on the intellectual left and thus one might expect them to be critical of neoliberalism, several of our subjects are located in the mainstream, at the center of university operations, and yet even these individuals offered serious criticism of neoliberal practices associated with globalization. It was apparent from many of the comments that the North-South separation of power has created much consternation about economic and cultural impositions from international banking agencies and the United States and that reservations about the potential soundness of neoliberal economic policies are no longer limited to a relatively small range of intellectuals.

Another significant finding points to the changing nature of the public, or the social, good that public universities historically have been charged with serving. As public universities increasingly become framed by market-driven practices, the traditional sense of a public good linked to communitarian and collectivist concerns shifts to more individualist, privatized interests. This same phenomenon has been described in the United States in the work of Slaughter and Rhoades (2004) in terms of the growing dominance of academic capitalism and a knowledge/learning/consumption regime framed by what we describe as "free marketeerism." Although such a shift in US higher education is barely distinguishable at times from the highly competitive, individualist society in which public universities are embedded, the same cannot be said of Latin America. Countries such as Argentina and Mexico have long-standing traditions and social contracts that have defined the relationship between the state and its citizens. Clearly, many of the values and beliefs associated with neoliberal versions of higher education are challenging fundamental elements of Argentine and Mexican culture.

At UBA, results of our conversations and data gathering suggest several pressing concerns. First, our subjects were quick to point out the weaknesses of neoliberal policies and their disastrous effects on the Argentine economy. Several reminded us that Argentina once had been the poster child of the IMF, yet in the spring of 2002, when we visited UBA, they were in economic ruin. In terms of higher education, several of our interview subjects noted the need for reform, but such reform seems implausible amid economic calamity. Nonetheless, a key concern of the reform agenda is the importance of access in a society wrestling with the challenges of globalization. Although many of the concerns about access relate to problems at the precollege level, issues of financial support and access at a postsecondary level, especially for low-income and working-class citizens, remain preeminent concerns as well. Another major concern centers on the lack of adequate support for scholarly and scientific endeavors. Building a strong full-time professorate is critical if public universities such as UBA are to play a key role in global processes. Related to this concern is the need to reconcile the role of the private sector, namely industry, in advancing science and technology at the university level. But reforms in public universities in Argentina will not come without increased support from the government and the larger society. One of our interview subjects said it best when he suggested that the biggest challenge is conveying to Argentine society the importance of higher education as part of a "democratic debt," believing, of course, that democratic societies demand an educated citizenry.

At UNAM several major challenges must be confronted in this age of globalization. First, advocates of public higher education must build support throughout the nation for public universities such as UNAM. Here, the challenge is not unlike that of Argentina. And, like Argentina, Mexican advocates of public higher education have had to battle structural adjustments that have sought to limit such support. Recently, however, there are indications that support for higher education may be on the rise. With promises of no more cuts and the implementation of funding programs to support faculty work, positive gains seem possible. But support programs are not without their critics, because such programs tend to follow the principles of individualism and competition so embedded in neoliberalism. Many of the professors with whom we spoke view such programs with derision, although they nonetheless participate simply because they are in dire need of financial support. From their perspective the programs are rooted in a culture of accountability and efficiency that damages the collective will and identity of Mexican intellectuals. They see such programs as emblematic of the US academy and the spirit of individualism that so dominates elite research universities in the North. They fear the Americanization of Mexican society and that the "spirit of collectivism" may be fading. Similar fears are expressed in the context of discussions of privatization and university-industry partnerships. Some see the public as a vanishing ideal, as private concerns move front and center. But the reality is that too much distrust exists between Mexican academics and the private sector, and so neoliberal initiatives likely will move slowly throughout the decade. In time, though, few doubt that Mexican universities such as UNAM will come to resemble those of their northern neighbors.

We cannot stress enough the importance and relevance of the uprisings at UNAM during the 1999–2000 academic year and on the streets of Buenos Aires following the collapse of the Argentine economy in December 2001. These seemingly disparate events had a common undercurrent to them: concerns among students and citizens that events within their countries were being orchestrated by powerful organizations quite removed from the economic hardships and sufferings of citizens in Mexico and Argentina. Student protesters complained about ongoing efforts to "globalize" the Mexican economy by pushing key institutions such as UNAM toward privatization. The students saw the proposed increase in fees as a sign of the shifting allegiance of the federal government away from long-standing social contracts and toward capital-driven free marketeerism. Similarly, protesters on the streets of Buenos Aires were highly critical of economic policies promoted by the IMF and embraced by the country's economic and political elites. They saw the growing gap between rich and poor and questioned how policies pushed by the IMF could ever produce economic well-being for the vast majority of Argentines. For both the student protesters at UNAM and the citizens taking to the streets in Buenos Aires, the time had come for grassroots resistance and insurrection. We no doubt can expect to see more of such forms of resistance if the hopes of average citizens continue to be snuffed out by economic policies favoring the most wealthy and powerful individuals and groups.

We are left with four overarching realities relative to neoliberal globalization and higher education in Latin America. First, it is inevitable that nation-states increasingly will be drawn into global economic, political, cultural, and social networks and that universities will play key roles in the unfolding of such processes. Second, for globalization processes to develop democratically, nation-states must have the ability, the opportunity, and the support to interpret and interact with global forces on their own terms. Economically advanced countries that forge trade policies from which they primarily benefit do not necessarily contribute to improved economic and social conditions in less developed countries. To impose postindustrial economic policies on countries such as Argentina and Mexico when, arguably, they have hardly advanced to a complex industrial stage may be disadvantageous as well as culturally and politically alienating. Third, although globalization can be understood as a historical reality, this is not to say that only one definition of globalization exists or should exist. Indeed, although globalization as economic expansionism rooted in the ideals of Western capitalism presently may be the dominant vision, other resistant and complementary views exist as well. Thus the democratization of globalization must include multivocality, or what we call multiglobality. Such a notion suggests that globalization is most likely to produce egalitarian relationships between nation-states if we can create networks and spaces where multiple definitions and belief systems around globalization are able to coexist. And finally, policy makers must recognize the key role that public universities such as UBA and UNAM play in global processes, both as agents of globalization and as sources of reflection and criticism concerning the deleterious hegemony of global endeavors. The university must remain a source of social reflection and criticism, lest societies lose all ability to be self-critical and domination proceeds unchecked.

References

Altbach, P. G. 2001. "Why Higher Education Is Not a Global Commodity." *Chronicle of Higher Education, The Chronicle Review*, May 11. Available at http://chronicle.com/weekly/V47/i35/35b02001.htm

Anderson, M. S. 2001. "The Complex Relations Between the Academy and Industry: View from the Literature." *Journal of Higher Education* 72(2): 226–246.

Apple, M. W. 2000. "Between Neoliberalism and Neoconservatism: Education and Conservatism in a Global Context." In *Globalization and Education: Critical Perspectives* (pp. 57–77), N. C. Burbules and C. A. Torres, eds. New York: Routledge.

BBC. 2004. "Argentina Blames IMF for Crisis." *BBC News* (31 July). Available at http://news.bbc.co.uk/1/hi/world/americas/3941809.stm

Blumenstyk, G. 2002. "Universities Try to Keep Inventions from Going 'Out the Back Door.'" *Chronicle of Higher Education*, May 17, A33–A34.

Blumenthal, D., E. G. Campbell, N. Causino, and K. S. Louis. 1996. "Participation of Life-Science Faculty in Research Relationships with Industry." *New England Journal of Medicine* 335(23): 1734–1739.

Boron, A. A. 1995. *State, Capitalism, and Democracy in Latin America*. Boulder, CO: Lynne Rienner.

Boron, A. A., and C. A. Torres. 1996. "The Impact of Neoliberal Restructuring on Education and Poverty in Latin America." *Alberto Journal of Education Research* 17(2): 102–114.

Breneman, D. W. 1993. *Higher Education: On a Collision Course with New Realities*. Washington, DC: Association of Governing Boards of Universities and Colleges.

Burbach, R. 2001. *Globalization and Postmodern Politics: From Zapatistas to High-Tech Robber Barons*. London: Pluto Press.

Burbules, N. C., and C. A. Torres. 2000. "Globalization and Education: An Introduction." In *Globalization and Education: Critical Perspectives* (pp. 1–26), N. C. Burbules and C. A. Torres, eds. New York: Routledge.

Campbell, T. I. D., and S. Slaughter. 1999. "Faculty and Administrators' Attitudes Toward Potential Conflicts of Interest, Commitment, and Equity in University-Industry Relationships." *Journal of Higher Education* 70(3): 309–352.

Cardoso, F. H. 1993. "North-South Relations in the Present Context: A New Dependency?" In *The New Global Economy in the Information Age: Reflections on Our Changing World* (pp. 149–159), M. Carnoy, M. Castells, S. S. Cohen, and F. H. Cardoso, eds. University Park: Pennsylvania State University Press.

Carnoy, M. 1993. "Multinationals in a Changing World Economy: Whither the

Nation-State?" In *The New Global Economy in the Information Age: Reflections on Our Changing World* (pp. 45–96), M. Carnoy, M. Castells, S. S. Cohen, and F. H. Cardoso, eds. University Park: Pennsylvania State University Press.

Carnoy, M., M. Castells, S. S. Cohen, and F. H. Cardoso, eds. 1993. *The New Global Economy in the Information Age: Reflections on Our Changing World.* University Park: Pennsylvania State University Press.

Carnoy, M., and H. Levin. 1985. *Schooling and Work in the Democratic State.* Palo Alto, CA: Stanford University Press.

Carnoy, M., and D. Rhoten. 2002. "What Does Globalization Mean for Educational Change? A Comparative Approach." *Comparative Education Review* 46(1): 1–9.

Casanova Cardiel, H., and R. Rodríguez Gómez. 2000. "El Conflicto de la UNAM." *Cuadernos Americanos* 81: 31–40.

Castells, M. 1993. "The Information Economy and the New International Division of Labor." In *The New Global Economy in the Information Age: Reflections on Our Changing World* (pp. 15–43), M. Carnoy, M. Castells, S. S. Cohen, and F. H. Cardoso, eds. University Park: Pennsylvania State University Press.

Castells, M. 1997. *The Power of Identity.* Boston: Blackwell.

Chomsky, N. 1998. *Profit over People: Neoliberalism and Global Order.* New York: Seven Stories Press.

Clark, B. R. 2000. "Creating Entrepreneurialism in Proactive Universities." *Change* (January/February): 10–19.

Clark, B. R. 2001. *Creating Entrepreneurial Universities: Organizational Pathways of Transformation,* 3rd ed. Oxford: Pergamon Press.

Consejo General de Huelga. 1999. "El Grito de los Excluidos." *Proceso* (special ed., no. 5, December 1): 14–19.

Cooper, M. 2002. "From Protest to Politics: A Report from Porto Alegre." *The Nation* 274(9): 11–16.

Domínguez Martínez, R., and J. E. Pérez Cruz. 2000. "La Secuencia Oculta de la Huelga." *Cuadernos Americanos* 81: 41–53.

Frasca, T. 2002. "The Sacking of Argentina." *The Nation* 274(17): 26–30.

Habermas, J. 1973. *Theory and Practice,* J. Vietel, trans. Boston: Beacon Press.

Hartcher, P. 2002. "$US 180 bn Farm Aid Trade Threat." *Australian Financial Review,* May 10. Available at http://afr.com/world/2002/05/10/FFX03NTIZ0D.html

Horkheimer, M. 1972. *Critical Theory,* M. J. O'Connell, trans. New York: Herder and Herder.

International Monetary Fund. 2003. *Lessons from the Crisis in Argentina.* Internal Report, October 8. Washington, DC: International Monetary Fund.

Lakoff, S. 1996. *Democracy: History, Theory, Practice.* Boulder, CO: Westview Press.

Lively, K. 2001. "AAUP Urges Professors to Play Key Role in Crafting Conflict-of-Interest Policies." *Chronicle of Higher Education, Today's News,* May 22. Available at http://chronicle.com.daily/2001/05/2001052206n.htm

Maldonado-Maldonado, A. 2002. "The National Autonomous University of Mexico: A Continuing Struggle." *International Higher Education* (winter) (online edition). Available at http://www.bc.edu/bc_org/avp/soe/cihe/newsletter/News26/texto11.htm

Marcuse, H. 1972. *Studies in Critical Philosophy*, J. De Bres, trans. Boston: Beacon Press.

"Mexico Sees U.S. Farm Bill Contradicts World Trade Rules." 2002. *Xinhua General News Service*, May 16.

Morales-Gómez, D. A., and C. A. Torres. 1990. *The State, Corporatist Politics, and Educational Policy Making in Mexico*. New York: Praeger.

Morrow, R. A., and C. A. Torres. 2000. "The State, Globalization, and Educational Policy." In *Globalization and Education: Critical Perspectives* (pp. 27–56), N. C. Burbules and C. A. Torres, eds. New York: Routledge.

Ordorika, I. 1996. "Reform at Mexico's National Autonomous University: Hegemony or Bureaucracy." *Higher Education* 31: 403–427.

Ordorika, I. 2003. *Power and Politics in University Governance: Organization and Change at the Universidad Nacional Autonoma de Mexico*. New York: Routledge Falmer.

Puiggrós, A. 1999. "The Consequences of Neo-Liberalism on the Educational Prospects of Latin American Youth." *Current Issues in Comparative Education* 1(2) (online edition). Available at http://www.tc.columbia.edu/cice/articles/ap112.htm (April 30).

Reich, R. B. 1991. *The Work of Nations*. New York: Vintage Books.

Rhoads, R. A. 2003. "Globalization and Resistance in the United States and Mexico: The Global Potemkin Village." *Higher Education* 45: 223–250.

Rhoads, R. A., and L. Mina. 2001. "The Student Strike at the National Autonomous University of Mexico: A Political Analysis." *Comparative Education Review* 45(3): 334–353.

Rhoads, R. A., and G. Rhoades. 2005. "Graduate Employee Unionization as Symbol of and Challenge to the Corporatization of U.S. Research Universities." *Journal of Higher Education* 76(3): 243–275.

Santos, B. S. 2001. "Os Procesos da Globalização." In *Globalização: Fatalidade ou Utopia* (pp. 31–105), B. de Sousa Santos et al., eds. Porto, Portugal: Editorial Afrontamento.

Santos, B. S. 2004. "A Universidade no Século XXI: Para uma Reforma Democrática e Emancipatória da Universidade." Keynote address at the IV International Paulo Freire Forum, Porto, Portugal, September 22.

Slaughter, S. 1998. "Federal Policy and Supply-Side Institutional Resource Allocation at Public Research Universities." *Review of Higher Education* 21(3): 209–244.

Slaughter, S., and L. L. Leslie. 1997. *Academic Capitalism: Politics, Policies, and the Entrepreneurial University*. Baltimore: Johns Hopkins University Press.

Slaughter, S., and G. Rhoades. 2004. *Academic Capitalism and the New Economy: Markets, State, and Higher Education*. Baltimore: Johns Hopkins University Press.

"South America Up in Arms over US Farm Bill." 2002. *Inter Press Service*, May 11.

Stiglitz, J. E. 2002. *Globalization and Its Discontents*. New York: W. W. Norton.

Thompson, G. 2000. "Unfulfilled Prophesy: The Evolution of Corporate Colleges." *Journal of Higher Education* 71(3): 322–341.

Torres, C. A. 2002. "Globalization, Education, and Citizenship: Solidarity Versus Markets?" *American Educational Research Journal* 39(2): 363–378.

Torres, C. A., and D. Schugurensky. 2002. "The Political Economy of Higher Education in the Era of Neoliberal Globalization: Latin America in Comparative Perspective." *Higher Education* 43: 429–455.

Urry, J. 1998. "Contemporary Transformations of Time and Space." In *The Globalization of Higher Education* (pp. 1–17), P. Scott, ed. Buckingham, UK: Open University.

Went, R. 2000. *Globalization: Neoliberal Challenge, Radical Responses*. London: Pluto Press.

CHAPTER SEVEN

Latin American Identities in Transition:
A Diagnosis of Argentine and Brazilian Universities
Marcela Mollis

Knowledge Institutions or Knowledge Supermarkets?

For some contemporary philosophers the words *wisdom and knowledge* are different; such differences are the basis of our preference for *wisdom*. Lyotard (1979) is of the opinion that "knowledge is that set of statements which denote or describe objects, with the exclusion of any other statement, and which may be declared true or false." *Wisdom* makes reference to a competence that exceeds the determination and application of criteria of truth and extends to criteria of efficiency (technical qualification), justice and/or happiness (ethical wisdom), and sound or chromatic beauty (auditory or visual sensitivity). Wisdom, so conceived, refers to a set of skills and, above all, to the individual who puts them into practice, that is, the "wise man." However, the increasing complexity of social activities throughout history has called for skills that were different, deep, and complex. Relatedly, the history of universities is the history of knowledge systematization, which had its origin in the wise man and which later gave rise to "the scientist, the professional, and the specialist" (Mollis 2002, p. 296). Knowledge gradually moved away from the individual who had it and started to be expressed through writing, accumulated outside the individual, and retained in books, thus giving rise to the modern book culture. Knowledge practices, which had been spontaneous, were organized and institutionalized, limited and fixed at the universities. In time the universities became the gatekeepers of specialized knowledge. To this day universities continue to be the guardians of all that is valued as knowledge. In a real sense, then, the history of universities is the history of the institutions where knowledge is kept, distributed, produced, invented, censored, or simply repeated.

Recent history in Argentina and Brazil has seen "northern winds," the influence of the powers to the North, most specifically the United States (Aboites 1999). These winds transformed the identity of universities and therefore the knowledge they produce and disseminate. Nowadays, Argentine and Brazilian universities—affected by neoliberal policies, budget restrictions, fiscal adjustments, and the transformation of the social contract between the state and the civil society—have denaturalized "university knowledge" and turned it into "mercantilist learning." Knowledge is measured with the language of finance and calculated through performance indicators and certificates and diplomas, duly and timely delivered with the highest market value possible; knowledge is represented in the allocation of human resources, an example of which is the declining resources for the humanities. Our universities have suffered an alteration in their identity as knowledge institutions and are constructing a new identity that equates them to a supermarket, where students are clients, knowledge is a piece of merchandise, and professors are salary earners who teach.

In this chapter I present a theoretical and practical critique of ongoing trends and outcomes of Latin American university reform, with special focus on the Argentine and Brazilian cases. I also provide elements and values of what could be an alternative model for the future of universities in the region.

Cultural Analysis of Universities

In previous writings I have recognized the existence of two approaches to the study of the functioning of higher education systems: organizational analysis and historical-social analysis (Mollis 1990, 2002). The approaches are mutually exclusive. Organizational analysis has been used mainly in the developed North, whereas historical-social analysis seems to prevail in Latin America and consequently in Argentina (Miranda 1993; Mollis 1990; Serrano 1993).

Organizational analysis is characterized by its internal and synchronic emphasis: Priority is given to learning, microprocesses are carefully analyzed, and much relevance is given to differentiation. Organizational analysis takes into account the relationships among disciplines and academicians and analyzes the internal organizational system. On the other hand, historical-social analysis emphasizes external and diachronic elements: It gives priority to public policies and then to university actors (fundamentally to professors and students); it gives relevance to macroprocesses by periods or stages, to the system, and to relations of power; and it takes into account the social, political, and economic context that operates as a source of transformation of university institutions (Mollis 1990, 1995, 1997).

Another useful approach to understanding university identity from a historical perspective is *cultural analysis*, so called by the institutional anthropologist Willem Frijhoff (1986). Such analysis requires the aid of a branch of anthropology that sees the university in articulation with culture (i.e., as a "space of cultural mediation"). For this reason cultural practices are taken into account; for example, the procedures of creation, appropriation, and transmission of knowledge, values, and representations at the highest level of the educational system may be defined as "superior" by a society (Mollis 1997). As a product of these processes, images, bylaws, and strategies are created, and the role of the aforementioned superior culture is unveiled by each society that has defined it as such.

The cultural analysis of universities refers to three interacting dimensions: historical, social, and anthropological. The historical dimension refers to the history of intellectual and aesthetic products considered of a superior order. The social dimension refers to the actions performed by a society to apply those ideas; such actions determine the place—either hierarchical or not—of art, science, and technology as referents to create the rules, values, images, and codes that govern social life. Last, the anthropological dimension refers to universities as spaces where some forms of basic social organization are elaborated, such as timetables, gestures, attitudes, and reflections. In this way a cultural web is created in which an elite's intellectual, social, and political conduct is reproduced. Such conduct, in turn, is expressed as a model to be followed by subordinate groups.

The cultural analysis of universities presents elements that are simultaneously constructive and challenging and serves the purpose of decodifying the current crisis of higher education institutions. It helps us to understand that the university is not an autonomous institution that produces ideas to be consumed or not by the society. On the contrary, the university is ruled by complex processes of interaction among the bylaws of science, professions, and disciplines, the expansion or contraction of the labor market, and the differences between social classes, ethnic minorities, gender, power, or the respective position of manual and intellectual work on the scale of social values. In this sense the university is constructed as an instance of production, control, and legitimization within a context of constant tension between what society, the state, and the production market delegate to it and its traditional functions of production and dissemination of knowledge. In addition, it should be taken into account that the traditional forms of organization, division, specialization, circulation, and appropriation of knowledge are obsolete in the face of the new structure of knowledge in the same way that the social status of traditional liberal professions such as medicine, engineering, and law underwent a crisis.

At present, economic globalization, which turned the welfare state into a neoliberal state, promotes significant change among university actors and the public sector. For instance, under conditions of structural adjustment and financial regulation, "multifunctionality," or the coexistence of different "missions" within the university itself (teaching, research, and extension), reduces the possibilities of complying with the missions assigned to the university at the expected level of excellence.

International Trends to Reform Higher Education in the 1990s

A number of common trends are indicated in the literature on the restructuring of higher education systems in many developed and underdeveloped economies in the late 20th century. These trends converge into a new orthodoxy about the value of higher education and how it should be managed (Altbach 1999; Marginson and Considine 2000; Mollis 2003b; Velloso, Cunha, and Velho 1999). According to Mala Sing (2001, pp. 24–25), some key trends include the following:

- The requirement of higher education to demonstrate efficiency, effectiveness, and value for money through external quality assurance systems and other accountability frameworks.
- Declining amounts of public funds to subsidize student fees and service costs, and the requirement to satisfy the incremental demand for higher education with less public investment.
- The requirement to run public universities according to private sector principles, and the dominance of managerial and entrepreneurial approaches to higher education.
- The requirement to diversify sources of funding, thus reducing the primary responsibility of the state for public education.
- The privatization of higher education (either as component parts of public institutions, such as cleaning services and even specialized fields of study, or through encouraged competition with public institutions).
- Market-responsive curriculum reforms, a shift from basic to applied research, increased emphasis on academy-industry links, and greater concern over issues of intellectual property rights and the prioritization of research for product development and commercialization.

In addition, the implementation of structural adjustment policies to liberalize the economies of Latin America and integrate them more tightly into the world capitalist system has provoked a number of crises throughout the region. With the diminished role of the state in the provision of basic social services—part of the cost-cutting policies recommended by the World Bank and the International Monetary Fund (IMF)—the social safety net provided for the most marginalized populations has been effectively removed. The gap between the wealthy and the poor is increasing. Moves to decentralize and privatize economies are paralleled by initiatives to dismantle centralized ministries of education and charge fees for educational services that were once provided free to all (Arnove et al. 1999). A recent report of the Latin American Studies Association (LASA) Task Force on Higher Education examined the functions, financing, and governance of tertiary education as well as the efforts to privatize and professionalize it. The report concluded that although democratization has often rescued higher education from government neglect, market orientations have not produced a coherent reform agenda. The report further noted that the reform agenda is highly polemical, with supporters arguing that neoliberal reforms have not been sufficiently implemented and opponents arguing that it brought to institutions nothing but an alteration of the social, political, and scientific identity of the universities (Mollis 2003a). The following features describe the consequences of the implementation of the international agenda to reform Latin American higher education in the 1990s (Mollis 2003b):

- Promulgation of higher education laws to regulate higher education within contexts of traditional autonomy.
- Institutional diversification (the creation of new tracks that changed the historical Latin American double-track system into a division of university and nonuniversity tertiary institutions); transformation of the structures of higher education systems (the creation of new institutions such as university colleges and university institutes); and the creation of short-term courses to grant vocational certificates within the university system (charging fees).
- Diversification of financial sources (e.g., charging user fees instead of providing service free of charge, and establishing services-for-profit partnerships).
- Strategic alliances between international agencies and governmental decision makers, and strategic alliances among the corporate sector, the public sector, and the universities.
- Incremental private investment in higher education and marketization of nonaccredited (or supervised) private tertiary institutions (nonuniversity sector), along with incremental growth of new providers, such as financial foundations, banking system, corporations, and so forth.
- New policies for accountability and institutional evaluation; institutional and program evaluation; and university and graduate program accreditation (combined with establishing national and central agencies for accreditation and institutional evaluation).
- New types of institutional coordination—national, regional, and inter-campus coordination, supported by new institutional regulations and agreements.

- Strong differentiation among faculty members through the implementation of incentive policies to award productivity indicators.

- Academic and curriculum reforms, including shortening of university professional programs, granting certificates for short-term courses at the university level, new learning models based on the "training of professional skills and competencies," and expansion of professional graduate courses (master's degrees).

- New methodologies for the dissemination of knowledge, such as the dominant presence of information technologies and electronic distance learning that shifts the traditional teaching role to remote tutorial activities.

In Search of the Lost Identity

Latin American universities have a long tradition. Many were established more than two centuries before their counterparts in North America, and most were state institutions, including Catholic universities during the Spanish period. From the beginning Spanish conquerors were concerned with educating the individuals who would govern the state and the Catholic Church and who at that time were from a single institution in Latin America. The first Latin American university was founded in 1538, only 45 years after Columbus's arrival in Santo Domingo. Universities were established in 1540 in Mexico, in 1551 in San Marcos, Perú, and in 1613 in Córdoba, Argentina. In contrast, the first Brazilian University, Lavras, was founded in 1908. In Latin America universities have had a unique role that is different from their role in the rest of the world. In addition to postsecondary teaching and research, they have assumed such social responsibilities as preparing political leaders, fostering ideological discussion, promoting social change, safeguarding tradition, and retaining and spreading the local culture.

To interpret the idea of the "university" underlying Latin American universities, many writers have made reference to the model proposed by Napoléon Bonaparte in the 19th century. However, the so-called Napoleonic university does not reflect the particularity of university institutions in Latin America. After the break with colonial Spain, secular professional knowledge came to characterize the Latin American university model by the end of the 19th century; this is what the German historian Hans Steger (1974,

p. 32) described as the "university of lawyers." Luis Sherz (1968) recognized a predominantly secular, pragmatic, and state-oriented conception in the professional university, which has the mission of shaping citizens, professionals, and public administrators. Sherz also affirmed that this model adapts to relatively static social systems and maintains a close link to the state, which recognizes privileges and rights of the university while financing it. Such universities appear as official state institutions. With Ministry of Education funding, the state became the "teaching state" and, as such, served as the administrator and inspector of the whole educational system and was situated as an "exclusive sovereign in educational matters" (Sherz 1968, p. 107).

Since the end of the 19th century, lawyers who graduated from these institutions were professionally and ideologically linked to agrarian property, and as statesmen and public officers they created the instruments of political control within state institutions (i.e., courts, prosecution offices, police headquarters, etc.). Through the schools and the press they carried out other activities, which allowed them to widen the expression of the hegemonic classes, whether as writers, poets, or educators: "This group gave rise to a bureaucratic elite and a political class with a formalistic and pompous style which adapted perfectly to the interests of the dominant classes" (Sherz 1968, p. 109). This affirmation is illustrated by the characterization of the members of the Argentine Congress at the end of the 19th century. By 1890 the typical member of the Congress and the Courts of Justice belonged to the class of landowners or was in some way related to cattle raising and agricultural activities. Most of the congressmen were *lawyers* who had worked for the government in positions of increasing importance. Four out of five members of the Congress had an activity linked to agriculture and cattle raising, and 80 percent of congressmen had a university education; also, 88 percent of their parents had a university education. They knew each other and, as a general rule, they also belonged to exclusive clubs and private associations, such as the Argentine Rural Society (see Allub 1989, p. 130; Cantón 1966, pp. 37–49).

Consequently, the Latin American university of the 19th century—recognized as a "university of lawyers"—shared or controlled political power, exerted a significant influence on the field of ideas, and held increasing weight over the system of cultural institutions (Mollis 1990). On the one hand, foreign university models in the 20th century had a relevant organizational influence: the German emphasis on research, the English development of institutional diversity, the French Napoleonic conception of the relationship between state and university, and the North American model of autonomy, funding, and private institutions. On the other hand, the academic model of Latin American universities is derived from the European model—specifically, the University of Paris, which had a strong influence on Latin America and whose influence can still be seen in the more traditional institutions. In this model the curricula are organized by professional programs, the universities have strong linkages with the state, and (despite academic autonomy) the state provides the funds and has indirect control over the institutions. For this reason these institutions met the demands of the ruling social class—mainly, their political and cultural demands. Thus since the 19th century professional training has been seen as the central task to be accomplished by Latin American universities.

These trends in and consequences of implementing the global and international agenda for reforming higher education systems are bringing universities in line with other social arrangements designed to position national economies for global competitiveness. According to Mala Sing, "The new policy framework for the restructuring of higher education in developed economies is functioning as a powerful and influential global paradigm, shaping higher education policies and practices in many developing countries' economies despite huge social, economic and historical differences" (2001, p. 25). The 1990s were marked by the presence of a neoliberal regime of truth that was driven by a clearly defined universalistic ambition. Although produced and practiced inside societies of the North, the most detrimental effects of neoliberalism have been felt in the South, particularly in its higher education systems.

The last document on higher education published jointly by the members of the Task Force on Higher Education and Society created by the World Bank and UNESCO begins by saying:

> The world economy is changing as knowledge supplants physical capital as the source of present (and future) wealth. Technology is driving much of this process, with information technology, biotechnology, and other innovations leading to remarkable changes in the way we live and work. As knowledge becomes more important, so does higher education. Countries need to

educate more of their young people to a higher standard—a degree is now
a basic qualification for many skilled jobs. The quality of knowledge generated within higher education institutions, and its accessibility to the wider
economy, is becoming increasingly critical to national competitiveness.
This poses a serious challenge to the developing world. (World Bank and
UNESCO 2000, p. 9)

This statement advances the global foundations so that developing countries
become aware of the economic imperative justifying the transformation of
higher education systems. Other sections of the report also convey the relevance of reforms linked to an economic imperative: "There are notable exceptions, but currently, across most of the developing world, the potential of
higher education to promote development is being realized only marginally"
(World Bank and UNESCO 2000, p. 10). What we see in all this is the tendency for the geopolitics of knowledge and power to divide the world into
countries that consume knowledge produced by the countries that dominate
globally, both economically and culturally, and countries that reassign the
economic function of training human resources to university institutions located in the periphery.

Two Examples of Identities in Transition:
Argentine and Brazilian Universities

Among the strategies promoted by the "agenda of modernization" to reshape the Latin American university (Brunner 1993; Levy 1993) and consistent with the positioning of financial rationalization at the core of universities, we can mention administrative deregulation and debureaucratization,
privatization, and the reduction of the state's responsibility in the provision
of public services. The implementation of modernizing processes in Latin
America is seen by politicians as an instrument to surmount obstacles in general, but the key role of the political actors involved in these processes is not
taken into account. As part of the modernization process, privatization became one of the fundamental instruments for the change of a liberal regime
in the region. From this process onward the intervention of the state in the
economy was modified and the "regulatory" function of state-owned com-

panies was abandoned, because all of them were privatized; all this was based on the illusion that a private market would bring about the greatest welfare to "client citizens."

Paradoxically, although the Argentine and Brazilian universities in the 21st century aim to educate professionals, these young graduates no longer participate in the historical process of training a political class committed to the national destiny and public morals. Training for the professions is moving from the public ethos to the search for a corporate ethos, which is influenced by the demands of a reduced job market and requires an instrumental and efficiency rationale in the practice of professions within private corporations. These transformations are delineated in research that compares the curriculum reform carried out in two medical schools in Argentina and Brazil in the 1990s (Koifman 2002). The policies for the privatization of "social benefit professions" in combination with the decline in public health direct the expectations of future professionals and physicians toward the practice of their profession in the private field. This also explains the lack of development of certain specialties linked to the public good, such as urban development architecture, public veterinary health, road engineering, or any other science-oriented courses.

In light of the growing power of the corporate ethos, the Argentine universities' public identity has been altered. Concomitantly, the political identity of the people's representatives who rule for the benefit of their private interests and not as representatives of the electorate's will is also altered.

None of this theoretical analysis about universities has backed up the recent descriptions of the quality crisis in developing countries' higher education systems. From the geopolitical perspective of knowledge, the triumph of the "university global identity" is evidenced, on the one hand, by the place assigned to instrumental knowledge at the service of economic development that benefits elites and, on the other hand, by the subordination of national and local development to the global dynamics of hegemonic countries.

In Argentina new private institutions and other private agents were promoted and remarkably expanded, the Law on Higher Education was promulgated, and the National University Evaluation and Accreditation Committee and the Fund for Quality Improvement (FOMEC) were created. Consequently, evaluation and accreditation processes and the search for alternative financing sources (e.g., voluntary contributions in graduate courses and payment of fees for postgraduate and distance or "virtual" courses) were set in motion, because the preeminent goal became the efficient management of resources (Mollis 2001, p. 209). These reforms are currently in force in other Latin American countries, including Mexico and Chile, which traveled the "modernization" route before the start of this process in Argentina (Aboites 1999; González 2001).

From an analysis of current higher education policies in Brazil, several writers—for example, Roberto Lehrer (in Mollis 2003b), Denise Leite (2001), and Helgio Trindade (2000)—have pointed out that recent trends are associated with a neoliberal project aimed at minimizing the state. These policies try to adapt the highest level of formal education to market demands and to the national state reconfiguration process. Dias Sobrinho (2000) explained:

> At present, a significant concern is to verify that diversification and differentiation policies under way in the country are based on four fundamental suppositions of neo-liberalism: a) they try to favor competition and the satisfaction of different demands and clients; b) they try to "naturalize," even more, individual differences through the gradual establishment of a meritocratic system where each individual will have access to the kind of higher education that he or she "may" afford; c) they increase the subordination of higher education to the market, particularly training and the privatization of activities and services; and d) they explain the method of operation of the system rather than its social purposes. (p. 58)

Another aspect of the new identity of the Brazilian university is related to the change in the curriculum. The importance of the curriculum for graduate courses began to grow after the start of higher education reform in 1995. Some of the elements that had a bearing on the matter were Law 9131/95, national and international discussions on professional profiles, the process started by the secretariat of higher education in 1997, and the position adopted by the Foro de Pró-Reitores de Graduaçao. The Ministry of Education intends to adapt the curriculum to the changes in the labor market on the basis of the following principles: flexibility in curricular organization, adaptation to job market demands, integration of graduate and postgraduate courses, emphasis on general training, and development of general skills. Professional training for the neoliberal labor market requires polyvalence and professional flexibility to adapt human skills to changing labor aims, tools, and environments. Other Brazilian writers, such as Leite (2001) and Trindade (2000), also have come to the conclusion that higher education in Brazil is being adapted to processes associated with the "academic capitalism" described quite nicely by Slaughter and Leslie (1997); in essence, this means adopting a mercantile rationality for the benefit of enterprises, rulers, and hegemonic classes (Catani and Ferreira de Oliveira 2000, p. 48).

Leite (2001) described the effect of values extrapolated from the market on some Brazilian university campuses: "Entrepreneurial professors are the result of such extrapolation: they sell their courses—i.e., they make their curricular offerings more attractive in search of students-clients. They adapt their conferences and papers to the sales codes of canned knowledge: efficiency and productivity indicators, evaluation of results, and leadership to win. The international agencies hire *entrepreneurial professors* as expert technicians in preestablished descriptions subject to the adjustment of theories and concepts" (Leite 2001, pp. 23–26). Overall, privatization and marketization are having a major impact throughout the higher education systems of Latin America.

The 1980s was a decade of "structural adjustments" and represented the deployment of the neoliberal doctrine through the imposition of a new scheme of financial discipline and modernization of the state. During this decade the strategic concepts were to reduce, differentiate, dismiss, and discipline. Quoting David Slater, "To adjust a structure is much more than an exercise for economists, it means to change the life of the people, the inhabitants and the citizens of a nation" (1992, p. 36).

The 1990s brought a theoretical adjustment of educational policy, which was reduced to the administration of reforms based on quantitative indicators and results of evaluations, giving up its democratic and civic potential to assist in the construction of a participatory citizenry and setting aside the consolidation of the public space as a guarantor of democratic culture.

Citizenry and Democracy:
Values Denied in the Idea of a Corporate University

New proposals, policies, and practices have replaced traditional values, concepts, and proposals in the Latin American university as the market takes on increasing importance. The role of government is being reinvented, and new technologies have replaced former perceptions of the role of universities and their participation in the configuration of a democratic citizenry (Mollis 2001). Globalization and internationalism have accelerated the dissemination of Fordist values of the entrepreneurial culture and are now extended to social and cultural institutions throughout Latin America. From the viewpoint of the doctrines that consider the "market" the only possible source of innovation, the value of "competition" increases and, consequently, the logic of the corporate-entrepreneurial sector gets reproduced within public good sectors. The privatization of the public ethos occurs in public and private universities, which become the prisoners of "marketing," as described by the Indian writer Tilak, who wrote about the transformation of higher education in India (Altbach 1999). Similarly, the Portuguese sociologist Boaventura de Sousa Santos describes the breach of the social contract characterizing the neoliberal state and reshaping the identities of our universities: "The neoliberal State is not a minimal State. . . . In fact, it does not regulate society any longer. . . . The Welfare State for the citizens turned into a Welfare State for the companies. Never before were so many incentives offered to the companies as nowadays" (2001, p. 1).

The idea of a Latin American public university during the 20th century (either publicly or privately managed, such as the universities managed by religious orders) implied scientific quality, social importance, pertinence, and equity. Clearly, the 21st-century idea of a corporate university differs from the earlier view: It appeals to profit in favor of public interests and contributes to social segmentation while placing the interests of ruling elites and capitalist ambitions at the center.

I support the idea that the efficient administration of a public university should not be based on profit earning but on the sense of the university's social function. Training independent and creative professionals as active citizens and future leaders, fostering epistemological diversity and disagreement, turning single-sided thinking into a plurality of alternative ways of thinking, enriching the cultural heritage, and making science sensitive to social needs—these are some of the missions necessary to respond to the global challenges of our impoverished societies. Expanding the scientific and cultural fields and producing scientific, technological, and cultural assets also create wealth and strengthen the economic development of the peripheral countries that the international agencies are so concerned about.

Quality in public institutions is directly related to the preparation of citizens to hold political, professional, cultural, or scientific offices for the benefit of "others." The democratic Latin American university contributed to the training of generations of young people in a "diversity" of interests, which made civic and democratic spaces more dynamic.

At present, the identities in transition of Argentine and Brazilian universities lead us toward the homogenization of knowledge and shapes us in the interest of corporate enterprises and international banking agencies. It is necessary and urgent to decontaminate the concept of quality from the connotations of "total quality" (as in "total quality management," or TQM, as it is also known), of financial logic from financial return, and of efficiency from academic excellence. We must demand that the university fulfill its social responsibility to its beneficiaries. It is urgent to recover the social, ethical, and humanistic significance of educational quality. The university does not just produce the technical and scientific knowledge necessary for the development of the country; above all, it must produce the knowledge necessary for a democratic, just, and more equitable construction of society. The Latin American university must invent knowledge not conditioned by the codes of profit; it must reconstruct its identity for the benefit of our societies, which are unprotected from possessive individualists who deny the value of culture because it is not listed on the stock exchange. If the Latin American university is considered a market entity, then there is no space for real and significant criticism. Institutional evaluation and assessment must be directed toward the deepening of the conditions of criticism at the university; public debate—among actors, sectors, and institutions—should be promoted and must be developed as a collective action focused on the criticism of the institution itself, both internally and in relation to the larger society. To end this diagnosis of Argentine and Brazilian universities, or rather, of the ideas supported by Argentine and Brazilian universities and their identities in transition, I cite the words of Santos: "We must recreate democracies of a high intensity. But a democracy of a high intensity cannot be made without democrats of a high intensity" (2001, p. 3).

Conclusion

I support the idea that the efficient administration of a Brazilian and Argentinean public university should not be based on profit earning but on the sense of its social function. Some necessary missions in response to the global challenges of our impoverished societies include the need to train independent and creative professionals as active citizens and future leaders, fostering epistemological diversity and disagreement, turning single-sided thinking into a plurality of alternative ways of thinking, enriching the cultural heritage, and making science sensitive to social needs. Furthermore, the expansion of scientific and cultural fields and the production of scientific, technological, and cultural assets create wealth and strengthen the economic development of the peripheral countries that the international agencies are so concerned about. Clearly, the university has an important role to play in the foreseeable future of both Argentina and Brazil as well as throughout the rest of Latin America.

References

Aboites, H. 1999. *Viento del Norte*. Mexico City: UAM Plaza & Valdés Editores.

Allub, L. 1989. "Estado y Sociedad Civil: Patrón de Emergencia y Desarrollo del Estado Argentino (1810–1930)." In *Estado y Sociedad en el Pensamiento Nacional*, W. Ansaldi and J. L. Moreno, eds. Buenos Aires: Editorial Cantaro.

Altbach, P., ed. 1999. *Private Prometheus: Private Higher Education and Development in the 21st Century*. Boston: Center for International Higher Education, Boston College.

Arnove, R. F., S. Franz, M. Mollis, and C. A. Torres. 1999. "Education in Latin America at the End of the 1990s." In *Comparative Education: The Dialectic of the Global and the Local* (pp. 305–329), R. F. Arnove and C. A. Torres, eds. New York: Rowman & Littlefield.

Brunner, J. J. 1993. "Evaluación y Financiamiento de la Educación Superior en América Latina: Bases para un Nuevo Contrato." In *Políticas Comparadas de Educación Superior en América Latina*, J. Balán et al., eds. Santiago, Chile: FLACSO.

Cantón, D. 1966. *El Parlamento Argentino en Épocas de Cambio: 1816–1916–1946*. Buenos Aires: Editorial Instituto.

Catani, A. M., and J. Ferreira de Oliveira. 2000. "A Reforma da Educação Superior no Brasil Nos Anos 90: Diretrizes, Bases e Ações." In *Reformas Educacionais em Portugal e no Brasil*, A. M. Catani, ed. Belo Horizonte, Brazil: Autentica.

Dias Sobrinho, J. 2000. "Avaliação e Privatização do Ensino Superior." In *Universidade em Ruinas: Na República Dos Professores*, H. Trindade, ed. Rio Grande do Sul, Brazil: Vozes, Petrópolis/CIPEDES.

Frijhoff, W. 1986. "La Universidad Como Espacio de Mediación Cultural." In *His-*

toria de la Educación. Revista Interuniversitaria No. 5. Salamanca, Spain: Universidad de Salamanca.

González, L. E. 2001. "Acreditación y Fomento de la Calidad: La Experiencia Chilena de las Últimas Décadas." Paper presented at the 20th General Assembly of CLACSO, Guadalajara, November 21–24.

Koifman, L. 2002. *Oprocesso de Reformulação Curricular do Curso de Medicina no Brasil e na Argentina: Uma Abordagem Comparada*. Ph.D. dissertation. Buenos Aires and Río de Janeiro: Universidad de Buenos Aires and Escola Nacional de Saúde Pública/FIOCRUZ.

Leite, D. 2001. "Avaliacao Institucional e Democracia: Posibilidades Contra-Hegemónicas ao Redesenho Capitalista das Universidades." Paper presented at the 20th General Assembly of CLACSO, Guadalajara, November 21–24.

Levy, D. 1993. "The New Pluralist Agenda for Latin American Higher Education: Honey, I Shrunk the State?" Introductory paper to the Seminar on Higher Education in Latin America. Bogotá, Colombia: Universidad de Los Andes, World Bank IDE.

Lyotard, J. F. 1979. *La Condition Post-Moderne*. Paris: Les Editions de Minuit.

Marginson, S., and M. Considine. 2000. *The Enterprise University: Governance and Reinvention in Australian Higher Education*. Cambridge, UK: Cambridge University Press.

Miranda, M. E. 1993. *La Formación del Sistema Universitario Nacional: Desarrollo y Crisis, 1880–1946*. Córdoba, Argentina: Dirección General de Publicaciones, Universidad Nacional del Córdoba.

Mollis, M. 1990. *Universidades y Estado Nacional: Argentina y Japón Entre 1880 y 1930*. Buenos Aires: Editorial Biblos.

Mollis, M. 1995. "En Busca de Respuesta a la Crisis Universitaria: Historia y Cultura." *Perfiles Educativos* 69(July–September).

Mollis, M. 1997. "The Paradox of the Autonomy of Argentine Universities: From Liberalism to Regulation." In *Latin American Education: Comparative Perspectives*, C. A. Torres and A. Puiggros, eds. Boulder, CO: Westview Press.

Mollis, M. 2001. *La Universidad Argentina en Tránsito*. Buenos Aires: Fondo de Cultura Económica.

Mollis, M. 2002. "La Geopolítica de las Reformas de la Educación Superior: El Norte da Créditos, el Sur Se Acredita." In *Reformas en los Sistemas Nacionales de Educación Superior* (pp. 321–353), R. Rodríguez, ed. Madrid: Netbiblo-RISEU (UNAM).

Mollis, M. 2003a. "A Decade of Reform in Argentina." *International Higher Education* 30(winter): 24–26.

Mollis, M., ed. 2003b. *Las Universidades en América Latina: Reformadas o Alteradas?* Buenos Aires: ASDI-CLACSO.

Santos, B. S. 2001. "Cuáles Son Los Límites y Posibilidades de la Ciudadanía Planetaria?" Paper presented at the World Social Forum. Available at http://www.forumsocialmundial.org.br

Serrano, S. 1993. *Universidad y Nación: Chile en el Siglo XIX.* Santiago, Chile: Editorial Universitaria.

Sherz, L. 1968. *El Camino de la Revolución Universitaria.* Santiago, Chile: Editorial Del Pacífico.

Sing, M. 2001. "Re-Inserting the Public Good into Higher Education Transformation." *International News* 46(November): 24–27.

Slater, D. 1992. "Poder y Resistencia en la Periferia: Replanteando Algunos Temas Críticos para los Años '90." *Nueva Sociedad* 122(November–December).

Slaughter, S., and L. L. Leslie. 1997. *Academic Capitalism: Politics, Policies, and the Entrepreneurial University.* Baltimore: Johns Hopkins University Press.

Steger, H. A. 1974. *Las Universidades en el Desarrollo Social de la América Latina.* Mexico City: Fondo de Cultura Económica.

Trindade, H., ed. 2000. *Universidade em Ruinas: Na República dos Profesores.* Rio Grande do Sul, Brazil: Vozes/CIPEDES.

Velloso, J., L. A. Cunha, and L. Velho, eds. 1999. *O Ensino Superior e o Mercosul.* Brasilia, Brazil: UNESCO-Garamond.

World Bank and UNESCO. 2000. *Higher Education in Developing Countries: Peril and Promise.* Washington, DC: Task Force on Higher Education.

CHAPTER EIGHT

Brazil's Local Solutions to Global Problems

Ken Kempner
Ana Loureiro Jurema

Argentina, Mexico, Brazil, and the Asian Tigers all provide excellent exam-ples of the successes and failures of globalization. Although the explanations of globalization are quite numerous, Giddens (1990, p. 64) provided a sim-ple and elegant definition that matches well the argument we advance in this chapter: "Globalization can thus be defined as the intensification of world-wide social relations which link distant localities in such a way that local hap-penings are shaped by events occurring many miles away and vice versa." This definition helps clarify Giddens's observation that "every cup of coffee contains within it the whole history of Western imperialism" (p. 120). This is, of course, a defining statement for our focus in this chapter on Brazil.

Our intent in this chapter is to discuss, first, the role that neoliberal the-ory plays in the economic, social, and cultural crisis in the developing world. In pursuit of our argument, we present supporting literature that addresses the failure of the Washington consensus, particularly in South America, where pressure to adapt the neoliberal policies of privatization and import substitution were strongest from external agencies. Our principal argument here is that nations have the inherent right of sovereignty to set their own economic and social policy. We argue further that these sovereign nations are also in the best position to understand the cultural and social consequences of externally imposed policies, particularly when such policies are not in the best interests of the country and its people. As the Commission of Economics for Latin America and the Caribbean (CEPAL—a UN agency) has argued, breaking out of the "iron circle of underdevelopment" should be the goal, as opposed to serving the hegemonic needs of the core (Folha de São Paulo 2002, p. A23). In our discussion we also note the rise of regionalism in the face of globalization. The consequences of globalization are confusing at best, especially for countries on the periphery that are losing their identities. Giddens (1990, p. 66) noted, "Nation-states, it is held, are becoming progressively less sovereign than they used to be in terms of controls over their own affairs." He divided the world system into three units: the core, the semiperiphery, and the periphery. Although such a division is fraught with difficulties, it does avoid the political relegation of countries to the "third world." Giddens's division does recognize, however, the economic reality of the major economic powers (United States, Japan, and Europe as the core), the newly industrialized or semiperipheral countries (e.g., Brazil, Mexico, and the Asian Tigers), and the peripheral countries that are primarily agricultural and can provide only cheap labor (e.g., Cambodia, Vietnam, and much of Africa).

Central to our argument on development in the face of globalization is the priority that education, principally higher education, must take in solving the economic and social problems at the regional and national levels. We are in complete agreement with Stiglitz (2002, p. 82) that "education is at the core of development." How education is to solve the problems of development at the national level is an unresolved issue that requires the integration of all levels of education within a country. As with the other contributors to this book, our focus is on how higher education in particular is necessary to mediate the effects of globalization through local educational solutions. Universities, as the major national institutions that produce knowledge, have a special social obligation to seek locally developed solutions to global problems. We argue, however, that globalization devalues the knowledge production of national universities. Under the dictates of neoliberal globalism, externally imposed solutions have the highest currency, so there is little need to support or develop an internal infrastructure of knowledge. From the perspective of the semiperiphery and periphery, local solutions and problems are rendered irrelevant, as are local universities and the intellectuals within them.

Following our consideration of the literature on the consequences of externally imposed solutions to globalization and the declining role of universities, we turn to Brazil as an example of a country that despite globalization is exercising its national sovereignty by developing locally derived alternatives to education. In particular, Brazil has created internally based educational programs through the Brazilian Service of Support to Micro and Small Enterprises (SEBRAE) and TELECURSO (a televised distance education program funded by the Roberto Marinho Foundation). SEBRAE is a Brazilian agency that focuses on the educational needs of small business owners, whereas TELECURSO provides education for young people and adult learners who missed the opportunities for basic education. This need to educate those who missed an earlier opportunity for education is a critical problem for Brazil and other newly industrialized countries. The continuing need to educate adults for whom advanced or even basic education was never a possibility prevents the full development of the workforce and continues exclusion on the basis of race and class. Educational and government agencies have a specific role to play in helping provide education to develop the capacity of the adult population. Whereas in developed countries education of adults is considered "continuing education," in developing countries the education of adults is basic education, or, as Paulo Freire (1970) named it, the "pedagogy of the oppressed." Universities, in particular, are in the best position to foster the educational development of adults because they are engaged in teacher education and social development programs. University economics and sociology professors in developing countries also are typically central figures in state welfare and employment policy debates and often move into the ministries, if not the presidency (former Brazilian president Fernando Henrique Cardoso was a sociology professor).

State educational agencies, labor organizations, and higher education institutions in Brazil provide excellent examples of how educational solutions are being developed at the local level to maintain the dignity and sovereignty of the people. This emphasis on local solutions to global problems is not just a national issue. In a country as vast as Brazil, regional differences and local culture are a critical issue of federal policy. The dictates out of Brasilia do not often match the regional needs of communities and states on the periphery that are far removed in distance and economic circumstances from Brazil's own core. Such regional comparisons are critical to understanding the cultural and economic reality within a country as well as between countries (Fry and Kempner 1996).

Finally, in this chapter we consider how SEBRAE offers an educational model of local solutions to global problems. These problems are not unique to Brazil, however, and are similar to the problems that many other countries face in opposing intrusions on their national and regional sovereignty by external agencies. Because only a small fraction of the Brazilian population has access to higher education, SEBRAE is an excellent example of a local solution for the advanced or "higher" education of poorly educated adults.

We conclude our discussion by addressing neoliberal theory's greatest failure: the cultural assumption that a unitary model of causes and solutions, as exemplified in the concept of developmental association (Kempner and Jurema 2002), is sufficient to solve each country's economic and social problems.

The Neoliberal Model of Development

Stiglitz (Chang 2001, p. 5) argued that the goals of the Washington consensus, which is responsible for implementing the neoliberal model, were "too narrowly defined in terms of economic growth." Therefore he maintained that "goals such as environmental sustainability, equity, and democracy" need to be "explicitly incorporated in policy design" (Chang 2001, p. 5). The failure of neoliberal theory and the consensus to understand the ramifications of such a restrictive strategy have led to CEPAL's conception of the "iron circle of underdevelopment." Because it appeared to be in the best interests of the core countries (the United States in particular) to control peripheral economies, the Washington consensus followed a modernization process that simply diffused the theories of Western hegemony rather than recognizing the unique economic, cultural, and social circumstances of each country—the basis for our argument in this chapter.

The Washington consensus has failed because, unfortunately, the cultural realities of developing countries do not uniformly fit the economic model or structural adjustment models of neoliberal theory imposed on them by external agencies. Paths to development are not linear, because each country faces its own unique cultural, geographic, and historical circumstances. The unexpected failures in Russia's transition to adapt to the shock therapy imposed by the neoliberal models of external agencies was, to quote Stiglitz (2002, p. 8), "fundamentally flawed in that it ignored informational inadequacies, opportunistic behavior and human fallibility." Stiglitz argued further that the key to economic success needs to be based on the "construction of a regulatory framework that ensures an effective financial system" (p. 31). The inability of global agencies to understand the unique cultural circumstances of each country and to account for this in the implementation of the imposed structural adjustment policies is clearly the reason for the failure. Again, Stiglitz explained: "In other words, development advice should be adapted to the circumstances of the country" (p. 62). This is the key to our argument in this chapter: Local solutions are necessary to resolve global problems.

The goals of the Washington consensus, under the premise of neoliberal theory, are often diametrically opposed to the social and cultural needs of the country allegedly being aided by external agencies. We have argued elsewhere (Kempner and Jurema 1999) that it is in the best interests of core countries to promote economic and political stability in all sectors of the periphery. Not to attend to these needs is to risk continued instability and uncertainty. How best to understand these social and cultural needs to avoid economic and political instability should be at the heart of any proposed solutions to a nation's difficulties. Unfortunately, external agencies have a mixed record on the effects of proposed solutions through structural adjustment policies. For example, Chossudovsky (1998, p. 201) attributed the breakdown of Peru's public health infrastructure and increased poverty to the results of International Monetary Fund (IMF) policies.

The inappropriateness of the neoliberal model uniformly imposed on developing countries is found in the economic difficulties faced by, among others, Argentina, Uruguay, and Mexico. Francisco Panizza (Folha de São Paulo 2002, p. A23), a Latin American specialist at the London School of Economics, explained: "The model has very clear systemic problems: excessive dependence on external capital, enhancement of social inequalities, and lack of politics to promote productive and technological changes, which can make these countries less dependent in exporting raw materials."

Although the 1990s began with great optimism in Latin America for the neoliberal imperative of privatization, commercial openness, and free markets, the decade ended with economic inequalities at the same levels or at even lower levels. "The virtuous circle announced by the liberal ideas of the early '90s was pure illusion," argued Clovis Rossi (Folha de São Paulo 2002, p. A24). In a recent report CEPAL noted that the economic deceleration in most Latin American countries, including Brazil, brings consequences:

> Poverty has affected more people than before. This phenomenon has been reinforced by the persistent inequalities in income distribution that persist in the region and by the characteristics of the performance of the labor market, which has been unable to incorporate workers into the formal economy with a consequent increase of informal workers and unemployment. (Folha de São Paulo 2002, p. A23)

The implications of growing economic inequalities and the increase of the informal sector place countries not just at economic risk but also at considerable political risk. Again, as we have argued (Kempner and Jurema 1999), the creation of a well-behaved economy is justified not only for economic purposes but also for cultural, social, and humanitarian reasons.

Our premise is that international agencies and their consequent policies should be guided as much by cultural and social concerns as by economic ones. Sen's (1999) concept of "development as freedom" provides what should be the basis for the formulation of global policy for individual countries and regions. Sen explained, "Social and economic factors such as basic education, elementary health care, and secure employment are important not only on their own, but also for the role they can play in giving people the opportunity to approach the world with courage and freedom" (p. 63). By not necessarily encouraging cultural freedom, the consequences of international agencies' policies on political stability and human agency have not been widely recognized. The IMF, for example, has typically been guided by one set of specific neoliberal policies (i.e., privatization, open markets, import substitution) that ignore the possibility of local-level solutions. Typically, little if any debate is allowed over alternative solutions to the unitary dictates of neoliberal theory.

The outcomes are quite clear in Latin America: Economic activity has declined, unemployment has increased, education has deteriorated, poverty and consequent malnutrition have increased, and violence has flourished (Stiglitz 2002). Stiglitz explained further that the IMF has compromised the ability of nations to preserve their social contracts with the people to maintain employment and to warrant social security. He noted elsewhere (Chang 2001, p. 17) that the Washington consensus needed to broaden its objectives of development "to include other goals, such as sustainable development, egalitarian development, and democratic development."

The perspective of the Washington consensus to see development principally as an economic pathology has led to a variety of national and regional crises and organized resistance to globalization, as evidenced by the World Trade Organization protests in Seattle and Cancun. In response to the external manipulations and intrusions by international agencies, under the guidance of the Washington consensus, developing countries have attempted to create their own internal solutions. Brazil, in particular, has engaged in its own defensive strategies by refusing to accept money from international agencies and multinational corporations: Paulo Freire refused to accept money from the World Bank when he was secretary of education for the city of São Paulo (Torres 1995); the governor of Amapá state refused to continue with a World Bank project (VEJA 1999), and the governor of the state of Rio Grande do Sul turned down Ford Motor Company's offer to build a plant in his state (Kempner and Jurema 2002).

Even with such resistance to the intrusion of international agencies into a nation's sovereignty, the demands of the IMF are sometimes perplexing. For example, in the Amazon region of Brazil a large number of individuals and institutions are involved in the creation of a system to watch and survey the Amazon. The goal of this organization, SIVAM (Sistema de Vigilancia da Amazonia), is to collect information to combat drug and weapons trafficking and mineral and resource theft—known as biobuccaneering. SIVAM was to have been in place by June 2003, but the connection between the regional centers to share data and integrate the radar system and network of computers has not been possible. This vital project for the protection of the Amazon was a victim of cuts that were necessary to meet the debt obligations to the IMF. For Brazil to meet its obligations to the IMF, it had to postpone efforts to protect the Amazon. The president of SIVAM's Coordination Committee, Ramon Borges Cardoso, said: "We have a Formula I Ferrari, with no wheels. It is the best car, but it does not move" (2003, p. 52).

As with most developing countries that are in debt to the IMF, Brazil had little choice but to cut funding for crucial social projects, such as SIVAM, in order to maintain the positive reserve balance demanded by the IMF. The problem for debtor nations is simply that more currency is leaving the country than is entering. When external payments are higher than the reserves available, the country falls into debt and is unable to meet its credit obligations. Because the IMF has such enormous control over a country's finances, the IMF can demand monetary reforms, such as the 4.25 percent primary surplus on the debt to GDP ratio. The IMF actually demands a ratio of 3.75 percent, but the Brazilian government decided on 4.25 percent, even though at this rate it is still a bitter pill for Brazil to swallow. To maintain such a positive reserve, Brazil has had to cut its expenses and control inflation through macroeconomic measures by reducing the federal deficit through reduction of federal jobs and cutbacks in retirement, health care, and other human resources. Although such fiscal austerity may be good for maintaining the deficit balance, it may destabilize the social fabric of society. The IMF may know what is best financially for a country, but it is the country itself that bears the burden for social instability. Brazilians, not an external agency, should decide which measures are safe to implement and at what risk.

These examples are indicative of the growing distrust of and resistance to the Washington consensus at the national and regional levels. Although neoliberal globalization is pervasive, it is not inevitable (Currie and Newson 1998). Brazil, for example, does have a large enough economy to provide some resistance to the Washington consensus that less developed countries do not have. We turn next to a discussion of a local alternative in Brazil, SEBRAE, which provides an education and economic program that is more appropriate to the cultural reality of its people.

The Case of Brazil

The outcome of the structural adjustment policies that developing countries must accept produces even greater inequalities. In opposition to the alleged benefits accrued from globalization, structural adjustment policies are bringing more poverty, more hunger, more unemployment, and more insecurity to daily life, according to Santos (2002, p. 41), "in a world that fragments and where social fractures are amplified." Santos continued, "Globalization affects the whole national territory, changing, brutally and blindly, balances and perspectives, and foremost, bringing a ferment of desegregation, an impulse to breaking cement patiently built, and putting in risk the idea of nation and of solidarity" (2002, p. 41).

The effects of globalization and the consequent imposition of structural adjustment policies by international agencies are not always immediately apparent on a nation's economic or social sectors. The consequences of such intrusions are manifested in the pressures and demands associated with the loans that cause the borrowing nation to fail in meeting the social demands of its citizens. Although the IMF's major concern is controlling inflation, the borrowing nation is more concerned with levels of unemployment, access to health care, availability of public education, and levels of nutrition for its families—its social contract with the people.

Globalization, as dictated from above by the core nations, imposes required methods of economic production, circulation, and distribution that alter the internal division of labor. Such imposed structural changes reinforce an international division of labor that determines how and what developing nations produce and export, what levels of employment they are to sustain, and how the distribution of political power is maintained on a global scale. Although currently it appears to be in the best interests of the core nations to subjugate peripheral nations, this may no longer be the case in a globalized future. Rifkin (1995) explained that with a "workforce in retreat in virtually every sector . . . at issue is the very concept of work itself. . . . New approaches to providing income and purchasing power will need to be implemented. Alternatives to formal work will have to be devised to engage the energies and talents of future generations" (pp. 168 and 217). By not attending to the changing nature of the workforce itself, advocates of the Washington consensus fail to recognize the ramifications of their policies on the economic and social future of developing nations and their workers.

Foremost in maintaining this social stability is recognition of the inherent conflict between knowledge workers and service workers. The social challenge for the future, both in developed and developing countries, is to understand the "class conflict between the two dominant groups in the post-capitalist society: knowledge workers and service workers" (Drucker, cited in Rifkin 1995, p. 176). The inherent conflict between workers who have access to education and those who do not is the foundation of "new and dangerous levels of stress" at the larger societal level (Rifkin 1995, p. 198).

Unfortunately, the ideological system of neoliberal theory that justifies globalization leads policy makers to ignore the dangerous levels of societal stress caused by class conflicts, particularly in developing countries fighting for economic and social stability. A notable example is the rioting in the streets of Buenos Aires following Argentina's economic collapse in 2001, despite Argentina having been the poster child for the IMF. But the effect of globalization is not uniform in every country, nor is there a true and inevitable path to economic development (Currie and Newson 1998). Unfortunately, under neoliberal policies of globalization, countries, places, and people are expected to organize their actions as if every crisis is the same and can be solved by the same recipe. This process of unconditional globalization from external agencies weakens the capacity of independent discovery of new solutions from within developing countries. The nation's universities and the intellectuals in them are disassociated from the problems of the larger society because solutions are dictated externally by international agencies rather than developed internally. Local research and the internal development of intellectuals in the national universities to solve local problems are devalued.

Within this context of globalization and imposed solutions, neoliberal policies compel economic reforms that make universities directly accountable to the market. Chauí (1999) observed that, gradually, neoliberal policies are moving universities from a condition of a public *institution* to a condition of a private *organization*. Similarly, Marginson and Considine (2000) used the term "enterprise university" to label the changing nature of universities whose priorities have shifted from the public good to profit seeking for the private good. The expansion of private universities in many countries coupled with the increased development of partnerships with private companies is creating what Chauí (1999) called an *operational university*—an organization focused on results and becoming a contract mediator rather than an institution devoted to creating knowledge. Such institutions can no longer afford to be focused on the public discovery of disinterested science and are no longer the exclusive place where knowledge is produced. Although the academic community does not respond alone to the emerging demands of society for information, the unfettered search for public knowledge is being substituted little by little by the operational, enterprise, or entrepreneurial university, the main goal of which is private profit. This profit-seeking behavior has created what Slaughter and Leslie (1997) called "academic capitalism." A principal concern over the capitalistic nature of universities is that having to engage in such economic competition displaces the focus of the university from its role as a social institution that preserves, inculcates, and creates dispassionate knowledge and science. As Readings observed, "The university is on the way to becoming a corporation" (1996, p. 22). Chauí explained further:

> Transformed into an administrative organization, the public university loses the idea and the practice of autonomy . . . [and] reduces its function to manage earnings and expenses, according to an administrative contract through which the State establishes goals and performance indicators. (1999, p. 216)

These policies, guided by neoliberal theory's focus on privatization, transform the ideology of the public's right of education into a private service that presents the university as a service-delivery enterprise with powerful economic interests rather than as a public institution. The pivotal point in moving from a public to a private entrepreneurial university is the shift from the society being viewed as the institution's referent to the university being guided by the principle of resource management, performance strategies, and competition. There is a permanent divorce between the public university devoted to the production of knowledge and creativity and the enterprise university that directs, orders, dictates, and controls the distribution of knowledge. The effects on academic life in this divorce are highly visible in the fragmented scenario presented by the public universities in Brazil. This fragmentation within the public universities does appear somewhat functional, however, because it offers a way for the institutions to survive the complex crises of Brazilian higher education. In reaction to this internal conflict and crisis within Brazilian universities, Trindade (2003) divided public higher education, euphemistically, into three different "universities":

1. "UNIMEC universities" are under the exclusive orientation of the Ministry of Education (MEC). These universities are noted for their poorly equipped classrooms, weak libraries, and professors with frozen

salaries. "Substitute professors" are the main professional workforce of UNIMECs. These temporary teachers have only master's degrees and teach undergraduate courses with no expectation for conducting research or producing academic work.

2. "UNICC universities" have the support of governmental higher education agencies such as CNPq (Conselho Nacional de Pesquisa [National Council for Research]), CAPES (Coordenação de Aperfeiçoamento de Passoal de Nível Superior [Coordination for Human Resources in Higher Education]), and FINEP (Financiadora de Estudos e Projectos [Funds for Studies and Projects]). Professors usually have a scholarship or stipend to complement their salary. Professors at UNICC universities receive allocations to participate in academic congresses along with money to equip their classrooms, libraries, and laboratories. UNICC professors also typically have a student team of researchers provided with scholarships.

3. "UFA universities" provide a support foundation for other institutions. UFA professors work as consultants and assessors on external projects for other universities.

Trindade's sarcastic observation of three "universities" coexisting within the same institution is, however, a realistic description of the fragmentation of Brazil's public universities. His three-part distinction highlights the extreme competitiveness among UNICC professors, who must contend with poor salaries, decreasing public funds for research, and systematic cuts in university budgets. Failure to support higher education has created a second-class professorate with "substitute professors" and distinctions between those faculty who can afford to do research and those who cannot based on "geography, gender, and class" (Kempner 1994, p. 287). The substitute professors are those who cannot afford to conduct research because they are teaching four or five classes per semester. They typically have only master's degrees, teach only undergraduate students, and are given two-year contracts with one two-year renewal. These faculty members have no attachments to their institutions, conduct no research, and do not participate in strikes for higher wages and better working conditions. They are merely functional workers delivering an educational product, as opposed to being professors and mentors of the country's next generation of intellectuals and knowledge workers.

Not only has the disintegration of Brazilian higher education affected the top levels of professional education that dispense high-status knowledge (medicine, engineering, law), but there is also a notable lack of education at the midlevel of technology (Kempner and Castro 1988). Whereas community colleges in the United States serve the postsecondary needs primarily of the lower and working classes, the Brazilian educational system has no comparable institutional level. Responding to the need for skilled technical workers, US community colleges have developed a vast array of two-year postsecondary programs ranging across computer technology, health care, manufacturing, aircraft maintenance, diesel mechanics, and home construction. Because so relatively few Brazilians in the lower classes graduate from secondary school, a US-style community college is not a viable educational alternative for these undereducated individuals. Therefore Brazil created the Serviço Nacional de Aprendizagem Indústrial (SENAI; the National Industrial Apprenticeship Service) as a way to deal with its undereducated population. SENAI provides an educational alternative for the lower classes who are denied the higher education that Brazilian elites receive. A similar national service (SENAC) in Brazil provides apprenticeship programs for commerce. Although both programs are quite effective, they are narrow in their focus on skilled manual occupations. Moreover, they are quite competitive among the lower working classes, creating occupational elites. SENAI and SENAC leave a large educational gap for working- and middle-class youths who cannot attain higher education but are seeking education for midlevel technical occupations—as the US community college provides. Because SENAI and SENAC are not truly postsecondary educational services, Brazil has been in need of an educational solution to fill this midlevel gap between skilled occupations and elite high-status knowledge at the university level.

A National Solution: SEBRAE

In an attempt to solve the dilemma of the educational system, Brazil created SEBRAE in 1990 as a technical institution to support the development of small entrepreneurial activities. Focused on increasing and empowering micro and small enterprises (*micro e pequenas empresas*, MPEs), SEBRAE is a government-sponsored institution composed of representatives from both the private and public sectors. These representatives work in partnership to stimulate and promote small enterprises in accordance with the national policies of development. SEBRAE is composed of a central coordinating agency with connected units distributed in all states and the federal district of Brasilia. The income to support SEBRAE's infrastructure is derived from a 3 percent salary tax on all Brazilian enterprises. This income supports the following (SEBRAE 2001, p. 2):

- Modernization of the management of Micro and Small Enterprises (MPEs).
- Increasing the MPEs' technological capacity and competitiveness.
- Diffusion of entrepreneurial information among the MPEs.
- Generation and dissemination of information about the MPEs' reality.
- Regulation and a differentiated legal status for the MPEs.
- Connecting the SEBRAE system with the supporting institutions to the MPEs.
- Technical support and implementation of the SEBRAE system for the MPEs.

SEBRAE makes these programs viable through a number of different activities, which include promotion of fairs and expositions and the development of training programs through courses and conferences. SEBRAE offers specialized consulting to MPEs on franchising and investments and distributes technical publications on issues of economic interest to MPEs. Since July 1995 SEBRAE has provided credit lines for development loans through the Banco do Brasil for small entrepreneurs. SEBRAE also has become engaged in advancing the federal government's social programs in the development of agricultural projects to support small rural properties, and SEBRAE works extensively on supporting tourism. Since 1994 SEBRAE has supported more than 6,000 enterprises through management support and technical courses. Such small enterprises are a significant part of the Brazilian economy, accounting for 48 percent of national production, 60 percent of employment openings, 42 percent of the paid salaries, and 21 percent of the gross domestic product (SEBRAE 2001, p. 3).

The central priorities in SEBRAE's strategic plan are the integral development of the human being, the growth of productivity, and the efficiency of the small entrepreneur. In this regard SEBRAE provides the local Brazilian solution to further education for adults. Because so many Brazilians are undereducated, it is perhaps more appropriate to think of SEBRAE as a "postelementary" educational solution, since it serves a similar population as the community college does in the United States. For example, US community colleges and many universities provide continuing education for individuals in small businesses and other entrepreneurial activities. Similarly, SEBRAE serves the needs of entrepreneurs who may be engaged in private business, public service agencies, nonprofit organizations, or philanthropic organizations. The foundation of SEBRAE's educational policy is (1) increasing access to continuing education and (2) creating and diffusing an entrepreneurial culture that fosters the growth of MPEs for sustainable development. This educational policy is drawn from the orientation of the UNESCO (1994) report *Education for the 21st Century*. This report proposes that education should be related to the principles of learning theories (cognitive, humanistic, and sociocritical); that is, "knowing how to do, how to be convivial and live together, how to share, and how to be" (SEBRAE 2001, p. 11).

The intent of SEBRAE's educational principles is to look at the entrepreneurial individual in a holistic way, not just as someone who simply needs and receives information. SEBRAE orients its educational process so that individuals not only will be able to perform their entrepreneurial activities with efficiency but also will know how to learn and how to enhance their personal abilities. This form of educational praxis is focused on preparing people to face problems, create and define solutions, and find alternatives both in their personal and entrepreneurial lives. SEBRAE's educational courses give emphasis not only to cultural and scientific knowledge but also to strategic abilities that enable individuals to be lifelong learners, able to continually grow and adapt to the changing social context (SEBRAE 2001, pp. 43–45). In many ways, SEBRAE is advanced or "higher" education for the underclasses that would never have had the opportunity for additional education. Because SEBRAE's pedagogical objective is to educate adults with little formal education, its intent is to "stimulate the transformation of the theory into action, the application of knowledge in planned and reflected practices" (SEBRAE 2001, p. 39). Based on the work of Paulo Freire, SEBRAE's goal is to "build knowledge in interaction with the world" (Freire 1979, p. 14) and to view individual learners as subjects, not objects. SEBRAE uses Freire's perspective of "learning how to do" to "shift knowledge into life, to self-development and to the student's enterprise" (SEBRAE 2001, p. 40). By connecting theory to practice, SEBRAE's pedagogy is related directly to action, initiative, and Freire's *conscientization*—personal awareness: "The education has an indirect action, and the learner has an active participation in the learning process applying different activities which stimulate reflection on meaningful and situated contents" (SEBRAE 2001, p. 40).

From this educational context of moving theory directly into practice, SEBRAE seeks to develop the capacity of the undereducated adult population of the informal sector, a characteristic of unstable and poor economies. Little attention is typically given by the state to the social and economic problems endemic to an informal economy and its educational needs. For this reason SEBRAE is an unusual government and private organization combination, because it works directly with the undereducated population of the formal and informal sectors. In Brazil, earning a traditional salary (wages subject to taxes that are paid by a legitimate business or government service) is not the dominant form of acquiring income, and therefore the higher education needs of these individuals are much different from those of the United States, for example. Because a relatively smaller percentage of Brazil's population have jobs in the formal sector, many individuals earn no salary paid by a traditional employer (i.e., legitimate income from equally legitimate employers). As we explained in an earlier work:

> The informal sector can be characterized as an unofficial part of a nation's economy that consists of relatively unskilled jobs not regulated by government, not susceptible to taxation, not providing job security or health insurance, as well as "outlaw jobs" where individuals make their living stealing or selling drugs or weapons. (Kempner and Jurema 1999, p. 111)

Although the informal economy may at first glance appear inefficient and disorganized, in reality many aspects of it are quite modern. The informal economy in Brazil provides a surprisingly dynamic economic environment with unique crafts, commerce, and finance that reveals a vibrant entrepreneurial capacity, well adapted to the local conditions. Brazilians know very well that the informal economy is responsible for the yearly success and pageantry of Carnival. The primary Samba Schools (the dancing and musical performance groups that compete in Carnival) are huge organizations expertly run by the black matriarchs of the *favelas* (slums). Within this highly dynamic informal sector, SEBRAE's challenge is to give individuals access to modern technology and provide a "higher" education. In this manner, SEBRAE enables individuals to acquire advanced knowledge while not neglecting the unique capacities for innovation and creativity that are based in the local context and culture of the informal sector.

Unrecognized sufficiently by neoliberal theory and its adherents in international agencies, the informal sector in Brazil and most developing countries is huge. For example, in September 2003 the Brazilian statistical agency, IBGE (2000), reported that there were 43.6 million formal workers in the country compared to an astounding 42.7 million informal workers. The city of Recife, capital of the state of Pernambuco, leads in the percentage of informal workers, with 49.4 percent of the workforce working informally, and only 34.3 percent of the local population is employed as registered formal workers (IBGE 2000, p. 10). Obviously, global solutions based on neoliberal theory's structural adjustment policies of privatization, opening capital markets, and lowering minimum wages make little sense in locations such as Recife, where most of the workforce is informal and receives *no* minimum wage to be reduced.

A Model of Action: SEBRAE-Pernambuco

To further explain the unique role that SEBRAE plays in Brazil's development and how SEBRAE parallels the US model of postsecondary education, we turn to the example of the program in the northeastern state of Pernambuco. Pernambuco is a small contributor to Brazil's overall GDP, with 2.71 percent of the nation's total output (IBGE 2000). The main industries in Pernambuco are involved in the processing and production of nonmetallic minerals, textiles, furniture, leather, and sugar. The Pernambuco government has invested mainly in developing economic sectors such as medicine, gypsum mining and processing, information technology, and tourism. The state's decision to concentrate its development policies and programs in these areas is aligned with SEBRAE's educational focus to provide support for these specific sectors. This regional focus allows a unified economic and social policy in keeping with the reality of the region, an understanding gained only with intimate knowledge of the local situation and culture. SEBRAE has a local educational role similar to community colleges in the United

States that provides workforce development and contract training for local employers.

In Pernambuco, small formal companies from the industrial, commercial, and service sectors total nearly 160,000. This total represents about 77 percent of the enterprises operating in the state, which accounts for almost 40 percent of the employed individuals in the economy of Pernambuco. These data, of course, do not include the contingent of informal activities and businesses that have no official recognition. Government estimates are that for each formal registered company there are four informal ones (SEBRAE-PE 2002, p. 23). The state and national economies are dominated by small businesses, mostly informal. This situation shows the critical role that small entrepreneurs (formal and informal) play in the national economy and the need these individuals have for some form of higher education. Even though many of these entrepreneurs never completed an elementary education, they have grown to be knowledgeable adults who would now benefit from advanced education. Data from IBGE indicate the existence of approximately 4.4 million formal MPEs in Brazil, corresponding to 98.5 percent of all formal productive companies that operate in the country (IBGE 2000). This percentage of companies is responsible for 21 percent of the GDP, absorbing about 59 percent of the occupied laborers.

Because the MPEs are such a large part of the Brazilian economy, formal and informal, they provide the path to Brazil's economic development. And herein lies the importance of SEBRAE in providing targeted education to small business owners, because they account for such a large portion of the economy. Because most of these individuals lack education beyond the eighth grade, they have no resources or little time to enroll in advanced training from traditional educational institutions. SEBRAE offers a local solution to fit the cultural context of Brazil and a parallel form of higher education for these adults. By working mainly with MPEs, SEBRAE attempts to focus the economic planning processes of the state and city government on the role of MPEs in the formal and informal sectors. The intention is to build a favorable environment to create, increase, and maintain MPEs in the state of Pernambuco. To support the MPEs, SEBRAE-Pernambuco (SEBRAE-PE) prioritizes joint working relationships based on the collaborator's needs, such as assistance from external consultants and partners and configuring a network of institutional agents.

An example of SEBRAE's local solution is in the Litoranea zone in northeastern Brazil, an area known for its sugar cane plantations. SEBRAE-PE has created a program to develop and energize the economy of the region based mainly on its sugar and alcohol production. There are 16 cities participating in this program. In an attempt to diversify the one-product economy of the region, sugar, SEBRAE-PE is using its educational and community resources to shift the regional focus from reliance on sugar to the creation of a sustained and competitive economy that embraces new products and services. In this manner SEBRAE-PE is bringing together local entrepreneurs, rural producers, *assentados* (those who received land through agrarian reforms), and MPEs of different sectors to diversify the economy across the areas of industry, commerce, services, agriculture, and cattle. Whereas the more traditional educational institutions, such as the universities or national services (SENAI, SENAC), provide education or apprentice programs, SEBRAE uses a holistic approach to the economy. Centered on integrating methods that sustain local development, SEBRAE-PE identifies and then addresses local agenda and priorities of the communities to provide appropriate opportunities—in the case of the Litoranea, going beyond its concentration on sugar cane plantation activities.

Yet another example of SEBRAE-PE's integration and understanding of local solutions is found in the sector of *Confecções* (fashion industry), which covers three cities in the Agreste region of Pernambuco (Caruaru, Toritama, and Santa Cruz do Capibaribe). In the *Confecções* there are 8,000 small companies generating more than 20,000 jobs, using about 600 tons of fabric a month. These enterprises sell the equivalent of US$21 million a month at more than 24,000 points of sale in the free markets of Pernambuco and other states. Research by SEBRAE-PE (2002, p. 17) has indicated that most administrative and marketing decisions in these myriad informal mini-industries were intuitive by nature. Therefore SEBRAE-PE created a partnership network to reach better solutions based less on intuition and more on knowledge of production activities, increased competition, and access to markets in the *Confecções* to achieve a greater level of sustainability among the MPEs. The solutions were to utilize continuing education to increase an MPE's knowledge of technological development and management and organizational skills. The creation of a fashion school by SENAI-PE (SEBRAE's partner in the service system—"S system") has made a recognized difference in this sector. The SEBRAE educational effort organizes MPEs according to different subjects, such as computerized modeling, industrial sewing in fabric and textiles (*malha* cloth), sewing machine mechanics, planning, and cutting and styling in sales techniques that attend to the specific demands of the local sector. Again, we see local educational and economic solutions that are particular to this region—cultural knowledge that is rarely available to international agencies and often to a nation's federal government.

DEFINING STRATEGIES

SEBRAE understands the necessity of knowing a regional culture and therefore uses informed and competent agents to respond to the needs and demands of local MPEs. SEBRAE's agents or experts are then responsible for accomplishing measurable and effective results for all involved MPEs, which results in stimulating sustainable development of the local economy. To achieve its goals, SEBRAE-PE has developed the following strategies (SEBRAE-PE 2002, p. 28):

- *Interiorização* ("interiorization"): Promotes inclusion and disseminates knowledge that enhances sustainability for small companies all over the state.
- Social capital/sustainability: Founded on citizenship and local governance, this is the competence to accomplish social and economic development through educational processes using Freire's (1970) *conscientização* (the act of becoming aware of one's own circumstances for which one is not necessarily responsible, especially poverty) so that local citizens are the agents of their own development.
- Valorization of cultural diversity: Focuses on cherishing local culture, seeking competitiveness in the differences among products and services.
- Internationalization of MPEs: Develops the capacity in technology and administration to promote competitiveness and entry into local, national, and international markets.
- Network action: Catalyzes, connects, and motivates a network of partners.

Among its strategic priorities in executing its projects, SEBRAE-PE provides entrepreneurial education for millions—the goal being to universalize entrepreneurial education (SEBRAE-PE 2002, p. 29) and to provide a higher education for those who have missed earlier educational opportunities not available to them. In its educational efforts SEBRAE-PE targets specifically (SEBRAE-PE 2002, p. 28):

- Micro and small businesses of all branches of activities, formal and informal, at any entrepreneurial level of development.
- Cooperatives and societies formed by micro and small producers and people dedicated to family businesses (rural and urban) organized around any branch of activity.
- Entrepreneurs and people in general, of any social class, social and economically excluded or integrated, dedicated to any nature of economic activities.
- Young people in the process of entering the social and economic sphere.

ACTING IN THE SEBRAE NETWORK

Central to the philosophy of SEBRAE in the state of Pernambuco is the creation of a network of individual entrepreneurs working together with institutional agents (see Figure 8.1). Establishing a connected, informed, and competent network allows individuals to respond to the demands of the MPEs and businesses with the ultimate goal of maintaining a sustainable economy for the state. As indicated in Figure 8.1, each SEBRAE-PE project has a manager who is responsible for connecting the various partners and for mobilizing the community to accomplish the planned results. These partners include a variety of educational, public, and private agencies. For each project manager there is a contact person, or "leader," at SEBRAE who is in charge of finding internal solutions to help meet the MPEs' demands. The SEBRAE leaders have at their disposal a variety of resources and cooperative arrangements. These resources include access to legal, banking, and management professionals in an "associativism" (*associativismo* in Portuguese) network, as it is termed in Portuguese, of entrepreneurs and small business leaders who work collectively with the SEBRAE leader to assist MPEs.

Herein lies the chief strength of the SEBRAE-PE model, which exists in opposition to externally created, prepackaged solutions or structural adjustment policies imposed by world organizations. Local solutions are found to

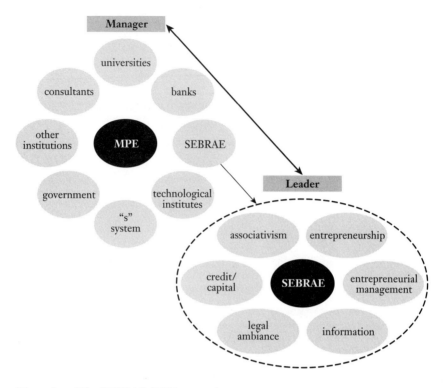

Figure 8.1 The SEBRAE-MPE network

local problems because of the mutual interaction and respect of SEBRAE's leadership through its institutional agents with the MPEs. The MPEs know their needs best when they are educated to articulate these needs through SEBRAE's educational programs. For example, in the dry lands of the Sertão in the state of Pernambuco, the focus on developing productive arrangements with the local MPEs has led to positive results for the group of *tecelões* (weavers) in the city of Tacaratu. This city concentrates on the manufacturing of textile products, such as hammocks, carpets, blankets, and other accessories. The local SEBRAE, in partnership with the Federal University, has financed several design workshops to help the *tecelões* create new textures, colors, patterns, and products closer to the buyer's taste. Such university-SEBRAE connections are growing in importance with the recognition of the need for intellectual-worker solidarity in the face of globalization.

EDUCATING ENTREPRENEURS AND WORKERS

The unique and decidedly local aspect of SEBRAE-PE is that it invests directly in young people's entrepreneurial and citizen education. SEBRAE-PE assists the next generation of MPEs by opening paths to education and community participation. The philosophy in assisting these youths is to insert them directly into the economy with an integrated emphasis on the sustainable development of the local economies. For example, Projeto Aprendiz ("Project Learner") works with young people, 16 to 21 years old, who are concurrently enrolled at the public high schools. The project's objectives are to identify labor opportunities and to establish business opportunities for these youths while they are still in school; the overarching goal is to provide a sustainable future for them within the context of the local economy. The project introduces young people to the ambiance of the local business culture and promotes, through work experience, the development of self-management skills and creative independence. The young people who join the project participate in meetings where they reflect on professional practices and evaluate the working environment, market, and public policies. This aspect of SEBRAE is similar to school-to-work programs in the United States but is directed toward local circumstances, educational capacity of the youths, and the local economy.

SEBRAE's accomplishments are based on its integrated view of development, which is typically lacking in externally imposed programs or projects. SEBRAE-PE, in particular, owes its success to the understanding and promotion of vocations that are suitable to and sustainable in the economic and cultural conditions of the immediate region. By reflecting on the local needs of social and human capital, SEBRAE-PE with its connections to business, industry, and educational institutions is in a unique position to assist contemporary MPEs and their future generations. Although SEBRAE-PE's knowledge of the life circumstances, conditions, and culture of Pernambuco's entrepreneurs and workers surpasses understanding by any international or national agency within Brazil, it is limited in its linkage across the spectrum of workers who need educational support. Although SEBRAE is able to meet the needs of many MPEs, it is still a limited educational solution for the needs of the larger Brazilian workforce. For this reason workers have had to look elsewhere for assistance with their educational needs. One promising solution, again at the local level, has been developed by the Integrar Institute of the Central Única de Trabalhadores (CUT; Workers Central Union) in conjunction with the public universities.

In 1996 the Integrar Institute of CUT developed and offered courses on different levels to union workers, the unemployed, union managers, and other *trabalhadores*. CUT took the initiative to contact the major public universities in Rio de Janeiro, Campinas, and São Paulo for assistance in the development of courses in basic education, management and planning, computing, and economics. CUT's purpose was to create other ways for workers to manage for themselves their collectively owned industries and enterprises and to improve their profits. This cooperative venture between CUT and the universities is an example of a union movement producing and developing its own professionals. By taking it upon themselves, CUT has created an internally developed alternative to public policy for the preparation of workers that unites them to fight unemployment and social exclusion of the underclasses. It is not coincidental that the president of Brazil, Luiz Inàcio Lula da Silva, is a worker and union organizer himself. Indeed, CUT's initiatives reflect the power of workers' movements within Brazil and the growing support for local solutions to global problems.

The initial offerings by CUT and the universities were considered "extension" courses because they were not of standard academic rigor. The State University of Campinas in São Paulo (UNICAMP) provided "Work Economy and Unionism" and the Federal University of São Carlos, São Paulo (UFSCar) offered "Planning and Public Management." Although the courses had little academic value in the traditional sense, they did give workers the opportunity for the first time to become familiar with academic work and the ways of academic culture. Because academe has its own rules and bureaucracy, these courses are not part of the official university curriculum, but they were offered at the initiative of individual schools or institutes operating within the university. The universities are now working with CUT to help build a professional strategy that educates workers to satisfy local needs of the workplace and the demands of labor. The universities therefore have introduced their own demands for the curriculum related to necessary qualifications for work and the development of workers who are able to exercise their citizenship—again, along the lines of conscientization.

All parties involved in this university-worker experiment agree that they want to offer answers to emerging social demands. However, this requires higher education to consider educational compromises aimed less at meeting academic standards than the needs of the workers. Obviously, the challenges to the universities are great, but this program with CUT has provoked an ongoing debate on university reform and the need of universities to attend to local demands for creating new fields of knowledge. The union movement is responsible for initiating this program, but universities have responded admirably with a need to merge the vision and needs of CUT with the social role of the university. The vision of the Integrar program team, which developed the concept, is "to open the university to the workers" (CUT 2002, p. 2). This vision and program has led to a dialogue between workers and academics that mirrors the larger political change in Brazil with the current president, Lula, a former labor leader, heading the discussion. The workers, who have accumulated vast experiences, now are having professors recognize the depth of their knowledge and raw intellect. In addition, the workers have given the universities an opportunity to adapt and redirect the curriculum to help satisfy local needs and contribute to social inclusion. The challenges ahead are to deepen this dialogue and to create public policy from the success of this program.

Conclusions and Implications

SEBRAE's holistic approach to the economy seeks sustainable development practices rather than the one-time inoculation of externally imposed and culturally inappropriate policies of structural adjustment. SEBRAE addresses local needs by providing educational opportunities appropriate to the circumstances of the individuals it is serving. Attending a university was not a possibility for most of Brazilian workers, but SEBRAE provides a "higher education" for these adult workers. As we have discussed, the worker-designed courses developed by CUT advance the role of a university-worker connection in higher education that is unique to the needs of Brazil's workforce. Such idiosyncratic differences of the local and regional economies can be served adequately only by agencies that understand the unique demands of the informal and formal sectors in each specific location. Even federal policy within a country is often incapable of understanding the needs of local communities, especially in a country as large as Brazil. SEBRAE is able to find local solutions because of the mutual interaction and respect created between its leadership (institutional agents) and the MPEs. This integrated view of development is successful because SEBRAE is able to promote sustainable businesses suitable to the economic and cultural conditions of the immediate region. Likewise, CUT provides a model for advanced education that connects the needs of workers with the role of universities to offer local solutions to Brazil's unique workforce.

Because there is no single path to economic development, the individual social reality of a nation must be considered by international lending agencies. Holding developing countries hostage to uniform neoliberal policies of globalization exacerbates social crises under the guise of economic recovery. Each country does not suffer from the same problems of development, and therefore uniform solutions are not likely to result in consistent outcomes. Much more economic variation is possible than allowed by the rules of neoliberal theory. Local and independent discovery of solutions, as SEBRAE has aptly shown, needs to be promoted by international agencies. Rather than imposing globalized solutions, international agencies should seek a greater understanding of local needs and promote local research and development. Developing countries with limited resources are typically forced to rely on imported knowledge that often has little relevance to the social and cultural reality of the country. Rather than forcing the implementation of solutions derived from external theory and research, international agencies should further assist countries in the development of their own research and researchers to seek local solutions to local needs. The relationship between universities and workers, developed by CUT, is indicative of the role that higher education can play in a nation's development of the underclasses. Nurturing programs that align universities with small entrepreneurs (SEBRAE) and with workers (CUT) are examples of how internally created solutions are more appropriate for the cultural and social circumstances of the country.

The disintegration of Brazilian higher education is especially troubling. The lack of education for the midlevels of technology is equally disconcerting, especially given IBGE's estimate that 98.5 percent of all formal companies are small and micro businesses. Brazil should be developing further its capacity for education at all levels, especially at the middle and lower levels of technology and business, but instead it is dismantling higher education to repay its international debt. Rather than strategically developing Brazil's capacity for educational development, the IMF is forcing short-term tactical decisions for immediate debt repayment at the risk of Brazil's educational and intellectual infrastructure.

The implications for all developing countries are that the economic and political hegemony of core countries has the potential for disastrous social consequences. The policies of the Washington consensus reinforce developing nation's dependency by keeping them on the periphery, further strengthening international inequalities and stimulating internal violence and instability. The distance to becoming a developed country is ever greater when generations rather than years are needed to rebuild the quality of the educational and social infrastructures. The viewpoint from the periphery is that the present policies of the Washington consensus are condemning generations to the technological hinterlands at a time when developing countries need a new, creative, well-educated workforce. Because undereducated citizens are unlikely to successfully compete in a global economy, short-term decisions for debt repayment at the cost of quality education doom a nation's youth in a globalized future. Unable to transform their lives or conceive of a brighter future, the young are unable to exert their citizenship and turn instead to alternative social futures. Certainly, more is at stake here than simply repaying a debt to the IMF.

References

Cardoso, R. B. 2003. "A Amazônia Protegida?" *Primeira Leitura* (October 20): 50–57.

Chang, H.-J., ed. 2001. *Joseph Stiglitz and the World Bank: The Rebel Within*. London: World Economics.

Chauí, M. 1999. "A Universidade em Ruínas." In *Universidade em ruínas na República dos professors* (pp. 211–222), H. Trindade, ed. Petrópolis, Brazil: Editora Vozes.

Chossudovsky, M. 1998. *The Globalization of Poverty: Impacts of IMF and World Bank Reforms*. New York: Zed Books.

Currie, J., and J. Newson, eds. 1998. *Universities and Globalization: Critical Perspectives*. Thousand Oaks, CA: Sage.

CUT (Central Única de Trabalhadores). 2002. *Programa Integrar*. Mimeo. Recife, Brazil: Integrar Institute.

Folha de São Paulo. 2002. "Crise Derruba 'Otimismo Histórico' da AL." *Folha de São Paulo Domingo* (June 23): A23–A24.

Freire, P. 1970. *Pedagogy of the Oppressed*, M. B. Ramos, trans. New York: Continuum.

Freire, P. 1979. *Educação e Mun dança*. Rio de Janeiro, Brazil: Paz e Terra.

Fry, G., and K. Kempner. 1996. "A Subnational Paradigm for Comparative Research: Education and Development in Northeast Brazil and Northeast Thailand." *Comparative Education* 32(3): 333–360.

Giddens, A. 1990. *The Consequences of Modernity*. Stanford, CA: Stanford University Press.

IBGE (Instituto Brasileiro de Geografia e Estatística). 2000. *Cadastro Central de Empresas*. Brasilia, Brazil: IBGE.

Kempner, K. 1994. "Constructing Knowledge in Brazilian Universities: Case Studies of Faculty Research." *Studies in Higher Education* 19(3): 281–293.

Kempner, K., and C. M. Castro. 1988. "Higher Education for Mid-Level Technology: A Comparative Analysis of Brazil and the United States." *Comparative Education Review* 32(4): 478–493.

Kempner, K., and A. L. Jurema. 1999. "On Becoming a Well-Behaved Economy: The Case of Brazilian Education." *Prospects* 29(1): 106–120.

Kempner, K., and A. L. Jurema. 2002. "The Global Politics of Education: Brazil and the World Bank." *Higher Education* 43: 331–354.

Marginson, S., and M. Considine. 2000. *The Enterprise University: Power, Governance, and Reinvention in Australia*. Cambridge, UK: Cambridge University Press.

Readings, B. 1996. *The University in Ruins*. Cambridge, MA: Harvard University Press.

Rifkin, J. 1995. *The End of Work: The Decline of the Global Labor Force and the Dawn of the Post-Market Era*. New York: Putnam.

Santos, M. 2002. *O País Distorcido: O Brasil, A Globalização e a Cidadania*. São Paulo, Brazil: Publifolha.

SEBRAE. 2001. *Referenciais para uma Nova Praxis Educacional*. Brasília, Brazil: Edição SEBRAE.

SEBRAE-PE. 2002. *Relatório de Atividades 2001–2002*. Recife, Brazil: SEBRAE-PE.

Sen, A. 1999. *Development as Freedom*. New York: Anchor.

Slaughter, S., and L. Leslie. 1997. *Academic Capitalism: Politics, Policies, and the Entrepreneurial University*. Baltimore: Johns Hopkins University Press.

Stiglitz, J. E. 2002. *Globalization and Its Discontents*. New York: W. W. Norton.

Torres, C. 1995. "Estado, Privatização e Polítia Educacional: Elementos para uma

Crítica do Neoliberalimso." In *Pedagogia da Exclusão: Crítica ao Neoliberalismo em Educação* (pp. 152–172), P. Gentili, ed. Petrópolis, Brazil: Editora Vozes.

Trindade, H. 2003. "Universidade e Estado." Paper presented at the 55 Reuniao Annual da SBPC, Recife, Brazil, July 14–18.

UNESCO International Committee on Education for the 21st Century. 1994. *Education for the 21st Century.* Paris: UNESCO.

VEJA. 1999. "Radar." *VEJA* (November 1): 13.

CHAPTER NINE

Mexico's *Estímulos*: Faculty Compensation Based on Piecework

Estela Mara Bensimon
Imanol Ordorika

Entrepreneurial models of the university (Marginson 1997; Slaughter and Leslie 1997) have had a profound effect on Latin American universities and on Mexican universities in particular (Ibarra Colado 2001b; Mollis 2003). Many of the structures, practices, behaviors, and values that we have come to associate with academic capitalism (Slaughter and Leslie 1997) or entrepreneurialism (Marginson and Considine 2000) are evident in Mexico's extreme form of incentive-based variable pay, or *estímulos*, as we refer to them in this chapter. Variable pay based on individual productivity has been in place in Mexico's higher education system for almost 20 years, thus making Mexico's compensation model a paradigm of entrepreneurial practices and their consequences for individuals, the university, and the production of knowledge.

The *estímulos* represent a differentiated system of monetary rewards specifically designed to "stimulate" or "incentivize" faculty to invest time and effort in the creation of knowledge products that can enhance the international standing of Mexico's higher education system. Under this system all full-time faculty members, regardless of their rank, are entitled to a base salary or "fixed salary" (*salario fijo*), as it is called in Mexico. The base or fixed salary is quite low and for many academics quite insignificant; upwards of 50 percent of an academic's[1] annual salary is based on a combination of national and institutional financial supplements determined on the basis of academic productivity. The system of *estímulos*—which has been portrayed as a "Darwinian nightmare," "perverse," and "savage"—encourages faculty members to be ultraconscious of maximizing the production of academic "pieces" in order to increase their earning capacity. Simply put, the base salary for an academic in Mexico falls far short of a salary considered adequate for a professional, whether in Mexico or elsewhere. Consequently, only those academics who produce the most prized goods (e.g., publications in international journals) and earn extra supplements receive a salary that is representative of a middle-class standard of living.

Critics of the system point out that the race to accumulate "pieces" as fast as possible has weakened the university as a political and moral institution (Suárez Zozaya and Muñoz García 2004), has turned faculty members into "*maquiladoras de* papers" (Díaz Barriga 1997a), and has created an academic culture that is hyperindividualist (Acosta Silva 2004). Scholars in Mexico have provided historical (Canales Sánchez 2001), political (Ordorika 2004a), and organizational (Ibarra Colado 1993, 2001b) analyses of the program. The *estímulos* have also been examined as a rational modernizing strategy (Grediaga 1998; Kent Serna 1995) and as a tool of the state to gain greater control of a university known for its rebellious and independent nature. However, outside Mexico this compensation model is mostly unknown because the many analyses and critiques it has generated have appeared in books and journals published in Mexico. Although systems of variable pay are not widespread in national systems of higher education, there is increased interest in performance-based compensation models, particularly as a viable strategy in times of limited financial resources and increased calls for accountability. The example of Mexico can be quite sobering for advocates of marketlike strategies and particularly merit-based faculty compensation.

In this chapter we examine the *estímulos* both as an outcome of globalization and as a means of transforming academics into agents of globalization. The framing questions for this chapter are:

In what ways are the *estímulos* a product of globalization?
In what ways do the *estímulos* transform the practices of academics?
In what ways do the *estímulos* reflect the logic and values of globalization?

We start with a brief definition of globalization, followed by a history of the emergence of the *estímulos* as a modernizing strategy. Next, we examine the ways in which the *estímulos* reproduce the worst effects of globalization in Mexico's academic community.

Globalization as Market Ideology

Globalization has become an all-encompassing concept in the analysis of contemporary society. It addresses, among other things, material transformations at the level of economic production (Castells 1996), the demise of the nation-state (Castells 1997; Evans, Rueschemeyer, and Skocpol 1985), changes in the nature and speed of communications (Carnoy 1998), incredibly fast exchanges in the financial and commercial realms, the preeminence of market and business practices and discourse in many spheres of societal interaction (Touraine 2000), the economization of social life (Wolin 1991), and the emergence of a hegemonic discourse based on deification of the free market (Touraine 2000).

Consequently, globalization has many definitions. In the realm of higher education, for example, globalization has been used in connection with the role of the university in producing "symbolic analysts" for a knowledge- and globally based economy (Altbach 2003; Morrow and Torres 1995). It also has been used to denote communication processes that have made the world smaller (Currie 1998).

Slaughter and Leslie (1997) identified two distinct processes through which globalization manifests itself in higher education. On the one hand, globalization becomes tangible through the reduction of public money for higher education institutions. On the other hand, globalization materializes in the emergence of new markets and market connections for higher education products and institutions. The adoption of market-oriented and marketlike behaviors in colleges and universities has become one of the most relevant features of contemporary higher education (Slaughter and Leslie 1997). Merit pay compensation for faculty in Mexico—the *estímulos* programs— is a significant example of the adoption of marketlike behavior in higher education. It is our understanding that *estímulos* policies are part of a redefinition of the relations between public higher education and the state in Mexico. These programs are a local expression of higher education policies and guidelines that have become hegemonic at the international level.

Estímulos policies are the product of both material constraints on higher education—financial deprivation—and market-oriented ideologies. Consequently, our analysis of the *estímulos* is informed specifically by the conceptualization of globalization as "a market ideology with a corresponding material set of practices drawn from the world of business" (Currie 1998, p. 1). In this chapter we examine how the market ideology that is characteristic of globalization is manifested in the rationality of the *estímulos* and in the practices that have ensued among those who implement them and among those who participate in the program.

The Estímulos *Programs*

We use the term *estímulos* in reference to the two largest sources of compensation that affect an academic's monthly paycheck in Mexico. These two sources are the Sistema Nacional de Investigadores (SNI; National System of Researchers) and the institutional programs that go by different names or acronyms at each university (e.g., PRIDE at the Universidad Nacional Autónoma de México [UNAM]).[2]

Even though the national and institutional programs are different, both of them emerged during periods of severe economic stress, the first in 1982 and the second in 1990. In 1982 the heavy reliance on the oil trade in the Mexican economy and the increase in foreign debt generated an economic crisis. The International Monetary Fund (IMF) put forward a "rescue package" with a corresponding structural adjustment plan for the Mexican economy. The conditions imposed by the IMF on Mexico were reorganization of public finances, control of inflation, reduction of public expenditure, and guaranteed foreign debt payment (Ordorika Sacristán 1996). These policies reduced the flows of resources to higher education. Faculty salaries, which had been declining steadily since the mid 1970s, hit an all-time low in the early 1980s. To make ends meet, faculty members were forced to moonlight at other universities or even secondary schools, an activity that in Mexico is referred to as *chambismo*. In the 1980s *chambismo* became a common practice of supplementing one's salary, and as more faculty members engaged in it, *chambismo* came to be seen as a threat to the integrity and quality of the higher education system. Along with *chambismo* the university faced the loss of its most reputable scholars, who were lured away by the higher salaries and better academic working conditions in systems of higher education in other countries—"brain drain."

The rise of *chambismo* and the occurrence of brain drain were particularly detrimental to the academic standing of UNAM and other public universities. According to government officials' and university administrators' accounts of this period, the national financial crisis made across-the-board adjustments of academic salaries prohibitively costly. Faculty salary increases, however, were contained below increases of national minimum wage and were well under increases of university budgets (Ordorika 2004b). On the one hand, this alleged scarcity of resources precluded the option that every academic would receive a fair salary. On the other hand, if academic salaries continued to deteriorate, Mexico was at risk of losing its most talented academics. This particular construction of the problem led university administrators and a small group of senior and well-positioned academics, primarily from UNAM and El Colegio de Mexico, to come up with the creation of the SNI as a solution (Canales et al. 1999).

The SNI was founded in 1984. It is no coincidence that this program was put in place at the height of the "quality" movement in higher education at the worldwide level. In this context the notion of a reward system tied to quality and productivity was highly appealing to individuals, primarily administrators and government officials, who thought that higher education, namely, UNAM, needed to be more businesslike in its operations.

Sistema Nacional de Investigadores

Official documents at the SNI website describe the purpose of the SNI as "strengthening and stimulating the efficiency and quality of basic and ap-

TABLE 9.1
Sistema Nacional de Investigadores *(SNI)*:
Amount of monthly supplemental compensation by rank

SNI rank	Compensation
Candidate to become a national investigator	Three times the monthly minimum wage
National Investigator Level I	Six times the monthly minimum wage
National Investigator Level II	Eight times the monthly minimum wage
National Investigator Level III	Fourteen times the monthly minimum wage
Emeritus National Investigator	Fourteen times the monthly minimum wage

SOURCE: *Reglamento del Sistema Nacional de Investigadores*, December 22, 2003; available at http://www.conacyt.mx/dac/sni/reglamento-sni-2004.html

plied research . . . [to] ensure that there [is] a national scientific community that has the resources needed to advance the production of knowledge and work toward the resolution of the nation's most hard-pressing problems." Because the SNI adopted the language of efficiency and quality, many see it as an instrument designed specifically to legitimize the corporatization of higher education. And, even though the emergence of SNI is represented as a strategy to protect the prestige of the university and prevent brain drain, advocates of the programs' incentives are seen by some as having had a convenient pretext to introduce the strategies of the new managerialism through a reward system that would bring the greatest benefits to individuals, who in normal financial times might have been its greatest foes.

The SNI consists of four ranks, plus an "emeritus" rank (see Table 9.1). Individual academics receive a monthly salary supplement based on their rank. The supplement is calculated on the basis of the national minimum wage.[3] For example, the monthly minimum wage in Mexico in 2003–2004 was 1,290.95 Mexican pesos.[4] Thus an academic who had the rank of Investigador Nacional II would qualify for eight times the minimum wage, that is, 10,327.60 pesos additional compensation per month. This compensation is roughly equivalent to US$920.00 a month.[5]

To be admitted to the SNI, an academic has to have a doctorate and has to be a full-time instructor or researcher—two criteria that rule out most of Mexico's faculty. Moving from Level I to Levels II and III (*Nivels* I, II, and III) is extremely difficult, and, as shown in Table 9.2, it is clear that most SNI members are concentrated at Level I. Needless to say, academics who rise to Level III wield a great deal of power and influence.

TABLE 9.2
Sistema Nacional de Investigadores (SNI): Members by year and level (1984–2001)

	1984	1985	1986	1987	1988	1989	1990	1991	1992	1993	1994	1995	1996	1997	1998	1999	2000	2001
Candidates	212	651	1,121	1,499	1,588	1,859	2,282	2,502	2,655	2,274	1,683	1,559	1,349	1,297	1,229	1,318	1,220	1,128
Level I	797	1,127	1,353	1,338	1,523	2,010	2,453	2,636	2,860	2,810	3,012	3,077	3,318	3,546	3,980	4,193	4,346	4,682
Level II	263	339	374	413	480	550	691	718	779	797	807	839	862	952	1,032	1,157	1,278	1,556
Level III	124	159	171	208	183	247	278	309	308	352	377	393	440	483	501	584	622	652
Total	1,396	2,276	3,019	3,458	3,774	4,666	5,704	6,165	6,602	6,233	5,879	5,868	5,969	6,278	6,742	7,252	7,466	8,018

SOURCE: SNI-CONACYT, Estadísticas Básicas 2001–2002 (mimeo).

Being admitted to the SNI is almost as prestigious as it is for US academics to be named a fellow of the National Academy of Sciences, except that in the United States this is exclusively an honorific title that accrues status but no additional compensation. In contrast, earning the SNI anointment represents a major attainment in terms of income (again, see Table 9.1) and status. To be a member of the SNI is to be a member of a select and exclusive academic club that gives access to all kinds of benefits, rewards, and coveted perks. The SNI represents Mexico's mandarin academic class, a sort of academic oligarchy. In addition to receiving a higher monthly salary, SNI members become eligible for research grants and for participation in high-level committees at their own universities, and they have access to administrative assistants, better offices, more travel funds, the use of international telephone calling cards, and so forth. In a research center of 80 full-time academics, of which only 5 are SNI members, being one of those five carries a lot of weight.

Academics who are admitted into the SNI are an important asset to their academic units because the number of SNI members is one of the measures used by UNAM's administration to evaluate and compare quality across research institutes and centers. From this condition—in addition to the prestige entailed by membership in SNI, and given the small relative amount of faculty included in the system—SNI members derive a certain degree of power within their institutions. The power and prestige associated with SNI membership for individuals, their departments, their universities, and the system as a whole are also stratified.

Access to SNI in each of its areas and levels is decided and overseen by the Comisiones Dictaminadoras (evaluation committees), which are made up of 12 Level III *investigadores*, whose responsibility it is to review the dossiers for applicants who seek admission, renewal, or promotion and then determine their eligibility. Level I members have to be reviewed every three years, Level II members every four years, and Level III members every five years.[6] Just as members can be approved for a new three-year term, they also can be demoted to a lower rank or eliminated if their productivity is judged to have declined in the interim period. Unlike in the United States where the possibility of losing tenure is a rare occurrence, being demoted or eliminated from the SNI is a real possibility and it represents a major embarrassment. As one academic put it, "To lose one's status in the SNI is as much of a disgrace as having one's stripes taken away." The small cadre of Level III members

TABLE 9.3
Sistema Nacional de Investigadores (SNI): Members by area, gender, and rank (1999)

Area and gender	Candidate		Level I		Level II		Level III		Total
	Number	%	Number	%	Number	%	Number	%	
Humanities and social sciences	258	100.00	1,222	100.00	331	100.00	193	100.00	2,004
Men	147	56.98	688	56.30	216	65.26	142	73.58	1,193
Women	111	43.02	534	43.70	115	34.74	51	26.42	811
Science and technology	1,060	100.00	2,971	100.00	826	100.00	391	100.00	5,248
Men	712	67.17	2,240	75.40	692	83.78	353	90.28	3,997
Women	348	32.83	731	24.60	134	16.22	38	9.72	1,251
Total	1,318		4,193		1,157		584		7,252

SOURCE: SNI-CONACYT, *Estadísticas Básicas 2001–2002* (mimeo).

plays a major role in running the system and controlling access to each level. Level III members have become the gatekeepers of the system. This control becomes apparent when looking at the number of members in each level (see Table 9.2).

The most recent statistics show that the SNI has grown from 1,396 members, when it was first established in 1984, to 8,018 members in 2001. Levels I and II have increased at a faster pace than Level III. In 2001 *candidatos* and Level I members made up 72.5 percent of the total membership in the system. On average, Level III membership has been about 6.6 percent of the total. It decreased from 8.88 percent in 1984 to 4.67 percent in 1992. Since 1992 it has grown slowly to 8.13 percent of the total in 2001.

SNI membership is organized into seven disciplinary areas: physics, mathematics, and earth sciences; biology and chemistry; medicine and health sciences; humanities; social science and administration; biotechnology and agriculture; and engineering. SNI membership is heavily skewed toward the sciences and technology, which in 1999 made up 72 percent of all SNI members (see Table 9.3). The SNI is also heavily male; men make up 72 percent of the membership. As the rank increases, so does the share of men; for example, men make up 70 percent of Level I but 85 percent of Level III. Among women, the reverse is true: Women's share decreases as rank increases. Not surprisingly, UNAM has the highest share of SNI members, 29 percent. In addition, among UNAM's academics, the likelihood of gaining access to the SNI is much greater for those individuals who are affiliated with one of the university's research institutes or centers (such as the Institute of Social Science or the Center for the Study of the University) than for those who are affiliated with one of the discipline-based departments (such as philosophy or history) or professional schools (such as law or engineering).

The Path to PRIDE

In February 1990, President Carlos Salinas announced the establishment of a new program of productivity incentives to compensate faculty members. The SNI was founded to provide incentives to Mexico's top academics and to stimulate the professionalization of academic personnel. The institutional *estímulos* were driven much more explicitly by a market ideology; to stimulate academic production, the state needed a system of rewards and punishments that had real and significant consequences on the lives of individuals. Salinas's announcement of the institutional *estímulos* marked the beginning of a policy change in higher education with regard to the role of the state versus the role of the university. PRIDE was an initiative that came directly from the government without participation from the academic body, faculty, or administrators.[7] In an analysis of the operation of PRIDE between 1990 and 1996 at UNAM, Alejandro Canales Sánchez (2001) observed that 20 years earlier such an intervention would have been inconceivable, least of all without the participation of the union. Because PRIDE encompasses a much larger number of academics, it has had a much greater impact on the academic culture than the SNI.

PRIDE is similar to the SNI in that it also represents a modernizing movement to spur scientific and technology activities (Canales Sánchez 2001, p. 65) by providing merit-based salary supplements to those individuals who choose to participate in the system. Like the SNI, the rationale behind PRIDE is that in order to stimulate academic production, incentives need to be put in place to make up for the loss of buying power among those academics with the greatest potential and motivation to be productive. PRIDE did away with across-the-board annual salary raises, and it further segmented the academic community on the basis of their ranks in PRIDE and the SNI. PRIDE also resulted in the institutionalization of an extensive and expensive evaluation apparatus.

PRIDE was established during a period in which higher education, particularly UNAM, came under great criticism from politicians. Canales Sánchez points out that, higher education institutions were being exhorted to improve their quality and to be more responsive to national and international needs and circumstances. Leftist politicians were also critical of the university, but for different reasons. The universities were seen as unresponsive to the masses who struggled for economic emancipation, and they were called on to improve their quality not to be more competitive in the global market of higher education but simply because it was their duty. Ironically, as we discuss later, one of the most detrimental consequences of the *estímulos* is to discourage social action research.

The PRIDE system of *estímulos* is different from the SNI in several ways. For example, although only 29 percent of UNAM's academics are members of the SNI, 83 percent qualify for PRIDE. PRIDE is less selective, and it

TABLE 9.4
PRIDE levels

	Level A	Level B	Level C	Level D
Amount of supplement as a percentage of the base salary	45%	65%	85%	105%

SOURCE: *Convocatoria PRIDE 2002*, available at http://dgapa.unam.mx/pride

functions much more like an entitlement. SNI's evaluation criteria are relatively stable and equivalent at a given time. Changes in evaluation policies and requirements from one selection period to another are relatively small. The SNI is basically a national and standardized program in which every applicant is usually evaluated on the basis of the same criteria regardless of whether their institutional affiliation is public or private. In contrast to the SNI, PRIDE is administered at the institutional level and there are inter- and intra-institutional variations in the evaluation criteria and in the approaches that are used to carry out the evaluation. For example, at UNAM the evaluation commissions, some of whose members are elected, have a great deal of latitude in determining what counts and by how much. The disparities in the definitions that are used create situations in which one unit might define teaching loosely (e.g., working individually with a couple of students), whereas in another unit teaching may be defined in precise terms (e.g., a six-hour course). The same disparities exist in how research is evaluated, with some commissions adhering to stricter standards and others accepting minimal standards.

PRIDE's salary supplement is calculated as a percentage of each faculty's base salary and seniority according to four ranks: A, B, C, and D (see Table 9.4).

In 2000 there were 8,249 participants in UNAM's PRIDE, and of these only 7 percent were in Level D. The criteria for participating in PRIDE are more flexible than for the SNI. Individuals with a master's degree qualify for Levels A and B; a doctorate is required for Levels C and D.

Living Under the Estímulos

To provide an idea of what an academic paycheck looks like, we have included a copy of a pay stub for a full-time academic who has reached Level C in

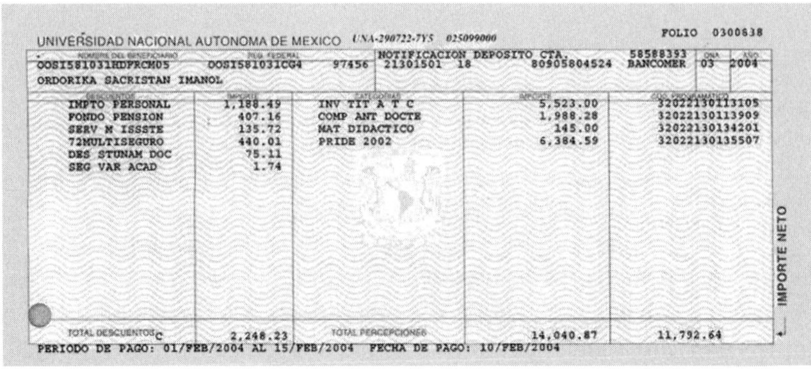
UNIVERSIDAD NACIONAL AUTONOMA DE MEXICO UNA-290722-7Y5 025099000 FOLIO 0300638

NOMBRE DEL BENEFICIARIO / REG. FEDERAL / NOTIFICACION DEPOSITO CTA. 58588393 / QNA / AÑO

OOSI581031HDFRCM05 OOSI581031CG4 97456 21301501 18 80905804524 BANCOMER 03 2004

ORDORIKA SACRISTAN IMANOL

DESCUENTOS	IMPORTE	CATEGORIAS	IMPORTE	COD. PROGRAMATICO
IMPTO PERSONAL	1,188.49	INV TIT A T C	5,523.00	32022130113105
FONDO PENSION	407.16	COMP ANT DOCTE	1,988.28	32022130113909
SERV M ISSSTE	135.72	MAT DIDACTICO	145.00	32022130134201
72MULTISEGURO	440.01	PRIDE 2002	6,384.59	32022130135507
DES STUNAM DOC	75.11			
SEG VAR ACAD	1.74			
TOTAL DESCUENTOS C	2,248.23	TOTAL PERCEPCIONES	14,040.87	11,792.64

IMPORTE NETO

PERIODO DE PAGO: 01/FEB/2004 AL 15/FEB/2004 FECHA DE PAGO: 10/FEB/2004

Figure 9.1 Pay stub for UNAM full-time academic at Level C in PRIDE

PRIDE (see Figure 9.1). This faculty member belongs to a research institute and has been an academic for 18 years. The second column, row one, "INV TIT A T C" ("Investigador Titular 'A' tiempo completo")[8] indicates that this individual's biweekly base salary amounts to 5,523.00 Mexican pesos (US$482.00). The fourth row in the second column, "PRIDE 2002," provides the supplemental amount, 6,384.59 pesos (US$558.00), which represents 85 percent of 5,523 pesos (the base salary, US$483.00) plus 1,988.28 pesos (US$174.00), which is the amount of compensation based on seniority. For this individual the PRIDE compensation represents 45.47 percent of his university salary. As a member of SNI Level II, he also qualifies for an additional 10,327.60 pesos (US$900.00) per month, which is not shown on this pay stub. This means that more than 60 percent of this individual's salary is made up of supplemental compensation.

The weight of merit-based supplements increases for *Titular* C's, PRIDE Level D's, and SNI Level III's. These are usually senior faculty, commonly referred to in jokingly as DC3's. A 30-year DC3 earns a total monthly salary of 72,663.91 pesos (US$6,346.00, including base salary, seniority compensation, PRIDE, and SNI). Before taxes, supplemental compensations (SNI and PRIDE) represent 63 percent of the DC3 salary.

At the Universidad Autónoma Metropolitana (UAM), the second largest university in Mexico, the situation is similar to that at UNAM, even though UAM uses a different system to distribute the PRIDE *estímulos*. A professor who is ranked at Level C in the UAM system can earn about 39,700 extra pe-

TABLE 9.5
Universidad Autónoma Metropolitana *point system*

Activities and products	Points
Textbook	2,200–6,600
Scientific book	2,200–6,600
Article or chapter in a book	880–3,300
Participation in faculty evaluation committees	1,100–1,100
Having earned a master's degree	6,600
Having earned a doctoral degree	15,400

sos per month, and if the professor is in the highest SNI level, his or her monthly salary can go up to 55,600 pesos. Of the 55,600 pesos, only 22.7 percent represents the base pay, and the remainder is subject to change from year to year depending on the professor's continued productivity.

Evaluation at UAM is based on a standard point system that is uniform for all faculty members regardless of discipline. According to Ibarra Colado (2001a), this point system represents the most radical approach to the implementation of the *estímulos*. The point system is divided into three areas: academic experience, professional experience, and education. A sample of what this point system looks like for a few of the indicators is provided in Table 9.5.

The Impact of Estímulos

Estímulos programs represent many of the characteristics that we have come to associate with the effects of globalization. We discuss four outcomes of globalization that are reflected in the *estímulos* programs: (1) labor flexibility and anti-unionism; (2) the polarizing consequences of knowledge-based economies; (3) the loss of academic identity, hyperindividualism, and competition; and (4) the dominance of the market.

LABOR FLEXIBILITY AND ANTI-UNIONISM

Institutionally based *estímulos* are described in Mexico as the program of salary *"deshomologación"* (Ibarra Colado 2001a; Suárez Zozaya and Muñoz García 2004), which literally translates into "dehomogenization" of compensation and marks the end of across-the-board raises. As we pointed out, more than 80 percent of the full-time academics at UNAM qualify for these *estímulos*, so they seem to have taken on the characteristics of a traditional system of annual salary raises.

The number of academics at UNAM alone who qualify for this supplement is almost as large as the number of academics nationally who qualify for membership in the SNI. So, given that the system now reaches just about everyone who meets the minimum expectations of academics, why continue to treat it as a supplement rather than as regular pay? For sure, the system does not represent a major savings, given that it covers more than 80 percent of the full-time academic personnel. Moreover, the administration of the program has resulted in an extensive and bureaucratic evaluation apparatus that, according to Ibarra Colado (2001b), is an extremely expensive system of regulation and surveillance.

The rationale behind the institutional *estímulos* is not so much that it accrues savings but that it is politically expedient in different ways (Ordorika 2004b). First, because *estímulos* represent "supplements" rather than regular pay, the government can bypass the requirements for negotiation with faculty unions. Second, *estímulos* embrace one of the most significant principles of flexible labor by linking wages to individual productivity on a variable basis. Third, *estímulos* produce a severe stratification of faculty on the basis of salary. They have created a significant group of marginalized academics who have no access to supplemental compensations and associated resources for academic work. University administrations assumed that marginal researchers and instructors would resign over time and in this way reduce the number of overall faculty by getting rid of the least productive members. Finally, *estímulos* were adopted because variable pay could increase administrators' control over faculty and become a powerful device to induce administration-directed change.

ACADEMIC *MAQUILADORAS*

Ibarra Colado (2001b) noted, "Today, those of us who participate daily in the university are very different from who we used to be" (p. 391). The primary instruments of control are the point systems that determine an academic's eligibility for the different incentives and that have become, "little by little, powerful instruments of planning and evaluation of the academic work, as they determine priorities in activities and privilege, [which] can be quantified" (p. 391). The mind-set and practices of academics as individuals and collectively change radically to fit into a context where monetary value is attached to academic products according to how much they weigh on the globalized scale of prestige and excellence.

The point systems, whether they are explicit, as at UAM, or implicit, as at UNAM, become powerful instruments of regulation in that academics become superconscious of what they should do to maximize their points. The point system makes it possible to differentiate academic work between those who generate the greatest economic benefit and those who do not. It converts individuals into academic *maquiladoras* who are pushed little by little to engage in certain activities and disregard others.

Under the rule of the *estímulos*, the "clearest example" of the most desirable academic is one who "generates original knowledge and disseminates the results in peer-reviewed publications and, particularly, in international journals" (Coordinacion de la Investigacion Científica 2001, p. 15). The image of the exemplary academic being promulgated under the influence of the *estímulos* represents a far more dangerous form of brain drain than the kind that the SNI *estímulos* were originally designed to prevent. The *estímulos* may be effective in keeping the most prestigious and productive academics in Mexico's universities, but the kind of work the *estímulos* encourage may represent wasted talent and the production of knowledge that is unresponsive to the most urgent educational, social, and economic needs of the people of Mexico. For example, this chapter, which is being published in a book by a prestigious press in the United States, represents the kind of scholarship that earns the highest amount of money and accrues the most prestige in Mexico's *estímulos* system. In contrast, if instead of this chapter, one of us (Ordorika) wrote about this very same topic and published it in a Mexican journal or as an opinion piece in the national press in order to increase awareness of how the *estímulos* stimulate knowledge products that are irrelevant to Mexico's most pressing needs, it would decrease significantly in monetary[9] and prestige value. In this way encouragement to adopt research topics and strategies according to research agendas from the central countries and for the publication of books and articles at the international level becomes a form of knowledge and capital transfer from peripheral to central countries.

Supplemental compensation—institutional *estímulos* and the SNI—have introduced two distinct dynamics into academic bodies. On the one hand, we have addressed the issue of faculty stratification. This is a process of differentiation based on salary levels and prestige associated with participation in *estímulos* and the SNI. On the other hand, faculty differentiation is enhanced by intense competition among academics, an intrinsic characteristic of any variable pay system.

Many higher education specialists in Mexico have pointed out that *estímulos* systems, at the institutional and national levels, have destroyed the social fabric of academic communities and eroded collegiality (Díaz Barriga 1997b). This is evidently a consequence of any variable pay system associated with productivity, given the fact that these systems stimulate competition among members of the organization and disarticulate the connections between individual and organizational objectives (Díaz Barriga 1997b; Ordorika 2004b). Competition favors confrontations between academics and erodes collective identities. It also increases faculty individualism. Traditional interactions of collegial life and shared academic activities are disrupted because they become burdensome and inefficient in the quest for productivity "points" or even dangerous in the competition with colleagues.

According to many academics' perceptions of *estímulos*, these systems have deeply transformed the nature of academic work and its products (Díaz Barriga 1997b; Ibarra Colado 1999, 2001b; Suárez Zozaya and Muñoz García 2004). Faculty members usually state that long-range research projects are abandoned in favor of others that yield results faster. It is also argued that work on books or broader academic projects has given way to article writing. Even the selection of research topics is biased toward those that yield the highest returns.

These practices play a major role in orienting academic production. Traditional concepts such as "academic freedom" and "disinterested pursuit of knowledge" are put into question (Díaz Barriga and Pacheco 1997). The search for high returns in academic activities in this competition for additional compensation transfers decisions about the degree of individual con-formity vis-à-vis institutional research programs and academic practices to each faculty member. The economic needs of academics create concrete limits to academic freedom for each individual at the university (Ordorika 2004b). In this way "market value" of academic products in this system of competition shapes the nature and content of academic work.

In an essay on economic globalization and its consequences for the com-mon good, Benjamin Barber (2000) put forth the idea that in countries such as Russia the adoption of free-market economies without the exis-tence of democratic institutions to control and regulate them leads to a "bru-tal Social Darwinism" and "wild capitalism" that end up worsening eco-nomic circumstances (p. 2). He reasoned that the expansion of US-like free-market economies to countries that do not have a history or tradition of democracy "means we have globalized our vices without globalizing our virtues" (p. 2). Although we recognize the faulty reasoning behind the idea that democratic states of the West possess safeguards against corrupt prac-tices and unfair competition, we agree with Barber's analysis that free-market practices do not automatically transform the system of governance and decision making.

Just as Barber suggests that the globalized marketplace produces "wild capitalism," we suggest that globalized definitions of academic quality, excel-lence, and productivity that are being promulgated through the system of *estímulos* unleash academic simulation, corruption, and credentialism (Acosta Silva 2004; Díaz Barriga 1997b). Similarly, we can say that the worst aspects of academic culture have become global: the quantification of scholarship, the academic star system, the obsession with university rankings and citation indexes, and so forth. In the United States the effects of these "academic vices" are moderated by the sheer size of the system and its diversity (in types of institutions). In a country such as Mexico, where higher education is smaller in number and in variety of institutions as well as in the proportion of academics who hold full-time appointments, the effects of globalization can be disastrous on several levels, as pointed out by Ibarra Colado's (2001b) indictment of the system:

[It] discourages long range projects, generates high levels of stress and anxiety, and disrupts academic communities and their internal cohesion. It discourages reflection and has awakened the most primitive appetites of individual self interest, opportunistic and selfish behaviors that rule the post-ethical society of men. This unregulated competition for money atrophies critical reflection, positing academic work and each of its products as simply mediums of getting money regardless of the quality of the work. All we have left are the procedures, isolation, an unwillingness to share ideas for fear of being stolen, and weakening dialogue and communication. (p. 401; translated from Spanish by E. M. Bensimon)

Accordingly, academic work under the rule of the *estímulos* becomes a "privatized affair whose aim is to produce competitive self-interested individuals vying for their own material and ideological gain" (Giroux 2002, p. 429). And, identity shifts from that of being a scholar to that of being an entrepreneur (Currie and Newson 1998; Marginson and Considine 2000). To be blunter, the *estímulos* represent a sizable amount of income and they can distort academics' relationships to one another in much the same way as someone in a commission-based sales job might scheme to out-compete his or her associates.[10]

To put it even more bluntly, the stakes in this system are high enough that some faculty members might respond by being conniving about the kinds of activities most worthy of time investment. Ibarra Colado (1993, 2001b) warned that some faculty members respond to this system of supplemental pay by thinking in terms of "If I do this, it counts; but if I do that, it will not count."

BOTTOM-LINE SCHOLARSHIP

The system of *estímulos* can also have disastrous consequences on the role and responsibility of academics to address the urgent social conditions of the great majority of Mexico's population. The structure of the system encourages academics to concentrate on the production and accumulation of various forms of academic products as rapidly as possible to maximize their pay. For social scientists the most efficient response to the compensation structure is to invest time on publications that are not labor intensive and that do not require extended periods of data gathering and analysis. The lack of funding for large-scale investigations of urgent social problems exacerbates the consequences of this structure on the quality of social science scholarship. Accordingly, the combination of the compensation structure and the lack of funded research engenders academic work that is heavily concentrated on literature synthesis, critical assessments of policies and practices, and historical accounts. For example, in the field of higher education studies, there is an abundance of publications on the history of UNAM and collections of edited books on topics that are primarily centered on the university as a political institution and on descriptions and analyses related to various aspects of the faculty. In contrast, there is almost no research on differential patterns of access and educational attainment for historically disenfranchised groups, such as those from low-income backgrounds, indigenous people, and women.

ACADEMIC HAVES AND HAVE-NOTS

One of the consequences of globalization is to polarize societies into a large group of individuals who fill the many low-level service jobs that are needed to support an information- and knowledge-based economy and a much smaller and elite group who control access and participation to the new economy. Mexico's academic compensation system has created a similar division in that resources are concentrated in a small group of privileged academics. A much larger group of academics—the majority of whom are part-time, lack a doctorate, and are outside the academic networks that provide opportunities for publication—carry out the lion's share of undergraduate teaching. Academics who are affiliated with one of UNAM's 39 research institutes and centers make up only 10 percent of the full-time academic personnel, but they constitute the majority of the SNI members from UNAM. The research centers' full-time researchers are required to teach much less, and when they teach, they typically do so in small graduate courses on topics of their own choice. At UAM the division between those who do research and those who teach is magnified by the criteria for the allocation of productivity points. Although research activities can generate 3,300 to 6,600 points, teaching activities generate only 110 to 660 points, or about one-tenth of what can be earned from activities that are labeled research and scholarship.

Conclusion

The Mexican case shows how policies and practices derived from globalization erode traditions and values entrenched within higher education. Notions of scholarship and academic work are challenged by these policies and practices. The academic implications of the adoption of marketlike procedures in higher education are seldom considered in advance. Proponents and supporters of systems such as the *estímulos* argue that the adverse effects that these policies have on collegiality, scholarship, and knowledge production are the consequence of deficient implementation. In our view the *estímulos* are functioning in ways that are consistent with and expected of market-based practices.

The *estímulos* can be seen as a "technology of control" that works in invisible ways and transforms the identity of the academic, but in ways that may seem rational and logical. In the United States university officials and academics deplore the competitive frenzy for prestige that has been created by the annual ranking of universities in *US News and World Report*. Yet they make its existence possible by complying with the magazine's annual survey. The same is true with regard to the *estímulos*; at the same time that academics are critical of them, they also participate in the legitimization of the system by complying with the evaluation requirements and doing what they can to maximize the number of points they accumulate.

It is indeed not rare for an academic to recognize the perversity of the system yet also to work very hard to ascend in the system and maintain a favorable position in it. The *estímulos* have been extraordinarily effective in getting individuals to submit to and perpetuate a system that is recognized as polarizing. As Currie (1998) observed, "The frightening aspect of globalization is the subtle way the process works to infiltrate institutions so that resistance to its agenda is weakened. It takes a mammoth effort to question these practices" (p. 6).

Compliance with variable pay systems in Mexico, however, is not surprising. It reveals how strong and far-reaching the ideological components of globalization are. Strategies based on business practices and a free-market orientation are now commonplace and quite legitimate in a variety of institutions, and universities are no exception. One of the most salient features of globalization is the escalation of competition, and Mexico's *estímulos* programs symbolize a response that, by all indications, is likely to become an option of increasing appeal to tertiary education systems worldwide that feel the pressure to be competitive despite diminishing resources.

Notes

1. Throughout this paper we use the term *academic* rather than *faculty member* or *professor*, because most of our discussion focuses on the enactment of the *estímulos* at the Universidad Nacional Autónoma de México (UNAM). The UNAM faculty consists of a large group of instructors, full- and part-time, and a much smaller but much more privileged group of *investigadores* (researchers), who are affiliated with research centers rather than with disciplinary colleges or departments. Accordingly, we use the term *academic* to refer to individuals who are instructors or researchers.

2. PRIDE stands for Primas al Desempeño del Personal Académico de Tiempo Completo (Primes [Incentives] for Full-Time Faculty Performance). The Universidad Autónoma Metropolitana (UAM) has three different incentive programs: Beca de Apoyo a la Permanencia (Permanent Scholarship), Estímulo a la Docencia y la Investigación (Incentives for Teaching and Research), and Estímulo a la Trayectoria Académica Sobresaliente (Incentives for Faculty with Extraordinary Academic Careers).

3. National minimum wages are established on a yearly basis by the Comisión Nacional de Salarios Mínimos de la Secretaría del Trabajo y Previsión Social (National Commission on Minimum Wages deriving from the Federal Secretary of Labor).

4. In 2004 the daily minimum wage was 43.297 pesos ("Salario mínimo general promedio de los Estados Unidos Mexicanos 1964–2004," available at http://www.conasami.gob.mx/estadisticas/ docs/Salminprom_64_04.pdf).

5. According to Banco de México, on September 20, 2004, exchange rates were US$1 to 11.45 Mexican pesos (http://www.banxico.org.mx).

6. According to SNI's regulations, after completing the first review in each level, Level I and II members are reviewed every four and five years, respectively. Level III members are reviewed every 15 years after they have completed two periods in that level (Reglamento del Sistema Nacional de Investigadores, December 22, 2003, available at http://www.conacyt.mx/dac/sni/reglamento-sni-2004.html).

7. We refer to the institutional program of incentives at UNAM as PRIDE. Originally called Programa de Estímulos a la Productividad y al Rendimiento Académico (Incentives for Academic Productivity and Performance Program, PEPRAC), this program was changed several times. It was established in its present form and under the name PRIDE in 1994.

8. This is the equivalent of a full professor. There are three levels of full professors at UNAM: A, B, and C. *Investigador* (or *Profesor*) *Titular "C"* is the highest level of faculty appointment at this university.

9. We also wish to note that the attachment of points to academic products is not unique to Mexico's system of higher education. At the Rossier School of Education at the University of Southern California, where Bensimon holds her academic appointment, this chapter will garner her four points in the school's performance index that is used annually to determine merit-based raises (see Bensimon and O'Neil 1998).

10. Not everyone agrees with the view that before the entrepreneurial university model the university was a more collegial and congenial place. For example, Carmen Luke (2001), a critical feminist theorist and policy analyst, suggested that "pastoral" pedagogies and administrative systems associated with the premanagerial university, such as "consensus style management," "collegiality," and "co-operation and support," were in fact the informal mechanisms of patriarchal culture and rule that managed to rule out difference (p. 436). She asked, "Indeed, was the 'Golden Age of Academic Autonomy Prior to Managerialism' an epoch of access, equity and enfranchisement for women and people of color?" (p. 436). Luke suggested that the transparency of the new tools may be a better system for women and others. However, as we have shown, the fact is that the kinds of productivity that are associated with garnering more points constitute activities that are enabled by academic social networks that are predominantly male.

References

Acosta Silva, A. 2004. "El Soborno de los Incentivos." In *La Academia en Jaque*, I. Ordorika, ed. Mexico City: CRIM-UNAM/Miguel Angel Porrua.

Altbach, P. G. 2003. "Globalization and the University: Myths and Realities in an Unequal World." *Current Issues in Catholic Higher Education* 23: 5–25.

Barber, B. R. 2000. "Challenges to the Common Good in the Age of Globalism." *Social Education* 64(1): 8–13.

Bensimon, E. M., and H. F. O'Neil Jr. 1998. "Collaborative Effort to Measure Faculty Work." *Liberal Education* 84(4): 22–31.

Canales, A., M. De Ibarrola, P. R. M. Latapi Sarre, J. Mendoza, and C. Munoz Izquierdo. 1999. "La Reforma del SNI." *Observatorio Ciudadano de la Educación*, June 25.

Canales Sánchez, A. 2001. *La Experiencia Institucional con los Programas de Estímulo: La UNAM en el Período 1990–1996*. Mexico City: DIE, CINVESTAV.

Carnoy, M. 1998. *Globalization and Educational Restructuring*. Paris: International Institute of Educational Planning.

Castells, M. 1996. *The Rise of the Network Society*. Cambridge, MA: Blackwell.

Castells, M. 1997. *The Power of Identity*. Malden, MA.: Blackwell.

Coordinacion de la Investigacion Científica. 2001. *Criterios Generales para la Evaluacion del Personal Academico del Subsistema de la Investigacion Cientifica*. Mexico City: Universidad Nacional Autónoma de México.

Currie, J. 1998. "Introduction." In *Universities and Globalization: Critical Perspectives*, J. Currie and J. A. Newson, eds. Thousand Oaks, CA: Sage.

Currie, J., and J. A. Newson. 1998. *Universities and Globalization: Critical Perspectives*. Thousand Oaks, CA: Sage.

Díaz Barriga, A. 1997a. "La Comunidad Académica de la UNAM ante los Programas de Estímulos al Rendimiento." In *Universitarios, Institucionalización Académica y Evaluación* (1st ed., Vol. Pensamiento Universitario), A. Díaz Barriga and T. Pacheco, eds. Coyoacán, Mexico: Universidad Nacional Autónoma de México, Coordinación de Humanidades Centro de Estudios sobre la Universidad.

Díaz Barriga, A. 1997b. "Los Programas de Evaluación (estímulos) en la Comunidad de Investigadores: Un Estudio en la UNAM." In *Universitarios, Institucionalización Académica y Evaluación* (1st ed., Vol. Pensamiento Universitario), A. Díaz Barriga and T. Pacheco, eds. Coyoacán: Universidad Nacional Autónoma de México, Coordinación de Humanidades Centro de Estudios sobre la Universidad.

Díaz Barriga, A., and T. Pacheco, eds. 1997. *Universitarios, Institucionalización Académica y Evaluación* (1st ed., Vol. Pensamiento Universitario). Coyoacán: Universidad Nacional Autónoma de México, Coordinación de Humanidades Centro de Estudios sobre la Universidad.

Evans, P. B., D. Rueschemeyer, and T. Skocpol. 1985. *Bringing the State Back In*. New York: Cambridge University Press.

Giroux, H. A. 2002. "Neoliberalism, Corporate Culture, and the Promise of Higher Education: The University as a Democratic Public Sphere." *Harvard Educational Review*, 72(4): 425–463.

Grediaga, R. 1998. "Cambios en el Sistema de Recompensa y Reconocimiento en la Profesión Académica en México: Estudio Exploratorio en Cuatro Áreas Disciplinarias." *Revista de la Educación Superior* 27: 125–205.

Ibarra Colado, E. 1993. *La Universidad ante el Espejo de la Excelencia: Enjuegos Organizaciones* (1st ed.). Mexico City: Universidad Autónoma Metropolitana, Unidad Iztapalapa División de Ciencias Sociales y Humanidades.

Ibarra Colado, E. 1999. "Evaluación, Productividad y Conocimiento: Barreras Institucionales al Desarrollo Académico." *Sociológica* 14(41): 41–59.

Ibarra Colado, E. 2001a. "Considering 'New Formulas' for a 'Renewed University': The Mexican Experience." *Organization* 8(2): 203–217.

Ibarra Colado, E. 2001b. *La Universidad en México Hoy: Gubernamentalidad y Modernización* (1st ed.). Mexico City: Universidad Nacional Autónoma de México, Dirección General de Estudios de Posgrado, Universidad Autónoma Metropolitana, Unidad Iztapalapa Asociación Nacional de Universidades e Instituciones de Educación Superior.

Kent Serna, R. 1995. *La Regulación de la Educación Superior en México: Una Visión Crítica* (1st ed.). Mexico City: Asociación Nacional de Universidades e Instituciones de Educación Superior.

Luke, C. 2001. *Globalization and Women in Academia: North/West–South/East*. Mahwah, NJ: Lawrence Erlbaum Associates.

Marginson, S. 1997. *Markets in Education*. St. Leonards, Canada: Allen & Unwin.

Marginson, S., and M. Considine. 2000. *The Enterprise University: Power, Governance, and Reinvention in Australia*. Cambridge, UK: Cambridge University Press.

Mollis, M., ed. 2003. *Las Universidades en América Latina: Reformadas o Alteradas?* (1st ed.). Buenos Aires: CLACSO.

Morrow, R. A., and C. A. Torres. 1995. *Social Theory and Education: A Critique of Theories of Social and Cultural Reproduction*. Albany: State University of New York Press.

Ordorika, I., ed. 2004a. *La Academia en Jaque: Perspectivas Políticas sobre la Evaluación de la Educación Superior en México*. Mexico City: CRIM-UNAM/Miguel Angel Porrua.

Ordorika, I. 2004b. "El Mercado en la Academia." In *La Academia en Jaque: Perspectivas Políticas sobre la Evaluación de la Educación Superior en México*, I. Ordorika, ed. Mexico City: CRIM-UNAM/Miguel Angel Porrua.

Ordorika Sacristán, I. 1996. "Mexican Higher Education in Transition: From Politically to Financially Driven Public Policies." *International Higher Education* 5(July): 7–8.

Slaughter, S., and L. L. Leslie. 1997. *Academic Capitalism: Politics, Policies, and the Entrepreneurial University*. Baltimore: Johns Hopkins University Press.

Suárez Zozaya, M. H., and H. Muñoz García. 2004. "Ruptura de la Institucionalidad Universitaria." In *La Academia en Jaque: Perspectivas Políticas sobre la Evaluación de la Educación Superior en México*, I. Ordorika, ed. Mexico City: CRIM-UNAM/Miguel Angel Porrua.

Touraine, A. 2000. *Can We Live Together? Equal and Different* (1st English ed.). Stanford, CA: Stanford University Press.

Wolin, S. S. 1991. "The New Public Philosophy." *Democracy: The Journal of Political Renewal and Radical Change* 1(October): 23–36.

CHAPTER TEN

Graduate Student Unionization as a Postindustrial Social Movement: Identity, Ideology, and the Contested US Academy

Robert A. Rhoads
Gary Rhoades

Based simply on size and expansion alone, graduate student unionizing in the United States warrants consideration as a significant social movement (Barba 1994a, 1994b; Rhoades and Rhoads 2003). For example, the number of union-ized graduate student employees has increased by 175 percent since 1990, and close to 40,000 graduate student employees are now unionized (Small-wood 2001). Also, at the beginning of the 1990s only a handful of graduate student unions existed; by the close of the decade more than 20 graduate stu-dent unions had formed, and a similar number of groups were mobilizing (Julius and Gumport 2003; Rhoades and Rhoads 2003; Smallwood 2001). Reflecting its rising prominence, graduate student unionization increasingly has captured the interest of scholars, who largely have focused on conflict between union organizers and university administrators (Barba 1994a, 1994b; Julius and Gumport 2003; Nelson 1995; Rhoades 1999; Vaughn 1998; Villa 1991). Other than a preliminary analysis of the public discourse contained on graduate union websites by Rhoades and Rhoads (2003), graduate student unionization as a social movement has yet to be examined in any serious manner.

Three recent studies have examined key aspects of graduate student unionization, but not specifically as a social movement. Lee et al. (2004) studied various cultural barriers to a graduate student union's mobilization efforts. They delineated several key barriers to mobilization, including the temporary employment status of graduate students, high levels of autonomy among faculty, the loosely coupled nature of academic institutions, and organizational paternalism among university administrators. Julius and Gumport (2003) examined causes and consequences of graduate student union activity. They identified economics as a fundamental concern contributing to graduate student organizing. They also pointed to the exploitative nature of the relationship between universities and graduate students, noting that a significant issue "is the explicit conceptualization of graduate students as resources for the university to use as they see fit, including as inexpensive substitutes to leverage faculty time" (p. 209). And Rhoads and Rhoades (2005) examined graduate student unionization as both a "symbol of and challenge to" the corporate turn within the US research university. This study provides some insight into the ways in which graduate student unionization can be understood as a resistance movement in the context of a global, neoliberal political and economic environment. Given the growing dominance of corporate models of the US university and the push toward increased business-mindedness and entrepreneurialism (Clark 2000, 2001; Slaughter and Rhoades 2004), the unionization of graduate teaching assistants stands in stark contrast to the effort of universities to casualize workforces through the use of part-time employees, outsourcing, and the use of contract and flexible workers. Seen in this light, it is easier to understand the steadfast resistance to graduate student unionization by so many academic managers mindful of the bottom line and the need to minimize labor costs above all else.

The New Social Movements and the Changing Academic Context

Since the early 1990s, scholarly work in the area of social movements has focused considerable attention on relationships among identity, ideology, and collective action (Calhoun 1994; Laraña, Johnston, and Gusfield 1994;

McAdam 1994; Scott 1990; Turner 1994). In placing identity, ideology, and collective action at the heart of the matter, we seek to examine the cultural terrain of the graduate student union movement in the United States. In essence, we study graduate student unionization at the microsociological level, exploring in the process key features of the movement's culture. Our turn to identity and ideology supports criticism of social movement theorizing offered by McAdam, who noted that "short shrift" has been given to "the more cultural or ideational dimensions of collective action" (1994, p. 36). He went on to argue, "Whatever the reason, the absence of any real emphasis on ideas, ideology, or identity has created, within the United States, a strong 'rationalist' and 'structural' bias in the current literature on social movements" (p. 36). McAdam further claimed that the literature on social movements lacks "real theoretical or empirical understanding of the processes that shape the ongoing development of distinctive movement cultures" (p. 46). Such a focus also is consistent with Scott's (1990) criticism of more traditional macrosociological analyses of social movements and his contention that insight lies in understanding the formation of group identity.

A key aspect of the emergent literature on social movements focuses on the link between identity and grievance. As Johnston and colleagues pointed out, "The traditional theories of social movements did not emphasize the link between grievances and identity as relevant to explaining movement formation, but it makes sense that the link was there. For laboring men and women, for peasants, and for anarchist militants, the substance of grievances, and their interpretation by ideologies, was embedded in everyday life" (1994, p. 22). A shared sense of injustice historically has proven to be a powerful source of affiliation. And although few who have forged collective lines of action as a response to perceived injustice are likely to have defined their struggle as a quest for identity, new social movement theory offers a conceptual direction that clearly reveals how lived experiences and social interactions are linked to the formation and vitality of collective struggle. "Collective identity and grievances are not the same, but their close association lies in the fact that the organization of how social movement adherents think about themselves is structured in important ways by how shared wrongs are experienced, interpreted, and reworked in the context of group interaction" (Johnston, Laraña, and Gusfield 1994, p. 22).

Marginality and collective identity thus become important constructs

278 FINDINGS FROM PARTICULAR COUNTRIES AND REGIONS

in exploring contemporary social movements (Calhoun 1994). Given that the forging of a collective identity often involves political struggle, it is no wonder that identity politics has taken on such a crucial role in social movement theorizing. Calhoun argued that identity politics are expressed through collective movements and involve "seeking recognition, legitimacy and sometimes power" (1994, p. 21). He went on to posit that such movements "are political because they involve refusing, diminishing or displacing identities others wish to recognize in individuals" (p. 21). Thus at the center of identity politics is the formation of a group identity oriented toward self-representation and political action (Rhoads 1998; Rhoads and Martínez 1998).

In addition to grounding our study in the new social movement literature, it is also helpful to explore research on student movements in general. Empirical studies of student movements proliferated as a consequence of campus unrest in the 1960s and early 1970s (Altbach 1973; Altbach and Laufer 1972; Altbach and Peterson 1971; Baird 1970; Heineman 1993; Lipset 1976; Lipset and Altbach 1969; McAdam 1988; Miller 1994). Activism of this era centered on civil rights, the war in Southeast Asia, free speech, and student rights, and early identity politics centered on such matters as curriculum inclusion and campus representation for African Americans, Chicanos, Asian Americans, women, and other groups. The 1980s saw the emergence of a strong anti-apartheid movement; college students throughout the United States supported the struggle for equality in South Africa through a variety of public protests, including the construction of shanty towns on university grounds (Hirsch 1990; Vellela 1988). More recently, Rhoads (1998) and Levine and Cureton (1998) have conducted studies of contemporary student activism. They described the key roles that multiculturalism and identity politics played in campus organizing during the 1990s.

Finally, the works of Castells (1997) and Touraine (1988) call attention to the relevance of social movements in a changing global context. Castells argued that a "network society," characterized by the dominance of computers and informational technologies and the "abstraction of power" from traditional organizational contexts, is "disintegrating existing mechanisms of social control and political representation" (p. 69). The consequence, for Castells, is in accordance with an "old law of social evolution": "Resistance confronts domination, empowerment reacts against powerlessness, and alternative projects challenge the logic embedded in the new global order, increasingly sensed as disorder by people around the planet" (p. 69). Consequently, in his book *The Power of Identity*, Castells examined how four social movements—the Zapatistas in Mexico, the American militia, the Aum Shinrikyo (a Japanese cult), and the environmental movement—posed challenges to the global order of the 1990s.

Similarly, Touraine sees traditional organizations and political structures as increasingly impotent within the context of rapidly changing global and postindustrial societies. "The idea of society," Touraine argued, "acquires a new meaning here, far less defined by institutions, a central power, values or permanent rules of social organization, than by this field of debates and conflicts which has as its global stake the social use of the symbolic goods that postindustrial society massively produces" (1998, p. 33). As part of his goal of forging a postindustrial sociology, Touraine maintained that the focus must turn to social movements, given that "social life loses its unity, its center, and its mechanisms of institutionalization, control, and socialization" (p. 27). Thus for both Castells and Touraine social movements take on increasing importance in generating resistance to the domination of a variety of powerful and complex organizations and networks framed to a large degree by the restructuring of global capitalism.

The work of Castells and Touraine is particularly relevant to the study of graduate student unionization, given the importance of universities in supporting the shift from an industrial to a postindustrial society. For example, in their studies of higher education in the United States, Great Britain, Canada, and Australia, Slaughter and Leslie (1997) argued that the last two decades saw higher education enter a global era. A consequence of globalization is that research universities are forced to play by new rules. Such considerations, described by Slaughter and Leslie as academic capitalism, revolve around the following four trends: (1) the constriction of funds for postsecondary education, (2) the growing centrality of technology and science and fields closely tied to markets, especially international markets, (3) the increasing ties between multinational corporations and state agencies involved with development and innovation, and (4) the increased interest by advanced industrial countries and multinational corporations in global intellectual property issues. Slaughter and Leslie went on to argue that all four countries in their study saw the central purpose of higher education shift from the liberal education of undergraduates to wealth creation.

Similarly, in his analysis of contracts among unionized faculty in the

United States, Rhoades (1998) found that faculty unions increasingly sought to mitigate the effects of the academy's turn toward academic capitalism. Part of what Rhoades saw happening in the academy was a reflection of changes in the broader society. One such change was a shift from full-time workers to a more contingent, part-time workforce. The shift to part-time labor is especially notable in the US academy, where the use of part-time instructors recently reached an all-time high, more than 40 percent (Wilson 2001). This is of utmost concern to graduate student employees, given that many hope to leave their assistantships and move on to full-time faculty positions.

　　What the preceding points suggest is that capital-driven models of management have influenced the academic culture of the university and challenged many of the traditional notions of academic work (Rhoades 1998; Slaughter and Leslie 1997). As a consequence of a shift from an industrial society characterized by manufacturing processes to a postindustrial society driven by the creation of new technologies and the management and communication of information, the US research university has taken center stage in an ever-changing global economic system. The battle over control of the university thus has become a key feature of what many have come to see as a political struggle to insert corporate capitalism at the center of the academic enterprise (Castells 1997; Chomsky 1998; Rhoads 2003). Thus it is within the context of the growing influence of academic capitalism and postindustrialization that we seek to make sense of the identity and ideologies of graduate student organizers seeking to forge collective lines of action.

A Study of Graduate Student Unionization

During the 2000–2001 academic year, we visited four universities as part of a study of graduate student unionization. In all, we conducted 36 formal interviews with graduate student organizers (we interviewed 5 union representatives and faculty as well). The four universities we visited were New York University, Michigan State University, the University of California, Los Angeles (UCLA), and the University of Michigan. The following research questions were key to our study: (1) What are the fundamental characteristics exhibited by graduate student unionization as a social movement? (To what extent does the movement reveal class sensibilities? Is the movement best characterized as modern or postmodern, industrial or postindustrial?) (2) What role does identity play in advancing graduate student union-ization? (3) In what ways (if at all) does unionization exhibit and/or foster a shared sense of identity? (4) What ideas and ideologies (if any) have been for-mulated as part of advancing unionization? Related to the final question, we were curious about the ways in which graduate student unionizing might pose a challenge to contemporary notions of the academy. Similarly, are there qualities reflective of the contemporary academy that might contribute to the movement's momentum during the late 1990s and early 2000s?

We frame a discussion of our study around central concerns deriving from our research questions as well as key points grounded in a more induc-tive analysis. In brief, our analysis of the data and the subsequent generation of key themes centered on issues of identity, ideology, and collective strug-gle (for a much more thorough discussion of the research methodology used in this study, including the data analysis, see Rhoads and Rhoades [2005]). Our concerns reflect a commitment to new social movement theorizing and the importance of how individuals experience, interpret, and rework shared wrongs (Johnston et al. 1994). Accordingly, we use four categories for pre-senting our findings: connecting with existing identities, forging a collective identity, ideological considerations, and the context of the contested academy.

CONNECTING WITH EXISTING IDENTITIES

An aspect of the unionization movement's strength has been its ability to connect graduate student organizers to existing points of self-identification. Here we speak of the identity some graduate student organizers embrace as activists, progressives, liberals, and, in some cases, radicals. One organizer described how union activity appealed to his identity as an activist. For sev-eral years he thought that the environmental movement held the potential to bring progressives together, but now he believes that labor struggle may be the "umbrella movement" for a broad social justice coalition. Another or-ganizer spoke of her need to connect closely held social justice values to ac-tive participation in an organized struggle. She feared becoming an armchair intellectual, "like so many of [her] left-wing friends had done during gradu-ate school." Graduate student unionization enabled her to pursue progres-sive values in a meaningful way; she described her involvement as a way to connect "theory and action."

Most of our interview subjects spoke of their turn to union organizing as a means of connecting with fundamental social justice ideals, such as democratizing the workforce. Clearly, existing identities play a key role in shaping the movement. The following comments highlight how various aspects of one's identity became connected to union organizing:

> I already saw myself as somebody who was kind of oppositional. Perhaps union organizing drew me for that reason. Maybe it just drew me because I knew that there would be other people here who would share the kind of values I hold, the kind that made me oppositional within my family structure.

> There's something about identity, sort of a personality element that has brought me to union organizing. But then there's also the element of engaging in politics and understanding what happens in politics. Identity and politics sort of build on each other.

> Politically, I've always been more liberal. I've always identified politically with Democrats and supported unions, even when I wasn't part of one. So, given the opportunity to be part of a union and take an active role organizing, it seemed like a natural thing to do.

> I feel like there are certain kinds of people who favor unions. There are people like me who have always wanted to be a member of a union and when they find out about GEO [Graduate Employees Organization] they get involved. They have to be involved. I think they tend to be on the left, tend to be really interested in organizing and activism.

Identity, in part, derives from the experiences one has in life and how such experiences become internalized. One student organizer addressed this point: "It's probably obvious, but I think we all believe unionization is a means to social justice. We all know each other, and I think that most of us have experienced or been witness to injustice. I think we channel that sort of experience into energy for organizing. We involve ourselves in ways that produce results."

Sometimes the experiences that shape one's political orientation are closely tied to family. One organizer noted how she was raised in a leftist family and was expected by her parents to become socially and politically engaged. Another student related his union organizing directly to family matters: "Being involved in the labor movement is about recognizing the importance of what my parents and so many of my relatives have done for their families, for themselves, as immigrants, for the country that they are a part of and have contributed to."

Certainly not everyone who becomes active in a graduate student union does so because of connections to his or her political identity. Many organizers pointed out that some students join because of the oppressive experiences they have as graduate students: "They gravitate toward the union because they're so appalled by their experience in graduate school," explained one organizer. A second organizer noted that he believed "bread-and-butter" issues—basic benefits such as wages and health care—are the primary reasons that graduate students support the union, especially in terms of the broader membership. In this regard, the connection between union involvement and one's political identity seems most germane to organizers, whereas bread-and-butter issues tend to appeal more to the broader membership.

FORGING A COLLECTIVE IDENTITY

Advancing a collective identity involves not only tapping into already existing self-definitions but also convincing fellow graduate students (particularly graduate student employees) that they have common concerns and a course of action as "workers"—the conversion component. By this, we suggest that graduate student organizers recognize the need for large groups of graduate student employees to define themselves in common struggle with one another—essentially to see themselves as a "we," amounting to what Blumer (1946) described as a "we consciousness." Consequently, a key aspect of the discourse used by organizers focuses on helping graduate student employees to envision themselves as workers, perhaps even marginalized workers. This has not been an easy task, given the context of the academy and the tendency to situate intellectual activity as something other than work. The following student organizers attest to these concerns:

> There are discussions among those against the union versus those for it. Most of us working for the union are comfortable with the notion of what we do as work and that unions are not just for factory workers. As one of my friends likes to say, if the university thinks we're not employees, then why don't we stop working for a while and see what they have to say about

284 FINDINGS FROM PARTICULAR COUNTRIES AND REGIONS

that. The fact that our work is intellectual doesn't mean that we aren't workers. I mean I wouldn't identify myself with an assembly line worker putting together widgets. I'm not so much a blue collar worker, but I'm a worker nonetheless. There are many workers in the service industry whose work is not so much different from mine.

I think that for all of us in the academy, for graduate students, for faculty, for administrators, all of us are coping with how does the work of the academy, the intellectual endeavors of the academy, how does this work differ fundamentally from other work done? Everyone has to recognize that all work relates to different aspects of how people define or think about themselves. It's not just true of the academy, but elsewhere as well. And so a movement has to make sense of that. This exceptionalism notion in the academy—that there are no intellectual workers in the academy— is troubling. For many people, their notion as an intellectual, as an individual, may be threatened by the union. Part of our job is to help people make peace with this notion—that sometimes they are an intellectual and a worker, and sometimes they are simply an intellectual. The point is to help them understand that their identity as an intellectual does not have to be threatened.

Exceptionalism and individualism, so dominant in the culture of the academy, poses a serious challenge to graduate student organizers. But although organizers are reluctant to liken themselves and what they do to factory workers and the grueling challenges of the assembly line, nonetheless they see themselves as workers and resist the notion that intellectual activities are something other than work.

One challenge of getting graduate student employees to commit to the union is that they see their current work as temporary. The following comments speak to this challenge:

There's a kind of identity politics related to whether or not unions are for me or not, or someone not identifying as a TA [teaching assistant]. Kind of like trying to sign waiters up—"I'm not really a waiter, I'm a writer." But the fact is that the average American is only in a job for four to six years, and when you point that out to a graduate student, they may say, "That makes a lot of sense." So there's that kind of identity politics—getting graduate students to see themselves as workers with union rights and to get them to see themselves with other union workers around the country as opposed to seeing themselves aligned with the university administration. So getting them to identify themselves with each other as employees instead of as individual scholars . . . that's an important form of identity and it gets played out in a variety of ways.

Part of the push to connect graduate student employees as workers has been in reaction to university administrations claiming otherwise—arguing that graduate student employees are apprentices. University administrators have maintained that it is difficult to separate the work graduate students do as part of their academic experience from their paid teaching or research experience. A student organizer at one university responded to a chancellor's claim that it was too difficult to distinguish between graduate students as TAs and graduate students as students: "When I'm teaching, and grading, or speaking in front of a class, or talking with students during office hours, or e-mailing students about assignments, then I'm a teacher and a worker. When I'm talking to my adviser, or working on my dissertation, or reading for one of my classes, then I'm a student. It may be that I'll take some ideas that come from my dissertation or from my coursework and use them in the class I'm teaching. But, in any case, it's pretty easy for me to distinguish them." This organizer went on to add, "If I don't show up to teach my class, they won't kick me out of the Ph.D. program. But they might fire me. They are separate things."

IDEOLOGICAL CONSIDERATIONS

At the heart of the ideological position of the graduate student organizers is the conviction that representation as workers is fundamental to democratic rights. As one student commented, "I believe that everybody has the right to be unionized, but also that it's a good idea for everybody to be unionized. . . . Also, unions represent democratic institutions and are a form of democratizing the workplace. They help to democratize higher education, both in terms of the profits of higher education and access to higher education." A second organizer added, "In terms of why people supported it, people realized that it could make a real difference in their lives, make a difference in the structures of the university, making them more democratic."

Although many of the union organizers may hold deep commitments to democracy in the workplace, this may not be as true of the larger body of graduate students who support the actions of the organizers. One graduate student organizer alluded to this fact in the following comments: "I think generally people came to the movement from one of two positions: They were either directly affected by the union and its efforts because they were TAs who worked or knew others who worked and thus identified in a deeply personal way. Or they came from liberal/progressive politics and they saw it as the right thing to do." Other organizers also noted that many union members are not as much interested in democratizing the workforce as they are concerned about supporting their families and having decent wages, health care, and so forth.

Differences between organizers and the larger body of graduate student employees may contribute to why several organizers denied that the movement has an ideological component at all. For example, a few organizers were quick to point out that their own local movement purposely sought to structure the union in nonideological terms. Nonetheless, these same organizers often proceeded to offer a substantial ideological critique of the academy and the role of unions. One might make sense of this somewhat contradictory position by thinking of the movement as having both a public and a private face. There is a desire by organizers to advance a relatively moderate vision of the movement, because of the need to generate greater support among members, some of whom are conservatives. As one organizer explained, "The union includes graduate students who are conservative and Republican. Obviously, it would not serve the cause to alienate a significant portion of our membership." At the same time, many of the organizers deeply embrace left-wing politics. A consequence of the split between the public side of the movement and its more subtextual ideological undergirding is that organizers have to continually balance their more left-wing views with the needs and interests of a broad constituency. A good example of this took place at Michigan State University. During the 2000 presidential campaign, Green Party candidate Ralph Nader visited the campus, and organizers debated whether the Graduate Employee Union (GEU) should come out in support of Nader or perhaps Al Gore. Although there was much debate, ultimately

GEU's steering committee decided it was not in the best interests of the movement to alienate a large body of potential union members by identifying GEU with a particular candidate.

Another key ideological concern addressed by organizers is the traditional chasm between theory and praxis, a divide that graduate student organizers see embedded in the very culture of the academy. Part of committing to union organizing is a desire to link one's ideological view of the world to lived experience. The following student addressed this matter:

> There is an implicit notion among most union organizers and activists that there is a deeper meaning to what we are doing. That theory matters. But at the same time, especially in the English department, we do a lot of things theoretical that have no material component to them. They have little connection to lived experience and remain much removed from something like unions. I mean even if you're a classic Marxist theorist in the English department, there often is no connection made to real-life issues, such as those that unions face. I have friends and colleagues who are really involved in these kind of left-wing ideas but will not do anything in terms of activism, such as supporting unions or helping to organize. There seems to be a suggestion that you trade off energy toward one endeavor for energy toward another—that there is an economics of activism and intellectualism, and if you spend time organizing, then you lose time intellectualizing.

A lack of commitment to connecting theory and action was a common criticism of left-leaning graduate students who support unions in theory but have not actively engaged in supporting the graduate student union movement. One student summarized the feelings of many graduate student organizers with whom we spoke: "It's especially frustrating when you realize that people don't just do theory, they teach it too. They teach it to undergraduates. And interestingly, the colleagues who were most adamant about teaching those students and who were the most reluctant to strike, they didn't quite buy into the idea that they had the right to assert themselves, as in striking. They could talk about Marx and left-wing ideas in the theoretical realm but didn't seem to be able to connect it to their own actions."

Part of the ideological basis for union organizing is rooted in a challenge to the middle-class bias of the academy and the limited opportunities open to graduate students from low-income backgrounds. Consistently, graduate student organizers expressed a view that graduate students from middle-, upper-middle-, and upper-class backgrounds can find the means to make it one way or another, often with some support from their parents, whereas students from low-income backgrounds do not have these additional means of support. Thus the call for better wages and benefits is about challenging the basic class structure of the academy. This is most interesting, given that out of 36 student organizers participating in our study, only 6 identified themselves as coming from lower- or working-class backgrounds. The following student spoke to the class concerns of the movement: "I think as long as people can't make ends meet, it limits the kind of people who can attend graduate school. Low-income people are essentially blocked from attending." A second organizer pointed out that without lower- and working-class graduate students participating in serious scholarly debate, the whole discussion is skewed toward middle- and upper-class values. She went on to add, "I want to make sure that all people have a chance to participate in those discussions. . . . Graduate work needs to be accessible to a larger body of people; people from low-income backgrounds need to have the same chance of participating in graduate studies. We need to demystify the elitist culture that undermines all aspects of the academy."

In suggesting that the movement has ideological components, we in no way intend to undermine the very real economic, health, and quality-of-work concerns addressed by graduate student organizers. Students shared countless stories of hardship, including a 60-year-old graduate student with breast cancer who described the trauma of having a "worthless" health insurance policy provided to her as part of her assistantship. Ideology is important in advancing the movement and building a complex discourse to counter administrative recalcitrance, but the significance of day-to-day bread-and-butter issues should not be underestimated.

THE CONTEXT OF THE CONTESTED ACADEMY

Associated with the ideological facets of the movement, we uncovered a fairly complex critique of the academy. At the heart of the graduate student union movement is a debate between graduate student organizers and university administrators over the nature of the academy. And although we write about the contested academy separate from the preceding section on ideological considerations, criticism of the academy is very much a part of an ideological assault on the contemporary research university.

A major source of tension fueling graduate student organizing is the sense that the academy has dramatically changed over the past few decades. From the perspective of graduate student organizers, the university is no longer a collegial community in which issues are resolved through fair and open debate. Instead, the university has become a corporation where the bottom line is almost always tied to economics. From such a perspective graduate student employees are, as one student maintained, "the line workers in the production of knowledge." The following students' comments address the critique of the academy as a corporate or business entity in which collegiality is a masquerade presented by administrators to serve economically driven interests:

> Universities are being run more and more like corporations, and graduate students provide a source of labor that universities can continue to use and take advantage of, especially as larger and larger numbers of undergraduates are being admitted. Given the limited benefits that graduate students have, it seems rather apparent that universities are not going to look out for their best interests.

> If we want to have jobs in the future, then we need to unionize. I think if faculty want to have jobs down the road, they may need to unionize. I think trustees no longer see a difference between running their businesses and running the university. I think unionization prevents university administrations and trustees from finding cheap labor. If we all unionize, then there is no more cheap labor. . . . Universities can't relocate. They are pretty much stuck where they are. They are trying not to be tied to their built environment, by virtual organizations and courses online. . . . They need to deal with us. They can't relocate.

> We need to protect graduate students so that we have access to education. The university more and more is trying to save money—"How can we cut down on our expenses?" The university is more and more acting like a corporation, and so we need to unionize so that we are not squeezed too tightly.

Part of the critique of the academy as a corporation reflects an ideological view of what the academy ought to be. From the perspective of graduate student organizers, compromising undergraduate instruction for the sake of economics is unacceptable. Hence much of their critique of the contemporary academy revolves around the deployment of part-time labor to handle instructional needs. One graduate organizer put it this way: "The systemic issue is that we're being used on a part-time basis so universities don't have to hire full-time faculty. And here's the paradox, that if universities quit hiring graduate students and hire full-time faculty, then wouldn't we be putting ourselves out of work as graduate students? But I actually don't think that that's the case, because there are so many large classes, and if the university used graduate students in conjunction with an adequate supply of faculty, we could reduce the size of those classes."

In part, the corporate academy is responding to a global postindustrial environment in which flexibility is highly valued by successful organizations. Often, flexibility is translated by employers as having a part-time labor force. Consequently, over the past few decades universities have increasingly come to rely on part-time faculty to meet instructional needs. Graduate student organizers recognize these trends as well. As one student pointed out, "Speaking at a more lofty level, we're temporary employees, and temporary employment is kind of the wave of the future, and at some point we need to stop and organize. When I was working as an engineer in a company where they actually fire a lot of people with master's and Ph.D.'s and then hire them back as temps, I said 'Oh my God, they're actually temping an entire workforce.'" Clearly, the fear that the number of full-time faculty positions will continue to decline as the academy increasingly moves toward a flexible workforce is a central concern of graduate student organizers.

Graduate Student Unionization and the Contemporary Academy

Graduate students engaged in collective action to mobilize for unionization or to advance already established graduate student employee unions may be seen as constituting a broad social movement committed to enhancing workers' rights. In terms of graduate student organizers, common identities associated with left or liberal political views often form a basis for collective struggle and their efforts to build a larger movement. As a social movement, graduate student organizers seek to bridge diverse identities by tapping into and fostering a collective identity framed around one's status as a "worker" and, in many cases, as a "marginalized worker." Furthermore, efforts to forge a collective worker identity involve the deployment of particular ideologies linked to progressive democratic politics and a critique of the corporate turn within the academy.

Sophisticated strategies on the part of graduate students and union supporters are demanded largely because the movement itself must negotiate and challenge academic culture and its deeply held beliefs rooted in individualism and exceptionalism—ideals seen to be antithetical to unions and collectivism. Furthermore, graduate student organizers see the academy as fundamentally different from 30 or 40 years ago and thus offer insight into why unionization is taking such a firm hold on the contemporary research university, when in the past such organizing was rare and often unsuccessful. The primary explanation offered by graduate students is that the contemporary academy has come to function more and more like a corporation and that the university has become a key location for advancing the structure of a global postindustrial economy. Consequently, graduate student organizers operating within what they increasingly define as a corporate enterprise see themselves as having little choice but to mobilize as part of an effort to advance their participation in organizational decision making.

In many respects the struggle of graduate students to unionize in light of administrative opposition brings two opposing discourses face to face. Although administrators make the argument that collegial communities ought to solve problems through fair and open dialogue, thus rejecting the need for unions, graduate student organizers accuse administrators of talking out the side of their collective mouth. Graduate student organizers argue that administrators know for a fact how far removed the academy is from the community-of-scholars ideal. To graduate student organizers such arguments are facades intended to conceal the true nature of the contemporary academy, which to them has become an extension of the corporate ideal.

In the corporate academy the bottom line takes precedence over quality education. To support this contention, organizers point to undergraduate education and the use of part-time labor as a source of instruction. If undergraduate education is valued, then why do universities place such a heavy burden on part-time graduate instructors and in turn offer them minimal pay and instructional development? These arguments are central to the resistance that graduate student organizers present to university administrations.

As a form of organizational resistance, graduate student unionization can be examined as a challenge to the instrumental rationality of the academy that places efficiency over other relevant educational values. In this regard graduate student unionization can be understood as a social movement that, in the words of Melucci, reveals "that the neutral rationality of means masks interests and forms of power; it makes clear that it is impossible to confront the massive challenge of living together on a planet, by now . . . a global society, without openly discussing the ends and values that make such cohabitation possible. Movements highlight the insuperable dilemmas facing complex societies, and by doing so force them openly to assume responsibility for their choices, their conflicts, and their limitation" (1994, pp. 102–103).

Social movements tend to confront the foundations of societies, and in the words of Castells, their outcome, in "victory as in defeat, transforms the values and institutions of society" (1997, p. 3). Similarly, Touraine wrote that social movements are in essence defined by "relations of domination and conflict" in which various groups are "in contention for the social management" of the society's culture and of what is produced by the culture (1988, p. 9); clearly, "culture is at stake, a set of resources and models that social actors seek to manage, to control, and which they appropriate or whose transformation into social organization they negotiate among themselves" (p. 8). Consequently, although neoliberal forms of globalization may be seen as forms of "globalization from above," in that they are largely shaped by powerful and wealthy forces acting transnationally, social movements such as the efforts of graduate students in the United States may be seen as forms of "globalization from below," not so much because they are global in their organizational structure or strategies but more so because the social forces that they oppose are shaped to a large degree by global processes, namely, neoliberalism. In contrast to "globalization from above"—globalization of the variety associated with corporate capitalism and the capitalist state—the notion of "globalization from below" suggests a process in which "oppositional individuals and social movements resist globalization and use its institutions and instruments to further democratization and social justice" (Kellner 2000, p. 301).

The new social movement literature often suggests that contemporary movements are more likely to be organized around social groups sharing common identities in the quest for meaning than by groups defined by their relationship to the means of production. The dilemma is often posed as an either-or proposition: Previous movements centered on conflict associated with the means of production, whereas today's movements center around identity and meaning. Part of the problem here is that theorists have only begun to take into account the fact that modes of production that so defined capitalism as the modernist project have dramatically split with the past as part of what might be described as a postmodern or postindustrial turn (at least in the most technologically advanced societies). Consequently, many social movement theorists now see the nature of social conflict in different terms. As Melucci explained, "Contemporary conflicts reveal the contradictions . . . and bring to the fore actors and forms of action that cannot be fitted into the conventional categories of industrial conflict or competition among interest groups. The production and reappropriation of meaning seem to lie at the core of contemporary conflicts; this understanding requires a careful redefinition of what a social movement is and what forms of action display its presence" (1994, pp. 109–110).

Graduate student employees seeking recognition as a union offer an excellent example of how actors and actions are not easily fitted into traditional notions of industrial conflict. Their struggle in a very real sense represents the shift from an industrial model defined by the manufacturing of raw materials to a postindustrial model defined by technology and the production of knowledge. At the same time, to say that their struggle is without a class quality is to underestimate the influence of the changing economy on the nature of class relations. Hence, although the new social movement thinking tends to shift the focus from class conflict to cultural tensions linked to identity and meaning making, we suggest that both may in fact exist in postindustrial conflicts.

Data collected from many organizers tended to support new social movement positions, suggesting that graduate student unionization fundamentally is about issues linked to dignity and respect for graduate students. Time and time again we heard comments about the struggle centering on the dignity of graduate work. Thus significant portions of the empirical data reinforce the cultural aspects of the graduate student unionization movement. However, although cultural facets of graduate life linked to dignity and respect were important, bread-and-butter issues also drew considerable concern. For example, when asked about the key issues that make unionization necessary, more times than not we heard comments about increased wages and better health benefits. Improving the benefits of graduate student employees was also connected to a social justice perspective; many organizers discussed the exclusion of lower-income students as evidence of class warfare inherent in the elitism of the academy. These wage and benefit concerns move beyond simple cultural facets linked to dignity and respect and deal in essence with institutional resources and an effort to reallocate such resources. Here we begin to see aspects of a class struggle as workers on the lower rungs of the organizational hierarchy engage in collective struggle to improve their benefits. Indeed, phrases such as "bread-and-butter" may be intentionally used, as Clemens (1996) suggested, to elicit certain frames of reference linked to "craft solidarities" and to forge a collective class consciousness.

Following a class-based analysis, we noted that graduate students working in less lucrative fields—the humanities and the social sciences—tend to be involved in union organizing in larger numbers than those graduate students positioned more closely to the center of academic capitalism—in natural science and engineering fields. For example, of our interview sample only 3 graduate students came from the natural sciences and engineering (9 percent) and of the broader pool of union organizers only 22 of 128 (17 percent) came from these fields.[1] Differences between high-revenue-generating and low-revenue-generating fields reinforce interpretations that class sensibilities are an important aspect of graduate student unionization.

If we move away from traditional notions of class in a modernist industrial world and adopt an information-based postindustrial conception of class, the tension between the cultural analysis and the class analysis becomes less compelling. Here we suggest that any analysis of graduate student unionization is likely to be incomplete if we fail to frame the struggle within the larger socioeconomic context—a context greatly shaped by neoliberal globalization. We contend that it is more than coincidence that at the turn of the 21st century graduate student employees have suddenly mustered the momentum to unionize, after having initiated such actions nearly 40 years ago. Certainly momentum is a factor. Through word of mouth, annual meetings, Internet correspondence, student movement from university to university, and cooperation among graduate student organizations, the movement is akin to a snowball gaining in size and pace as it speeds down a steep and slip-pery slope. But there is more to the movement than this. Clearly, graduate student unionization in the United States must be understood as part of the changing context of the broader economy and the shift from an industrial sector economy to a service-, information-, and technology-centered global economy.

In the industrial economy workers waged battle with industrialists as they sought their share of profits from a variety of manufacturing processes. But much of this industry has left the United States. Whereas workers in the context of a grand industrial structure shoveled coal, fastened bolts to cars on an assembly line, or ran a drill press, today's service and technology work-ers flip burgers, send faxes, repair and program computers, and, yes, provide educational instruction. Now it is certainly true that higher education in the United States has long been involved in educational services—namely, edu-cating undergraduates—but the form that such instruction takes has changed in significant ways over the past few decades. At the heart of such changes— and here we speak primarily of research universities—is the employment of graduate students as instructors, who often individually serve hundreds of students in large classes. This, of course, enables the research university to maximize its most highly skilled resource—faculty as researchers and scientists.

Finally, as graduate students cover large portions of the undergraduate curriculum, faculty are freed to pursue the research and development inter-ests of the university, as the university both explicitly and implicitly elevates research and development over teaching. This shift in the basic structure of the research university—and interpretations of this shift—has produced some of the most powerful ideological warfare offered by graduate student organizers, and it has situated their work as lower-level knowledge produc-tion. The consequence is the emergence of working-class sensibilities among groups of graduate student employees who serve as postindustrial line work-ers engaged in the production of knowledge.

Notes

1. Although we interviewed 36 graduate student organizers at the four universi-ties we studied, we identified 128 graduate students actively involved in the four

unions. We then proceeded to collect basic background information about these 128 organizers, including gender, race, and area of study.

References

Altbach, P. G. 1973. *Student Politics in America: A Historical Analysis*. New York: McGraw-Hill.

Altbach, P. G., and R. S. Laufer. 1972. *The New Pilgrims: Youth Protest in Transition*. New York: McKay.

Altbach, P. G., and P. Peterson. 1971. "Before Berkeley: Historical Perspectives on American Student Activism." *Annals of the American Academy of Political and Social Science* 395: 1–14.

Baird, L. 1970. "Who Protests: A Study of Student Activists." In *Protest: Student Activism in America* (pp. 123–133), J. Foster and D. Long, eds. New York: William Morrow.

Barba, W. C. 1994a. "The Graduate Student Employee Union in SUNY: A History." *Journal of Higher Education Management* 10(1): 39–48.

Barba, W. C. 1994b. "The Unionization Movement: An Analysis of Graduate Student Employee Union Contracts." *NACUBO Business Officer* 27(5): 35–43.

Blumer, H. 1946. "Social Movements." In *Principles of Sociology* (2nd ed.) (pp. 199–220), A. McLung Lee, ed. New York: Barnes & Noble.

Calhoun, C. 1994. "Social Theory and the Politics of Identity." In *Social Theory and the Politics of Identity* (pp. 9–36), C. Calhoun, ed. Cambridge, MA: Blackwell.

Castells, M. 1997. *The Power of Identity*. Cambridge, MA: Blackwell.

Chomsky, N. 1998. *Profit over People: Neoliberalism and Global Order*. New York: Seven Stories Press.

Clark, B. R. 2000. "Creating Entrepreneurialism in Proactive Universities." *Change* (January/February): 10–19.

Clark, B. R. 2001. *Creating Entrepreneurial Universities: Organizational Pathways of Transformation* (3rd ed.). Oxford: Pergamon Press.

Clemens, E. 1996. "Organization Form as Frame: Collective Identity and Political Strategy in the American Labor Movement, 1880–1920." In *Comparative Perspectives on Social Movements* (pp. 205–226), D. McAdam, J. D. McCarthy, and M. N. Zald, eds. New York: Cambridge University Press.

Heineman, K. J. 1993. *Campus Wars: The Peace Movement at American State Universities in the Vietnam Era*. New York: New York University Press.

Hirsch, E. L. 1990. "Sacrifice for the Cause: Group Process, Recruitment, and Commitment in a Student Social Movement." *American Sociological Review* 55: 243–254.

Johnston, H., E. Laraña, and J. R. Gusfield. 1994. "Identities, Grievances, and New

Social Movements." In *New Social Movements: From Ideology to Identity* (pp. 3–35), E. Laraña, H. Johnston, and J. R. Gusfield, eds. Philadelphia: Temple University Press.

Julius, D., and P. Gumport. 2003. "Graduate Student Unionization: Catalysts and Consequences." *Review of Higher Education* 26(2): 187–216.

Kellner, D. 2000. "Globalization and New Social Movements: Lessons for Critical Theory and Pedagogy." In *Globalization and Education: Critical Perspectives* (pp. 299–321), N. C. Burbules and C. A. Torres, eds. New York: Routledge.

Laraña, E., H. Johnston, and J. R. Gusfield, eds. 1994. *New Social Movements: From Ideology to Identity*. Philadelphia: Temple University Press.

Lee, J., L. Oseguera, K. A. Kim, A. Fann, T. M. Davis, and R. A. Rhoads. 2004. "Tangles in the Tapestry: Cultural Barriers to Graduate Student Unionization." *Journal of Higher Education* 75(3): 340–361.

Levine, A., and J. S. Cureton. 1998. "Student Politics: The New Localism." *Review of Higher Education* 21(2): 137–150.

Lipset, S. M. 1976. *Rebellion in the University*. Chicago: University of Chicago Press.

Lipset, S. M., and P. G. Altbach. 1969. *Students in Revolt*. Boston: Houghton Mifflin.

McAdam, D. 1988. *Freedom Summer*. New York: Oxford University.

McAdam, D. 1994. "Culture and Social Movements." In *New Social Movements: From Ideology to Identity* (pp. 36–57), E. Laraña, H. Johnston, and J. R. Gusfield, eds. Philadelphia: Temple University Press.

Melucci, A. 1994. "A Strange Kind of Newness: What's 'New' in New Social Movements?" In *New Social Movements: From Ideology to Identity* (pp. 101–130), E. Laraña, H. Johnston, and J. R. Gusfield, eds. Philadelphia: Temple University Press.

Miller, J. 1994. *Democracy Is in the Streets: From Port Huron to the Siege of Chicago*. Cambridge, MA: Harvard University Press.

Nelson, C. 1995. "Lessons from the Job Wars: What Is to Be Done?" *Academe* 81(6): 18–25.

Rhoades, G. 1998. *Managed Professionals: Unionized Faculty and Restructuring Academic Labor*. Albany: State University of New York Press.

Rhoades, G. 1999. "Medieval or Modern Status in the Postindustrial University: Beyond Binaries for Graduate Students." *Workplace* 2(2): 1–9.

Rhoades, G., and R. A. Rhoads. 2003. "The Public Discourse of U.S. Graduate Student Unions: Social Movement Identities, Ideologies, and Strategies." *Review of Higher Education* 26(2): 163–186.

Rhoads, R. A. 1998. *Freedom's Web: Student Activism in an Age of Cultural Diversity*. Baltimore: Johns Hopkins University Press.

Rhoads, R. A. 2003. "Globalization and Resistance in the United States and Mexico: The Global Potemkin Village." *Higher Education* 45: 223–250.

Rhoads, R. A., and J. G. Martínez. 1998. "Chicana/o Students as Agents of Social Change: A Case Study of Identity Politics in Higher Education." *Bilingual Review/La Revista Bilingüe* 23(2): 124–136.

Rhoads, R. A., and G. Rhoades. 2005. "Graduate Employee Unionization as Symbol of and Challenge to the Corporatization of U.S. Research Universities." *Journal of Higher Education* 76(3): 243–275.

Scott, A. 1990. *Ideology and the New Social Movement.* London: Unwin & Hyman.

Slaughter, S., and L. L. Leslie. 1997. *Academic Capitalism: Politics, Policies, and the Entrepreneurial University.* Baltimore: Johns Hopkins University Press.

Slaughter, S., and G. Rhoades. 2004. *Academic Capitalism and the New Economy: Markets, State, and Higher Education.* Baltimore: Johns Hopkins University Press.

Smallwood, S. 2001. "Success and New Hurdles for T.A. Unions." *Chronicle of Higher Education* (July 6): A10–A12.

Touraine, A. 1988. *Return of the Actor: Social Theory in a Postindustrial Society,* Myrna Godzich, trans. Minneapolis: University of Minnesota Press.

Turner, R. H. 1994. "Ideology and Utopia after Socialism." In *New Social Movements: From Ideology to Identity* (pp. 79–100), E. Laraña, H. Johnston, and J. R. Gusfield, eds. Philadelphia: Temple University Press.

Vaughn, W. 1998. "Apprentice or Employee? Graduate Students and Their Unions." *Academe* 84(6): 43–49.

Vellela, T. 1988. *New Voices: Student Activism in the '80s and '90s.* Boston: South End Press.

Villa, J. 1991. "Graduate Student Organizing: Examining the Issues." *CUPA Journal* 42(4): 33–40.

Wilson, R. 2001. "Percentage of Part-Timers on College Faculties Holds Steady After Years of Big Gains." *Chronicle of Higher Education* (April 23). Available at http://chronicle.com/daily/2001/04/2001042301n.htm

PART THREE

Concluding Analyses

The Political Economy of Higher Education in the Time of Global Markets: Whither the Social Responsibility of the University?

Daniel Schugurensky

After three decades of promises and realities, it is becoming more and more evident that neoliberal economic globalization is not an engine for universal prosperity. Certainly, global markets brought prosperity to a minority, but for most of the world population it has been a race to the bottom. With global capitalism as the hegemonic model, the gap between rich and poor nations—and between rich and poor people—has continued to grow. Coupled with increasing inequalities, exclusions, and poverty, we are experiencing an upsurge of financial and personal insecurity, social breakdown, environmental destruction, spiritual emptiness, intolerance, and military conflicts (Chomsky 2004; Clark 2003; Hedley 2003; Ibsister 2003; Korten 2001). Indeed, neoliberal globalization promised a trickle-down effect from which everyone would benefit, but in the last decades what we have experienced was a "vacuum-up" effect that concentrates wealth in fewer hands than before.

At the same time many of our most cherished public institutions are becoming more commercialized than ever. Even well-established altruistic traditions such as humanitarianism and international charitable work are now shaped by market forces. For instance, in the conclusion to their last study researchers Smillie and Minear (2004) argued that much of what passes for humanitarianism today is a commercial enterprise, which they call "the business of humanitarianism" or the "humanitarian enterprise."

Educational institutions, and universities in particular, have not been immune to these developments. As universities become more heteronomous in nature (i.e., more susceptible to the impositions of the market and the state), they are losing the capacity to promote the common good or even to pursue knowledge and truth in an autonomous way. As Giroux and Searls Giroux (2004, p. 265) pointed out, "Neoliberalism, fueled by its unwavering belief in market values and the unyielding logic of corporate profit-making, has little patience with noncommodified knowledge or with the more lofty ideals that have defined higher education as a public service." Indeed, universities are becoming embedded in the logic of academic capitalism, a logic that requires an appropriate policy and cultural climate, specific regulations, and a variety of administrative arrangements and academic regimes (Slaughter and Rhoades 2004).

With the preceding in mind, I have organized this chapter in five sections. In the first section I describe the prevailing university visions that were contended until the 1980s and the rapid transit of the "service university" from a project to an inescapable reality in most university campuses. In the second section I broaden the concept of "service university" to the notion of "heteronomous university" (a combination of laissez-faire and control mechanisms that erode university autonomy) as a contribution to our understanding of the role of the state in this process. In the third section I raise some concerns about the potential risks of an academic world dominated by a heteronomous model. In the fourth section I put on the table for discussion the question of social responsibility and the university's role. Finally, in the last section I provide a summary and seek to formulate some preliminary conclusions.

University Visions: The Rise of the Service University

Almost two decades ago Janice Newson and Howard Buchbinder, two professors from York University in Toronto, wrote an insightful and to some extent prophetic book titled *The University Means Business*. In this book, pub lished in 1988, Newson and Buchbinder identified three main visions for the direction of higher education that competed for hegemony during the preceding decades: academic haven, tools for economic growth, and means for social transformation.

The first vision, academic haven, followed the liberal education tradition and was influenced by Cardinal Newman's classic *Idea of a University*, first published in 1873. Proponents of this vision argued that the academic and moral integrity of Western higher education was being eroded by the pursuit of utilitarian aims, by the politicization of knowledge, by massive expansion, and by the lowering of standards. To address this problem, advocates of the academic haven viewpoint called for the strengthening of university autonomy and academic freedom, so that universities could better resist pressures alien to intellectual discipline, excellence, the pursuit of truth, and cognitive rationality. This would imply the development of strategies to raise standards, eliminate vocational programs, reduce enrollments, and withdraw from involvement in the surrounding community. Some of the many articulations of the academic haven argument (combined with elements of elitism) can be found in the work of US scholars during the 20th century, including Hutchins's "The THREAT to American Education" (1944), Bloom's *The Closing of the American Mind* (1987), and D'Souza's *Illiberal Education* (1991).

The second vision, inspired by the tenets of human capital theory (Schultz 1961), argued that the intellectual infrastructure, the professional training, and the scientific technical capability provided by the university are prerequisites for economic development, particularly in emerging "knowledge-based" societies. Hence advocates of the university as a tool for economic growth called for enrollment expansion, closer linkages with industry, vocational programs, entrepreneurialism, and the development of incubators in high-tech areas.

The third vision, the "university as a means of social transformation," was able to attract a critical mass of faculty and students during the 1960s and early 1970s in many parts of the world. Its proponents argued that universities have an obligation to contribute not only to the equalization of educational opportunities but also to collective projects that promote social and environmental justice and ultimately alter existing social, economic, and political relationships. This vision was influenced by Marx's original formulation of polytechnic education, the Córdoba Reform of 1918, and the effervescence of the late 1960s, including the university movements (particularly the French May) and the writings of such authors as Freire, Althusser, and Illich. Among other things this vision proposed a reduction in the gulf between mental and manual work (and thereby the stratified social relations that derive from the division of labor) and an integration of theoretical and practical knowledge. It also called for making students subjects—rather than objects—of their learning process, so that they will be active, critical, and creative citizens as well as good workers and to nurture among them a comprehensive understanding of the relations between productive forces and the social, political, and cultural spheres. Although advocates of this vision did not challenge basic research, in general they expressed a preference for "socially relevant" research that addressed the needs of the most marginalized members of society or that contributed to the project of social transformation.

As Newson and Buchbinder (1988) noted, these competing visions of the university are not just speculative exercises of academics. As with other visions of societies and institutions, they mobilize people in certain directions and away from others. Moreover, these three visions invoke values (an important dimension of academic culture) that include clear principles about the purposes and ways of conceiving of the main university missions (research, teaching, and extension) in their relationship to larger society. These visions are also embedded in material (rather than abstract) social processes and in concrete structures of rewards and punishments shaped by political and economic forces. In turn, these forces are not impersonal but are brought into play through human agency.

When their book was written, Newson and Buchbinder noted that a fourth competing vision, which they labeled "service university," had began to emerge and gain prominence. This vision, which conceives of the university as an enterprise, academics as entrepreneurs, and knowledge as a commodity, has been able to attract the attention of a critical mass of university actors and to compete successfully with the other three visions. Indeed, during the last decades such a vision consolidated and paralleled significant changes in the academic culture of the university (Altbach 2002; Fisher and Rubenson 1998; Newson 1998; Turk 2000).

Needless to say, in Newson and Buchbinder's book, the title, *The University Means Business*, was used in a critical and negative way to the extent that some readers thought that it reflected an exaggerated and unfair portrayal of contemporary higher education. Interestingly enough, today the same phrase is not used as an indictment; quite to the contrary, it is used with a positive connotation by public relations departments of some universities. For instance, in May 2002 a press release from the University of Reading (United Kingdom) was precisely titled "University Means Business":

> Release date: May 24, 2002. Newbury MP David Rendel will see at first hand how weather-sensitive businesses across the world can improve their management of weather-related risks, view cutting-edge video graphic technology and hear the latest on developments for the prevention of thrombosis. The MP is visiting The University of Reading today for presentations on a variety of commercially exploitable research projects and to visit spin out and spin in companies in the University's Science and Technology Centre.

Similarly, a press release submitted by the public relations team of the University of Portsmouth (also in the United Kingdom) on December 16, 2003, titled "University Means Business with New Appointment," announced the appointment of its first regional development manager. The newly appointed development manager was depicted as having a broad range of business and marketing experience, including having been responsible for the market research for Sony's PlayStation. It seems that unintentionally, inadvertently, and especially paradoxically, Newson and Buchbinder provided public relations departments of contemporary universities with a catchy slogan.

Service University, Academic Capitalism,
and the Transition to the Heteronomous Model

The concept of the service university advanced by Newson and Buchbinder (1988) bears similarities to the notion of the entrepreneurial university proposed by Slaughter and Leslie (1997). For Slaughter and Leslie the entrepreneurial university is part and parcel of a phenomenon that they identified as academic capitalism, which refers to institutional and professional market (or marketlike) efforts to secure external monies. In some countries academic capitalism has nurtured the development of a new class of faculty and professional staff who are in essence entrepreneurs subsidized by the public purse.

Although the concept of a service university or an entrepreneurial university (also known as commercial, market, or business university) is a central one to understanding current changes in higher education, I suggest that its connotation does not provide a full picture of what is going on. In other words, the service university is a necessary but insufficient concept to provide a comprehensive descriptor of the nature of the changes. From my perspective, by focusing on the relationships between the universities and the market, the concept of the service university tacitly overlooks the new relationship between the university and the state.

Thus I submit that a more comprehensive account of current changes in higher education can be found in the transition from an autonomous to a heteronomous university (Schugurensky 1999). Etymologically, autonomy is the quality or state of being independent, free, and self-directed, whereas heteronomy refers to subjection to external controls and impositions—that is, subordination to the law or domination of another. The heteronomous university results from a combination of two apparently contradictory dimensions: laissez-faire and interventionism. In the heteronomous model the university agenda is increasingly conditioned by market demands and state imperatives. Hence it encompasses a "commercial" (or service) university and a "controlled" (also known as "responsive" or "accountable") university.

The commercial university consists of a privatization package based on a combination of policy instruments, including the proliferation and strengthening of private institutions, entrepreneurial management, and a multiplicity of cost-recovering mechanisms. The controlled university is characterized by decreased funding as well as conditional funding. Combined, the idea of the commercial and controlled university, captured by the heteronomous university, can be summarized in ten "C's"—the first seven C's derive from the commercial university and the final three derive from the controlled university. The commercial university, a model in which the traditional research and teaching activities are reoriented toward a dynamic relationship with industry and the job market, can be summarized by the following C's: (1) cultivation of private and foreign universities, (2) customer fees, (3) client-oriented programs, (4) corporate rationality, (5) cooperation with business, (6) casualization of labor, and (7) contracting out. The con-

TABLE II.I
The 10 C's of the heteronomous university

Commercial university	Controlled university
Cultivation of private and foreign universities	Cutbacks
Customer fees	Conditional funding
Client-oriented programs	Coordination (collaboration and competition)
Cooperation with business	
Corporate rationality	
Casualization of labor	
Contracting out	

trolled university consists of a triad of (8) cutbacks, (9) conditional funding, and (10) coordination, which in turn combines dynamics of "collaboration" and "competition" in the system (see Table 11.1).

Four clarifications regarding the use of the term *heteronomy* are worth mentioning here. First, it is true that universities have been conditioned by state and private interests before. However, the emerging pattern constitutes a new structural and globalized model of dependency to the market and subjection to the state that goes beyond the classic control of a specific institution by a businessperson through endowments or donations and beyond conjunctural infringements on institutional autonomy by the government in a particular university or nation-state. Second, the term *heteronomy*, as used in this context, does not imply that universities are being (or are going to be in the near future) stripped of any vestige of institutional autonomy. It rather indicates that this space is being reduced, or gradually taken over if you prefer, by external powers that are increasingly capable of imposing their own logic and interests. It is not so much that the university is operated by nonacademic actors as that its daily practices (its functions, internal organization, activities, structure of rewards, etc.) are subsumed into the logic imposed by the state and by the market. Third, heteronomy is an abstract concept, and hence its application to the analysis of a specific reality should be appropriately contextualized. Finally, the transition to the heteronomous university is not a smooth, linear, and consensual process that is welcomed by all members of the academic community; this process is usually obstructed by the resistance of those who espouse alternative visions of the university.

It would take more space than available here to discuss each one of the 10 C's of the heteronomous university (a detailed description of each one of these features can be found elsewhere, in Schugurensky [1994]). In these pages I prefer to discuss four of these trends that are particularly significant in terms of the issues discussed in this book. The first one is the cultivation of private and foreign universities, a development that has been especially evident in Latin America. In the last two decades this region has experienced a faster growth of the private sector than any other region in the world. A few decades ago the private sector was relatively insignificant in terms of student enrollment, but today they represent approximately 40 percent of total enrollments. Moreover, in the mid-1990s five Latin American countries had a higher enrollment rate in the private sector than in the public one, an unusual situation in the university system anywhere in the world (García Guadilla 2002).

A second important trend is the steady consolidation of a corporate rationality. This can be observed not only in the adoption of a variety of corporate values and practices (see Slaughter and Leslie [1997] and Slaughter and Rhoades [2004]), but also in the growth of a distinct administrative class, including specialists in public relations, fund-raising, and marketing. Analyzing data from the United States, Lewis (1996, 1998) noted that in the 1930s institutions of higher learning spent 19 cents on administration for every dollar spent on instruction, a figure that rose to 27 cents in 1950 and to 45 cents by the end of the 1980s. Moreover, between 1975 and 1990 college and university enrollments rose only 10 percent, full-time faculty members increased 21 percent, and administrative positions grew 42 percent. In contrast, in the period 1985–1990 institutions of higher learning hired about twice as many nonteaching staff members as faculty members, who were then faced with larger classes and workloads. In addition, administrative salaries are usually higher than faculty salaries, and in the last three decades this taken-for-granted inequality has grown significantly.

Indeed, the earnings of many top university presidents in the United States are spiraling up toward $1 million a year, a trend that was inconceivable just a few years ago; the number of university presidents earning $500,000 or more annually doubled in 2003–2004 from the previous year. The faster rise of administrative budgets relative to teaching budgets (faculty pay has been growing at half the rate of that of presidents) is a particularly disturbing trend for public universities, which are recurrently faced with budget crises, forcing them to raise tuition and fees and freeze staff positions.

Ironically, this happens at the same time that universities are marketing themselves as institutions committed to teaching and learning. Above all, as university presidents begin to act as corporate CEOs, a new market logic comes to dominate the academic environment (Bowen and Buck 2004; Dillon 2004; Lewis 1996; Zemsky 2004).

A third significant feature of the heteronomous university is the imposition (or increase, when they are already in place) of so-called customer fees. To take Canada as an example, during the 1990s university tuition and fees have more than doubled on average, and with it student debt went up. These twin developments had noticeably negative consequences in terms of accessibility and equality of opportunity to succeed in postsecondary education (Doherty-Delorme and Shaker 2000; Quirke 2001; Statistics Canada 2003). To remind ourselves of the "heteronomous dimension" of tuition and fees, during part of the 1990s the federal government froze the per capita transfers to postsecondary institutions, which led to substantial drops in cash transfers that same year. These budget cuts placed several institutions in a position of financial exigency, applying enough pressure to force them to raise tuition and fees. In some provinces, for example, Ontario, no other transfer sector suffered so much during the 1990s as university funding. Year after year, operating budgets went down and tuition and fees went up, and in only a decade average class sizes and student faculty ratios nearly doubled (Jacek 2003; Wiseman 2003). This also reminds us of the connections between the different C's, because customer fees cannot be understood in isolation from cutbacks. Indeed, in Canada as a whole, the rapid decline in core state funding has forced universities to aggressively pursue other sources of revenue. This has come primarily in the form of increased student fees, private research contracts, donations, and endowments. The greatest sources of relative growth in university revenues in 2002–2003 were sponsored research and tuition income (both at 13.6 percent). At the same time, academic rank salaries have shrunk to a 30-year low of 22 percent of total noncapital spending (Canadian Association of University Teachers 2004).

The reference to cutbacks leads us to the controlled dimension of the heteronomous model, where we can find another important feature in the process of contemporary higher education restructuring, which is coordination. By coordination I refer to a set of policies, agreements, and regulations at the national and supranational level that regulate the amount of collaboration and competition that should exist among higher education institutions. Particularly momentous in this regard is the development of the General Agreement on Trade in Services (GATS) by the World Trade Organization (WTO). This agreement proposed an unprecedented liberalization of the higher education sector, to transform it into a multimillion dollar industry (Robertson 2003). Proponents of GATS for higher education assume the existence of a free market in which fierce competition for students will take place and the best universities will be rewarded for their efforts. Such an assumption is difficult to prove in the real world. For the Americas it is relatively easy to predict that the most powerful and wealthy players are more likely to take advantage of the so-called free market. As Philip Altbach noted, US institutions already have advantages in overseas markets, and a market liberalization would only reinforce those advantages. In his words, "The further opening of higher education markets worldwide will help US institutions without any reciprocal effects to other countries" (2003, p. 7).

Some Words of Caution About the Heteronomous University

Advocates of the heteronomous university argue that multiple sources of sponsorship and supervision will promote diversity and healthy competition, which in turn will lead to greater efficiency and accountability. They also proclaim that closer links with industry will make both teaching and research more relevant, promote technological development, and hence increase international competitiveness. Finally, they expect that stricter government controls will reduce waste and bring more relevance to research and teaching activities. Without denying the validity of these assumptions and expectations, the rise of the heteronomous university raises some areas of concern; that is, the advance of the heteronomous university raises some red flags about risks and dangers that should be seriously considered.

For instance, the heteronomous university can lead to the development of new priorities that would widen the gap between "rich" disciplines (those closer to the marketplace) and "poor" ones. A personal visit to any university campus will allow for an observation of such differences firsthand, starting with the quality of the buildings and the state and quality of the facilities. Moreover, the typical low status and low funding of the arts, social sciences, and humanities are striking in comparison to such areas as the applied sciences, business, or engineering. Although these differences are not new, the gap is certainly widening.

Let us consider, for instance, recent trends in terms of faculty salaries in different fields in the United States. In 1976 a newly hired assistant professor teaching literature earned $3,000 less than a new assistant professor in business. By 1984 that gap had grown to $10,000, by 1990 it reached $20,000, and by 1996 it exceeded $25,000. Business is not the only field with high rewards. The salaries of assistant professors in economics, law, engineering, and computer science, for instance, also averaged $10,000 a year higher than those in literature in 1990 and more than $15,000 a year higher by 1996. And literature professors are not the ones with the lowest salaries. Faculty members in the fine arts, foreign languages, and education are paid even lower salaries. In addition, consulting fees and second jobs in the humanities represent less than one-third of the average "extra" income earned by professors in all disciplines. This means that professors in other fields, who are already more highly paid by their universities, spend more time on outside ventures and less on duties at the institution itself (Engell and Dangerfield 1998).

Another concern is that the heteronomous university could lead to a proliferation of conflicts of interests among industry-sponsored researchers and to restrictions in the dissemination of research findings, as occurred in the paradigmatic case of Dr. Nancy Olivieri and Apotex in Canada during the late 1990s. Olivieri, a specialist in hereditary blood diseases who was working in the Hospital for Sick Children (University of Toronto), was conducting trials on a drug (deferiprone) as a treatment for thalassemia (a group of genetic blood disorders). The research was funded by a pharmaceutical company (Apotex), which also owned the patent for the drug. At some point, Olivieri discovered that the drug had a potential to harm the children who were participating in the experiments. She decided that she had the duty to contact her patients immediately to let them know about the situation, but Apotex denied her findings and ordered her not to disclose them. Challenging the orders of the company, Olivieri made her findings public, which led her into a long and painful litigation process with Apotex.

This situation is exceptional because the researcher dared to challenge the interests of the private sponsor and dared to go public with her research findings. In many other cases researchers may simply act as employees of the research sponsor. Indeed, it is not uncommon on today's campuses that private corporations provide university units with capital or operating grants in exchange for exclusive licenses on patentable discoveries made in laboratories or for influence over the direction of research (Newson 1998; Turk 2000). In such a system a symbiotic relationship between client and researcher evolves. The corporation expects the researcher to find certain results, and the researcher may end up finding them to please the client. In fact, one of the risks of contracted research is that the researcher or the research institution may aim at collecting and analyzing data in such a way that the conclusions of the final report coincide with the needs and interests of the paying research client.

A fascinating case that clearly illustrates this situation took place in the province of Ontario, Canada. In 2004 the Ontario government considered a research report that claimed that provincial hospitals could save almost $200 million a year if they reduced inefficiencies. At the same time the hospitals released findings of another research report that stated that Ontario hospitals are the most efficiently run in the country and that provincial funding is $600 million short of their needs. The first study was contracted by the Ontario government to a research company called the Hay Group. Interestingly, the second study was contracted by the hospitals to the same research group (Metro 2004; Urquhart 2004). The two studies conducted by the same consulting firm were paid for by the taxpayers of the province, who are still unclear as to whether or not hospitals are efficient or inefficient and whether or not they deserve more or less funds. I suggest that a more reasonable way to use these public monies would have been for the two parties to combine their budgets and ask for only one study to be conducted by researchers without any vested interests in the research outcomes.

The tensions derived from research for hire sometimes result in delays in publication, secrecy, and concealment of negative results. In a study on pharmaceutical companies and intellectual property rights that resonates with the Olivieri case, Lexchin found that "gaining a competitive edge on rival firms leads to a restriction in sharing of research results and delays in publication of findings because of commercial concerns" (2003, p. 21). In a subsequent paper, Lexchin (2004) reported that drug regulation in Canada is carried out in a secretive manner because of the "unique" relationship between the pharmaceutical industry and the unit of Health Canada in charge of testing and approving new drugs. Because of drastic budget cuts by the federal government in the 1990s, this unit turned to cost-recovery methods to continue its work. As a result, today the pharmaceutical industry contributes almost half the agency's $70 million annual operating budget to cover its drug tests. The study found that the directorate's close ties with the pharmaceutical firms has led to the concealment of scientific or technical information about the safety and efficacy of new drugs.

A related issue for concern is that university researchers may have a financial interest in the company, a situation that provides fertile soil for conflicts of interest. In some fields, for instance, biomedical research, nearly one in four scientists has financial ties to industry, and more than two-thirds of academic institutions in the United States and Canada hold shares and other equity in firms that sponsor biomedical research (Bekelman, Li, and Gross 2003). This does not prove that the potential conflict of interest actually influences the nature of the research findings, but it certainly creates enough suspicions to raise serious doubts about the ethics of industry-contracted research, especially if the researchers and universities are in some way aligned with the financial interests of the sponsoring company. As Jerome Kassirer (former editor of the *New England Journal of Medicine* who currently teaches at Yale University) has noted, physicians who participate in research studies often become spokespeople for the very companies that sponsor their research or they go on to join their advisory boards (Kassirer 2005).

As a result of all this, there is a general concern that the heteronomous university can gradually lead to the erosion of the academic environment and the ascendance of a business environment. In this transition, traditional academic values and practices, such as free flow of information, collegiality, co-governance, or public access to knowledge, may be replaced with values and practices from the business world, such as secrecy, competition, hierarchical management systems, or the commodification of knowledge. This concern is not just based on speculation. A former president of the University of Waterloo (Canada) recently published an essay in which he lamented that "we have become a little too economy-centric in our focus, at the expense of some other values and considerations that go to the heart of our enterprise" (Downey 2003, p. 29). It is true that this is not a new development. In *Higher Learning in America*, published in 1918, Thornstein Veblen described how the business world (particularly business culture) dominated the inner life of universities to the detriment of the free production of knowledge. However, the concern is that today, in the midst of 21st-century global neoliberal capitalism, we are reaching a point in this trajectory that has quantitative and qualitative differences with Veblen's times.

Other potential risks of the heteronomous university are an increased emphasis on applied (market-oriented) research at the expense of pure (curiosity-driven or basic) research and an increase of benefits to private groups, although disguised by a progressive discourse invoking public interest, "social relevance," and accountability.

Whither the Social Responsibility of the University?

Never before in the history of humanity have there been so many people, either in absolute or in relative terms, enrolled in higher education institutions. During the 1960s and 1970s, when higher education enrollments expanded significantly, it was hoped (and even expected) that a more educated populace, together with new scientific discoveries, would lead to a better world—one that is more peaceful, more democratic, more livable. Unfortunately, such expectations largely are unfulfilled. As the 21st century unfolds, it is becoming increasingly clear that technical progress has not necessarily been matched by social or moral progress and that a dramatic expansion of higher education has not necessarily resulted in a more democratic, peaceful, and ethical world.

Perhaps one of the reasons for this is that an increase in the average years of education of the population per se does not result necessarily in a society with better citizens. When educational institutions, including universities, are not seriously concerned with the preservation and transmission of basic moral values, they become merely places for workplace and professional training and for research and teaching that are indifferent to human suffering and to social justice. The late Haim Ginot (1972), a child psychologist who was also a principal, copied in a book for teachers the following words from a Holocaust survivor:

> I am a survivor of a concentration camp. My eyes saw what no man should witness: Gas chambers built by learned engineers, children poisoned by educated physicians, infants killed by trained nurses. Women and babies shot and buried by high school and college graduates. So, I am suspicious of edu-

cation. My request is: Help your students become human. Your efforts should never produce learned monsters, skilled psychopaths, educated Eichmans. Reading, writing, and arithmetic are important only if they serve to make our children more humane.

In the same vein, Hannah Arendt observed with outrage that intellectuals cooperated with the Nazis more than ordinary folks, an awareness that moved her away from academic disciplines and toward activism. Half a century later, unfortunately, many universities are not rising to the circumstances.

Thus it is fair to ask the question: Do universities have a social responsibility? If so, what exactly does this mean?

It could mean that universities have an obligation to nurture democratic, caring citizens and to promote the common good though processes of knowledge creation and dissemination and through the development of decent institutional values. Unfortunately, the heteronomous university is becoming less an affordable and accessible public institution that encourages critical thinking and moral responsibilities and more a private business, less accountable to the public interest and more beholden to private interests.

A typical metaphor to describe the university in social context is a triangle, as in the models advanced by Sábato and Botana (1968) in Latin America and Clark (1983) in North America. Sábato and Botana referred to the three vertices of the triangle as "productive structure, government, and scientific-technological infrastructure," whereas Clark called them "market, state, and academic oligarchy." It is intriguing, however, that in both models there is an absence of a fourth actor: the community (or "civil society," or "the public"). Perhaps in the original triangle it was assumed that the community could be subsumed under the market, but such conflation of the market and society is problematic. However, this conflation is not infrequent in neoliberal discourse, which tends to equate "service to industry" with "service to society" and "economic relevance" with "social relevance." I submit that a more inclusive metaphor for the university and its context is a square that allows for the inclusion of community and service to society.

If a key mission of universities is to serve the public and to improve the communities and regions in which they operate, it is not self-evident that by serving business interests they are automatically serving the community. Even the World Bank has already admitted in its 1999 world development report that the trickle-down (or spillover) effects of the "free market" have been overestimated, as capital accumulation tends to remain at the top of the social pyramid. Because our universities are becoming more corporate, more technocratic, more utilitarian, and far more concerned with selling products than education (Fisher and Rubenson 1998), it is time to bring back the interests and needs of the majority of the population to the research agenda.

This does not mean that universities should stop interacting with the market or avoid any type of sponsored research. It means that such interactions should be regulated by clear guidelines that reduce potential conflicts of interest, ensure the free flow of information, eliminate the gap between the haves and the have-nots in the academy, protect the common good and the environment, and put the public interest before profits. Let us not forget that in most societies university systems are by and large publicly funded and that most scientific research is conducted in public universities. Hence, in an era in which universities are developing a cozy relationship with the market, it is not inappropriate to remind ourselves that, first and foremost, academics also need to be accountable to the public.

Back to Hannah Arendt, she stated once that "nothing is more important to the integrity of universities than a rigorously enforced divorce from war-oriented research and all connected enterprises" (1972, pp. 118–119). Unfortunately again, many universities are not enforcing such a divorce, and there is much research going on at university campuses that is connected to the development of weapons systems and to military training (Feldman 1989). Likewise, research contracts are established with the tobacco industry and with companies that are big polluters or that exploit child labor. In the meantime, issues of peace, health, environment, and social justice must take a backseat. In a world that faces massive poverty, inequality, starvation, environmental degradation, and militaristic exploitation, it is imperative that those selected institutions that have a traditional commitment to the common good take a leadership role in guiding us away from the present deplorable conditions. Clearly, the university is one such institution.

Summary and Conclusions

Current changes in higher education throughout the Americas cannot be examined in isolation from larger international political and economic trends.

With the decline of socialist and welfare-state models, neoliberal regimes have become hegemonic in many parts of the world, including the Americas. In most countries changes in financial arrangements coupled with accountability mechanisms have forced universities to reconsider their social missions, academic priorities, and organizational structures. Concerns about equity, accessibility, autonomy, and the contribution of higher education to social transformation, which were prevalent during previous decades, now are overshadowed by new priorities, funding arrangements, and market-oriented values, urgencies, and practices.

The full impact of a heteronomous model on university life is still to be seen, but given past and present developments, it is prudent to raise a few concerns about this trend. First, the heteronomous model could widen the gap between "rich" and "poor" disciplines. Second, it could overemphasize applied (market-oriented) research at the expense of pure (curiosity-driven) research. Third, it could result in the general erosion of the academic environment and in the replacement of traditional academic values and practices (e.g., collegiality, autonomy, academic freedom, and protection of the common good) with practices shaped by market dynamics and corporate logic (e.g., hierarchical administration, competition, and profit-oriented rationales). Finally, the heteronomous model could result in a proliferation of conflicts of interests among industry-sponsored researchers and to restrictions in the free flow of information. As Westheimer (2003) noted:

> When the weeding [out of nonconforming faculty] is completed, the anti-intellectual mission of the corporate university becomes clearest. The bottom line is raised to the top. Research that promotes the financial and hierarchical health of the administration is rewarded, and independent scholarly thought is punished. Institutions of higher education become ones of education for hire. (pp. 134–135)

Indeed, institutions for hire that are reactive to the market are incompatible with autonomous public institutions in pursuit of truth and the common good. In this era of global capitalism and neoliberal economics, it is time to ask once again, clearly and loudly: Do universities have a social responsibility? If so, what does this mean? Academics and citizens in all societies deserve the opportunity to have an open debate about these pressing questions.

References

Altbach, P. 2002. "Knowledge and Education as International Commodities: The Collapse of the Common Good." *International Higher Education* 28(August). Available at http://www.bc.edu/bc_org/avp/soe/cihe/newsletter/News28/newlet28.html (retrieved June 18, 2004).

Altbach, P. 2003. "Why the United States Will Not Be a Market for Foreign Higher Education Products: A Case Against GATS." *International Higher Education* 31(spring): 5–7.

Arendt, H. 1972. *Crises of the Republic*. Orlando, FL: Harcourt Brace Jovanovich.

Bekelman, J., Y. Li, and C. P. Gross. 2003. "Scope and Impact of Financial Conflicts of Interest in Biomedical Research: A Systematic Review." *Journal of the American Medical Association* 289: 454–465.

Bloom, A. 1987. *The Closing of the American Mind: How Higher Education Has Failed Democracy and Impoverished the Souls of Today's Students*. New York: Simon and Schuster.

Bowen, R., and J. Buck. 2004. "College Presidents Are Hard-Working, Talented, and Vastly Overpaid." *Chronicle of Higher Education* 50(35): B24.

Canadian Association of University Teachers. 2004. "Public or Private University Finances, 2002–2003." *CAUT Education Review* 6(3): 1–6.

Chomsky, N. 2004. *Hegemony or Survival: America's Quest for Global Dominance (The American Empire Project)*. New York: Henry Holt.

Clark, B. R. 1983. *The Higher Education System: Academic Organization in Cross-National Perspective*. Berkeley: University of California Press.

Clark, J. 2003. *Worlds Apart: Civil Society and the Battle for Ethical Globalization*. Bloomfield, CT: Kumarian Press.

Dillon, S. 2004. "Ivory Tower Executive Suite Gets C.E.O.-Level Salaries." *New York Times*, November 15. Available at http://www.nytimes.com/2004/11/15/education/15salary.html

Doherty-Delorme, D., and E. Shaker. 2000. "What Should We Spend on Education? Highlights from the Year 2000 Alternative Federal Budget and the Ontario Alternative Budget." Available at http://www.policyalternatives.ca/eduproj/ososaltbudgets.html (accessed April 8, 2004).

Downey, J. 2003. *The Heart of Our Enterprise: Insider Essay*. Ottawa, Canada: University Affairs.

D'Souza, D. 1991. *Illiberal Education: The Politics of Race and Sex on Campus*. New York: Free Press.

Engell, J., and A. Dangerfield. 1998. "The Market-Model University: Humanities in the Age of Money." *Harvard Magazine* (May-June): 48–55.

Feldman, J. 1989. *Universities in the Business of Repression: The Academic-Military-Industrial Complex and Central America*. Boston: South End Press.

Fisher, D., and K. Rubenson. 1998. "The Changing Political Economy: The Private and Public Lives of Canadian Universities." In *Universities and Globalization: Critical Perspectives*, J. Currie and J. Newson, eds. Thousand Oaks, CA: Sage.

García Guadilla, C. 2002. "General Agreement on Trade in Services (GATS) and Higher Education in Latin America: Some Ideas to Contribute to the Discussion." Paper presented at the Convention of Universities Members of Columbus, Paris, July.

Ginot, H. 1972. *Teacher and Child: A Book for Parents and Teachers*. New York: Macmillan.

Giroux, H., and S. Searls Giroux. 2004. *Take Back Higher Education: Race, Youth, and the Crisis of Democracy in the Post–Civil Rights Era*. New York: Palgrave Macmillan.

Hedley, A. 2003. *Running Out of Control: Dilemmas of Globalization*. Bloomfield, CT: Kumarian Press.

Hutchins, R. 1944. "The THREAT to American Education." *Colliers* 114: 20–21.

Ibsister, J. 2003. *Promises Not Kept: Poverty and Betrayal of Third World Development*. Bloomfield, CT: Kumarian Press.

Jacek, H. 2003. "The Universities Are Not Ready." *Ontario Confederation of University Faculty Associations Forum* (spring): 4–6.

Kassirer, J. 2005. *On the Take: How Medicine's Complicity with Big Business Can Endanger Your Health*. New York: Oxford University Press.

Korten, D. 2001. *When Corporations Rule the World*. Bloomfield, CT: Kumarian Press.

Lewis, L. 1996. *Marginal Worth: Teaching and the Academic Labor Market*. New Brunswick, NJ: Transaction.

Lewis, L. 1998. "Budget Cuts and Administrative Bloat." *International Higher Education* 11(spring): 18–19.

Lexchin, J. 2003. *Intellectual Property Rights and the Canadian Pharmaceutical Marketplace: Where Do We Go from Here?* Ottawa: Canadian Centre for Policy Alternatives. Available at http://www.policyalternatives.ca/publications/ipr.pdf (accessed October 21, 2004).

Lexchin, J. 2004. *Transparency in Drug Regulation: Mirage or Oasis?* Ottawa: Canadian Centre for Policy Alternatives. Available at http://www.policyalternatives.ca/publications/transparency.pdf (accessed October 21, 2004).

Metro. 2004. "Ontario Looks to Save $200M in Hospitals." *Metronews* (September 22): 1.

Newson, J. 1998. "The Corporate-Linked University: From Social Project to Market Force." *Canadian Journal of Communications* 23(1): 107–124.

Newson, J., and H. Buchbinder. 1988. *The University Means Business: Universities, Corporations, and Academic Work*. Toronto: Garamond Press.

Quirke, L. 2001. "Access in Jeopardy? Social Class, Finances and University Attendance." In *Missing Pieces II: An Alternative Guide to Canadian Post-Secondary Edu-*

cation (pp. 63–74), D. Doherty-Delorme and E. Shaker, eds. Ottawa: Canadian Centre for Policy Alternatives.

Robertson, S. 2003. "WTO/GATS and the Global Education Services Industry." *Globalisation, Societies, and Education* 1(3): 259–266.

Sábato, J., and N. Botana. 1968. "La Ciencia y la Tecnología en el Desarrollo Futuro de América Latina." *Revista de la Integración, INTAL* 1(3): 15–36.

Schugurensky, D. 1994. *Global Economic Restructuring and University Change: The Case of Universidad of Buenos Aires*. Ph.D. dissertation, University of Alberta, Edmonton, Canada.

Schugurensky, D. 1999. "Higher Education Restructuring in the Era of Globalization: Toward a Heteronomous Model?" In *Comparative Education: The Dialectic of the Global and the Local*, R. Arnove and C. A. Torres, eds. Lanham, MD: Rowman & Littlefield.

Schultz, T. W. 1961. "Investment in Human Capital." *American Economic Review* 1(2): 1–17.

Slaughter, S., and L. Leslie. 1997. *Academic Capitalism: Politics, Policies, and the Entrepreneurial University*. Baltimore: Johns Hopkins University Press.

Slaughter, S., and G. Rhoades. 2004. *Academic Capitalism and the New Economy: Markets, State, and Higher Education*. Baltimore: Johns Hopkins University Press.

Smillie, I., and L. Minear. 2004. *The Charity of Nations: Humanitarian Action in a Calculating World*. Bloomfield, CT: Kumarian Press.

Statistics Canada. 2003. "University Tuition Fees." *The Daily* (August 12).

Turk, J. 2000. "What Commercialization Means for Education?" In *The Corporate Campus: Commercialization and the Dangers to Canada's Colleges and Universities*, J. Turk, ed. Halifax, Canada: James Lorimer.

Urquhart, I. 2004. "Hospitals Wary of Cuts." *Toronto Star* (September 22), A1 and A8.

Veblen, T. 1918. *Higher Learning in America: A Memorandum on the Conduct of Universities by Business*. New York: B. W. Huebsch.

Westheimer, J. 2003. "Tenure Denied: Union Busting in the Corporate University." In *Steal This University: The Rise of the Corporate University and the Academic Labor Movement*, B. Johnson, P. Kavanagh, and K. Mattson, eds. New York: Routledge.

Wiseman, N. 2003. "Conservative Stewardship of Postsecondary Education." *Ontario Confederation of University Faculty Associations Forum* (spring): 14–16.

Zemsky, R. 2004. "Have We Lost the 'Public' in Higher Education?" *Chronicle of Higher Education* 49(38): B7.

CHAPTER TWELVE

The Global Economy, the State, Social Movements, and the University: Concluding Remarks and an Agenda for Action

Robert A. Rhoads
Carlos Alberto Torres

Globalization as defined by the neoliberal project is not inevitable. Grass-roots movements and sound analysis and criticism have altered the strategies of those individuals and organizations seeking to advance a corporate-driven model of global trade relations. We have even witnessed a confessional of sorts in the International Monetary Fund's 2003 report, *Lessons from the Crisis in Argentina*, in which the organization acknowledged a variety of strategic mistakes in working with the Argentine government. Elsewhere, global trade representatives now speak of the need to treat each country as a unique case and avoid the "one size fits all" approach that so dominated policies of the IMF and the World Bank during the 1980s and 1990s and into the 21st century. But is this a shift in substance or simply a shift in rhetorical strategy aimed at handling increased resistance? Has "globalization from above" become more sensitive to the grassroots movements seeking to challenge economic policies largely crafted by economic elites?

Clearly, leaders of the neoliberal project see the growing resistance among workers, intellectuals, human rights advocates, environmentalists, students, citizens, and the economically disenfranchised. Because of efforts described in this book as "globalization from below," individuals and institutions leading the neoliberal advance have had to react to mounting resistance. One way that neoliberalists have responded is with public relations devices and the clever use of media. For example, the official website for the Free Trade Area of the Americas (FTAA) now offers an "Invitation to Civil Society," that reads as follows: "We recognize and welcome the interests and concerns that different sectors of society have expressed in relation to the FTAA. Business and other sectors of production, labor, environmental and academic groups have been particularly active in this matter. We encourage these and other sectors of civil societies to present their views." The website goes on to explain how individuals can send letters to the organization as a way of offering ideas and criticism. But inviting input is a far cry from restructuring global decision-making bodies.

In keeping with the trend to use public relations measures as a form of damage control, the World Trade Organization (WTO) has a cleverly captioned *10 Benefits of the WTO Trading System*, complete with cartoon characters (World Trade Organization 2004). According to this document, the benefits include the following: (1) The system helps promote peace; (2) disputes are handled constructively; (3) rules make life easier for all; (4) freer trade cuts the costs of living; (5) freer trade provides more choice of products and qualities; (6) trade raises incomes; (7) trade stimulates economic growth; (8) the basic principles make life more efficient; (9) governments are shielded from lobbying; and (10) the system encourages good government. With regard to fostering peace, we might note that this sounds like an exaggerated claim, but the WTO beat us to the punch by acknowledging this very fact in its own document: "This sounds like an exaggerated claim, and it would be wrong to make too much of it," notes the WTO, adding, "Sales people are usually reluctant to fight their customers." At best there is a lack of economic and historical foundation to some of these claims; at worst they are outright fabrications. Certainly, the case of Argentina offers much counterevidence to several of these claims.

Not to be outdone by the FTAA or the WTO, the IMF now directs first-time visitors to a document that seeks to address some of the criticism aimed at the organization. *Common Criticisms of the IMF* (International Monetary

Fund 2004a) pays particular attention to the following questions: Do IMF-supported programs impose austerity on countries in financial crisis? Do IMF-supported programs favor bankers and elites? Does the availability of IMF lending encourage "moral hazard"? Does the IMF obstruct debt reduction for the poorest countries? Is the IMF dominated by the G-7 (especially the US Treasury)? Is the IMF unaccountable? In responding to the question about whether IMF-supported programs favor bankers and elites, the IMF explains, "IMF support to a country includes: (i) advising the country on what the appropriate policies should be; (ii) providing resources to the country to tide it over its difficulties. Corrective policies will restore investor confidence, so that capital will once again flow into the country. This should not be seen as 'favoring' bankers and elites" (International Monetary Fund 2004b). Is this a public relations machine at work, or is there a grain of truth here? Perhaps a better question is whether the IMF is able to "advise" a government on what the "appropriate" policies should be. Based on its own internal report—*Lessons from the Crisis in Argentina* (International Monetary Fund 2003)—the organization seems to be lacking in this important area. Perhaps the problems lie with the basic philosophy of neoliberalism to which the IMF and other global trade organizations subscribe. Is there a place for alternative economic views? Is there any understanding of the informal and formal social contracts that have existed for years in countries such as Argentina, Brazil, and Mexico?

Can it be that some deep changes are taking place in the global trade governing bodies? The World Bank announced a revision of its lending program in 2004 so that the uniqueness of each country's economic and social situation can be considered in developing financial strategies (World Bank 2004b). In shifting from "adjustment lending" to "development policy lending," the World Bank acknowledged that "there is no one blueprint for reform that will work in all countries. Therefore, governments must take ownership of reforms to develop a program that meets their countries' needs" (World Bank 2004a). James Adams, vice president and head of the Operations Policy and Country Services Network at the World Bank stated, "We have abandoned the prescriptive character of the old policy statement, in which we essentially enshrined goals and methods" (World Bank 2004a). Is this a significant shift in the World Bank and in its commitment to neoliberalism? Hardly. Adams went on to add, "This is how you do public sector reform, this is how you privatize. We have learned that a wide variety of approaches can work but we've also learned that the key ingredients to successful economic growth include giving greater space to the private sector." And so the beat of neoliberal privatization goes on, and the *cacerolazos* that once claimed the streets of Buenos Aires, as "Don't cry for me, Argentina" echoed in the distance, may soon spread to other global cities. Changes in strategies and tactics cannot conceal an unyielding commitment to capital over people, or "profit over people," as Noam Chomsky (1998) described it.

The *cacerolazos* of Buenos Aires are a telling indicator of the level of dissatisfaction and hopelessness afflicting the lives of average citizens in these troubled times. As globalization advances and the discrepancy between the poorest and the wealthiest of our societies grows ever wider, as the differential access to decision-making bodies between the disempowered and the influential elites grows ever further, and as the educational differences between the rural and the urban and between the lower and the upper classes expands even greater, tensions will continue to surface. We witnessed the tensions in the streets of Seattle during a meeting of the WTO in 1999, at the World Economic Forum in Davos in 2001, at the G-8 summit in Genoa in 2001, and also in Buenos Aires in 2001, when Argentina's economy collapsed under the direction of the IMF and thousands of citizens carried their misfortune and discouragement to the streets.

But resistance can yield positive results. The powerful voice of Argentina's unemployed and dispossessed marching in the streets provided the political support for a dramatic change and enabled President Nestor Kirchner to redirect the country's economy and reject the dictates of the IMF. To the surprise of the IMF, Argentina's economy grew by more than 8 percent in 2003, despite an emphasis on public spending at the cost of attracting private capital; the economic growth in 2003 followed an 11 percent decline the previous year, a year during which the country followed the dictates of the IMF. And so it seems that privatization is not the only way to bring about economic growth.

Opponents of neoliberalism have had their own summits, such as the one that took place in Porto Alegre, Brazil, in 2002, when the World Social Forum (WSF) met. Chomsky, in his keynote address, discussed the connections between neoliberalism and war and the role of the United States in maintaining "discipline" for the sake of reinforcing the neoliberal project.

History reveals the willingness of the US government to engage in war as a means of protecting and/or advancing its economic interests. For example, in *Perpetual War for Perpetual Peace*, Gore Vidal (2002b) documented roughly 200 overseas military "adventures" conducted by the United States to protect or advance its interests. In *Culture and Imperialism*, Edward Said (1994) developed the connection between US economic and military interests as part of a foreign policy rooted in imperialism. He argued that the United States sets the "ground rules for economic development and military deployment across the planet" (p. 286). In discussing the first Gulf War, Said (1994) argued that

> the entire premise was colonial: that a small Third World dictatorship, nurtured and supported by the West, did not have the right to challenge America, which was white and superior. Britain bombed Iraqi troops in the 1920s for daring to resist colonial rule; seventy years later the United States did it but with a more moralistic tone, which did little to conceal the thesis that Middle East oil reserves were an American trust. Such practices are anachronistic and supremely mischievous, since they not only make wars continuously possible and attractive, but also prevent a secure knowledge of history, diplomacy, and politics from having the importance it should. (pp. 296–297)

Said also noted that "global thinking tends to reproduce the superpower. . . . The powerful are likely to get more powerful and richer, the weak less powerful and poorer" (1994, pp. 283–284). And so we are left with little doubt that war and neoliberalism go hand in hand, and at the WSF summit Chomsky reinforced the correctness of such a view.

Vidal (2002b) suggested that it is the law of physics, and history too, that every action produces a reaction; Said posited that "history also teaches us that domination breeds resistance, and that the violence inherent in the imperial contest—for all its occasional profit or pleasure—is an impoverishment for both sides" (1994, p. 288). Thus the US military strikes and then is struck, often in some convoluted "terrorist" fashion, for how else would a group respond to the greatest military might in world history? Or the United States is attacked and then strikes back. It is never really clear who started "it" or what the real reason is for the attacks, because history is an endless chain and the justifications are just as endless. And so the United

States draws the wrath of much of the world, a fact evidenced once again at the 2004 Olympic Games in Greece, when Secretary of State Colin Powell was forced to cancel his appearance at the closing ceremonies because of protests in the streets of Athens. The protests targeted the US occupation of Iraq, which continued to serve as a reminder of the global character of contemporary war and terrorism and the lack of clarity between what constitutes an act of war and an act of terrorism. The United States defines its attackers as terrorists, and the attackers of the United States define the US government as the terrorists. Along these lines it should come as no surprise that Osama bin Laden and the Taliban in Afghanistan had received threats of a possible US strike against them months before their terrorist attack on New York and Washington and thus arguably were engaged in an act of preemption (Vidal 2002a, p. 15), essentially adopting the policies advanced by Condoleezza Rice, former national security adviser to President Bush, later promoted to secretary of state. Hence the definition of terrorism clearly has become, as Chomsky noted in Chapter 2, "what *they* carry out against *us*," with the *us* switching back and forth between more privatized warring factions and more state-sanctioned warring factions, principally the United States. It may be the ultimate irony that a form of privatization—the privatization of war in the form of terrorism—has become so powerful in affecting a nation's psyche and economy—and a nation so deeply entrenched in the ideology of privatization. But this is one form of privatization that even the neoliberalists cannot support—that is, terrorism as an act of governmental deregulation accessible to any group with sufficient capital to fund its weaponry and its labor.

And so there is no doubt that the world faces new levels of global tension as the shrinking of time and space continues and the connections between and among countries grows tighter. Serious considerations must be given to these growing ties and the ways in which global trends are affecting our institutions and our lives. This book is but one attempt to examine globalization and its growing impact, and we have done so by adopting perspectives firmly rooted in critical social science. Cultural theorist Douglas Kellner validated the key goals of this work when he wrote, "Rather than just denouncing globalization, or engaging in celebration and legitimation, a critical theory of globalization reproaches those aspects that are oppressive, while seizing upon opportunities to fight domination and exploitation and to promote democratization, justice, and a progressive reconstruction of education and society" (2000, p. 308). Our goal from the outset has been to study globalization and its intersection with universities, states, and markets, with democratic ideals guiding our analysis. This is in keeping with the tradition of critical theory.

The chapters in this book explore the many ways in which the political economy of globalization is altering the landscape of the Americas. As the various contributors elaborate, universities, states, and markets interact with and contribute to the growing influence of transnationalism, international integration, and economic interdependence in many complex ways. With particular focus on the Americas, it is increasingly obvious that decisions of political and economic leaders throughout this region will continue to reflect the growing interdependence of the countries contained therein.

With the preceding in mind, we use the remainder of this chapter to more clearly articulate the theoretical and practical challenges posed by globalization, with a focus, of course, on the university, state, and market. We rely on important points offered throughout this text by our many contributors and on additional understandings acquired through our reading and observations as well as our global travels. Let us begin by formulating a more cohesive understanding of what we mean by the "global economy."

Globalization, the Global Economy, and the State

One could quite easily argue that just as "postmodernism" was the central theoretical concept of the 1980s, globalization may be key to the 1990s and the early part of the 21st century (Nash 2000; Waters 1995). "Globalization" as a concept may in fact represent the central lens through which we seek to make sense of complex and dynamic social environments throughout the present century. For the emerging relationships among the university, state, and market, the theoretical problem of globalization provides a more grounded and empirically analyzable set of questions than the slippery formulations associated with postmodernism and postcolonialism (Morrow and Torres 1995, 2000).

Although globalization in general has a longer history, its more specific meaning today is linked to the ways in which, by the mid 20th century, cer-

tain processes associated with social interaction, exchange, and human mobility became increasingly accelerated. In this respect globalization overlaps
with processes variously described as postindustrialization, postmoderniza-
tion, post-Fordism, and the information society. Economic globalization, a
central concern of this book, is the result of a worldwide economic restructuring involving the globalization of commerce, science, technology, and
culture as well as a profound transformation in the international division of
labor (Burbules and Torres 2000; Giddens 1990; Harvey 1989). This transformation in the international division of labor has been accompanied by a
readjustment of economic integration among national, state or provincial,
and regional economies (Torres 1998a). As discussed throughout this book,
in large part this new phase of globalization is a result of changes in communications and technology and is related to post-Fordist production strategies that have become the basis of a "network society" (Castells 1996, 1997).
These changes are redefining relations among nations, and they involve
the mobility of capital by means of international exchanges as well as short-
term, high-risk financial instruments and ventures. There is an enormous
concentration and centralization of capital and production at the international level (Carnoy 1993; Carnoy et al. 1993).

With regard to labor in contemporary capitalism, globalization affects labor markets, which are not homogeneous but segmented. The segmentation
of labor markets implies that there are at least four kinds of markets: (1) One
market responds to the demands of monopoly capitalism, usually transnational; (2) a second market responds to the demands of competitive capitalism, representing the secondary labor market; (3) a third market is the public sector, one of the few labor markets relatively protected from international
competition (many public universities in Canada, the United States, and
Latin America definitely fall within this category of labor market, with a bit
more flexibility than simply state or civil labor markets); and finally, (4) a
rapidly growing marginal labor market includes everything from illegal
transactions (such as narcotrafficking) to self-employment, domestic work,
family enterprises, small-scale subsistence production, and numerous other
economic activities that have been called marginal, underground, or informal work.

One of the central characteristics of this highly globalized capitalism is
that the factors of production are not located in close geographic proximity.

Furthermore, marginal profit rates are growing because of the continued increase in per capita productivity (the rate of growth of which continues to increase in advanced capitalism) and the reduction of costs (by means of lay-offs, intensification of production, and the replacement of more expensive workers with less expensive ones). With the growing segmentation of labor markets in which the primary markets offer more income, stability, and perquisites, hourly wages are increasingly being replaced by payment through piecework. This creates a clear distinction between the nominal and real salaries and wages of workers and the social wage by means of indirect loans and state actions. At the same time this set of transformations implies the decline of the working class and a reduction of the power of organized labor in negotiating economic policies and in the constitution of the social pact underscoring state domination. Following the secular tendency of the last three to four decades, service sectors continue to grow, reducing the importance of the gross national product in the primary sector and manufacturing—although there are clear indications of substitution of "middlemen" by technology, as is evident in the declining importance of certain professions.

These changes in the global composition of labor and capital are taking place at a time when there is an abundance of "surplus" labor and when the overt conflicts between labor and capital are decreasing. The increase of supernumerary workers is also associated with an increase in international competition and the conviction on the part of the working class and labor unions that it is dangerous and counterproductive to exclusively pressure the companies in search of more and better social services or salaries. This is made possible because of the abundance of labor, the awareness of falling profit margins of companies in the transnational and competitive environment, and the resulting loss of jobs and the accelerated migration of capital from regional markets in advanced capitalistic countries to areas where labor may be highly skilled but more likely poorly paid.

The threat of free trade agreements such as NAFTA, the proposed ALCA (Area de Libre Comercio de las Américas), or FTAA and the new arrangements proposed previously by the General Agreement on Tariffs and Trade (GATT) and now by the WTO marks the limits of protectionist policies. One well-known example is that of engineers and computer experts from India entering the payroll information for North American companies in databases for a fraction of the cost that white-collar workers in the United States or Canada would command. Another example is the low-cost mass production of goods by Chinese workers, who are sometimes subject to forced labor. A final, idiotic if not funny example is the attempt in the late 1990s by the conservative educational minister in the Province of Alberta, Canada, who floated the idea of having university professors record their lectures on videotape, which then could be widely distributed as a way to cut costs in universities. This "genial" idea was shelved not because of opposition from unions representing professors or teachers but because of the opposition voiced by the actors guild, concerned that no copyrights would be applied to the lectures and therefore that the "performers" would not be paid a fair wage. The thinking, of course, was that if this were to happen in higher education, then surely it could happen in the entertainment industry.

The new global economy is very different from the former national economy. National economies were previously based on standardized mass production, with a few managers controlling the production process from above and a great number of workers following orders. This economy of mass production was stable so long as it could reduce the costs of production (including the cost of labor) and retool quickly enough to remain competitive at the international level. Because of advances in communications and transportation technology and the growth of service industries, production has become fragmented around the world. As a consequence of outsourcing, production is moving to areas of the world where any of the following exist, individually or in combination: cheaper or better trained labor, favorable political conditions, access to better infrastructure and national resources, and larger markets and tax incentives.

The new global economy is more fluid and flexible, with multiple lines of power and decision-making mechanisms, analogous to a spider's web, as opposed to the static pyramidal organization of power that characterized the traditional capitalist system (Ohmae 1990; Przeworski 1991; Reich 1991; Thurow 1992). Whereas the public education system in the old capitalist order was oriented toward the production of a disciplined and reliable workforce, the new global economy requires workers with the capacity to learn quickly and to work in teams in reliable and creative ways. These workers are described by Robert Reich (1991) as "symbolic analysts," and they will make up the most productive and dynamic segments of the labor force, although they are likely to account for only about one-third of the labor force.

The growing power of the market, as reflected by the hegemony of one particular strain of globalization, suggests a specific vision of the state. The neoliberal state, characterized by a substantial change in the logic of public action and involvement of the people's representatives, has emerged in place of the welfare state. Government is seen to exist for the primary purpose of advancing the free market and ensuring the protection, even expansion, of investment interests, privatization, consumerism, and so forth. Thus corporate interests take precedence over traditional activities associated with the public good, including public education, health, and welfare.

Theories of the state have particular relevance to higher education. In fact, the origins and specific characteristics of mass higher education can be understood only in relation to a theory of the state. For example, if a particular state seeks to operate on fundamental principles associated with progressive democratic ideals, such as those advanced by John Dewey, then access and equity within the context of higher education take on much relevance. Alternatively, if a given state is primarily framed by competitive markets and individualism, such as was advanced in the thinking of Adam Smith, then higher education is likely to be constructed in an entirely different manner, with greater emphasis placed on consumerism, decreased public investment, and increased private competition. In the second case access is primarily determined by who can afford tuition, just as any other good or commodity becomes readily available only to those "paying customers." Likewise, university research also is framed by the particular vision of the state. From a more democratic perspective, university research must meet the demands of the broader social good, as determined by the citizenry. From a market-oriented view of the state, university research responds to the flow of revenue, as scholars circulate proposal after proposal in quest of funds, often being forced to transform their interests to match revenue streams driven by private capital oriented toward its own interests or state capital oriented toward advancing consumerism, privatization, the free market, and any other supporting activity, including the expansion of the military industrial complex.

Particular visions of the state also shape the way we think about higher education reform; the definition, interpretation, and analysis of contemporary educational problems and their solutions depend to a large extent on theories of the state, which justify and underlie the diagnosis and solution. For example, when US higher education underwent a period of expansion with the Higher Education Acts of 1965 and 1972, significant changes took place at US colleges and universities. With increased financial support made available by the state, students from low-income backgrounds, including many students of color, found a college education accessible. Many of these individuals were first-generation college students, and as a consequence of the democratic vision that guided the Higher Education Acts, they were able to begin to break the chains of social stratification and seek a degree of social and economic mobility. But these changes were made possible only by a particular vision of the state grounded in the progressive social movements of the 1960s and a vision often termed the Great Society. Alternatively, since the 1980s, US progressivism has witnessed a reversal of fortune; the new liberalism of the era aligned to a certain extent with conservatism (neoconservatism) and produced a dramatic antidemocratic turn that included attacks on affirmative action, assaults on state support for college tuition (this includes the channeling of state money to "merit-based" scholarships largely benefiting the middle and upper classes), and a general decline in overall support for higher education as a public trust. This turn was the clear result of a redefinition of the state, beginning with the election of Ronald Reagan (Apple 2000; Rhoads, Saenz, and Carducci 2004).

Thus, as we seek to understand higher education reform (university reform more specifically), we cannot do so without developing clear conceptions of higher education's relationship with the global economy and changing conceptions of the state. We also need to understand the role that social movements play as vehicles for shaping the state and influencing various educational reforms.

The State and Social Movements

The neglect of the relations between states and social movements has reinforced the even greater lack of explicit attention given to relationships between education and social movements. Although educational change and reform are central to analyses of social progress, functionalist approaches have dominated and have tended to focus on the imperatives of differentiation as an autonomous process, as opposed to the dynamics of the struggle between the state and collective movements (Morrow and Torres 1999; Ringer 1987; Smelser 1985).

The problem of social movements, however, does enter into the educational field in various contexts of conflict theories of educational change. First, theories of educational practice (i.e., pedagogies) have had a significant impact as part of cultural reformist movements, which generally have been aligned with broader social movements. Notable cases here include the progressive education movement and the form of liberalism associated with Dewey in the United States and more recently the liberational movements of South and Central America associated to some extent with the work of Paulo Freire. More typically, the affiliation of educational theories with social movements has remained marginalized, as in the 20th-century "modern school" movement inspired by Spaniard Francisco Ferrer; the modern school movement was closely related to the anarchist movement in the context of the United States (Avrich 1980; Lawson 1971). Today, the "back to basics" movement in education is broadly affiliated with New Right political movements, much as "critical pedagogy" and "feminist pedagogy" have ties with New Left movements.

Second, the problem of student movements is largely associated with contexts in which the university itself becomes the site of social movement activity. Such student movements have had periodic influence in advanced industrial societies. Examples are numerous: the revolutionary uprisings in Europe after World War I; the 1930s in the context of European confrontations between fascists, socialists, and communists; the worldwide student revolts of the late 1960s; and, more recently, the spasmodic student struggles in Latin America (Cohen 1993; Lipset 1971; Touraine 1968; Willener 1970). In many underdeveloped contexts student movements have remained virtually a continuous source of agitation against more or less authoritarian states that serve to reproduce vast inequality of income and opportunity. In these settings struggles over university "autonomy" have been in part triggered by political threats posed by student movements (Ordorika 2003; Rhoads 2003; Rhoads and Mina 2001).

Third, educational policy may be an explicit part of a general social movement, as in the case of "old" social movement theory concerned with working-class mobilization. The classic example here is the role of education as part of the demands of European labor movements in the 19th and 20th centuries (Simon 1965, 1987; Wrigley 1982). The rise of public schooling in the West can be broadly described as the outcome of the struggles of class-based social movements to gain state support for inclusion as part of a universal citizenship (Boli, Ramirez, and Meyer 1985). Some of these have been associated with major social transformations. Following the Mexican revolution, for example, educational reform was officially linked with extensive efforts to expand rural schooling and assimilate the *campesino* and indigenous populations. Changes in higher education with the University Reform in Córdoba in 1918 sought increased access to the university in the context of diminishing authoritarian relationships in the classroom, and the possibility of linking research and knowledge production to middle-class social mobility. Similar mass educational programs were initiated in Cuba in 1959; important activities took place in Argentina during the return of Peronism in 1973 until the right-wing sector of the Peronist coalition took control of the government in 1975; and extraordinary new relationships between university students, secondary students, and *campesinos* took place in Nicaragua in 1979 in the context of the National Crusade Against Illiteracy (Arnove 1986; Arnove and Torres 1996; Carnoy and Torres 1990; Schugurensky and Torres 1994; Torres 1991).

With the decline of various single-factor theories of educational growth (e.g., human capital theory, modernization theory), more comprehensive models of educational expansion have stressed the competitive struggle between institutionalized corporate and potential primary actors—meaning those capable of collective action (Archer 1982, 1984). In Europe, for example, the contention between Protestants and Catholics provided the initial impetus for primary action, whereas class-based movements emerged later in response to the Industrial Revolution. And the English case represents a complex process in which the Chartist and Owenite movements played an important role in the development of public education (Dobbs 1969 [1919]). Similarly, in this century aspirations for basic education rights in third world contexts typically have been part of both modern urban and agrarian class-based movements (largely composed of peasants). Teachers have generally played important roles in these movements as well (Lorena Cook 1996).

One of the few explicit contemporary attempts to link the state, social movements, and education as part of a general theory can be found in Carnoy and Levin's "social-conflict" theory of the state; their work "provides a framework for developing a dialectical analysis of education in capitalist society, because it views social movements as playing a vital role in affecting educational policy" (Carnoy and Levin 1985, pp. 46–47). On this basis an effort can be made to "predict" educational reforms and assess the potential and limits of struggles over schooling. Nevertheless, this approach remains largely within the framework of the class-based assumptions of old social movement theory, ignoring the peculiarities of the new social movements, including the prominence of identity politics within the university context (Rhoads 1998).

Finally, new social movement theory has provided the basis for a dramatic shift in understanding the relationships among social movements, educational policy, and citizenship. A distinctive characteristic of new social movements is their focus on rethinking preexisting social and cultural paradigms as part of a politics of identity (Calhoun 1994). As a consequence, one of their key strategies is broadly educational, as opposed to a singular focus on gaining power. Despite numerous setbacks at the level of public policy, the new social movements have been more successful in educational efforts, a process reflected in significant shifts in public opinion on various issues related to gender, race, sexual orientation, the environment, and peace. In the case of the racially based civil rights movement in the United States, the dismantling of segregated schools constituted perhaps the most fundamental and far-reaching demands linking race and education (Eyerman and Jamison 1991).

Many new social movements have been characterized by the advocacy of curricular change and have generally found a few sympathetic listeners within teacher education and universities and among educational policy makers. Moreover, the pluralist mandate of public education systems in most liberal democracies requires ongoing updates of the agenda of "legitimate" issues to be presented as part of mass education. Such effects increase dramatically at the higher levels, thus precipitating recent debates about "political correctness" on university campuses, especially in the United States (Bérubé 1994). To a great extent, this whole debate can be viewed in terms of the significant success of new social movements in reforming—if not fundamentally transforming—the content of higher education in the humanities. This is true to a lesser extent in the social sciences (which have long been more attuned to inputs from social movements). For the most part these changes have proceeded along the lines of the single-issue demands often typical of identity politics. One consequence has been the need to rethink the relationships among race, class, and gender in education (Morrow and Torres 1994).

With the preceding in mind, let us now turn more pointedly to the university. Obviously, like the contributors to this book, we see the powerful influence of globalization on universities and their relations to states and markets. No serious reform efforts can neglect a proper analysis of such relationships and their changing nature in light of global processes.

Higher Education Reform in the Age of Globalization

The university clearly is a key institution in the ongoing advance of globalization (Santos 2004; Stromquist 2002). In her book *Education in a Globalized World*, Nelly Stromquist noted, "In the era of globalization, a time in which a 'knowledge-based economy' is expected to be the driving force behind many applied developments, the university becomes a special place from which to advance new visions and ambitions" (2002, p. 103). New visions and ambitions certainly lie ahead for universities throughout the Americas. However, many of these institutions also face serious funding challenges as nation-states struggle to adequately support higher education. If countries are to compete in a global economy, supporting public forms of higher education obviously is critical.

Stromquist astutely observed how the changing context of knowledge and communication has altered the landscape of higher education and increased competition among institutions in the adult education arena: "A clear sign of change in universities is the rapid differentiation in the kinds of existing institutions of higher or postsecondary education. Universities no longer enjoy a monopoly in providing high-status information to adults; numerous other institutions, ranging from minor private universities to technical universities to computer training institutes, compete for students" (2002, p. 104). To her point we would add this: Not only are the kinds of institutions expanding, but so are the kinds of interinstitutional partnerships. Universities throughout the Americas increasingly are engaged in collaborative partnerships aimed at strengthening local, regional, national, and even global economies. Indeed, the role of universities in strengthening economies has never been as front and center as it is today. Globalization and the growing interdependence of economies obviously have contributed to this trend.

But just as universities contribute to economies, they also are increasingly shaped by economic forces and concerns. Stromquist, for example, argued, "The escalation of economic globalization has driven a demand for instrumental education—that which can be clearly tied to the goals of production, productivity, and employment" (2002, p. 105). Instrumental education is apparent in the ways in which academic majors and programs that directly affect the economy or that lead to specific careers within economic sectors are increasingly elevated over other fields of study. Consequently, business and science disciplines that directly connect to emerging technologies and revenue streams receive higher levels of funding and support than more traditional fields in the arts, humanities, and social sciences. Various contributors to this book raise fundamental questions about this trend and what may be lost as the social and cultural facets of societies increasingly take a backseat to science, technology, and business.

The push to increase the connection between universities and economic sectors, of course, does not end simply with academic programs and fields of study. The entire operation of universities, especially research universities, is increasingly shaped by forms of "academic capitalism" described in the work of Slaughter and Leslie (1997) and Slaughter and Rhoades (2004). Any examination of universities and their relationship to the political economy of globalization is quite lacking if it does not address the role of academic capitalism in today's higher education context. US higher education offers clear evidence of the growing influence of entrepreneurialism and the efforts that universities must now undertake to support complex structures and programs linked to research and development and the generation of capital. Although none of the contributors to this book suggest that universities abandon their economic obligations, questions are raised about the degree to which the "public good" is increasingly defined only in economic terms. Phrased in the form of a question: What becomes of public concerns and issues that do not generate streams of revenue for universities?

Although instrumentalism and academic capitalism are clearly flourishing and are seen by neoliberalists as key contributions that universities ought to make to the global economy, the issue of access to higher education is less widely embraced and often is contested terrain between those advancing a free-market position and others stressing a more democratic or social justice perspective. Throughout this book the role that global trade and banking organizations have played in advancing the privatization of higher education has been pointed out time and time again. The concern of every writer who worked on this project is the degree to which access to a sound postsecondary education will be available if the neoliberal privatization movement fully succeeds. What becomes of those citizens of Argentina, Brazil, Mexico, and, yes, the United States who cannot afford education beyond the secondary level? The movement away from accessible forms of higher education already is taking root in the United States, as states increasingly fund a smaller portion of the budgets of public institutions and consequently virtually force such institutions to increase tuition and fees. In California, for instance, funding issues have gotten so bad that the California Master Plan—a heralded plan that defines the relationships among community colleges, state comprehensive universities (the California State University system), and universities (the University of California system) and their joint obligation to the state's citizens—may have to be scrapped because these institutions cannot meet the educational demands of its citizens and because many cannot afford the cost of attending such institutions. Relatedly, a 2004 report by the National Center for Public Policy and Higher Education in San Jose, California, confirmed that colleges and universities throughout the United States are increasingly less affordable and that rates of college enrollment are in decline.

Another expression of globalization is the increasing international links among social movements. For example, it has been argued that globalization has contradictory cultural effects, provoking fundamentalist religious and ethnic movements that challenge the secularization of education while encouraging other ecumenical tendencies that force religious and ethnic movements to "relativize" their positions through the discovery of common principles (Robertson 1992). But the primary impact of globalization—whether political, economic, or cultural—is reflected in a broad shift toward an international standardization of educational curricula and credentials that goes beyond but has not altogether escaped earlier forms of educational colonialism (Carnoy 1974). Such standardization is most explicit in the European community, with the demand to reconcile higher educational credentials. In the third world it is expressed through the emergence of private colleges and universities where instruction is primarily in English and oriented toward the international economy (e.g., the technological institutes originating in Monterey, Mexico). Another fundamental change in the wings is the attempt by multilateral and bilateral organizations—and now present in the discussions of the WTO—to commodify higher education and treat it like any other service (e.g., financial services). Not surprisingly, most of the groups and networks associated with "globalization from below" (grassroots movements that oppose neoliberal globalization) are denouncing this WTO project as totally detrimental to free and gratuitous education, detrimental to the autonomy of the institutions of higher education, particularly in developing countries, and detrimental to the autonomy of nation-states, which will have no way to control or even tax this fast-growing market.

There is no question, then, that the relationship between globalization and higher education remains an emergent form of inquiry—and one posing important questions to specific colleges and universities as well as to systems of higher education. One promising line of analysis builds on the concept of the *creolization* of culture, a notion drawn from linguistics that provides a more empirically grounded basis for issues that have been taken up in the postcolonial literature under the heading of hybridity (Bhabha 1994). As Ulf Hannerz stressed, "The cultural processes of creolization are not merely a matter of constant pressure from the center toward the periphery, but a more creative interplay" (1996, p. 68). In short, "creolist concepts also intimate that there is hope yet for cultural variety. Globalization need not be a matter only of far-reaching or complete homogenization; the increasing interconnectedness of the world also results in some cultural gains" (p. 66). In the context of peripheral societies, cultural flows are framed primarily by the state and markets. On the one hand, the most common focus of attention is on how states typically use education to construct citizens and to inculcate "an almost universally replicated set of basic skills, including literacy and numeracy" (p. 71). But there is also a very different process whereby the state serves as a "transnational cultural mediator" through which education becomes the filter between the metropolitan culture and the indigenous culture, which remains more marginally influenced and necessarily appropriates global culture on its own terms. Although the state channels transnational influences, it cannot fully control their relation to local practices. Although many with higher levels of formal education reflect in their consumption patterns the rhetoric of globalization as market-based homogenization, less visible are the opposite processes in which "creolized music, art, literature, fashion, cuisine, often religion as well, come about through such processes" (p. 74). Intellectually, such developments could serve as counterhegemonic reference points of a new kind. Clearly, such issues should become the basis of a research agenda concerned with globalization, higher education, and cultural change.

On the other hand, neoliberal globalization has provided an impetus for efforts to reorganize education and teacher's work and curricula along lines that are held by neoconservatives and neoliberals to reflect the imperatives of the new world economy, a process reinforced by the pressures of international organizations such as the World Bank. As a consequence, the demands of local movement-based struggles are often marginalized in the name of strategies of "national" development that just happen to coincide with the long-term interests of global transnational capital. Although most obvious in underdeveloped countries under pressure from international agencies, such processes can also be seen at work on a more voluntary basis in neoliberal "post-Fordist" educational policies in advanced societies (Soucek 1995, 1996; Torres et al. 2005). This poses the question of what happens in universities with a growingly diverse population in terms of race, class, and gender, and, of course, in terms of the connection of all these dynamics to the form of the state and its educational policy.

Concerns about academic standards and accountability have gone hand in hand with globalization, because a variety of international agencies and global governing bodies have pressured universities to conform to similar standards. In the United States this movement largely has been framed as "assessment" or "institutional assessment." Assessment, however, tends to be rooted in schemas in which comparisons are drawn between and among similar types of institutions, as opposed to basing the assessment on some measure of the institution's contribution to society. Reflecting the influence of total quality management, academic programs and departments often engage in "benchmarking" by identifying comparable programs and then seeking to attain similar standards, measured by a variety of performance indicators. In academic programs the measures tend to be such things as the number of publications by the faculty, the number of faculty grants (or the amount of revenue generated by the faculty), the number of students, the number of degrees or certificates awarded, and the time to degree. The same kinds of analyses are conducted at the institutional level, of course. Stromquist pointed out the problems with such schemas: "While assessment procedures could be devised to gain greater understanding of the contribution of universities to the overall improvement of their societies, this is not the case. The assessments focus instead on quantitative indicators that pit one university against others" (2002, p. 111). Stromquist continued, "Moreover, the focus on performance and the consequent competition that it generates among universities result ultimately in taking away the autonomy of purpose and the function of those universities" (p. 111).

The evaluation and assessment push is playing a major role in reform of higher education throughout the Americas. Unfortunately, too much of the reform effort reflects a narrow conception of the university. Such a conception is largely based on the US model, with its heavy emphasis on entrepreneurialism and academic capitalism. Global trade and economic organizations such as the IMF and the World Bank play a key role in such reform efforts, because it is their funding programs that play a major part in reshaping societal values and the nature of the state's relationship to the universities. The push toward the entrepreneurial university in countries such as Argentina and Mexico consequently is not only shaping the nature of the universities but also fundamentally altering the identity of the citizens of these countries.

Universities obviously have a central role to play in a world increasingly shaped by global ties. Issues linked to the changing landscape of higher education, instrumentalism, academic capitalism and entrepreneurialism, access and affordability, and evaluation and assessment have a major effect on restructuring the university in a global age. In short, the university has never been more important to society than it is today, and globalization is a telling force in the elevation of the university's prominence.

Generative Themes for an Action Agenda

The preceding points lead us to consider an action agenda for challenging the hegemony of neoliberal globalization and its powerful influence on the university, state, and market. Here we turn to the work of Paulo Freire and the deployment of "generative themes."

Paulo Freire (1970) argued that the prevailing ethos of educational systems and structures is to follow the direction of authoritarian technocrats;

he spent much of his life challenging the mindlessness of technocracy and harshly criticized education as a pedagogy of the oppressed. Technocrats seek to distance education from power and politics, but Freire maintained that education cannot be dissociated from power, and he inaugurated a rich and growing theoretical perspective sometimes termed critical education, critical pedagogy, or pedagogy for liberation (Torres 1998b). In fact, Freire argued that there is a politicity of education and an educability of politics.

Generative themes à la Freire may provide us with a reasonable set of guiding principles for action (Morrow and Torres 2000). By generative themes we refer to sets of issues that reflect a particular epoch and which bring to mind a particular set of ideas, values, beliefs, hopes, doubts, and challenges, all of which call forth their opposites in a dialectical fashion. Generative themes pose obstacles to people becoming something more than they are, and, consequently, understanding these themes and wrestling with them is a step toward a fuller and more meaningful life (Bohorques 2005).

Generative themes as a group constitute the thematic universe of the epoch, where people take dialectical and contradictory positions, supporting either the maintenance or the transformation of social structures. Freire noted that as the antagonism between the themes increases, a tendency toward mystification, irrationality, and sectarianism arises. Therefore reality is emptied of its dynamic and historic sense. This happens when the themes are wrapped in and concealed by "limit situations," which are presented to people as unavoidable determinants. The contrary, liberatory action is to overcome the "limit situations" in which people find themselves reified (Bohorques 2005).

What are these generative themes today, considering the political economy of globalization and the relevance of the university, state, and market in the Americas? And what have we learned from the studies in this book that could help an agenda for action?

ANTIHEGEMONIC GLOBALIZATION

The need for universities, social movements, scholars, intellectuals, and communities to confront the dilemmas of the global and the local should not distract us from a most pressing concern: to challenge authoritarian neoliberal globalization and its hegemonic pretension through networks, institutions, and practices that have changed the intensity and dynamics of social interaction and the actual lives of people in impoverished societies. Yet a most pressing need is to challenge the narratives of neoliberal globalization, such as the idea of *un pensamiento único*, "the only possible thinking," so prevalent among economists, who, following rational choice models and engaging occasionally in the practice of game theory, have come to conclude that in a post-Fordist society the only possible theoretical model is neoliberal economics. This, coupled with the practical implementation of a class alliance so well analyzed by Michael Apple in many of his books and articles, has resulted in the adoption of neoliberal economics by neoconservative governments (see Apple [2000, 2004], for example). Challenging, defying, and demystifying this technocratic approach to social sciences, and particularly economics, is a most important generative theme of contemporary struggles.

FREEDOM IS EMANCIPATION, NOT TUTELAGE

One of the most important insights of a critical analysis of educational policy is that the attempt to highlight representative democracy as the only viable model that characterizes the form, content, and method of democratic practice is also an attempt to create freedom that is controlled; this is a notion of freedom as the selective device of elites, who control the freedom of the masses. What we have come to see is that representative democracy represents a dictatorship of capital, or at least the dictatorship of the economic elites. Obviously there are other alternatives, starting with a liberal notion of participatory democracy that will exploit the limitations of representative democracy and enhance the quality and texture of democratic life (Torres 1998b), or, to a more radical palate, the notion of radical democracy as practiced in the implementation of participatory budgeting for more than a decade in Porto Alegre, Brazil.

Redemocratizing democracy emerges as a most central notion in the context of higher education and societies. Movements to reform political campaign contributions or to increase the transparency of civil servants' and politicians' financial statements as well as attempts to create better ways to increase the connections between education and citizenship or between citizenship and the practice of democracy at the local level are nothing but attempts to make democracy work. However, there are more specific roles when it comes to linking the university with the social movements opposing hegemonic globalization. This is important for a number of reasons. With growing unemployment the unemployed are beginning to question the foundations of capitalist democracies and the role of universities. Are public universities ready to include more and more of the poor, the underemployed, the unemployed, the indigenous peoples, and the people asking for a more clear assessment of how contemporary modes of production are deteriorating the planet? Are the demands of these individuals and groups being incorporated into the curricula of higher education, as a way to begin a dialogue between popular education and scientific knowledge? Is it possible to use the science and technology of universities to facilitate, train, and even finance new micro-enterprises and local economic initiatives as a way not only to provide employment but also to create new avenues for local initiatives to come to fruition, taking advantage of old traditions and long-standing cultural, social, and economic practices?

DEFENSE OF PUBLIC HIGHER EDUCATION

It is clear that the defense of public education is one of the central concerns of innumerable social movements and public declarations, from the World Social Forum, to the World Educational Forum, to the student strike at UNAM, to students protests over tuition around the world, to teachers unions worldwide, and to a large and complex amalgam of institutions, individuals, practices, and narratives. For those to whom participatory democracy is more than a phrase of a bygone era, a robust defense of the importance of public support for higher education must be waged; similarly, we must defend the achievements of some of the most cherished ideals of the democratic pact—equality, freedom, solidarity—and not allow the hegemony of neoliberalism to erode such ideals.

DEFENSE OF THE DEMOCRATIC STATE

Given the intense dynamics between the local and the global, the nation-state takes on even greater importance within the context of globalization (Santos 2004). Yet it is clear that without resorting to a serious defense of the principles of representation and participation in the democratic state, we may not be able to make much of the generative themes outlined earlier. Here we present four critical concerns that cannot be ignored.

First, we must adequately fund public services. Without serious regulations, particularly of the financial transactions that cross borders, as proposed by some public policy analysts, such as the Tobin tax in France, we may not be able to sustain a reasonable level of investment in the public sector with regard to essential social services. This point is valid to the central, semiperipheral, and peripheral countries in the world system.

Second, if we do not defend domestic markets against the wild capitalist logic of outsourcing and the predatory practices of corporations, we may find ourselves in the heart of a most serious crisis of unemployment; this in turn could produce a most serious crisis in social security.

Third, some level of correction to the growing liberalization of the markets needs to be implemented. Otherwise, we face a most challenging set of deregulations, some of which are likely to damage higher education drastically. A clear example is the proposal by the WTO, heavily resisted by the third world and peripheral countries, to consider education, and particularly higher education, a service comparable to financial services. The effects of this model, if implemented, will amount to nothing less than neocolonialism. Universities in the central countries, through aggressive recruitment, superior technology and support systems, and distance education, will capture a larger share of the educational market in the world system, especially in peripheral nations. This will diminish the autonomy of national institutions on the periphery, diminish the autonomy and financial resources of their public universities, and increase the force and vigor of the expansion of culture from the center to the periphery.

Finally, without a democratic state we may not be able to work toward the construction of a more just world, with growing planetary sensibilities, less prone to war and the dominance of the strongest military nations in the world, and more equipped to deal with conflict resolution through dialogue and negotiation.

A PLANETARIAN MULTICULTURAL CITIZENSHIP

Advancing a planetarian multicultural citizenship is perhaps one of the most important actions to be undertaken by universities as part of their responsibility to the public good. With increased immigration and the slippage of cultures and languages in local communities and national societies, it is imperative to work toward a cosmopolitan democracy based on a planetarian multicultural citizenship. Indeed, as utopian as this model may sound—and remember that many of the most astute and critical social scientists, such as Immanuel Wallerstein (2001), have called for a science of "utopistics"—there are really few options but to create new social and human horizons. We need to seek new horizons based on an educational model that facilitates a new encounter between human culture and nature and that recognizes the vulnerability of the environment given our present tendencies toward ecological destruction. We need a new model of relationships between mind and body, one that moves beyond the logocentrism characteristic of European and North American white cultures. We need a new model for building and sustaining global relationships, one not based on the threat of a nuclear holocaust but rooted in ideals anchored to a more peaceful world.

This call for generative themes for social action is not pure speculation but the result of countless meetings and conversations around the world, the reading of many manifests for action, and our own sensibility about how serious the situation is today. As the thousands of deaths in Iraq exemplify, we cannot simply resort to a model of rationality based on instrumental reason or economic gain, nor can we rely on a model of policy guided by specific interests of certain corporate sectors, such as the powerful influence of global energy companies in the United States.

The responsibilities of universities to the survival of the species on this planet, to social justice, to peace and solidarity among individuals, local and global communities, and nations cannot simply be a subject of study within ivory tower walls. The knowledge and ideals advanced by our greatest minds must impact our societies, our social policies, and indeed global practices. Consequently, we call for a transformation of higher education throughout the Americas and are particularly concerned about the movement toward privatization and the decline of prominence of the public good. The university must be an institution of social action for the commonweal, not simply an economic resource for the corporate world.

We need a vision for the future, because, as the book of Proverbs cautions us: "When there is no vision, the people perish." Or, to put it in more contemporary terms and echoing the sentiments of Paulo Freire, we need to build a world in which it will be easier to love. Universities must be at the center of such an endeavor.

References

Apple, M. W. 2000. "Between Neoliberalism and Neoconservatism: Education and Conservatism in a Global Context." In *Globalization and Education: Critical Perspectives* (pp. 57–77), N. C. Burbules and C. A. Torres, eds. New York: Routledge.

Apple, M. 2004. *Ideology and Curriculum* (3rd ed.). New York: Routledge.

Archer, M. S. 1982. "Introduction: Theorizing About the Expansion of Educational Systems." In *The Sociology of Educational Expansion* (pp. 3–64), M. S. Archer, ed. Beverly Hills, CA: Sage.

Archer, M. S. 1984. *Social Origins of Educational Systems*. London: Sage.

Arnove, R. F. 1986. *Education and Revolution in Nicaragua*. New York: Praeger.

Arnove, R. F., and C. A. Torres. 1996. "Adult Education and State Policy in Latin America: The Contrasting Cases of Mexico and Nicaragua." *Comparative Education* 31(3): 311–326.

Avrich, P. 1980. *The Modern School Movements: Anarchism and Education in the United States*. Princeton, NJ: Princeton University Press.

Bérubé, M. 1994. *Public Access: Literary Theory and American Campus Politics*. London: Verso.

Bhabha, H. K. 1994. *The Location of Culture*. London: Routledge.

Bohorques, I. 2005. "Untested Feasibility in Paulo Freire: Behind the Profile of a Dream." In *Paulo Freire, Education, and the Possible Dream*, C. A. Torres, ed. Urbana-Champaign: University of Illinois Press (in press).

Boli, J., F. O. Ramirez, and J. W. Meyer. 1985. "Explaining the Origins and Expansion of Mass Education." *Comparative Education Review* 29(2): 145–170.

Burbules, N. C., and C. A. Torres, eds. 2000. *Education and Globalization: Critical Perspectives*. New York: Routledge.

Calhoun, C., ed. 1994. *Social Theory and the Politics of Identity*. Cambridge, MA: Blackwell.

Carnoy, M. 1974. *Education as Cultural Imperialism*. New York: David McKay.

Carnoy, M. 1993. "Multinationals in a Changing World Economy: Whither the Nation-State? In *The New Global Economy in the Information Age: Reflections on Our Changing World* (pp. 45–96), M. Carnoy, M. Castells, S. S. Cohen, and F. H. Cardoso, eds. University Park: Pennsylvania State University Press.

Carnoy, M., M. Castells, S. S. Cohen, and F. H. Cardoso, eds. 1993. *The New Global Economy in the Information Age: Reflections on Our Changing World*. University Park: Pennsylvania State University Press.

Carnoy, M., and H. M. Levin. 1985. *Schooling and Work in the Democratic State.* Stanford, CA: Stanford University Press.

Carnoy, M., and C. A. Torres. 1990. "Education and Social Transformation in Nicaragua (1979–1989)." In *Education and the Social Transition in the Third World: China, Cuba, Tanzania, Mozambique, and Nicaragua*, M. Carnoy and J. Samoff, eds. (with A. M. Burris, A. Jonhston, and C. A. Torres). Princeton, NJ: Princeton University Press.

Castells, M. 1996. *The Rise of the Network Society.* Boston: Blackwell.

Castells, M. 1997. *The Power of Identity.* Boston: Blackwell.

Chomsky, N. 1998. *Profit over People: Neoliberalism and Global Order.* New York: Seven Stories Press.

Cohen, R. 1993. *When the Old Left Was Young: Student Radicals and America's First Mass Student Movement, 1929–1941.* New York: Oxford University Press.

Dobbs, A. E. 1969 [1919]. *Education and Social Movements 1700–1850.* New York: Augustus M. Kelley.

Eyerman, R., and A. Jamison. 1991. *Social Movements: A Cognitive Approach.* Cambridge, MA: Polity Press.

Freire, P. 1970. *Pedagogy of the Oppressed*, M. B. Ramos, trans. New York: Continuum.

Giddens, A. 1990. *The Consequences of Modernity.* Stanford, CA: Stanford University Press.

Hannerz, U. 1996. *Transnational Connections: Culture, People, Places.* London: Routledge.

Harvey, D. 1989. *The Condition of Postmodernity.* Oxford, UK: Blackwell.

International Monetary Fund. 2003. *Lessons from the Crisis in Argentina.* Internal Report, October 8. Washington, DC: International Monetary Fund.

International Monetary Fund. 2004a. *Common Criticism of the IMF.* IMF informational document. Available at http://www.imf.org/external/np/ext/ccrit/eng/cri.htm

International Monetary Fund. 2004b. *Common Criticism of the IMF: Some Responses.* IMF informational document. Available at http://www.imf.org/external/np/ext/ccrit/eng/crans.htm

Kellner, D. 2000. "Globalization and New Social Movements: Lessons for Critical Theory and Pedagogy." In *Globalization and Education: Critical Perspectives* (pp. 299–321), N. C. Burbules and C. A. Torres, eds. New York: Routledge.

Lawson, R. A. 1971. *The Failure of Independent Liberalism, 1930–1941.* New York: Capricorn Books.

Lipset, S. M. 1971. *Rebellion in the University.* Chicago: University of Chicago Press.

Lorena Cook, M. 1996. *Organizing Dissent: Unions, the State, and the Democratic Teachers Movement in Mexico.* University Park: Pennsylvania State University Press.

Morrow, R. A., and C. A. Torres. 1994. "Education and the Reproduction of Class,

Gender, and Race: Responding to the Postmodern Challenge." *Educational Theory* 44(1): 43–61.

Morrow, R. A., and C. A. Torres. 1995. *Social Theory and Education: A Critique of Theories of Social and Cultural Reproduction*. Albany: State University of New York Press.

Morrow, R. A., and C. A. Torres. 1999. "The State, Social Movements, and Educational Reform." In *Comparative Education: The Dialectics of the Global and the Local*, R. Arnove and C. A. Torres, eds. Lanham, MD: Rowman & Littlefield.

Morrow, R. A., and C. A. Torres. 2000. *Reading Freire and Habermas*. New York: Teachers College Press.

Nash, K. 2000. *Contemporary Political Sociology, Globalization, Politics, and Power*. Oxford, UK: Blackwell.

National Center for Public Policy and Higher Education. 2004. *Measuring Up 2004*. San Jose, CA: NCPPHE.

Ohmae, K. 1990. *The Borderless World: Power and Strategy in the Interlinked World Economy*. New York: Harper Business.

Ordorika, I. 2003. *Power and Politics in University Governance: Organization and Change at the Universidad Nacional Autonoma de Mexico*. New York: Routledge Falmer.

Przeworski, A. 1991. *Democracy and the Market: Political and Economic Reforms in Eastern Europe and Latin America*. New York: Cambridge University Press.

Reich, R. B. 1991. *The Work of Nations*. New York: Vintage Books.

Rhoads, R. A. 1998. *Freedom's Web: Student Activism in an Age of Cultural Diversity*. Baltimore: Johns Hopkins University Press.

Rhoads, R. A. 2003. "Globalization and Resistance in the United States and Mexico: The Global Potemkin Village." *Higher Education* 45: 223–250.

Rhoads, R. A., and L. Mina. 2001. "The Student Strike at the National Autonomous University of Mexico: A Political Analysis." *Comparative Education Review* 45(3): 334–353.

Rhoads, R. A., V. Saenz, and R. Carducci. 2004. "Higher Education Reform as a Social Movement: The Case of Affirmative Action." *Review of Higher Education* 28(2): 191–220.

Ringer, F. 1987. "Introduction." In *The Rise of the Modern Educational System* (pp. 1–14), D. Müller, F. Ringer, and B. Simon, eds. Cambridge, UK: Cambridge University Press.

Robertson, R. 1992. *Globalization*. London: Sage.

Said, E. 1994. *Culture and Imperialism*. New York: Vintage Books.

Santos, B. S. 2004. "A Universidade no Século XXI: Para uma Reforma Democrática e Emancipatória da Universidade." Keynote address at the IV International Paulo Freire Forum, Porto, Portugal, September 22.

Schugurensky, D., and C. A. Torres. 1994. "Adult Education and Political Education: Lessons from Comparative, Cross-National Research in Cuba, Mexico,

Nicaragua, and Tanzania." In *Aspects of Globalization and Internationalization of Political Education*, B. Claussen, ed. Hamburg, Germany: Krämer.

Simon, B. 1965. *Education and the Labour Movement: 1870–1920*. London: Lawrence & Wishart.

Simon, B. 1987. *The Rise of the Modern Educational System*. Cambridge, UK: Cambridge University Press.

Slaughter, S., and L. L. Leslie. 1997. *Academic Capitalism: Politics, Policies, and the Entrepreneurial University*. Baltimore: Johns Hopkins University Press.

Slaughter, S., and G. Rhoades. 2004. *Academic Capitalism in the New Economy*. Baltimore: Johns Hopkins University Press.

Smelser, N. 1985. "Evaluating the Model of Structural Differentiation in Relation to Educational Change in the Nineteenth Century." In *Neofunctionalism* (pp. 113–130), J. Alexander, ed. Beverly Hills, CA: Sage.

Soucek, V. 1995. "Public Education and the Post-Fordist Accumulation Regime: A Case Study of Australia." *Interchange* 26(2): 127–159.

Soucek, V. 1996. *Education Policy Formation in the Post-Fordist Era and Its Implications on the Nature of Teachers' Work*. Ph.D. dissertation, Department of Educational Policy, University of Alberta.

Stromquist, N. 2002. *Education in a Globalized World: The Connectivity of Economic Power, Technology, and Knowledge*. Lanham, MD: Rowman & Littlefield.

Thurow, L. 1992. *Head to Head: The Coming Economic Battle Among Japan, Europe, and America*. New York: William Morrow.

Torres, C. A. 1991. "The State, Nonformal Education, and Socialism in Cuba, Nicaragua, and Grenada." *Comparative Education Review* 35(1): 92–114.

Torres, C. A. 1998a. *Democracy, Education, and Multiculturalism: Dilemmas of Citizenship in a Global World*. Lanham, MD: Rowman & Littlefield.

Torres, C. A. 1998b. *Education, Power, and Personal Biography*. New York: Routledge.

Torres, C. A., S. Cho, J. Kachur, A. Loyo, M. Mollis, A. Nagao, and J. Thompson. 2005. "Political Capital, Teachers' Unions, and the State: Value Conflicts and Collaborative Strategies in Educational Reform in the United States, Canada, Japan, Korea, Mexico, and Argentina." Unpublished.

Touraine, A. 1968. *Le Communisme Utopique: Le Mouvement de Mai 1968*. Paris: Seuil.

Vidal, G. 2002a. *Dreaming War: Blood for Oil and the Cheney-Bush Junta*. New York: Nation Books.

Vidal, G. 2002b. *Perpetual War for Perpetual Peace: How We Got to Be So Hated*. New York: Nation Books.

Wallerstein, I. 2001. *The End of the War as We Know It: Social Science for the Twenty-First Century*. Minneapolis: University of Minnesota Press.

Waters, M. 1995. *Globalization*. London: Routledge.

Willener, A. 1970. *The Action-Image of Society: On Cultural Politicization*, A. M. Sheridan Smith, ed. London: Tavistock.

World Bank. 2004a. *Development Policy Lending Replaces Adjustment Lending.* DevNews Media Center, World Bank publication. Available at http://web .worldbank.org

World Bank. 2004b. *From Adjustment Lending to Development Policy Support Lending.* World Bank publication. Available at http://1nweb18.worldbank.org

World Trade Organization. 2004. *10 Benefits of the WTO Trading System.* WTO informational document. Available at http://www.wto.org/english/thewto_e/ whatis_e?10ben_10b00_e.htm

Wrigley, J. 1982. *Class Politics and Public Schools.* New Brunswick, NJ: Rutgers University Press.

Index